Center for Basque Studies
Occasional Papers Series, No. 10

BEGOÑA ARETXAGA

States of Terror

Begoña Aretxaga's Essays

Edited by
Joseba Zulaika

Introduction by
Kay B. Warren

Prologue and Epilogue by
Joseba Zulaika

Center for Basque Studies
University of Nevada, Reno
Reno, Nevada

This book was published with generous financial support from the Basque Government.

Center for Basque Studies
Occasional Papers Series, No. 10

Center for Basque Studies
University of Nevada, Reno
Reno, Nevada 89557
http://basque.unr.edu

Library of Congress Cataloging-in-Publication Data

Aretxaga, Begoña.
  States of terror : Begoña Aretxaga's essays / edited by Joseba Zulaika.
      p. cm. – (Occasional papers series / Center for Basque Studies ; no. 10)
  Two articles translated from Spanish.
  Summary: "Collection of essays by Basque anthropologist Begoña Aretxaga on political violence, gender and nationalism, and the political culture of Basque youth"–Provided by publisher.
  Includes bibliographical references and index.
  ISBN 1-877802-57-3 (pbk.)
  1. Political violence–Spain–País Vasco. 2. Political violence–Northern Ireland. 3. Terrorism. 4. Sex–Political aspects–Northern Ireland. 5. País Vasco (Spain)–Politics and government–20th century. 6. Northern Ireland–Politics and government–20th century. I. Zulaika, Joseba. II. University of Nevada, Reno. Center for Basque Studies. III. Title. IV. Series: Occasional papers series (University of Nevada, Reno. Center for Basque Studies) ; no. 10.

 JC328.65.S7A74 2005
  303.60946'6–dc22

2005030476

CONTENTS

Manuscript

Mourning

J. Rose → War And failure to
mourn —
uninterrupted mourning as affective bond
alongside love (of friendship, love,
etc)
politics of friendship — in Deridda —
mourning as in nostalgia object of the
past — in Melly Ivy in rel. to Japan.
— Difference — and relation w/ Svengali —
just worth noting
State/tenement: a mourning object

+ Autonomia — Insurgency — tenant —
Youth — chapter

+ State — Sovereignty — paranoic — Law —

chapters —
1) Dirty war /2/secret papers / CSTS /pleasure etc
3) Sovereignty / Law : Otegi —
5) State + action : MADNESS?
— Ambivalence — desire —
Conclusion Rethinking the political +
the political subject.

A page from Begoña Aretxaga's notes for States of Terror.

PROLOGUE[1]

JOSEBA ZULAIKA

Begoña Aretxaga, the author of these essays, died in Austin on December 28, 2002. She was forty-two years old.

Begoña was born in the city of San Sebastián, Spain. After completing a bachelor's degree in philosophy and psychology and a master's degree in cultural anthropology at the University of the Basque Country, she joined the Anthropology Department at Princeton. She worked there with Professors James Fernandez, Gananath Obeyesekere, Joan Scott, and Kay Warren. After her doctorate in 1992, she took a position as assistant professor at Harvard University, where she was promoted to associate professor in 1997. In 1999 she accepted a position at the University of Texas, Austin, where she was tenured in 2001. She also served as a visiting professor at the University of Chicago in the spring of 2001.

Her colleagues in the Anthropology Department at Austin have written: "Her untimely death occurred after a graceful and courageous struggle with cancer. Known internationally for her work in political and psychological anthropology, Begoña was active in the Center for Women's Studies as well as the Department of Anthropology. She has a wide circle of friends, relatives, colleagues, and students throughout the world who will fondly remember her brilliant mind, passion for life, infectious good humor, and gift for friendship. Her death is a tremendous loss, and she is sorely missed."

They continue, "Her innovative publications on oppositional nationalisms, gender and sexuality, and political violence have won international acclaim. Two books and numerous

1. I am thankful to several colleagues and friends of Begoña Aretxaga who have been involved in this project from the beginning, giving me encouragement and advice on how to publish the volume. Among them are Kay Warren, William Christian, James Brow, James Fernandez, Yael Navaro-Yashin and Davida Woods. Jill Berner and Cameron have been in charge of editing and proofreading the volume with their usual care. Kate Camino helped in various ways. I owe a particular debt of gratitude to Begoña's loving family, her mother Mertxe Santos, her sisters Amaia and Arantxa, and her brother Koldo who took care of her during her illness. Koldo provided me with the typed texts of the essays and the copyright permissions. Their presence has been a major motivation to publish this volume.

articles draw on extensive research in troubled areas of Western Europe: the Basque Country and Northern Ireland. Her 1989 book on Basque separatist funerals, *Los Funerales en el Nacionalismo Radical Vasco,* is a classic in her field. Her 1997 study of separatist women in Northern Ireland, *Shattering Silence: Women, Nationalism and Political Subjectivity in Northern Ireland*, has been influential in ethnic studies, European cultural studies, and women's studies as well as in anthropology."

Begoña's research was supported by fellowships from the MacArthur Foundation, Social Science Research Council, Mellon Foundation, American Council for Learned Societies, Wenner-Gren Foundation for Anthropological Research, and Harry Frank Guggenheim Foundation, among others. She was invited to participate in numerous international conferences and workshops, and served on the advisory boards of the *Journal of Spanish Cultural Studies* and the Center for Basque Studies at the University of Nevada, Reno. A major symposium honoring Begoña's scholarship and legacy was held in Chicago in November 2003, in conjunction with the annual meeting of the American Anthropological Association, and the proceedings will be published as a special issue of *Anthropological Theory.*

At the time of her death, Begoña was working on a book tentatively entitled *States of Terror: Nationalist Youth and Political Violence in the Basque Country*. Previously, before going to Princeton and while still an undergraduate, she wrote her first book on the funerary rituals of Basque radical nationalism, and the ethnographic and mediatic contexts in which these funerals were performed by the comrades of the killed militants. She examined these rituals as a site for the construction of Basque national identity, as well as political action against the Spanish state. Her book showed that these political rituals were highly gendered performances, in which women figured as mediators to ensure the permanence of a transcendent Basque nation while sanctioning nationalist violence.

Begoña rebelled against the male bias in most anthropological studies of political violence. The violent actions, discourses, and bodies were all male. She found such analyses incomplete. Her special contribution was to pay attention to the gendered structure and sexualized forms of the violence. She chose as her dissertation topic the relationship between gender and political violence in the parallel scenario of Northern Ireland. The work focused on social practice and the nature of agency as indicators of the ways in which social transformation is accomplished. The final result, published by Princeton University Press, is an extraordinary ethnography on the political subjectivity of working-class, activist women who defy common representations of women as victims of a male war. Begoña drew from interpretive anthropology and post-structural feminist theory to investigate the social processes that shaped the political agency of Nationalist women. Her exploration of the dynamics between the gender structure of ethnic politics and the political structuring of power is unique in the literature, for it raises questions about the possibilities of feminist transformation in a situation over-determined by the practices of colonialism and nationalism, both of which strategically use gender to legitimize either colonial subordination or national liberation. The study bears powerful evidence for the need to theorize subjectivity and affect as crucial dimensions of political agency.

In addition to this book, she wrote essays on political resistance, border crossing, and gender politics in Ireland and Northern Ireland. Five of these essays are included in this volume. A powerful example of her ethnographic skill and theoretical sophistication can be seen in "Dirty Protest," which won the 1993 Stirling Prize of the Society for Psychological Anthropology. It analyzes the various meanings and political effects of violence on the bodies of Irish men and women prisoners. The article, "Striking with Hunger," examines male models of redemption and agency through a selective interpretation of historical memory and contemporary practices. "What the Border Hides" studies the consequences of the partition of Ireland on gender policies north and south of the Irish border, and theorizes the border as phantasmatic wound that turns into an emblem of the incompleteness of the Irish nation. The instability and mutual dependence of the concepts of gender and nationalism are analyzed in "Does the Nation Have a Sex?" by focusing on the Irish historical contingency; while in "The Sexual Games of the Body Politic," Aretxaga examines the practice of strip searches as an institutional technology of control sustained by violent sexual fantasies.

After a decade dedicated to working on Northern Ireland, during the late 1990s she decided to return to her Basque ethnography. If her previous research focused on the mutual constitution of gender and nationalism, now she changed emphasis toward youth culture and the cultural construction of the state. She centered her work on the new generation of Basque radicals, born and raised within the context of a parliamentary democracy, who perceive "the state" as an omnipresent authoritarian force that threatens the very existence of Basque identity. The manuscript examines the political culture of this new generation engaged in various forms of sabotage and intimidation, thus creating deep antagonisms between radical and moderate nationalists. Her relational approach investigates the forms in which the government and police forces partake in the reproduction of violence by their own transgressions of democratic legality. She pays particular attention to the phantasmatic oppositional representations between "terrorism" and "the state" and how such collective representations end up having a life of their own, powerfully conditioning the imagination and experience of everyday life (see chapters 8–14 of Part II).

At the time of her death, the book manuscript was nearing its completion, as six essays dealing with the research had already been published and two more were ready for publication. She even wrote the first draft of an introduction to the book and during her year of illness, she hoped she would find the time and energy to complete it. The reason for publishing this volume is to bring these pieces together. Needless to say, even if I have decided to replicate her own tentative title of *States of Terror*, this is not the book she would have published. All I have done is to give some order to the materials, based on the chronology of her development and the proximity of the themes. Since they are essays written for separate publications, there is some repetition of background information that she would have deleted; she also makes references to the same revelatory incidents across various papers. It is, in fact, fascinating to see how the same emblematic event provides the author avenues for quite diverse and original analyses while examining the realms of law, the fictional reality of the political, its cultural and metaphoric contexts, or the nature of madness.

The introduction to her unfinished manuscript, while clearly a first draft, is uniquely self-revealing. It is vintage Aretxaga, with nothing hyperbolic or self-aggrandizing, only the bare and piercing narration of what led her into political activism first and intellectual pursuit later. It is left unconcluded with the following sentence: "Since this [the logic of sovereignty] will be discussed at length in the different chapters of this book, I will only outline here the main lines of the discussion." Among her manuscripts, there is another draft describing the project of the book which provides such an "outline"; and I have added it here as the last section of the Introduction under the heading "Historical Background and Theoretical Significance."

I have placed her early essay, "The Death of Yoyes," at the beginning of the "States of Terror" group of papers. She wrote it while a graduate student at Princeton; a decade later she added an introductory note, perhaps thinking of including it in her unfinished book. This paper, on a high-level ETA militant who, six years after quitting the organization, was murdered by her former colleagues as a traitor, is a little-known but path-breaking piece. Begoña had been intimately involved in politics and could identify with Yoyes' commitment to activism, followed by disappointment and refuge in writing. By the time Yoyes was executed in 1986 in front of her five-year-old son, more than three hundred ETA ex-militants had taken advantage of the "reinsertion" measures to become ordinary civilians. Why was Yoyes, a woman, more culpable than the other "repented" ones? By turning this murder into a paradigmatic case that encapsulates the dilemmas of Basque politics, Begoña inquired into the cultural meanings of Yoyes' roles as a hero, traitor, martyr, as well as the condition that contradicts those exceptional roles, that of motherhood. Even without the theoretical sophistication that her writing would later display, the essay is still unique in unveiling the use of gender categories in ETA. This was a most difficult piece to write, yet Begoña had to do it because intellectual work was, for her, in the end, a tug-of-war, almost an exorcism, to elucidate and transform experience, in this case the experience of herself and her generation involved in radical nationalist politics. Much as she had taken political risks during the late Franco period for the sake of freedom, she was now again risking her subjectivity, but this time by writing.

During her later work on *States of Terror*, Begoña was attempting a new theoretical amalgam on nationalism, political violence, and the state. She went far beyond Anderson's celebrated notion of the "imagined community" by incorporating the concept of the political imaginary, borrowed in part from the work of the political theorist Cornelius Castoriadis and psychoanalyst Jacques Lacan. The complex dynamic of identifications, projections, and fantasies, central to understanding the affective bonds that constitute nationalism as well as the state, required such a notion of the imaginary. Her goal is to illuminate the phantasmatic structures of political violence. The great originality of Aretxaga's work relies on the combination of ethnographic insight and theoretical sophistication regarding the imaginary present in each of her essays. This enterprise leads her to explore intersubjective dynamics and often unconscious processes by means of concepts such as fantasy, fetish, and mourning, which she finds particularly effective for an ethnographic study of the state. Regarding the state, she is particularly concerned, beyond it being the reification of an idea, about the social life and the psychic dynamics that sustain such an idea as the ultimate political reality. These issues are addressed directly in her essay "Maddening States."

Begoña's goal was to describe "the discourse of the unconscious in Basque political violence," the subtitle of her essay "Before the Law," published for the first time in this volume. The essay examines at length an unusual political trial that captured her attention. The defendant killed two Basque policemen while in a state that he claimed was a loss of consciousness, and against all odds he was set free. An inquiry into the discourses of madness and fantasy become a central aspect of the reality at hand. And the essay delves into the social reactions to the outcome of the trial, while exploring the consequences of such discourses in configuring the political conflict. Begoña further developed the theme of madness in her remarkable "Out of Their Minds? On Political Madness in the Basque Country." The starting point of this article is another puzzling killing, in March 2001, of a Basque policeman—the first such killing by "a mad ETA ready to burn all bridges," and one that signaled the highest point in the Basque nationalist dystopia between its moderate and radical forces. This essay takes seriously the trope of madness as a domain of knowledge in the Lacanian sense of a rupture in the everyday experience, while paying special attention to the intolerable ambiguities and ambivalences of nationalist identities. The text concludes with a section on "national intimacy," a topic she insightfully explored in "The Intimacy of Violence." Contrary to the image in the media of the terrorist as a tabooed stranger, it is argued that terrorism among Basques displays the uncanny character of the intimately and strangely familiar.

"Of Hens, Hoods, and Other Political Beasts" explores the social reality of the complex political metaphor, *cipayo*, a word applied to Basque policemen which signifies betrayal, and is used to reconfigure their identity from Basque civil servants to national traitors, thus legitimizing disdain and violence against them. Various levels of metonymic associations from different positionings within Basque identity are analyzed. The metaphor also presents a solution to the ambiguity of a police force which symbolizes a fantasized Basque state while in fact upholding the law of the Spanish state.

The implications of political fantasy in the creation of actual terror are analyzed in "Playing Terrorist," where it is argued that Spanish state terror practices known as the "dirty war" made democracy into more a fetish than a process. It shows how the state may acquire a social and psychological reality, as if it were a subject of feeling and desire, by mimetically enacting the fantasies of terrorist transgression. Aretxaga suggests that the ineluctable, yet elusive, realities of "the state" and "terrorism" are ghostly presences produced through the mirroring projections of a threatening enemy. Another aspect of this argument was elaborated in "A Hall of Mirrors: On the Spectral Character of Basque Violence." It views the violence between the radical nationalist youth and the Basque police as a traumatic repetition that is acted out while denying the split character of Basque identity. This analysis of the spectral and intimate character of Basque violence, animated by ambivalence and metaphors of betrayal, is based on various stories and rumors recounted by both sides of the conflict.

Finally, invited by *Anthropological Quarterly* to comment on the 9/11 tragedy, Begoña applied these approaches to the phenomenon of international terrorism in the essay "Terror as Thrill." In Madrid, she had just seen and been impacted by Goya's exhibit, "The Disasters of War." She found one of this series of paintings, entitled "Truth Died," to be poignantly applicable to America's "war on terror." She had watched the World Trade Center towers collapse while in her native city of San Sebastián, and her anxiety grew as she saw President Bush declare a "crusade" of good against evil "to save the world." The unreality of it all brought back memories of her childhood during the dark years of Francisco Franco, the dictator who also called for a "crusade" against an elected republican government, and who claimed to have saved Spain for God. A few months earlier, in her introduction to the "States of Terror" manuscript, Begoña had written about this childhood under Franco and how it had influenced her life permanently. Now it seemed she was back in the same dark period again.

On her return from San Sebastián to Austin in October, Begoña discovered that her persistent cough was, in fact, lung cancer. She had to put aside her writing and concentrate on saving her life. The following spring she was still able to attend a conference at the University of Nevada, Reno on Terrorism and Globalization, of which she was a co-organizer. (The papers from this conference were published by the Center for Basque Studies under the title *Empire and Terror*.) Despite her frail health, she was an active participant. For a storyteller, the most salient fact about Begoña's life might be that it ended so soon. For us, colleagues, friends, and now readers of her work, her life cycle and intellectual achievement hold a remarkable integrity and fulfillment.

Begoña's brilliance, common sense, and unassuming capacity for empathy and friendship touched the lives of many of her colleagues and students. But she never lost sight of her militant and intellectual beginnings, the struggle against all forms of dictatorship and patriarchy. Her uncanny ability for "displacement," for bringing to the situation at hand the experiences and sights of other times and places, was at the root of her creativity. This included her displacement from her native place of origin, as well her place of residence. As she wrote in the Introduction, her position was first of all "characterized by a displacement from militancy by academic writing and a displacement from academic writing by past militancy." That she could hold both worlds simultaneously was the source of her inner strength and her clarity of mind. If displacement was the main figure she predicated upon herself, it is perhaps fitting that even the publication of her book should have bccn displaced into the posthumous decisions of an editor. It is left to us, readers of her striking essays, to see the ultimate pattern and beauty in her displacements.

A line I read in the Introduction while preparing this volume has pulled me back to that hospital bed in Houston almost three years ago. While discussing the irruption of the Lacanian Real in everyday life, the intolerable reality devoid of ideological justifications and palatable fantasies, Begoña Aretxaga pays particular attention to the "sensual encounter with death," to then add: "But what might be traumatic of such encounters with the Real might well be the unbearable lucidity of being." These words were written a few months before she found out about her fatal illness. It was such unbearable lucidity on her part that hit me when I visited her for that last time. There was no fear and no self-pity in her eyes. By then all she could say was a final embrace, each second an eternity, and all that was left was her quiet and fierce determination to experience and be a witness and endure open-eyed whatever love and death had in store for her.

Part I

Gender and Political Violence in Northern Ireland

INTRODUCTION

Critical Voices and Representational Strategies from Begoña Aretxaga's Ethnography on Northern Ireland

KAY B. WARREN

During her life, Begoña Aretxaga was interested in the cultural politics of state violence in Northern Ireland and Spain in very specific ways. Her work focused on the formation of political subjectivities—the dialectics of images and story-like creations through which people understand their world, the emotional force of resistance, the unconscious dimensions of social experience, and the meanings of violence for those caught in between. The quest for her was an experiential and a theoretical one. Aretxaga sought to open an alternative line of ethnographic research[1] and post-structural theoretical engagement drawing on post-colonial and Lacanian perspectives to examine democracy, ethnic nationalist opposition and state repression, the mimesis of violence, heterogeneous formations of resistance, and the activism of marginalized women in Northern Ireland and youths from the Basque north in Spain.[2]

This essay discusses Aretxaga's intellectual project and her critique of other social scientific perspectives on violence. The analysis moves on to consider her work as an ethnographer. To offer readers an opportunity to see aspects of the knowledge production behind the pages of her published works, this essay examines examples of Aretxaga's

---

1. In this essay, I draw on materials from Begoña Aretxaga's published writings, her field research, grant proposals, and my notes from our seminars, conferences, and, finally, from the 2002 School of American Research seminar on the Poetics of Violence seven months before her death. The archive of Begoña's field notes, publication drafts, and teaching materials belongs to her brother, Koldo Aretxaga, in San Sebastián, Spain. I thank him for permission to quote her work in this essay.

2. Begoña Aretxaga and I discussed anthropological perspectives on violence and shared field work experiences from the time when she first came to the U.S. for graduate school at Princeton University. She was a wonderful contributor to the MacArthur Foundation seminar I convened that produced *The Violence Within* (1992). Our careers intersected again at Harvard where we were colleagues for two years before her move to the University of Texas at Austin. I also spent a very powerful time with Begoña and her sister during Bego's final hospitalization at the M. D. Anderson Cancer Center in Houston, Texas.

ethnographic narratives and representational strategies from her Northern Ireland field research.[3] I focus on this project because of our close personal association at Princeton from 1985–1992 as she took courses from me, wrote research grants, went to Ireland from 1987–1989, and finished her dissertation in 1992. Clearly another essay could be written about parallel issues for her Basque research.

Aretxaga saw her own work as an experimental form of anthropology that offered vibrant critiques of the social scientific impulse to search for universals across formations of violence, fix typologies of violence, and read narratives of violence with a surprising literalism as a quest for the facts.[4] Rather, her projects pursued novel lines of questioning to confront important but underappreciated issues that serve as windows on the experience of violence and the reimagining of political subjectivities reshaped at critical junctures (Aretxaga 1993). She pursued "the processes that make Nationalist women in Northern Ireland political subjects of a particular kind, differentiated among themselves and different from the men" (1997: ix–x). Her approach to these issues was grounded in the politics and ordinary people's experiences of the state, Republican nationalism, and feminism. In her view, experience is never raw but rather individually, socially, and ideologically mediated in a complex variety of ways that need to be established ethnographically and historically (Scott 1991). This anthropological rendering of discourse and experience stands in critical tension with Foucault while drawing inspiration from a range of other theorists, including Taussig, Butler, de Certeau, Das, Mohanty, Spivak, and Obeyesekere. Aretxaga's project was also a direct challenge to the flat realism of much scholarship in the social sciences and in the media which offers artificially bounded human interest narratives as exhaustive.

In this brief commentary I want to illustrate Begoña Aretxaga's critical voice on these matters and show the significance for her work of living within Belfast's daily tensions. In Aretxaga's field notes, we see an astute observer, poetic writer, and insightful analyst who continually represented the diaological nature of her ethnographic encounters with all sorts of individuals and their memories of Belfast's past. These compelling narratives beg to be read in multilayered ways. One sees why she felt so strongly about post-structuralist currents in the anthropology of violence.

---

3. This essay focuses on community activists; I plan to write another essay on Aretxaga's research for her writings on the no-wash protests at the Armagh prison.

4. The debates I mention here occurred during Neil Whitehead's seminar on the poetics of violence, sponsored by the School of American Research (Whitehead 2004). Whitehead defined the poetics of violence in the following terms: "There have been few attempts to map how the cultural conceptions of violence are used discursively to amplify and extend the cultural force of violent acts or how those violent acts themselves can generate a shared idiom of meaning for violent death—and this is precisely what is meant by the 'poetics of violent practice.' " As one would expect in a research seminar composed of a heterogeneous group of anthropologists joined by a literary critic and a historian, there were lively discussions and heated arguments about these very terms. Particularly for the anthropological majority, the issue was how to conceptualize and analyze the variety of discourses and practices of violence in diverse places and situations. While there was a rough consensus on the salience of local meanings imputed to violence and traces of wider historical conflicts embedded in memory, history, and practice, much else was in dispute.

Aretxaga was critically concerned with the *multiple genealogies of violence*. She argued that we should reject the conventional move of beginning analyses by defining violence, creating typologies of violence, or using Riches' perpetrator-victim-audience paradigm to frame investigations (Riches 1986; Stewart and Strathern 2002). Aretxaga was particularly critical of Riches' distinction between expressive and instrumental violence—which she regarded as "false"—noting that all violence is expressive. For her, defending one's own (or critically deconstructing others') definitions of violence, typologizing genocide, or using Riches' structural model all detract from the more challenging project of generating rich ethnographic accounts of events that require local understandings to interpret and historical and transnational contextualization to fully comprehend. The challenge is to do justice to the multiple genealogies of violence. Many would agree with Aretxaga that the limitation of most typologies is their codification and reification of the phenomena they seek to represent, often stripping away history, and, thus, failing to deal adequately with power, inequality, and signification. Their predictive research paradigm misses the heart of the matter, the human cost, dynamic power relations, and identity politics which can be examined to yield new understandings of the state and the internalization of violence by many parties in these situations.

Aretxaga was interested in *theorizing genealogies and political formations of violence in democracies* as part of a wider self-reflexive political critique of institutionalized violence in Europe. This framing is a corrective to anthropology's focus on the "other," on the subaltern and on the periphery of the Western great powers. Her second book, *Shattering Silence* (1997), and her many essays on Northern Ireland dealt with British state terrorism in Northern Ireland, Irish nationalist resistance, and women's gendered politicization through activism on the streets and in prison. Her later project on Basque youth violence, state repression, and community responses continued her concern with "states of exception," situations where states suspend the rule of law, propagate ideologies of radical otherness elaborated to exclude certain sectors from their rights of citizens, and normalize violence against targeted civilians in the name of preserving order. She was struck, as many others have been, by the radical blurring of perpetrators, victims, and audiences in these situations, marked by state induced fragmentation, ambiguity, and uncertainty. Her own line of questioning was concerned with portraying moments of rupture that show how violence disrupts systems of interpretation and leads to the proliferation of discourses. In her work on Basque violence, she was especially interested in ethnographically pursuing shock and the space of rumor and panic at what she found to be the brink of interpretation. Here she pressed on with Lacanian concerns about the unconscious as revealing other dimensions of state and oppositional politics and meanings beyond the discursive. To capture the intimacy of violence, Aretxaga wrote experimental ethnography that engaged silence and madness, the circulation of oblique narratives in daily life and events narrativized in the news, marked as unintelligible.

In both research projects, Aretxaga was interested in multiple histories of violence, the recognition that analytical commentaries—by academics and others—about violence came not just from anthropologists in the U.S. and Europe, but from peer intellectuals in the community and in social movements. She wanted to represent the generative and fragmenting effects of violence, the production of certain forms of the political, of statehood, of political consciousness/unconsciousness. The key question for Aretxaga was what is at stake in the particular expressiveness of violent acts by representatives of the state power and its opposition—competing ways of politicizing violence, revealing surreal subversions of state power, legacies of colonial and oppositional histories, positionalities of protest and power, and memories that both recognize and forget.

Ethnographic Narratives and Their Representational Strategies

Aretxaga thought of her Northern Ireland research as a project that continued unfinished business from her early work in *Los Funerales en el Nacionalismo Radical Vasco: Ensayo Antropológico* (1987). She was interested in raising a new range of gendered questions about state terror and radical political nationalism. Sometimes she talked about the limits of popular leftist politics in Spain, the lack of a gendered agenda in social and political critique at that time. The move to the U.S., where she pursued graduate studies in anthropology, was complicated, given her close ties to her family in Spain and many contacts in Europe. Aretxaga continued to see the U.S. as a place of great personal freedom and terrible political contradiction.

She faced the challenge of the transition. She had come from the Basque Country with only a few words of English after having said so much politically and anthropologically in Spanish. She quickly created her own cultural amalgam, just as her writing in English took on a special Basque-Spanish-English rhythm and inflection. It was clear to everyone at Princeton, where she did her PhD, that her background as a leftist youth activist and her identity as a Basque would give her unique legitimacy and access to the Nationalist community in Belfast. In reading her field notes, it is also clear that the Basque situation was often on her mind.

Aretxaga knew that field research in a war zone would have to be circumscribed, so she framed her project as one dealing with the history of British colonialism, community political activism, and political prisoners in Northern Ireland. It would have been next to impossible to ethnographically research the armed wing of the IRA in the late 1980s. As it turned out, this was a powerful decision because history was such an important aspect of everyday life and conversation in Belfast. Aretxaga argues that it is a mistake to start with the "troubles" of the 1970s in and of themselves because they cannot be understood without still deeper historical referents.

Aretxaga's field notes, written in 6 x 8" bound notebooks with lined pages, model a particular kind of fieldwork. Sometimes she quickly jotted down cryptic notes, who she planned to meet, where, when. These notes are mixed with materials from news sources or other media, observations of an event, and detailed notes on passing conversations or formal talks. There are no lists of questions for formal interviews, no surveys that I have ever seen; rather more of an ethnographic diary, filmic in quality, of people talking to her as events unfolded or in chance encounters. Sometimes there are dialogues, amusing moments, as when she is tired of telling her story and answering more questions. To a passing stranger she becomes a simple student rather than an academic researcher. Sometimes there are frustrated comments about doing anthropology at all in a difficult situation without a clear political exit for the people she is studying.

Aretxaga burnished some of her handwritten field notes and interviews from her notebooks into typescripts which can be seen as stepping stones to the arguments she developed and contextualized theoretically in her published works. It would be a mistake, of course, to see these field notes as not theoretically engaged or as somehow pre-theoretical for several reasons. Aretxaga's own research proposals were driven by emerging anthropological debates. She was concerned with contesting conventional portrayals of violence and examining issues that many scholars of Northern Ireland had ignored—gendered politics, discourses, and activism. Throughout her time in Belfast, she was a voracious reader of philosophy, social theory, post-colonial studies, feminist theory, and European scholarship. There are often scribbles in her field notebooks of suggestions from friends, readings lists, and notes on passages of interest in the books she was reading or from talks she attended.

What stands out in her field notes is her desire to capture the individual voices of working-class women and men as they lived and remembered events which in other studies become abstracted as "policies" or "periods" of strife, for instance, the 1970 curfew policy of the counterinsurgency state. Many of these notes deal with retrospective oral histories that place people in the contexts of their lives and wider political events. As in a documentary film, we do not see her questions but we feel her presence. Sometimes the field notes are transcriptions of interviews, on other occasions they are a recounting of a discussion or meeting. The style of her field notes is self-reflexive in that Aretxaga always narrates the context of the encounter, leading to the representational strategy of "a story within a story." As often as not the traces of this initial framing are lost when these narratives are divided up and woven into longer analytical texts.

In this essay, I have maintained the original form of the refined notes Aretxaga prepared for herself. I quote passages at their "natural" length[5] rather than excerpting cross-sections of all her notes over time. This allows me to offer close readings of some of the longer passages in this essay. The results are fascinating. It becomes clear how richly polyphonic the individual accounts are, how many more layers of intersubjective meaning and irony there are in the recounted memories to the anthropologist as an engaged audience. In Aretxaga's published essays, the passages become oral histories. They are given new contexts, driven by the lines of analysis and argumentation Aretxaga advances, by theoretical concerns, thematics, and debates central to her intellectual project. What I find

---

5. Of course, there is no unmediated length for these stories, no original, so to speak, but only copies of copies by the speaker and the notetaker.

impressive is that Aretxaga chose to keep some of the longer passages intact, offering readers a chance to see the play of meanings in the original encounters.

In *Shattering Silence* (1997), Aretxaga quotes one of her first conversations in 1987 Belfast. This woman responded to her plan to write a book on Nationalist women with the assertion that, "women are the backbone of the struggle; they are the ones carrying the war here and they are not receiving the recognition they deserve." Aretxaga wondered, if this were the case, "why after almost twenty years had women not become part of the visible body of the struggle…why were they still politically unrecognized?" (1997: ix). Aretxaga's ethnographic exploration of the gendering of politics and the politics of gender brought her into very interesting tension with feminist activism of the U.S. and Northern Ireland. In her field notes, one can see her grappling with the challenge of representing political subjectivity and violence. She listened as individual women reflected on key periods of state intervention, community life violently torn apart, and IRA militancy. In her field notes, many of her interviews become stories within stories of ordinary people reliving the wave of popular resistance that began with the civil rights movement in 1969 and the subsequent curfew in 1970, women's activism finding milk for their family's children and participating in the hen patrols, and young women's dirty protests at the Armagh prison in 1980, before Bobby Sands' fast to the death a year later. Let me quote from her field notes to illustrate the genre Aretxaga created for herself to explore the ways that people remembered and reflected their own histories. In this "story within the story" narrative, Aretxaga uses a representational strategy that begins and closes with political friends drinking and singing together in the present and includes one woman's gentle reminder that women should also be the subject of songs of political glory.

6 Feb. 89.

Last Saturday (two days ago) went out with M, N, O, P. After the pub closed we went to a party. I asked Pauline about her memories of '69. She was 13 at the time. She didn't know what was happening. She remembered the smell of houses being burned at Bombay St. A neighbor came and told them there was serious trouble going on and they had to leave the house, it was better to get out. They got out only with some clothes in plastic bags. They left everything else behind. They started walking. They didn't know where to go. They ended up in Andersontown. They were lucky, a family looked after them. After a while they went back home. The house was wrecked by the army. Everything surrounded by barbed wire.

Then the curfew came. Her mother just had a baby and was sick in the bed. Her father was in England working. The baby needed food and there was no milk. Without thinking about it, she run into the streets to get to the shop for milk. The soldiers shouted at her to stop or they'll kill her. She didn't care, she run through the Brits. She says she didn't realize the risk at the time. It just had to be done. "It was all for the family, you know, got to the shop and got the milk for the baby." She did not know what was happening at the time but she learned soon what the British army meant. Just for experience. "They came to defend us but soon they were harassing and attacking." In school they were also told the British army should not be there. It was not right. "Some people think this is a question of religion but it's not. My father was a protestant. I don't care which religion anyone is. This is not a war of religion, this is a political war. Nothing is gonna be resolved until the Brits get out. That's the first thing for any chance of peace. Some people say you don't have to look back into history. But you do have to look at history, because history repeats itself. Learning from history you can go forward."

The party goes on. Men and women, all young, are singing. They are quite drunk. They are singing, "Glory, oh glory to the fenian men." The voice of a woman substitutes the word men for women and repeats it, "Women, there are fenian women too you know." She was Pauline's sister.

Here we see how Arextaga's concern with history in this violent neo-colonial situation is echoed in people's commitment to a policitized learning, when history is remembered to highlight the lesson of British protection morphing into violent domination. The voice in this passage is one of an adult activist remembering her childhood, the smell of burning houses, their own sudden displacement, only to return to their home, a war zone surrounded by barbed wire.

In Aretxaga's research, the imagery of unarmed women breaking through British lines to find milk to feed their families' babies—"because it had to be done"—is a recurrent theme. It naturalizes women's connections to political action so successfully that women often portray themselves as unaware of the risks they are taking. In recounting these stories, women highlighted their great frustration during the curfews of not being able to carry out their most basic family responsibilities for the children.

In this woman's account, other sectarian divisions pale in significance as the community copes with curfews, invasions, and state violence by the British forces in 1969. In the following passages from Aretxaga's notes, one can see the gendered themes of neighborhood and home invasions converge with growing threats of personal invasion as body search and strip search policies are implemented. This echoes Aretxaga's comment:

> The feeling of being overpowered experienced by working-class Catholics in Northern Ireland was inscribed at the border in the bodies of these women who felt poked and searched, manipulated and surveyed, and deprived of autonomy—just like the streets where they live were surveyed and controlled by the continuous occupation of the police and British army. And just as their bodies were appropriated by the security forces, these nationalist women also felt that the Irish nation—still under British control in the political imaginary of the nationalists—was deprived of autonomy and held hostage within its own boundaries (Aretxaga 1998: 20).

In another account from the period of state terror after the emergence of the civil rights movement, Aretxaga's interview produces as nesting stories of British violence with the violence of the armed resistance:

> Talking to Christine. Housewife. Four children, all married. Very ordinary woman. Works at a public institution.

> She was living at Conway Street when the curfew [happened]: *It was terrifying, so it was, unbelievable. You know how Jews felt in Germany, it was the same. When I see it on TV there was no difference. You really know how a Jew or Black person feels. There were soldiers all around. The helicopter announced nobody could come of out of the houses. In those days the soldiers were much worse than today.*

They were dragging men out of the houses kicking and beating them with the butts of their rifles, thrown to the ground, terrible to have to see that and not being able to do nothing. Is that feeling the worse that you can do nothing. And it was terrifying. A Brit came asking who were the men in the house, and I said a lie and thank God they believed it. They wrecked houses, you could not believe it. My house was searched, the TV smashed to pieces on the floor, everything broken, and I knew what it was in the roof. It seemed to me that because I knew it everybody could see it, but they never searched the roof. It was a nightmare, how do you explain a nightmare? And there were no food, some people had tins of beans, others had nothing and no milk. Then the women came from the upper Falls with bread and milk and everything they could, oh they were welcome! They got a lot of guns, but they were the sticks' guns so nobody cared. A bad lot the sticks, to kill your own people . . . bad lot. There was a lad that was caught with some stuff and surrounded by the army, and some people came to my husband if we could go talk to the sticks and make them come with a few guns to divert the attention so the lad could escape and they refused. They didn't give any explanation, they just refused and the lad was killed.

It was women who did everything. Husband: *What women did was unbelievable. They patrolled the streets at night, rain or not, from ten to six in the morning, fought the Brits, went to the jails . . . everything and they haven't got any recognition.* Wife: *Women became stronger and stronger as they were trying to let us down. I don't know how women did it, how they carry on. Well you see, love, you had to, you had no choice. And as they were getting worse and greater resolution grew among the women that they will not turn us down. See, love, women are the mothers and any mother would do anything for her children. I remember once we went to court to protest for two lads who had been arrested for wearing combat jackets. All women with hurlic sticks, something Irish we thought. As we got there, there was a crowd of orangies [loyalists]. We were beaten up by men and women alike. One woman got the little finger in her hand broke and hanging from her hand. And they would not leave her. And the police were there and they would not move a finger. Finally we were arrested and charged with disorderly behavior. Taken to the station and they wanted to search us, you know a strip search. I was so embarrassed, I would not have done it for the doctor, you know what I mean, we Catholic women. So I said, "No way, I'm not stripping, no way." Finally we were brought to the judge and the charges of disorderly behavior were dropped. So I raised my hand and said, "Your honor, if we are not charged with disorderly behavior can I have my hurlic stick back?" Everybody applauded and the judge said, "Yes, you can have it back." If someone had told me before that I was going to go to court protesting, I would not have believed it, you know, I would have said, "No, not me." But you learned, and that bad was you had to.*

One can see in this last passage—selectively quoted from Aretxaga's book (1997: 56–57, 60)—a range of issues that are central to her analysis. In the book version, the first section of the passage is used to characterize the extreme violence and terror of the moment. The final section is used to talk about the lessons women learn from their activism and the metaphor of space filled by these memories. What appears to be lost are references to near escapes during the searches and violence in the community itself.

A close reading of the exchange between Christine and her husband for Aretxaga's interviews reveals the terms in which women became politicized. What is missing, however, in the published version is the dialogical quality of the original interview and the ironies of a husband who now remembers men's failure to recognize women's public activism through the hen patrols during the curfews. The husband's own self-awareness is ambiguously represented here: Was he remembering or forgetting his own past? The patrols he refers to were spontaneously organized actions by working-class women. They alerted the community of approaching of the army patrols at night when the community was most vulnerable. The women were gleeful whenever the noise they raised rattled the soldiers (1997: 68).

Rose also speaks of the special terror that body and strip searches held for Catholic women. In her writings, Aretxaga shows how state terror was made manifest and how intimate assaults were enjoyed by the torturers. Both men and women implemented the policy of humiliation in police and prison settings. The feeling of violence was intensified for Catholic women by their special revulsion at having to reveal their bodies to men. This was especially so for young unmarried women prisoners who experienced these random, seemingly retaliatory strip searches as rape (1997: 122–28; 1998). Here the significance of Margaret's resistance to the threat of strip searches becomes clear, and readers can understand why the momentary triumph pushes her to press for the return of her possession when the women are released by the judge.

As becomes clear in the following passage, women had to endure a humiliating routine of searches in order to visit their family members in jail:

> Rose's son was arrested when he was 16 and spent 2 years. She talks about going to jail and getting searched. *You had to cope with everything. I've seen women with two, three children left to their own, finding out about benefits, getting the house searched once again, even if they knew their husband was in jail. And still cheering up for the visits, getting well dressed, your hair done and being cheerful because the men were so depressed in the jails. And then if they had a bad day and were depressed the women will go with that home. I've seen women coming out of the visits crying because the men were in a bad way, and I've said, "They are relatively well inside, they are secure there, they don't have to worry about anything. The children are looked after, they got the comradeship, the education." Now that I think about it, the men got the easy way, the women were left to cope with all the mess that was going on, the searches, the poverty, the children, the abuse, and the constant worry. Because worry never goes away. And they are in jail and you think about them all the time and worry. And still having to keep morale up for the men. But when you were back home alone again that was another thing, you know, you went down then.*

One of Aretxaga's ethnographic goals was to capture the *feeling* of making a life in this political situation rather than just documenting the techniques of repression. In this passage, one can see the ways women and men coped with the impact of having political prisoners, classified as criminals, in their families. Women's double consciousness and resentment is revealed in these statements, their awareness of the conventional contrast between home and politics that was upended and blurred during "the troubles" (Aretxaga 1997: 55). One can see how women's bodies anchored these ironic, multi-layered representations: they were physically harassed by the guards when they visited the jails at the same time as they dressed in their best to reassure the men in their families that all was well. Clearly it was not. The power of this narrative comes from these cross-currents of emotion. Aretxaga's interview does a very insightful job of unlocking the personal double-binds women navigated and constructed through these embodied imageries.

The final example from Artxtaga's field notes represents a story within a story of Aretxaga's evolving understanding of women's subjectivity among community activists who learned to work around male dominated organizations such as Sinn Fein and adopted alternative forms of activism. One can see this as a self-reflection on transformations in Aretxaga's subjectivity, a deepening of her understanding of the emotional power of religious allegory with its immediate connection to the existential dilemmas of people's lives and their experience of suffering. Aretxaga describes the way feelings and ethics came to trump abstract rational discourse whether the arguments were about women's equality or nationalist political strategy. Her meditation on feelings and tragedy explains how people became such astute critics of the church and the state as institutions and why some women largely decided on a non-feminist path for their activism, one that avoided challenging male control of their organizations.[6] The issues become personal as Aretxaga's mind turns for a moment to her own people's struggle in Spain.

May 10th, 89

There was an electoral do last Tuesday, the 2nd of May. It was called "Twenty Years of Resistance." It was a kind of internal ritual for the SF people. The club was not full, of course it was a Tuesday. The purpose was not to gather votes because the people there were already SF. It consisted of music (songs), play sketches, video and speeches. The main speech was given by Danny Morrison. The video and slides portrayed the different moments of the struggle during the last 20 years. Repression was the dominant note and the hunger strike the high point. There was a sketch about the women's part in the protests with the trash bin lids. While this portrayed the fight of ordinary women in the streets, the slide of Mairead Farrell and the Armagh protestors remained the women in the traditional male spaces: the military and the jail. Suffering is the main metaphor. The idea is that so much suffering only can conduct to victory, it legitimizes the struggle and it's the proof of its rightness [Aretxaga's hand written note to herself: suffering as purification.] *When the part of women is emphasized,* [what is underscored is not so much] *where or how they have participated (although also that) but how much they have suffered. This is understandable since the heroes or martyrs become so by means of suffering like the hunger strikers. There is a care in the language of the speakers to include women, but I've got the sense that most of the people present in the do are the middle range politicians . . . About the end, Fergus dedicated a song to all the mothers and especially the mother of M. Farrell, it's "Four Green Fields" where Ireland is featured as a woman, a mother from whom a son has been taken away. With the imagery of the hunger strikers starving to death for Ireland and their mothers protesting in the streets, the symbolism becomes literal, the allegory incarnates in flesh and endows politics with tremendous emotional power. The rational programmatic speeches about women, equality seem irrelevant compared with the images that the song and the experience of actually suffering sons and mothers convey. It provokes rage and determination. I have also sensed it in Euskadi. I've had to make an effort now to remember not the mechanics of how it was but the feeling. This is also like a tragedy. There is no choice. People oppose violence, mothers and relatives see how their sons are denied dignity which for them is unquestionable. Independently of* [whether] *they agree or not with their sons' deeds they support them because what they're dying for is a matter of ethical principle. In so doing they come against the state, and against their church. After that confrontation they can never be the same. The state structures have lost their respect. The unbelievable happened and now they cannot believe again . . . They were taught that there was good and bad, that there was justice. They've realized that what they learned did not work. That there was something*

---

6. For a fuller discussion of women's debates on gender and politics in organizational life, see Aretxaga (1997: 151–69).

called power who took their families away with the blessing of their church. Suddenly the model for behavior was not anymore in the church but in Christ, directly, because their representatives seemed to have turned their backs on him. Their sons suffering in the H-Block [prison for Nationalists] *incarnated the real Jesus. Most of the women who formed such a powerful movement as the RAC* [Relatives Action Committees] *did not bother with endless political arguments, did not discuss tactics and strategies and conjunctures. They did discuss them but never knew their name, more important they used them and used them right, in a manner that neither SF nor any other political party could. They ended exhausted. That's why women are usually more steady and stronger, for them it is not a matter of political competition among different factions, it is a matter of getting things done as effectively as possible with as many people as possible. Used to being the second citizen at home, being the top person of the group is not their priority. Used to caring for many more before considering herself, attention to others' opinions and suggestions does not come hard. Used to administering a house, organizing a thousand things at once, and making ends meet, organization and strategy comes easy to them, by training and instinct, even if they don't call it strategy.*

Here she outlines women's alternative militancy derived from their own experiences and skills, one that is effective precisely because it does not enter the small *p* politics of Sinn Fein organizational culture and sidesteps the political abstractions that have led to clashes of will and politics elsewhere in their communities. There are hints of tensions in this subjectivity, of the feeling of what Aretxaga terms choiceless decisions (1997: 60). And in her published works, there are indications of her continual questioning of both the neglect of gender issues in major works on Northern Ireland and her desire to contribute to critiques of liberal feminism when it became the measure of women's activisms in radical nationalist settings.

Conclusion

This overview of Begoña Aretxaga's work began with her critiques of conventional social scientific approaches to violence that recreate flat realism by stressing structural understandings of perpetrators and victims, typologies of violence, and predictive explanations. Instead, in her own work, Aretxaga was an advocate of anthropological approaches to multiple genealogies of violence that consider the interplay of imaginaries, stories, and experience in the lives of individuals who have faced great violence. Her interest was in capturing feelings and the power of narrativized experience rather than simply documenting the techniques of repression. This is an interesting rejection of the conventional study of radical nationalist movements as an investigation that presumes consensus and commitment to elite generated ideologies.

This analysis has examined Aretxaga's Northern Ireland research with the goal of showing some of the choices she made as she engaged working class community activists in the field and Aretxaga's strategies for representing their political subjectivity for her own consumption during the fieldwork phase of the research. The genre she crafted for these field notes registers her presence in an almost filmic way; that is, without revealing the questions that generated the long narratives she recorded in her notes. We have seen from this sampling of Aretxaga's polished field notes the way her ethnographic work informed her theoretical arguments, and how the driving arguments of her published work compelled her to limit the intersubjective dimension of her interviews and discussions in the published ethnography. There are moments when she talks abut internalized violence in the community and other moments when shc decides not to pursue the issue in her written work. All of us who have worked on counterinsurgency states have faced this dilemma in our work.[7] In the process, this essay has attempted to illustrate aspects of the production of anthropological knowledge behind the published page.

As a politically engaged feminist, lesbian, and post-Marxist, Aretxaga is famed for the power and humanism of her ethnographies of political movements and state repression, and for sophisticated theoretical engagements with post-structural and post-colonial literatures on subjectivity, power, and the state in the face of chronic violence and intensified globalization. Her published works charted new agendas for the study of oppositional nationalisms, political violence, and gender and sexuality. At the end of her life, she was interested in the clash of discourses of citizenship with the lived experience of violent marginalization in democratic societies and with the undercurrents of fantasy that animate rational technologies of state control. The importance of her questions and the richness of her ethnography as an engaged anthropologist live on in her books and in the published essays and the drafts that have been assembled in this collection. We miss her so as a gifted anthropologist, marvelous colleague, and dear friend.

---

7. See Warren (1998, 2002) for examples of how I have negotiated these issues in my work on indigenous mobilization and state violence in Guatemala.

CHAPTER 1

Striking with Hunger: Cultural Meanings of Political Violence in Northern Ireland[1]

> This entire book is a novel in the form of variations. The individual parts follow each other like individual stretches of a journey leading towards a theme, a thought, a single situation, the sense of which fades into the distance.
>
> Milan Kundera, *The Book of Laughter and Forgetting*.

In 1981, ten Republican men fasted to their deaths in the Long Kesh prison of Belfast to achieve Special Category (political) status denied to them by the British government. For the prisoners, political status amounted to five concrete demands: use of their own clothes instead of prison uniforms; no prison work; free association inside the jail; a parcel, a letter, and a visit per week; and restoration of lost remission of sentence. The strike was the culmination of a long fight in which dirt and nakedness were the prisoners' weapons. During this fight, the refusal of prison uniform became an encompassing and emotionally loaded symbol of a transforming political culture. At first, the fact that four hundred men would be willing to live for years naked, surrounded by their own excreta and face death by starvation, before putting on a prison uniform, may seem perhaps a bizarre show of stubbornness. After all, the Nationalist community (the main IRA audience) did not accept British standards on Irish affairs, and did not consider IRA prisoners to be regular criminals.[2] The British administration, on the other hand, implicitly acknowledged the prisoners' special character by de facto applying special legislation to them. Why, then,

---

1. Originally published in *The Violence Within: Cultural and Political Opposition in Divided Nations*, edited by Kay B. Warren (Boulder, CO: Westview Press, 1993), 219–54.

2. People in Northern Ireland use the terms Catholic or Nationalist community to signal an ethnic-political identity vis-à-vis Protestant-Loyalist or British. Thus, "the Nationalist community" is, in this sense, a homogeneous "imagined community"—to use Benedict Anderson's celebrated notion—of shared history, cultural forms, and ethos. Far from being homogeneous, however, the Nationalist community is characterized by dissenting social and political positions that at times have accounted for acute intracommunal conflict. With this in mind, it is possible, however, to talk about a Nationalist community to refer to that shared culture and ethnic identity in which Nationalists of different persuasions partake. It is in this sense that the notion of Nationalist community is used in this chapter.

engage in a long and torturous battle to settle an identity—political versus criminal—that seemed obvious from the start? The struggle over political identity was a struggle over the power to define the terms of the conflict in Northern Ireland. But this is clearly insufficient to understand the powerful motivations and symbolic constructions that enabled the prisoners to create and endure horrific living conditions and orchestrate their own death. It also does not explain why the British administration did not accede to the prisoners' demands, when their refusal was strangling political relations with Ireland and increasing the already high level of political tension in Northern Ireland.

This chapter is an exploration into the cultural construction of political violence, both as a form of colonial domination and of resistance to that domination, through an interpretation of the 1981 Irish hunger strike. I consider this hunger strike a complex political event and a rich multilayered cultural text in which different political, historical and personal strands converge—overdetermining and deconstructing each other—to create a situation generative of cultural meaning and social change. I do not present here, however, a full history of the multiple political and social relations that resulted in the hunger strike. Nor do I assess its political implications for the different parties involved (Nationalists, Loyalists, the British administration, the Irish administration). My attempt, rather, is to apprehend the "bizarre" reality of a group of men who forced their way out of a prison in a line of coffins.

I suggest that the hunger strike is best understood when placed into the larger context of the Anglo-Irish colonial relationship and the set of meanings and cultural identities that relationship created. In this light, I interpret Nationalist narratives of history and personal memories of dispossession. I also examine key categories used by colonial England in defining its political and economic relations with Ireland and their bearing on the British view of the current Northern Ireland conflict.

The meaning of the prisoners' identity is a central question in understanding the experience of political relations in Northern Ireland Nationalist communities. This experience is condensed in the 1981 hunger strike, a historical event that renewed old scars and added new ones to the heavily burdened political consciousness of Northern Ireland.

The "Troubles:" Historical Notes and Theoretical Considerations

The current conflict in Northern Ireland—or, as the locals call it, the "troubles"—began in 1968 with the campaign for Catholic civil rights. Its roots, however, are grounded in the formation of the Northern Ireland statelet[3] and extend back to the seventeenth century when the native Ulster population was dispossessed and displaced by Protestant Scottish and English settlers.[4] In the eighteenth century, the ill-fated rebellion of the Jacobin United

---

3. Although not completely independent, from the start, Northern Ireland enjoyed a high degree of autonomy with its own parliament, government, judiciary, and police bodies. The term statelet is generally used to refer to the small size as well as the quasi-independent character of Northern Ireland.

4. In relation to the Ulster Plantation, see Canny (1987) and Foster (1988).

Irishmen against the British colonial government gave rise to the Republican tradition in Ireland. The nineteenth century saw the growth of the Industrial Revolution in what is now called Northern Ireland, the beginning of communal riots between Protestants and Catholics, and the organization of Protestant Ulster in favor of the union with Britain and against self-government for Ireland.

The identification of the Conservative party in Britain with Ulster Unionists fostered the growth of the latter, and set the political conditions leading to the partition of Ireland in 1921. The partition was a product of British imperialist contradictions, which—having fed Ulster Unionism with its opposition to Irish autonomy—devised no better form of reconciling the conflicting interests of Ireland's Nationalist majority and Ulster's Unionist minority than to create a new statelet in which Protestant Unionists would constitute a permanent majority over Catholic Nationalists. To this end, the boundaries of Northern Ireland were explicitly drawn to include six of the traditional nine counties of Ulster, ensuring a religious cleavage of 820,000 Protestants (most of whom supported the British connection) and 430,000 Catholics (most of whom were against it) (Darby 1983a). The result was an inherently unstable state, riddled with discrimination and political violence.

Northern Ireland was born amid bloodshed and social disturbance. The formal opening of its parliament in June 1921 was preceded and followed by riots and attacks on Catholic districts. Between July 1920 and July 1922, 453 people were killed in Belfast: 37 members of the Crown forces, 257 Catholics, 157 Protestants, and 2 of unknown religion. Of the 93,000 Catholics in Belfast, 11,000 were fired or intimidated into leaving their jobs, and 23,000 were driven out of their homes by police forces and Protestant mobs (Farrell 1976).

Soon after the formation of Northern Ireland, the Unionist government established the bases for the political and economic discrimination of the Catholic minority. In 1922, the existing electoral system of proportional representation, which hitherto had given Nationalists certain control in local government, was abolished. Simultaneously, electoral boundaries were redrawn to ensure a Unionist majority, even in the councils of Nationalist enclaves such as the city of Derry. The government of Northern Ireland also restricted franchise by excluding nonratepayers from voting.[5] Because the Unionist councils actively discriminated against Catholics in housing allocation and public employment, while also encouraging discrimination in the private sector, Catholics were twice as likely to be poor as were Protestants and therefore much more likely to be left out of electoral politics. As a result, a quarter of the adult population was disenfranchised, the majority of whom were Catholics (Cameron Report 1969).

The structure of Northern Ireland was underpinned by a heavy security apparatus (Flackes and Elliott 1989). The regular police force, the Royal Ulster Constabulary

---

5. The term "ratepayers" refers to people who own houses or who rent them from the local council. An adult person without a tenancy did not pay rates (nonratepayer) and according to the Northern Ireland legislation, was not entitled to vote in local elections.

(RUC), was overwhelmingly Protestant; while the part-time voluntary police known as B-Specials were exclusively Protestant and were known for their anti-Catholic practices (Farrell 1976). Repressive legislation gave the police wide-ranging powers. The Civil Authorities (Special Powers) Act of 1922, used most often against the Catholic population, provided extensively for actions that represented a practical abrogation of civil and legal rights in the rest of Britain (Hillyard 1983). Such actions included arrests and internment without trial, house searches without a warrant, and censorship. This piece of legislation also introduced the death penalty for possession of explosives, and gave the minister of Home Affairs power to examine the bank accounts of citizens and to seize money if he suspected them of involvement in terrorism (Rowthorn and Wayne 1988).

The judiciary also gave Catholics little confidence. The majority of judges who have been appointed since 1922 in Northern Ireland have been associated with the Unionist party and therefore have been openly anti-Nationalist. The formation of Northern Ireland exacerbated tensions between Catholics and Protestants, deepening existing resentments and creating new fears and suspicions. Rioting and violence occurred during the economic depression of the 1930s, and again during the 1950s.[6]

In 1967, the Northern Ireland Civil Rights Association (NICRA) was formed to campaign for housing, an end to job discrimination, and a universal franchise. The government failed to make the minimal reforms necessary to appease Catholic discontent, and the campaign intensified. Political tension reached a breaking point in August 1969, when Protestant mobs and local police attacked and burned houses in the Catholic Bogside district of Derry and the Catholic Lower Falls area of Belfast. On August 14, the day after the attack of the Lower Falls and two days after that on Derry, the British government sent its army into Northern Ireland. The scene was set for the rebirth of the IRA and the longest violent conflict in Irish history.

Since 1969, a range of social scientists has contributed to the rapidly growing literature about the conflict in Northern Ireland.[7] Most researchers have used categories from political economy to explain the crisis. They locate the knot of the problem in clashing economic interests and market relations, thus seeing political violence as the result of British or Unionist capitalism in its different shapes and contradictions (Collins 1984; Farrell 1976; O'Dowd et al. 1980). The assumption here is that colonialism is first and foremost an economic phenomenon, masked as religious sectarianism, in Northern Ireland. There is no question about the economic motivations of colonialism; yet as interpretative sociology has suggested since Max Weber, economics is not devoid of cultural meaning. Colonialism not only exploits and despoils, it also creates meanings and shapes feelings. As with other political categories (for example, class) that appear to be "natural," colonialism

---

6. The 1930s also witnessed a short-lived alliance between the Catholic and Protestant working class in response to the terrible economic conditions of life. The brief coalescence, however, was dismantled by selective repression against Catholics and the stirring up of the Protestant supremacist ideology by Unionist leaders and members of the government, who constituted the landowners and financial class of Northern Ireland. For more information, see Farrell (1976).

7. For a guide to and a recent appraisal of this literature, see Darby (1983a) and Whyte (1990).

is also a historically made cultural phenomenon.[8] The political conflict in Northern Ireland, I argue, is shaped by, and interpreted through, cultural models and symbols deeply rooted in the history of the Anglo-Irish colonial relationship. Anthropologists (Burton 1978; Feldman 1991; Sluka 1989) working in Belfast have been more concerned than other social scientists about the cultural conceptions permeating the structures of inequality in Northern Ireland.

The importance of cultural narratives has been also addressed by historians (Foster 1988; Lyons 1979; Steward 1986), and cultural critics (Deane 1983, 1984; Kearney 1988). Yet these cultural critiques have frequently ignored the webs of power through which cultural narratives are spun. There is still a need to develop a view of political behavior that is capable of apprehending historical actors as they move through cultural space interpreting, manipulating, and changing power relationships. The notion of culture as multidimensional space though which people move in purposive action has been elaborated by James W. Fernandez (1986). In this chapter I attempt to endow this space with those relations of power and dominance that so strongly delineate the contours of people's experience in Northern Ireland. This chapter has a twofold aim: first, to show the weaknesses of simplistic political causality, by showing political relations as culturally constructed through time, and second, to critique a view of culture as decontextualized structural systems.

The 1981 Irish hunger strike provides a frame in which it is possible to meaningfully explore the interweaving of historical, political and cultural processes. When Bobby Sands decided to fast to death as a protest against Britain, he was following an international political legacy that had gained moral legitimacy since the time of Gandhi. At the same time, he was reinterpreting and enacting the cultural model of Christian sacrifice. Furthermore, he was introducing a cultural change, because in the process of reinterpretation and enactment, he gave this model new meaning by infusing it with mythological images of Gaelic warriors and modern ideas of national liberation.[9]

But Sands was also simultaneously fighting a concrete political battle in a way that influenced, at least temporarily, the balance of power between Britain and the Republican movement in Northern Ireland. For the people in Northern Ireland, history took a new, unexpected turn. By history, I do not mean simply a chronology of events or a determining cultural narrative, or the interplay of both, as Marshall Sahlins (1981, 1985) has suggested. The Irish writer Colm Toibin (1987) has compared narratives of Irish history to poetry in the sense that both enable similar emotional moves. I take this emotional quality seriously because I think it is what empowers people in political action. In Northern Ireland, history is understood primarily in existential terms—as a predicament that gives

---

8. For an excellent and now-classic account of the cultural construction of a political phenomenon, see Thompson (1963).

9. The polyvalent significations of the sacrifice model can be seen in the Republican funerary memorials as well as in murals seen throughout the Catholic districts. The use of these mythical models, such as the Gaelic warrior Cuchulain and Jesus Christ, in the political arena has its main antecedent in Patrick Pearse, leader of the 1916 uprising.

meaning to people's lives, legitimizing their politics and charging their actions with emotional power. This history is condensed in key events that, taken from Irish historical chronology, have become part of the cultural consciousness of people. To miss the existential quality in the "making" of history, both as event and narrative, is to disown history of agency and leave the creative force of human emotion unaccounted for or reduced to structural determinism. In this chapter, I see history as a continuous attempt to resolve existential paradoxes, on both the individual and collective levels, in a cultural field inscribed with the changing meanings of the colonial relationship. Bobby Sands died and another nine men died, and the horror of these deaths created a new space of meaning.[10] It is to the exploration of that space that I now turn.

Fasting against Britain

The 1981 Irish hunger strike became an international event, so much so that representatives of different foreign countries attended the funeral of, or sent their official respects to, Bobby Sands, the first hunger striker to die.[11] The British political establishment termed the hunger strike "suicide" and reasserted its resolve not to give in to criminals. Although eager to negotiate a way out, the Catholic Church also condemned the strike as suicide and warned the prisoners they were committing a mortal sin. The prisoners and their supporters—that diverse community of relatives, friends, neighbors, acquaintances and fellow Republicans of the Catholic ghettos—believed the prisoners, far from being suicidal, were fighting for their dignity with the last weapon left to them: their bodies—their lives.

When conversing about the social impact of these deaths with Republican people, I was surprised to hear a local cultural argument. Hunger striking has become part of modern political culture since the time of Gandhi and has been widely used by political movements in different parts of the world. Yet the lack of allusion to this internationally shared political weapon is striking. Instead, the prisoners and their supporters drew on a past native tradition for the meaning of the fast. The hunger strike, I was told, had a deep cultural resonance because it was an ancient Gaelic practice that if one were unjustly wronged and the wrong was not recognized and remedied, one was entitled to fast at the door of the wrongdoer until justice was done. If one died, moral and social responsibility for that death fell onto the person against whom the fast had been carried out.[12]

---

10. Michael Taussig (1987) has insisted on the need to examine the cultural meanings created in contexts in which political terror and violence are endemic. In these contexts torture and death become a privileged space in the creation of meaning.

11. The U.S. government expressed deep regret. The president of the Italian senate sent his condolences to the Sands family. Thousands marched in Paris. The town of Le Mans named a street after him. In India, the *Hindustan Times* accused Britain of allowing a member of the Parliament to die of starvation, and the opposition of the Upper House stood for a minute of silence. Iran sent an ambassador to the funeral. The Soviet Union condemned Britain for its policies in Northern Ireland. Poland paid tribute to Sands. Bombs exploded near British premises in France, Milan, and Lisbon; and there were demonstrations in several countries (Beresford 1987: 132).

There is evidence of fasting as a juridical mechanism for arbitration of certain disputes in Gaelic Brehon law (Foster 1989; Kelly 1988). Yet there is probably little resemblance between the cultural milieus of Gaelic Ireland and industrial Belfast. The link between ancient Gaelic practices and contemporary political ones is an imagined (in the sense of culturally constructed), though a powerful, one. For the Republican people I talked to, however, the linkage was not a cultural construction but an "objective fact"; it made up a clear historical continuity. It is interesting that the existence of this Gaelic practice was being used in the 1980s to confer meaning and legitimacy to a controversial political action and to fashion it—not in terms of an international political culture, but in terms of Irish history. In Northern Ireland, where national identity is perennially questioned, Republicans were reconstructing their Irish identity by establishing a lineal historical continuity between them and their preconquest ancestors.

The reinterpretation of Irish mythology and folklore for political purposes was not novel. It had its precedent in the literary renaissance that characterized the cultural and political turmoil in turn-of-the-century Ireland. W.B. Yeats elaborated on the theme of the hunger strike in his play *The King's Threshold*, in which a poet fasts against the king who abolished the customary right of the poets to sit at the king's council.[13]

By the 1970s, hunger strikes in Ireland were, if not a survival of ancient custom, at least a well-known practice in political culture. Ironically, political fasting owes its popularity in Ireland not to Republican men but to suffragist women, who were the first to resort to hunger striking as a means of political pressure during 1911–1913.[14] The tactic proved quite successful and was soon adopted by Republican Nationalists. In 1917, Tomas Ashe, president of the Irish Republican Brotherhood (a forerunner of the IRA) died on a hunger strike for refusing to wear the prison uniform and do prison work. Terence MacSwiney, Lord Mayor of Cork and officer commanding the local IRA, died similarly in 1920.[15] There were further hunger strikes in 1923, 1940, and 1946. But by the 1960s, all this history was fairly distant for Nationalists in the north.

It would appear that the young Republicans of the late 1970s, many of whom grew up in the urban ghettoes of the northern working class during the relative calm of the 1950s, shared little with the Irish heroes of the first part of the century, many of whom belonged to a cultural or social elite and who for the most part had not directly experienced sectarian or class oppression. Furthermore, that Republicans have resorted to hunger strikes in different historical moments does not necessarily imply they endowed it

---

12. The interpretation of Irish political hunger strikes in the light of the ancient Gaelic practice of fasting is not idiosyncratic of Republican Nationalists. Researchers have often referred to it in their analysis; see, for example, Beresford (1987), Fallon (1987), and O'Malley (1990).

13. W.B. Yeats wrote *The King's Threshold* in 1904. The first version of the play ended with the poet still alive. In 1924, after the death of Terence MacSwiney, he rewrote it. In his second version, the poet dies and so do his followers.

14. These women must have been influenced by the history of political fasting in other parts of the British Empire, especially India and overseas (Morris 1978). For discussion of the Irish suffragists, see Fallon (1987) and Owens (1984).

15. MacSwiney was a poet, playwright, and philosopher. The symbolism of the single, ultimate sacrifice is transparent in his writings. Like Pearse, he believed a symbolic act would awaken the consciousness of Ireland.

with the same meanings. We must ask, therefore: What was the meaning of the fasting that resulted in ten dead men in 1981? A Republican woman recalled that time in these terms: "It was so bad during the hunger strike that people actually turned to praying; 'cause if they [the British army] killed children [in the streets], what wouldn't they do? We thought we all were going to die."[16]

Republicans talk about the hunger strike with a deferential respect, almost awe. Voices are lowered, and their gaze gets lost in distant space. In many houses, portraits of the hunger strikers or memorials of Bobby Sands can be seen hanging on the wall under the rubric "our martyrs," beside a picture of the Sacred Heart or the Virgin Mary, and the Victorian landscape of Catholic West Belfast still shows the vestiges of that time. For Republicans it was a point of no return. As with Easter 1916,[17] for them, May 1981 was "the beginning of the end." The end of what beginning?

Out of the Ashes Arose the IRA[18]

In 1934, Lord Craigavon, first minister of Northern Ireland, declared in a memorable discourse: "All I boast is that we have a Protestant parliament and a Protestant state."[19] In 1968, when the Northern Ireland Civil Rights Association increased the pressure to change the sectarian character of Northern Ireland and win civil rights for Catholics, the inner contradictions of the state had became so entrenched that it proved impossible to reform. Repression was unleashed, riots broke out, and the conflict came to a head with the burning of Catholic houses in Belfast and Derry by Loyalist mobs and B-specials in August 1969. It was after what one participant called "this nightmare," that the Provisional IRA was formed in January 1970.

In 1969, the IRA had practically disappeared, leaving Catholic districts without the community defense force the IRA had become during the riots of the 1920s and 1930s. People expressed their mounting helplessness and frustration on the walls, where graffiti bitterly screamed: "IRA = *I Run Away.*" The IRA, which had remained practically inactive after the violence of the 1920s, launched a campaign in the late 1950s. Operation Harvest, as it was called, consisted of a series of attacks on police stations along the border with the Irish Republic. This was conceived to stir up nationalist feeling and create an insurrectionary mood. The Catholic population, however, was unreceptive to an armed campaign. The result was a political failure reflected in the 1959 Westminster elections, with the vote for Sinn Fein (the political wing of the IRA) declining drastically (Farrell,

---

16. Unless otherwise indicated, unidentified quotes come from discussions I had with Republican people during fieldwork in Belfast. To preserve anonymity, I have left the quotes unidentified in some cases and I have used pseudonyms for the sake of the narrative in others.

17. The Easter 1916 rebellion, with its subsequent executions, was the prelude to the war of independence and the Anglo-Irish treaty that gave rise to the Irish Free State and Northern Ireland.

18. Graffiti in Catholic West Belfast.

19. Northern Ireland Parliamentary Debates, House of Commons, vol. 16, cols. 1,091–1,095, cited in Farrell (1976). Lord Craigavon was a company director and a landowner; he also held various positions at Westminster Parliament.

1976: 216). Following this, the IRA leadership—embittered by the lack of popular support and divided over future tactics—called the campaign off.

The 1962 IRA convention marked the beginning of a turn toward a more socialist Republicanism that was increasingly concerned with socioeconomic issues. The shift from military struggle to agitational politics left the IRA ill prepared for the upsurge of sectarian violence in 1969. The Catholic Lower Falls area of Belfast, which suffered the brunt of intimidation and house burning, had only a handful of IRA volunteers and a few rusty weapons. The lack of infrastructure made the IRA deeply reluctant to intervene, because it feared the use of arms would justify harsh repression from local police (RUC) and B-specials, to which it would be unable to respond logistically. In addition, the leadership—which at the time was located in Dublin, far from the unfolding reality of the north—feared armed intervention would further polarize the Protestant and Catholic working class and preclude their alliance along common class interests.

From the vantage point of the community, however, the situation was quite different because people were being intimidated, threatened, and burned out of their homes by voluntary police and hostile Protestant mobs. In their view, if the IRA had a role it was as a defense force—as in the 1920s and 1930s—and in August 1969 they expected the IRA to take on that role. One citizen told me a story that illustrates the mood of the community in those early days:

> I think everybody was involved then, everybody. But there were no arms. I was driving with Tony one night and we had a flat tire, and Tony suddenly pulls out a gun and gets out of the car and says to me to change the tire, and we went around the corner because the Loyalist mobs were getting closer and closer. I had not a clue he had a gun, but thank God he had it. And he fired a few shots to scare them [the Loyalists], and then our people [were] shouting for him to fire more and becoming angry [that] he was not shooting enough. And I remember a man shouting at him, "Give it [the gun] to me if you are not going to shoot." But he couldn't because he didn't have enough bullets, and the Loyalists had [ammunition] and they were many.

There was increased community pressure for the IRA to use whatever weapons it had. Its reluctance and inadequate preparation resulted in resentment and discomfort on the part of many people in the Catholic ghettoes. Some IRA volunteers disagreed with the organization's leadership and its policy of subordinating armed struggle to other political tactics. Under these circumstances the IRA was split at its annual convention in January 1970, and a new organization—the Provisional Irish Republican Army (PIRA)[20]—, was established. The PIRA immediately attracted hundreds of young men, especially in Belfast and Derry where the violence of 1969 and the ensuing presence of the British army had left them eager to take some "real" action.

---

20. The other part of the split, the Official IRA, laid down its arms in 1972. I use the general term IRA, or the Provisionals, to refer to the PIRA. For a comprehensive history of the IRA, see Bell (1980) and Coogan (1980a).

In April 1971, the PIRA launched a major bombing campaign against commercial targets. Four months later, internment without trial was introduced by the government of Northern Ireland upon consent of the British government, and thousands of people in the Catholic ghettos were arrested (Farrell 1976: 281). After increasing pressure from the internees, the British Secretary of State for Northern Ireland, William Whitelaw, conceded political status to Republican prisoners in June 1972. In March 1976, however, under the so-called Policy of Normalization, the British government put an end to internment and abolished Special Category status for political prisoners. From then on, Republican prisoners were to be considered and treated as ordinary criminals and be forced to wear prison uniform and to do prison work.

Republican prisoners rejected the criminal label. Ciaran Nuget—the first political prisoner to experience the new policy—could wear only a blanket when he spurned the prison uniform, thus inaugurating what became known as "the blanket protest," which lasted four-and-a-half years. Protesting Republican prisoners were confined to isolation without reading materials or other sorts of stimulation, locked up in their cells twenty-four hours a day—naked except for a blanket—and routinely sentenced to punishment cells. The only time the prisoners—three-quarters of whom were between seventeen and twenty-one years of age—left their cells was for their monthly visit, weekly shower, and daily slop out.

In March 1977, the prison authorities decided that the prisoners would not be allowed to wear a blanket while outside the cells. This meant they had to leave their cells naked, exposing themselves to the warders' jeering at their bodies—especially their genitals—as well as to frequent beatings.[21] After eighteen months of this treatment, the prisoners responded with the "no-wash protest." They refused to leave their cells either to wash or to slop out. At first, chamber pots were emptied through the spy holes of the cell doors and the windows. When these were blocked by the warders, the prisoners began to smear their excreta on the walls of their cells (Fairweather et al. 1984). The indefinite continuation of this stalemate led, in 1980, to the first hunger strike,[22] and in March 1981, to the second which left ten men dead.

For Margaret Thatcher, the suffering of the prisoners was self-inflicted since it would end at once if they conformed to the law and wore the prison uniform. For the Republican prisoners, however, to do so was to renounce their very identity. The meaning of this identity, as soldiers of an army of liberation fighting a war with Britain, transcends the individual self to constitute the defining terms of a power struggle. The philosopher Albert Memmi (1965: 128) noted the political significance of military identity in the colonial context in his discussion of the use of khaki uniforms by Tunisian rebels: "Obviously they

---

21. The Long Kesh medical officer recorded 114 cases of injury to H Block prisoners in 1978. The Minister of State, Don Concannon, denied the abuse of prisoners, stating that no punishment had ever been imposed on warders for that reason.

22. The first hunger strike, led by Brendan Hughes, began in 1980. It was called off after fifty-three days when the British administration produced a document that seemed to concede implicitly to the prisoners' five demands. Once the hunger strike was abandoned, the British government claimed the demands were not contained in the document, a position that prompted the second hunger strike.

hoped to be considered soldiers and [be] treated in accordance with the rules of war. There is profound meaning in this emphatic desire as it was by this tactic that they laid claim to and wore the dress of history."

For the IRA prisoners, to wear a prison uniform meant to assume Britain's definition of reality and accept the judgment that Ireland's history was no more than a concatenation of criminal acts. That attitude contradicted not only their symbolic construction of nationality but, as we see later, their very existential experience. Furthermore, the prison uniform meant downgrading to the level of criminals not only themselves, but also their families and the community to which they belonged. Ultimately, wearing the uniform was to admit that moral and ethical distinctions lay only in the weight of the dominant force.

Only an arbitrary date marked the distinction between a political prisoner and a criminal. Those Republicans sentenced before March 1976 were considered prisoners of war and enjoyed the privileges accorded to this status. Those sentenced after that date were regarded as criminals. For members of the same organization—sharing principles, goals and jail—nothing but a "decree" differentiated them; a decree that, cast as "the Law,"[23] exempted the British establishment from political responsibility for the prison crisis while forcing Republicans into the last line of subversion. For Republicans, to reject the moral value of the law that classified them into opposed categories was to defy the arbitrariness of a superior power, to reassert their dignity and humanity. Paradoxically, to achieve that aim, Republicans sentenced after March 1976 lived in the most degrading and inhuman conditions and ultimately died.

The criminal-political dichotomy that converted the prison uniform into such a charged symbol is ultimately about ethical distinctions and political legitimation. Most people I talked to emphasized the low level of criminality in Northern Ireland. With internment, the jails filled with Catholics, and prisons took a central place in people's lives. This was a difficult adjustment that was made only because of the shared knowledge of the political reasons for imprisonment. The pretense of criminality was not only unbelievable for people but unpalatable, especially for Republicans for whom the new policy represented a criminalization of Irish history. A popular song of the time expressed this sentiment clearly:

> But I wear no convict's uniform
> Nor meekly serve my time
> That Britain's might call Ireland's fight
> Eight hundred years of crime.

The importance of the word *dignity* was soon evident in my fieldwork. It epitomized the accumulated feelings of the experience of being a Catholic in Northern Ireland: "Some

---

23. Corrigan and Sayer (1985) have shown the centrality of the ideology of "the Law" in the development of the British state, and the role it played in different historical moments in advancing upper-class and imperialist interests.

outsiders think they understand what is going on here, but they don't. They don't know what it means to be observed, humiliated, made to feel inferior, day by day in your own country." That the Republican prisoners saw the prison uniform as a denial of their identity and therefore of their human dignity was clearly expressed by Bobby Sands (1982: 93):

> That's a word: "Dignity." They can't take that from me either. Naked as I am, treated worse than an animal, I am what I am. They can't and won't change that . . . Of course I can be murdered, but while I remain alive, I remain what I am, a political prisoner of war, and no one can change that.

Bobby Sands legitimized his politics on a plane surpassing contingent law. The premises guiding his actions rest on an ethically superior order. It is precisely this transcendental conviction, along with a deep emotional bond among the prisoners, that allowed them to create moral value out of the most degrading conditions. On the first day of his hunger strike, Bobby Sands (1982: 153) wrote, no doubt as testament for the future:

> I am a political prisoner because I am a casualty of a perennial war that is being fought between the oppressed Irish people and an alien, oppressive, unwanted regime that refuses to withdraw from our land. I believe and stand by the God-given right of the Irish nation to sovereign independence, and the right of any Irishman or woman to assert this right in armed revolution. That is why I am incarcerated, naked and tortured.

I agree with Michael Taussig (1987) when he says that it is not in conscious ideology, as customarily defined, but in a dialectics of images and story-like creations that people delineate their world, including their politics. How did those young men and women prisoners of the late 1970s arrive there? What supported them during those years in which they survived practically naked and surrounded by their own excreta? What was the meaning of such apparently stubborn and irrational conduct? As an anthropologist, I am interested in the cultural formations of meaning and their articulation through personal experience, because it is at the intersection at which cultural constructions blend together with unique personal (or collective) experience that modes of feeling are shaped and new meanings created.

The protesting prisoners in the late 1970s were the children caught in the riots of a decade before. Mairead, twenty-nine years old when I met her, was sentenced to twenty years imprisonment in March 1981. She was nine years old when the troubles started and twelve when she and her family moved—as a consequence of intimidation—from their predominantly Protestant district to Twinbrook, a new Catholic housing estate at the outskirts of West Belfast. Mairead's grandparents lived in the Falls Road—the heart of Catholic West Belfast—at the center of the intimidation, burnings, and killings during the early stage of the present conflict. When the troubles began, Mairead and her sister stayed with their grandparents on the weekends and witnessed some of what was going on:

At eleven years of age we had to be actually escorted to and from the school buses by our teachers because the local Protestant youths living near our school would gather and throw bottles and stones at us. One day I can remember witnessing them trailing three young Catholic boys from the bus—a crowd of about twenty of them did it—and they gave them really bad beatings with sticks, and the rest of us were terrified and turned to get help from the other people standing by, but whether because of fear of whatever, none of them would interfere. The young boys in question had to be taken to hospital, they were that badly beaten.

As with many other refugees fleeing from other parts of Belfast, Mairead's family went back to the ghetto they had left in 1966, and began to live in unfinished houses without doors, windows, electricity, water, or anything else:

I'm not kidding you; in fact the BBC made a Panorama film about the slum conditions the people in Twinbrook had to live in, and in the film they interviewed my mother and filmed us sitting eating on the floor by candlelight. I can remember hearing of a young boy of seventeen from the Twinbrook state being shot dead by Loyalist gunmen at the garage where he was apprenticed at the Lisburn Road—that happened the night we moved to the [housing] estate.

Mairead later came to know the sisters of this boy, and they told her the details of his killing. Mairead's world was changing dramatically; and this change was becoming meaningful through whispers, memories and stories: "My granny would take us around the Falls and explain who had been killed. They'd recall the Belfast riots of the 1920s and 1930s, the execution of Tom Williams and other such things."

When she tells me about why she got involved in the armed struggle, it is not a conventional ideology or set of doctrinal ideas about socialism or national liberation that is described. That came later during the obligatory reflection that imprisonment imposes on so many people. When she recalls her early motivations, what comes to her is experience encapsulated and conveyed—as it always is—in images and stories: "Witnessing RUC/British army brutality left a profound image on most of the young teenagers then." Witnessing violence is mentioned again and again in the reminiscences of the people I talk to. "I learned my politics in the street, by witnessing what was going on," said Anne, another protesting prisoner.

A friend, Pauline, evoked the smell of the houses burning in the Lower Falls where she was living and the terror of abandoning the house with only a trash bag full of clothes, not knowing where to go or what was happening. The world shaped by those early impressions created a mode of feeling that led these young teenagers to get involved in a war they came to interpret as theirs. That world was also rendered meaningful by earlier memories, those of parents and grandparents who were marked by the riots of the 1920s and 1930s. Individual experience was embedded in collective memory as a frame of interpretation.

Bobby Sands was no exception in the formation of those early modes of feeling. He was fifteen when the troubles began. He was living in Rathcoole, a predominantly Protestant area. There were only six Catholic families on his street. One day, the Ulster Defense Association (UDA), a paramilitary group that became notorious for assassinating Catholics, staged a march down his street. The Sands family kept the lights out while Bobby waited on the stairs clutching a carving knife. On another occasion, he was coming home when two men stopped him. One produced a knife and cut him. Groups of youths began to gather outside the house shouting "taigs out!"[24] The intimidation increased until the Sands fled Rathcoole for a new place in Twinbrook in 1972. Shortly afterwards, Bobby Sands joined the IRA (Beresford 1987: 58–59).

The Creation of the Wild Irish

The Irish intellectual Seamus Deane (1983: 11) has observed that,

> The language of politics in Ireland and England, especially when the subject is Northern Ireland, is still dominated by the putative division between barbarism and civilization. Civilization still defines itself as a system of law; and it defines barbarism (which by the nature of the distinction cannot be capable of defining itself) as a chaos of arbitrary wills, a Hobbesian state of nature.

The use of the barbarism-civilization dichotomy to convey colonial relationships between Ireland and Britain has a long history which goes back to the sixteenth century. In 1600, Elizabethan England undertook a massive colonizing effort in Ireland, which until then had been very much under the control of Gaelic chiefs and their native Brehon laws, with the one exception of "the Pale," as the area around Dublin was known. Prior to 1600, during the years 1565–76, there were a number of privately sponsored colonizing efforts in Ireland. These campaigns were accompanied by an outpouring of rhetorical justifications underlying the uncivil and savage nature of the Irish (Canny 1973). Queen Elizabeth I, who wanted her Irish subjects to be "well used" during the colonizing campaign, was later willing to condone the massacres of colonizers, such as Essex in Ulster and Gilbert in Munster, on the grounds that the Irish were a "rude and barbarious nation . . . whom reason and duty cannot bridle" (Canny 1973: 581). This posture was not unusual; it had previously been adopted by the Spaniards to justify the massacres of Indians in the New World.

In the sixteenth century, the newly "discovered" people were still very much perceived through a medieval prism deformed with the fantasies of the marvelous and the monstrous. Despite evidence to the contrary, voyagers and explorers presented the natives of Africa and America to the European public as "half-human, hairy wild men, degraded by daily tumults, fears, doubts, and barbarous cruelties" (Hodgen 1964: 362). The Renais-

---

24. "Taig" is a derogatory word for Catholic, something like "nigger" in the United States.

sance "savage" (with its profound pejorative connotations) replaced the medieval human monster, becoming a central category in European thought. Not only was savagery projected onto people of distant lands, but the Irish neighbors fell into this category as well. Edmund Spenser's *A View of the Present State of Ireland*, written in 1596, summarized the then-current arguments for the wildness and barbarity of the Irish, and advocated harsh military policy as the only path by which to civilize them.

Elizabethan colonizers not only were familiar with travel writings and Spanish literature on the conquest of the New World and their images of barbarism; they were also well versed on available "knowledge" of the Irish. Two popular sources dealing with the Irish were Sebastian Muenster's *Cosmographiae Universalis*, written in 1544, and *Theatrum Orbis Terrarum*, written by the geographer Abraham Ortelius in 1570. Both describe the Irish as wild, uncivil, and cruel. Sixteenth-century colonizers in Ireland were also strict Protestants to whom the Catholicism of Gaelic Ireland (which did not fully conform to Roman liturgy) was simply paganism. The Irish, said historian William Camden in 1610, were "in some places wilde and very uncivill," among whom there was "neither divine service; nor any form of chapella . . . no Altars at all . . . the Missal or Masse booke all torne" (quoted in Hodgen 1965: 365).

The social structure was similarly interpreted according to medieval models of barbarism. Although Gaelic society was structured in a complex and hierarchical form, its positions of political authority, as well as land tenure, were not fixed by right of inheritance, but had a contractual character and could be redefined in every generation. This, coupled with the Gaelic practice of transhumance, accounted for a great deal of fluidity in Gaelic society, which the English interpreted as barbaric chaos (Foster 1988). Once the barbarous and pagan character of the native Irish was established, Elizabethan England concluded that "it was England's duty to educate the Irish brutes" (Smyth as quoted in Canny 1973: 588). Many English colonizers cited Spanish sources to justify their harsh measures in dealing with barbarous people.[25] By the beginning of the seventeenth century, eighty-five percent of the land in Ireland had been expropriated and given to Protestant planters and Cromwellian soldiers.

The sixteenth-century English held a dualistic conception of barbarian societies. Against all evidence, there were—for Smyth as well as for Spenser—two kinds of people in Ireland: the tyrannical and cruel lords governing the docile and simple tenants. It was part of the civilizing mission to liberate the latter from the tyranny of the former (Canny 1973). The official English view in the 1600s argued that it was not a war of conquest that was being waged in Ireland, but the "rooting out" of a few "unnatural and barbarous rebels" (Foster 1989: 35). In a similar vein, it has been characteristic of British officials since the early 1970s to portray the Catholic community in Northern Ireland as com-

---

25. The most extended Spanish influence was *De Orbe Novo* ("On the New World"), written by Peter Martyr D'Anghiera in 1555. According to Margaret T. Hodgen (1964), Peter Martyr was an "inveterate gossip" whose account of the discovery of America departed greatly from Columbus' descriptions, employing the fabulous invention of the medieval travel genre more than any kind of realist description.

posed of ordinary peace-loving people who are sick of the wicked terrorists who dominate them. The British army has been portrayed as a neutral third party whose duty it is to defend the common people from the tyranny of terrorists cast as brutal gangsters.

As with the English of four centuries ago, during the last twenty years in Northern Ireland the British government has combined the imagery of a murderous and hated group of terrorists with generalized intimidation against the Catholic minority. The incongruity of this policy has not deterred British governments, who seem systematically reluctant to learn from their own history.[26] When the military occupation and the policy of criminalization failed to "normalize" the political climate in Northern Ireland, the British establishment—instead of reassessing its policies—went back to its deep-rooted anti-Irish prejudices and concluded that the Irish were irrational and intractable. From the standpoint of British dominant ideology, the 1981 hunger strike was the ultimate proof of Irish irrationality because it was perceived as totally arbitrary and self-inflicted action (O'Malley: 1990). The situation was blamed on prisoners' depravity, in the same way seventeenth-century colonizers, such as Moryson, blamed Irish ills on Gaelic perversity (Foster: 1989). That they still think of the Irish—at least in Northern Ireland—as basically barbarian is expressed by many comments; two will suffice as examples.

The BBC broadcast a series of interviews on the *Tonight* program in the spring of 1977, with Bernard O'Connor, a schoolteacher, and Michael Lavelle, a production controller at a factory, in which they made allegations about the use of torture by the interrogators at Castlereagh interrogation center. After the program, conservatives in England and Northern Ireland protested strongly, accusing the BBC of aiding terrorism, and demanding tougher security measures. The respected *Sunday Times* newspaper added to the controversy by stating that "the notorious problem is how a civilized country can overpower uncivilized people without becoming less civilized in the process" (quoted in Curtis 1984: 55). If the Tories saw the allegations of torture as a sign of the strength of terrorist propaganda in the media, the liberal English were concerned about degeneration. The dilemma is an old one. The problem is not the legitimacy of overpowering others—that is granted by the other's inferiority—but how to avoid degradation while in contact with them. Far from being "naturally" superior, civilized morality seems quite easily corruptible.

A more recent instance of the resilience of British anti-Irish prejudice is the reply of former lord chancellor, Lord Hailsham, to the suggestion made by the Irish government in September 1989 that the Diplock courts—trials without jury presided over by only one judge—in Northern Ireland should be replaced by a more suitable alternative, such as a three-judge court. Lord Hailsham dismissed the suggestion as silly and ignorant. When a journalist challenged him, saying the Diplock courts were a cause of deep grievance for the Nationalist community, Lord Hailsham answered: "That is because they don't think. It's as simple as that, they just don't think and on certain subjects they are incapable of

---

26. The British introduced internment, despite its having been proven disastrous in the past. The same applies to the criminalization policy.

thought."[27] Nationalists responded to this statement with sarcasm. For them it was nothing new; they had heard it many times and felt it many more.

Perhaps nothing embodies the image of the wild Irish people more clearly than the image of the terrorist. They are the "other" par excellence, criminals depicted with apelike features maintaining an armed tyranny over the Nationalist community.[28] This image legitimizes the permanent deployment of the British army and local police, who—according to the British master narrative—are in Northern Ireland to defend "ordinary people" from the tyranny of the terrorists. That this idea is challenged by the everyday contempt of these "ordinary people" for the security forces in the Catholic districts, has not changed British officials' perceptions of the problem.

In a 1989 TV program about British troops in Northern Ireland, soldiers openly expressed their anxiety at moving in a terrain that was perceived as impenetrable, unknown, and filled with danger.[29] It is interesting that British soldiers perceived Belfast ghettoes as exotic and untamed, much as sixteenth-century Elizabethan soldiers perceived the Irish landscape—whose dense woods, bogs, lakes, and mountains concealed and sustained resistance (Foster: 1989). Yet little in West Belfast distinguishes it from the working-class neighborhoods of Liverpool, Newcastle, or Glasgow—the hometowns of the British soldiers. Little differentiates their styles of life, customs, or language—except, of course, the multiple army posts and police barracks dotting the area as landmarks competing with the chimneys of the now abandoned linen mills for historical hegemony and the murals and political graffiti endlessly painted over by the army and repainted by the natives.

The impoverished landscape of West Belfast is familiar; yet, like the remote Irish woods, it still conceals resistance. For the British soldiers it remains impenetrable, even when every household is under surveillance; by virtue of this perceived impenetrability, the landscape becomes defamiliarized and the people who inhabit it become strangers. The soldiers' perception, however, is far from innocent or spontaneous estrangement. They are trained in special sessions to see the population and the environment as things to be wary of and to tame. When they get to Belfast, they see what they are conditioned to see: potential criminals on every corner rather than people too similar to themselves to be aliens. Some soldiers admitted seeing every person as a potential terrorist who could slay them at any moment. Others spoke of being seduced in the vertigo of the game, of having fun by beating someone now and then. The cultural dynamic reinforces itself. Their patrolling, arbitrary searches, and continuous harassment anger the population, which views them with obvious disdain; this in turn reinforces the soldiers' perceptions of the

---

27. "Hailsham in Bitter Attack on Irish," *Irish News*, September 19, 1989, 1.

28. This is not only reserved for Nationalists. When it comes to British mainstream perceptions of Ireland, Catholics and Protestants alike are frequently portrayed as brutish and irrational.

29. Kay B. Warren (1993) calls attention to the cultural construction of space as a symbolic map of interethnic power relationships. In Guatemala, the army manipulates Mayan cultural meanings to infuse the local geography with new symbolic marks of violence and institutionalized terror. See also Warren (1989: 40–44).

Irish as hostile strangers. The contradiction is clear: although the problem of Northern Ireland is defined by the British government as one provoked by an organized bunch of criminals, the British policy criminalizes—de facto—the whole Catholic population.

In 1976, the British government defined IRA members as criminals, yet the treatment of these criminals was insidiously different from standard procedure. Torture was used to extract confessions, and special courts without juries were created to try IRA members. Yet for Britain, the prisoners' refusal to accept this disparity was a new example of their barbarism. The horrific imagery of degradation the "no-wash" protest provided only demonstrated, to the British mind, proof of a bizarre nature.[30]

When Bobby Sands began to fast, all attempts at mediation by Irish politicians, human rights organizations, and the Catholic Church were in vain. When, in the middle of his fast, Sands was elected to Westminster (the British Parliament) by 30,492 votes, people in the Catholic ghettoes thought that the British government would be obliged to recognize the political character of the prisoners. But their hopes were frustrated. Margaret Thatcher's response was her by now-famous phrase: "A crime is a crime is a crime. It is not political, it is a crime" (Beresford 1987: 115). This answer further alienated the Nationalist community and convinced many people that the only language Britain would understand was the language of force.[31] If Thatcher's intransigence was aimed at breaking the Republican movement and undermining its popular support, it achieved the opposite: The IRA and Sinn Fein rose in popularity. After the success of Sands' electoral campaign, Sinn Fein initiated a process of reorganization to lead a more comprehensive political strategy known as "the armalite and the ballot box" (a combination of political organizing, electoral campaigning and armed struggle), which has consistently secured it representatives in the local and Westminster elections. Most important, perhaps, the British strategy during the hunger strike left a deep scar in the consciousness of many Nationalists: "Nobody who went through that experience can say that it didn't profoundly affect their lives. No matter what happens we cannot give up the struggle now."

The Symbolism of the Hunger Strike

> You gather strength when you think of the people in the outside and your comrades, from their deaths, because you know they have died for you.
>
>   Republican prisoner

Some commentators on Irish Republicanism have emphasized the ideology of martyrdom that impinges on this movement. It has frequently been claimed that the mythology of sac-

---

30. I refer here to that dominant ideology that creates and shapes public opinion. This dominant ideology was contested in Britain, if only by small groups who campaigned in favor of the Irish prisoners.

31. Despite general perception that Thatcher was the main obstacle to a political resolution, the leaders of the other main political parties, including the Liberal and Labour parties, shared her position on the issue.

rifice determines IRA violence and the support it receives in the Catholic ghettos (Kearney 1988). This explanation assumes that myths have a force of their own and are capable, by themselves, of inducing people's behavior. It implies a vision of human conduct devoid of consciousness and choice. This view also presupposes both a powerful IRA leadership skillfully using its militants' suffering to draw people's support and a blind following of the rank and file. These interpretations fail to explain why people have responded at certain moments but not at others. It is important to remember that Nationalists have not always supported the IRA to the degree that they may do now. As mentioned previously, the IRA campaign of the late 1950s had to be abandoned for lack of popular support, and the IRA was bitter about this. Little attention was paid to the IRA prior to 1969. People from the Catholic ghettoes of Belfast voted mainly for the conservative and parliamentary Nationalist Party or the moderate Labour Party.

The mythology of sacrifice as the alleged cause of the current political violence in Northern Ireland seems to me to be a new origin myth which conveniently allows one to ignore the field of power relations at play in the use of such violence, both by the state and by the IRA, and its ramifications. Further, this mythology reinforces the too common view of Irish people as irrational myth followers. This is not to deny the existence of a mythology of sacrifice in the Nationalist community, especially in the Republican section; rather, it is to deny that the sacrificial narrative constitutes the etiology of the IRA violence. Such violence belongs more to the history of British colonization in Ireland and, in its contemporary fashion, to the peculiarly sectarian form that colonization took in the North. I thus wish to explore how the symbolism of sacrifice embedded in Catholic mythology becomes at certain political conjunctures, such as that of the 1981 hunger strike, a meaningful frame for political action.

The heroic symbolism of Republican culture has its origins in the Irish cultural revival of the turn of the century. W.B. Yeats perhaps did the most to create the image of the sacrificial hero that became so important to the imagination of the 1916 uprising.[32] And if Yeats reinvented a glorious mythological past populated with Gaelic warriors, Patrick Pearse infused it with Christian imagery and revolutionary action. One of the artificers of the 1916 uprising, Pearse conceived heroic sacrifice as an act of renewal, firmly believing that the sacrifice of a selected few would stir the dormant spirit of the nation and lead it to statehood. Not coincidentally, the day chosen for the revolt was Easter Monday.[33] The rebellion, which lacked popular support and was badly organized, was crushed rapidly; the participants were arrested and their leaders executed. Yet Pearse was right in a sense, because the intended exemplary executions provoked generalized social disturbances in Ireland, leading ultimately to the war of independence and the Anglo-Irish treaty of 1922, which severed the north-eastern corner of Ireland from the rest of the country.

---

32. For the imagery of the 1916 uprising, see Thompson (1982). For an account of the 1916 rebellion in Ireland in the broader context of the British Empire, see Morris (1978).

33. For an excellent biography of Patrick Pearse, see Edwards (1977).

Easter 1916 became a glorified, crucial event—not only in Republican mythology but also in the official historical narrative of the new Irish state.

Myths as meaningful frames of interpretation require a social context in order to become more than interesting stories. By the 1950s, the political significance of the symbolism of sacrifice was eclipsed for Nationalists in Northern Ireland. It was after the violence of 1969 that this symbolism was endowed with a new life and meaning in terms of political behavior. The imagery of sacrificial heroism then took on a new "force," in Renato Rosaldo's sense of the term—that is, it became not only a cognitive structure but also an emotional experience defined by the subjects' position within the field of social relations (Rosaldo 1989). During the "blanket protest," a profusion of religious imagery emphasized the Christ-like sacrifice of the Republican prisoners. Yet it was not the leadership of the IRA or Sinn Fein who created this imagery. In fact, Sinn Fein paid little attention to the prisoners in the early stages of the protest, and the IRA was opposed to the hunger strike.[34] It was the prisoners themselves, and their relatives, who increasingly saw in their existential predicament a parallel with the Christian narrative.

When I asked Pauline, a Republican supporter who had been in jail herself, what the era of the hunger strike was like, she said: "It was a dramatic time for all of us but especially for the families. They say about Jesus, well, Bobby Sands died for us all." There is virtually no house in Catholic West Belfast that does not have an image of the Sacred Heart and one of the Virgin Mary, just as there is no house that has not experienced military searches, police harassment, or the loss of a loved one. Religion is as deeply anchored in the Catholic experience of the world in Northern Ireland as is dispossession. Starting with the Penal Laws introduced by Britain in 1695, to be a Catholic became progressively synonymous with being Irish.[35] After Ireland was partitioned in 1922, religion in Northern Ireland became—more clearly than ever before—a parameter of one's position in the web of social relations. Being Catholic in the new statelet signified being disadvantaged and discriminated against. Religion continued to be another word for national identity. Eamon McCann (1980: 9) begins his story of growing up in a Catholic ghetto by saying: "One learned quite literally at one's mother's knee, that Christ died for the human race and Patrick Pearse for the Irish section of it."

The Catholic Church was not eager to propagate revolutionary values, however. The Church was careful to keep on good terms with the political establishment, systematically condemning the IRA and any serious attempt to challenge the status quo by polit-

---

34. The Relatives Action Committee was formed in 1976 by relatives of Republican prisoners (mainly women) to campaign in support of the prisoners' demands. The organization was a response to the apparent indifference of political parties, including Sinn Fein, to the prisoners' predicament.

35. The Penal Laws disenfranchised Catholic and Presbyterian religious practice. They denied Catholics and dissenting Protestants (that is, non-Anglicans) access to education, the right to vote, and access to government jobs. In the case of Catholics, they drastically curtailed land rights so that in 1775, Catholics held only five percent of the land. The Penal Laws must be understood in relation to the role of Protestantism in the formation of the English state. To Corrigan and Sayer (1985), it was the establishment of a state church in the 1530s that laid the ground for a potent fusion of Protestantism and English nationalism. Catholics in England and Ireland became the immediate "Papist" enemy that reinforced English national unity.

ical or military means. The emergence of the IRA in 1970 seriously threatened the tight control priests had maintained on the Catholic community. This is how Siobhan (a Nationalist woman) recalls it:

> They [the priests] had complete control of people then; if there was trouble in a family or in the street, the priest would come with a stick and beat up the troublemakers or sort out the family problem. Because, even in those days [before the troubles] Catholics did not call the police. There were the priests who had the social control and knew everything about everybody.

The generalized violence which accompanied the beginning of the troubles upset these traditional relations of authority just as it upset social relations in general.

People did not mechanically apply religious models to the political arena; they were re-created and infused with new meanings. Thus, if the Christian ideal of sacrifice and endurance had served the Church in preaching resignation to the suffering of this world, Republicans transformed it into a model of resistance. Suffering and endurance were now understood as active ways of changing this world. The statement of Terence MacSwiney (the Republican Mayor of Cork who died in a hunger strike in 1920) was revived: "It is not he who inflicts the most but he who suffers the most that will conquer." Church condemnation of IRA violence and the prisoners' protest alienated many people who found too great a disjuncture among religious convictions, priests' political opinions, and their own experience:

> My cutting point was when "so and so" was killed and the priest would not allow his coffin into the church for his funeral. I thought that was terrible, because let's put things straight, if somebody steals you something, that's stealing isn't it? Well that's what England has done: steal a part of this country. And I thought, this priest has been in the war and what is the difference? People go to war and kill hundreds of other people for no other reason than to steal somebody else's land, and they get a proper funeral. And what is the IRA doing? Fighting a war against Britain who stole this land! And they are Catholic men, and they cannot get a proper Catholic funeral? I told this to the priest and he had no answers, so I said this is it, and I didn't go back to church.

Forced out of the institutional frame, people discovered new meanings for their religiosity and new expression in the readily available political field. A Republican prisoner put it this way: "I am not an atheist; I don't think I could ever be, but I don't believe in the church. It is difficult to be critical of the church because it is so much a part of your upbringing, and we had never heard before of a feminist Christian or a socialist Christian. But people [are] looking now for other models, like the theology of liberation for instance."

During the years of the "blanket protest" and the hunger strike, a proliferation of leaflets and murals in support of the prisoners portrayed them as Christ-like figures. The physical appearance of the prisoners (with long hair and beards, their bodies covered only with blankets) strengthened this identification. As conditions worsened in the jail and solutions to the stalemate seemed far from sight, the parallel with the religious model of Christ became stronger. For the relatives and prisoners, this model contained the moral legitimation for their struggle in the face of widespread condemnation from the church, the media, and the political establishment. The Yugoslavian philosopher Elias Canetti observed that praying is a rehearsal of wishes. During the "blanket protest," the prisoners went to mass and prayed the rosary daily. When the hunger strike began, they started praying the rosary twice a day, while relatives and supporters prayed it on the street at the same time. "Praying was a form of drawing strength," said the former prisoner Eileen. "Even I who am not very much of a believer prayed when I was arrested." Many of the prisoners were believers, and so were their supporters on the outside. Bobby Sands was a strong believer, and he defended his political position in religious terms when the chaplain of the jail, Father Faul, tried to dissuade him from his strike on moral grounds: "What greater love hath a man than to lay down his life for the life of his friends?" Bobby Sands told him. And that is how much of the Nationalist community felt as well.[36]

Sands' writings are filled with religious imagery. Metaphors of sacrifice and also of hell transpire from his imagination. Sacrifice and hell are intimately woven together to capture an experience bordering on the surreal. "The Crime of Castlereagh" is a poem of 145 stanzas in which Sands talks about interrogation and jail.[37] Sands (1982: 44) imagines the space of Castlereagh interrogation center—with its cells and its corridors—as hell, with its devils torturing him, trying to eat his mind and rip his soul apart, tricking him into evil deals, and offering comforts in exchange for his secrets:

> This Citadel, this house of hell
> Is worshipped by the law.
> Some bear the stain of cruel Cain,
> These are the men of doom.
> The torture-men who go no end
> To fix you in that room.
> To brutalize they utilize
> Contrivances of hell,
> For great duress can mean success
> When tortured start to tell.

---

36. There were other feelings as well—a sense of powerlessness produced as much by the British attitude as by the inability to disengage from the hunger strikes. The situation was so polarized that not to support the hunger strikers was to support the British. There was also anger at the IRA, even among supporters of the hunger strikers, because many people believed that the IRA had the power to order an end to the fast.

37. It falls outside the margins of this chapter to explore the larger cultural tradition of the Irish ballad wherein much of Sands' poetry is embedded. Suffice it to mention the interesting resemblance between "The Crime of Castlereagh" and "The Ballad of Reading Gaol"—the celebrated work of that other great Irish poet, Oscar Wilde, who was also condemned to jail for being an outcast (if of a different type) by a British court.

In a space that is neither life nor death, Bobby Sands (1982: 50) perceives other prisoners as nightmare phantoms carrying the burden of a fate heavier than themselves: "Each looked like a loss, each bore a cross / Upon his bended back."[38]

In the interrogation center the parameters of reality blur. Space is distorted, not mastered, changing, and pregnant with fear, threats and promised comfort. Nor is there control of time; permanent lights make day and night indistinguishable. Creating uncertainty and confusion in the detainee is a big part of the interrogation game. There, one is left to one's most inner solitude to confront the ultimate dilemma of confession, that crucial operation of power producing truth through "the body of the condemned" (Foucault 1979). The production of truth was, in Northern Ireland as in any society founded on the degradation of a human group, vital to its justification and survival. In extracting confessions, the point is not the congruity of fact and evidence, but the fabrication of social truths. "The truth-power relation remains at the heart of all mechanisms of punishment," Michael Foucault (1979: 55) has said. An important component of this relation is, of course, the humiliation of the confessant. Obliged sometimes to confess nonexistent realities incriminating him or her and others, the confessant is deprived of individuality and of the last ground from which to resist normalization. Yet confession also represents a tempting relief from the agony of interrogation. Hence the dilemma, the distorted reality, the displacement of meanings that frequently produce a hallucinatory quality. Sands' devils turn into serpents, and he sees himself surrounded by the inferno's beasts (1982: 56):

> A demon came his eyes aflame
> And round him was the law.
> They danced like in Hades and rats in plagues
> And Christ I froze in awe.
> They spun a cord this gruesome horde
> On loom of doom and sin,
> To make a noose that would induce
> A tortured soul within.

His is a journey between life and death. Despite its nightmarish quality, there is a literalness in this space of death because Sands does not know if he is going to come out of it alive or (like detainee Brian Maguire) die on the way. This literalness becomes chillingly real during the hunger strike. As Michael Taussig (1987) has shown, the meaning of this experience cannot be conveyed in rational discourse because reality loses its cleavages and appears as a bad dream, leaving an indelible print. Sean, a blanket prisoner, expressed it one night: "For some people prison time is like a nightmare from where they never come out again even if the sentence is served and they can go home." As another

---

38. For an account of the uncertainty and surrealism of the experience of interrogation, see Timmerman (1981). For an excellent interpretation of this experience, see Taussig (1987). The experience of living in a space between life and death, where the line between the real and the imagined blurs, has been exceptionally captured by Mexican writer, Juan Rulfo, in his novel *Pedro Páramo* (1987).

woman said, "How do you explain a nightmare?" Only deep-rooted metaphors and images can convey the inexpressible. For Sands, religious imagery and poetic language provided the semantic and emotional space to interpret and transmit his experience.[39]

In the horror of incarceration, amidst deprivation and dirt, there is always the temptation of giving in, of ending the torture by conforming to prison rules. But salvation—that is, victory over the evil wrongs of Britain—demands endurance. Sands (1982: 64) saw in his predicament a Christ-like Calvary:

> The time had come to be,
> To walk the lonely road
> Like that of Calvary.
> And take up the cross of Irishmen
> Who've carried liberty.

If Bobby Sands saw himself walking to Calvary, the last step would be the ultimate sacrifice. Sands' decision to go on a hunger strike against Britain was a coldly weighted one. It was made, contrary to the media interpretations of the time, against the wishes of the IRA leadership.[40] Sands and the other prisoners saw it as a political last resort; but once the crisis escalated and the decision to fast to death was taken, it was the Christian myth of sacrifice—deeply rooted in his upbringing—that he seized.

If the Christian myth provided Bobby Sands with a "model for action" (Geertz 1973), it also constituted an interpretative frame for Nationalist supporters. The "force" of the sacrifice metaphor can thus be seen not only in the graffiti and murals of the urban landscape, but also in how it moved people in the political arena. I agree with James Fernandez (1986: 6) that the metaphoric assertions people make about themselves, or about others, "provide images in relation to which the organization of behavior can take place." In the Catholic ghettoes, demonstrations and riots escalated. If the Nationalist community moved in the direction of revolt, the Loyalist community was affected in the opposite direction. Among Protestants, the hunger strike stirred deep fears and anxieties about Catholics. As Padraig O'Malley (1990) has pointed out, the "no-wash" protest reaffirmed their belief in the inherent dirtiness and inadequacy of Catholics: "If cleanliness is next to godliness," asked Peter Robinson, MP, leader of the Democratic Unionist party, "then to whom are these men close?" (quoted in O'Malley 1990: 163). The prisoners' deprivation

39. As Lila Abu-Lughod (1986) has suggested, poetry can provide an alternative cultural discourse that allows people not only to express deep experiential feelings but also to persuade others to action, especially in situations of intense personal suffering. By using a stylized cultural form, poetry can resort to images and metaphors that may differ greatly from everyday discourse. Thus, the religious imagery and emotional vulnerability contained in Bobby Sands' poetry contrast strongly with the hardened, uncompromising attitude of Sands, the military strategist and officer in the IRA, in Long Kesh prison. Both the poetic and politico-military discourses were inextricably linked cultural devices through which collective and personal meanings were constructed, articulated, and enacted by Bobby Sands during the prison protest.

40. For the IRA leadership, priority had to be given to the military effort. A hunger strike was seen as divesting its resources because of the need to give attention to campaigns and propaganda and due to the political risk of the unsure outcome.

was, from the viewpoint of Protestants, as self-imposed as their second-class status and only deserved disdain. If Catholic walls cried "Don't let Sands die," Protestant wards demanded, "The time is now for Sands to die" (Rolston: 1987). Tension rose as the count-down went on. Assassinations of Catholics by paramilitary Loyalists increased,[41] as did the number of people killed by British troops in non-riot situations. Among the latter were seven children.

Sean McBride (1983: 5), winner of the Nobel Peace Prize in 1974 and the Lenin Prize for Peace in 1977, and founding member of Amnesty International, concluded: "The hunger strike must be understood in terms of the historical memory of British colonial misrule."[42] This historical memory is a contested subject in Ireland. Yet whatever the dif-ferent constructions, historical memory plays a deep role in political legitimacy. Historic actors do not function in an atemporal space or in a symbolic vacuum. The prisoners protesting in Long Kesh, especially the hunger strikers, saw themselves as the perpetua-tors of a long tradition of resistance that went back eight centuries. The force and imme-diacy of this history transpires in Bobby Sands' writings, when he juxtaposes men from different generations and sociopolitical contexts to create a single, identical tradition: "I remember and I shall never forget, how this monster took the lives of Tom Ashe, Terence MacSwiney, Michael Gaughan, Frank Stagg, and Hugh Coney" (1982: 91).

History for Republicans is not merely an intellectual legacy. If religious symbolism gives meaning to the incomprehensible—people willing to die of starvation—history makes meaningful the present as it unfolds in existential experience, directing action in the world. As Siobhan commented, "some people say we have to forget history, but we have to remember it because history repeats itself, and we have to be prepared." And Mary: "The troubles in 1969 caught us completely unprepared, but that shouldn't have happened. We should have known better with the history we got."

History for the Republican prisoners was not a detached knowledge learned at school but the crystallization of a mode of feeling: "History was forced on me," said Anne. It conveyed for Republicans the kind of inevitability contained in tragedy because tragedy is ultimately about facing paradoxical dilemmas. For the hunger strikers, the choice was to accept the criminal definition, in which case they were psychologically, if not politically, defeated, or to die, in which case they were also damned. Feeling deprived of everything else—their country, their history, and their self-definitions—death became the only act to preserve their humanity. Yet the nature of the tragedy appears strongest in the experience of the women, mainly mothers, who had to decide between saving the lives of their sons by betraying them or being loyal to them by losing them:

---

41. Bernardette Devlin, elected Member of Parliament in 1971 and forefront campaigner for the prisoners, was badly wounded; and several outspoken supporters were killed by Loyalist paramilitary organizations.

42. A key event in this sense was the Irish Famine of 1845–49, when English economic policies in Ireland allowed one million people to die of hunger. Without doubt, the 1981 fast had deep historical resonances; many people in Ireland, although disagreeing with the hunger strikers, still thought the English were again starving Irish people.

It was traumatic for the mothers because it's a reversal of all [that] it means to be a mother, a reversal of all [that] you have done for your son. You've struggled all your life to put food in their bellies, sometimes at the expense of yourself, and to watch them die of starvation . . .

Conclusion

The scars of the past are slow to disappear
the cries of the dead are always in our ears
Only the very safe
Can talk about right and wrong . . .

    Paul Doran

The hunger strike was a watershed in Irish history, the social and political consequences of which are only still being assessed. My concern here has been to reflect on a kind of experience that appeared to me as inexpressible. I have tried to show meaning in what seemed bizarre, meaningless, and futile. In the process, what seemed rational and civilized has become irrational and strange. Is it not the task of the anthropologist to show how porous, vulnerable, and context bound our categorizations of reality are? The leading question of this paper was how the ten Irish men—terrorists, criminals, martyrs: that for us matters little—who died voluntarily in 1981 came to make that decision. In answering this question, I have tried to decipher the interlocking contexts encompassing their actions with meaning, and the new cultural meanings created through their own interpretation and the interpretation of others. It is not for me to decide whether the hunger strikers were right or wrong or if what they achieved was worse than what they were trying to overcome. In her superb novel, *Beloved*, Toni Morrison tackles this dilemma. When it is suggested to Sethe that killing her baby to save her from slavery might be worse than slavery itself, she answers: "It ain't my job to know what's worse. It is my job to know what is and to keep them away from what I know is terrible. I did that" (Morrison 1987: 165). And that, too, is what the hunger strikers did. Just as Sethe's killing her baby cannot be understood without the unforgettable scar of slavery, so the starved bodies of the Irish hunger strikers are meaningless outside the ongoing imprint of British colonization.

CHAPTER 2

Dirty Protest: Symbolic Overdetermination and Gender in Northern Ireland Ethnic Violence[1]

Introduction

In a personal interview, a man arrested for Irish Republican Army (IRA) activity described a prison scene of the late 1970s that became known as the Dirty Protest. He recalled the first contact with his comrades—already immersed in the protest—shortly upon arrival at Long Kesh prison:

> We went to Mass—it was Sunday. Afterwards I walk into the canteen and if you can imagine this yourself . . . there were about 150 people in the canteen and all that they were wearing was trousers. Other than that they were naked, and had nothing on their feet. They had matted, long beards and long hair, and they were stinking, really filthy . . . can you imagine? I walked in there and I said to myself, "They are all mad!" Everybody had big staring eyes, and they were all talking fast, firing questions and very nervous . . . you know, all this. And I was seeing fellows in the canteen I had known outside [prison] and they were all just ribs, very thin. I thought they were really crazy . . . mad. I was really taken aback.

From 1978 to 1981, IRA and Irish National Liberation Army (INLA) male prisoners in Northern Ireland undertook an extraordinary form of protest against prison authorities and the British government. They refused to leave their cells either to wash or to use the toilets, living instead in the midst of their own dirt and body waste. In 1980, they were joined by their female comrades, thus adding menstrual blood to the horrendous excretal imagery of the protest. Unlike the hunger strike on which the prisoners

1. 1993 Stirling Award Essay. Originally published in *Ethos* 23.2 (1995): 123–48. This article is based on archival and field research conducted in Belfast, Northern Ireland, from October 1988 to January 1990, and in October 1991. Research was funded by the American Council of Learned Societies, the Social Science Research Council, and the MacArthur Foundation. I am especially indebted to Gananath Obeyesekere, Joan Scott, Kay Warren, Abdellah Hammoudi, and Davida Wood for their encouragement to write this article, and their insightful suggestions during successive drafts. Comments offered by the students and faculty of the departments of anthropology at Princeton University, the University of Texas-Austin, Harvard University, and Columbia University, where I delivered a shorter version of this article, helped to clarify and greatly enhance its final form. I am deeply honored by the Society for Psychological Anthropology, which awarded this article with the 1993 Stirling Award.

would embark in 1981, the Dirty Protest had no precedent in the existing political culture. This action, which resonated with notions of savagery, irrationality, and madness, was shocking and largely incomprehensible to the public in Ireland and Britain. Not only did relatives and supporters of the prisoners admit this popular incomprehensibility, but the main newspapers treated the protest as "a bizarre and foul exercise," to use the not uncommon words of *The Times* of London. The striking form of this political action, coupled, on the one hand, with the strong emotional reactions that it provoked and, on the other, with its genderized character, makes the Dirty Protest a particularly suitable case for the exploration of how subjectivity, gender, and power are articulated in situations of heightened political violence.

Bodily violence has been extensively theorized as a disciplinary mechanism (Asad 1983; Feldman 1991; Foucault 1979; Scarry 1985). In *Discipline and Punish*, Foucault has powerfully analyzed punishment as a political technology of the body aimed at the production of submissive subjects. In the modern prison, discipline and punishment are directed at the subjective transformation of individuals from dangerous criminals to docile citizens. In Foucault's analysis, the body ceases to be the repository of signs to become the material through which subjectivities are molded (1979: 23). What Foucault has not addressed are the points at which the technology of normalization breaks down, the moments in which rational disciplines of the body fail to produce docile subjects; either because the subjects refuse to be normalized, even at the cost of death, or because the exercise of punishment indulges in an excess that betrays its rational aims, becoming a drama of its own rather than merely a political tactic, as recent work has well shown (Graziano 1992; Obeyesekere 1992; Suarez-Orozco 1992; Taussig 1987).

In his extensive study of the Dirty Protest, Allen Feldman (1991) has criticized the unidirectionality of Foucault's analysis. For Feldman, the prisoners themselves instrumentalized their bodies against the technologies of domination first applied to them. Feldman's critique of Foucault remains, however, inside the Foucaudian paradigm. In his analysis, the body continues to be an artifact, an instrument subject to political technologies managed now by both the prisoners and the guards. Feldman, like Foucault, belies the question of subjectivity. Disciplines of the body are permeated by an emotional dynamic that includes powerful feelings of fear, desire, and hate that are crucial to the political operativity of the body. This emotional dynamic is entangled in cultural forms such as myth, religious images, stories, and the like. It is not only a product of the disciplines of the body used in the prison; it also plays an important part in the excess of violence characterizing those disciplines. Carceral violence has been used against political prisoners all over the world, including Ireland, yet there is no other case in which prisoners resisted with something like the Dirty Protest. The excreta and menstrual blood that characterized the protest expose an excess of meaning that reveals the very character of violence as an intersubjective relation that must necessarily be interpreted. This interpretative approach does not negate, however, Foucault's important understanding of the body as political field. Instead, it invests such political field (the body) with the intersubjective dynamic through which power takes place. For Lacan (1977: 50–52), subjectivity is always grounded in history—a history that includes the scars left by forgotten episodes and hidden discourses, as much as conscious narratives.

The Dirty Protest is a good case for an approach that combines a Foucaudian critique of power with an interpretative anthropology sensitive to the "deep play" of subjectivity. To develop this analysis, I conceptualized the feces and menstrual blood that characterized the Dirty Protest not as artifacts, but as overdetermined primordial symbols. I do not mean by *primordial* an ontological essence. I use primordial symbols here, for lack of a better word, to refer to those symbols that resort to physiological material of great psychological significance, and that are elaborated, in one form or another, in all cultures. Following Sapir, Victor Turner (1967) called them "condensation symbols," and Mary Douglas (1966), "natural symbols." I mean overdetermination in the Freudian sense of the term, as the condensation of different strands of meaning, none of which are in themselves necessarily determinant. Obeyesekere has noted that the power of symbols is derived from their capacity to tap into diverse areas of experience (1990: 280). The prisoners' excreta and menstrual blood tap into the interconnected domains of prison violence, colonial history, unconscious motivation, and gender discourses.

Resisting Normalization

With the escalation of the political crisis that followed the riots of 1969 in Northern Ireland, large numbers of people in the working class Catholic communities of Belfast were arrested. Most of them were accused of crimes against the state, a general label that included a wide variety of actions, ranging from the wearing of combat jackets to participation in demonstrations, to the use of firearms. After a hunger strike in 1972, the British government agreed to give the prisoners "special category" status, regarding them as de facto political prisoners. These included members of Irish paramilitary organizations, both Republican and Loyalists.[2]

In 1976, the British Government, as part of a more general counterinsurgency operation, withdrew "special category" status from Republican and Loyalist prisoners, who were then to be considered and treated as ODCs (Ordinary Decent Criminals), in British legal parlance. This entailed the use of prison uniforms instead of personal clothes, and the cancellation of rights of association, internal organization, and free disposal of time. Republican prisoners resisted government regulations by refusing to wear the prison uniforms. Since other clothes were lacking, the prisoners covered themselves with blankets. The prison administration penalized their insubordination with an array of disciplinary measures: 24-hour cell confinement, inadequate food, lack of exercise and intellectual stimulation, curtailment of visits, frequent beatings, and recurrent body and cell searches. The prisoners (three-quarters of whom were between the ages of seventeen and twenty-one)

---

2. Republicans favor Irish reunification and independence from Britain; they include the IRA and the INLA. Loyalists are pro-British and radically opposed to Irish reunification.

left their cells only for trips to the toilet, weekly showers, Sunday mass, and monthly visits. Physiological necessities such as food and excretory functions became a focus of
humiliating practices. The already inadequate diet was frequently spoiled with defiling sub-
stances such as spit, urine, roaches, or maggots. Access to the toilet was controlled by the
permission of guards who would delay or deny it at will. After a year of this situation,
the prison administration forbade wearing blankets outside the cells. Prisoners had to
leave their cells naked on their way to toilets and showers. Harassment increased at these
times, leaving prisoners especially vulnerable to beatings, guards' mockery and sexual
insults, as well as the hated body searches. These were thus described to me by an IRA
ex-prisoner:

> They made you squat on the floor on your haunches. You wouldn't do that so they beat
> you, they sat over you and probe your back passage, and then with the same finger some
> would search your mouth, your nose, your hair, your beard, every part of your body, there
> was nothing private about your body.

According to prisoners, it was the increased harassment and heightened violence
accompanying the use of toilets that sparked the Dirty Protest in 1978. In a coordinated
action, prisoners refused to leave their cells except to go to Mass and visits. At first, they
emptied the chamber pots through windows and peepholes of the doors. When the
guards boarded them up, prisoners began to dispose of feces by leaving them in a corner of their cells. This, however, allowed the guards to mess the mattresses and blankets
of prisoners with the feces during cell searches. Finally, prisoners began to smear their
excreta on the walls of their cells.

In 1980, Republican women in Armagh prison joined their male comrades in the
Dirty Protest. They had also been resisting the change of status from political prisoners
to criminals since 1976 by refusing to do mandatory prison work, and were also enduring similar disciplinary measures. But in contrast to the male prisoners in Long Kesh,
Republican women were allowed to use their own clothes—as were all female prisoners in
Britain. Although harassment and tension had been rising inside the jail, what prompted
women into the Dirty Protest was not humiliation accompanying use of the toilets, but
an assault by male officers—the second of its kind—followed by two days' lock-up in their
cells. What justified this assault was the search of "subversive garments." If in Long Kesh
male prisoners spurned the prison uniform to assert their political identity, in a similar
metonymic move, Armagh women used their clothes to improvise IRA uniforms. It was
in search of those small pieces of apparel—berets, black skirts; trivial in themselves yet
full of significance in the encoded world of the prison—that military men in full riot gear
entered the cells of IRA prisoners on February 7, 1980, kicking and punching the women.
The following quote from a report smuggled out of jail by one of the prisoners illustrates
the sexual overtones of the assault:

> At around 3:45pm on Thursday, Feb. 7th, numerous male and female screws [guards]
> invaded my cell in order to get me down to the governor. They charged in full riot gear

equipped with shields. I sat unprotected but aware of what was going to happen as I had heard my comrades screaming in pain. I was suddenly pinned to the bed by a shield and the weight of a male screw on top of me. Then my shoes were dragged off my feet. I was bodily assaulted, thumped, trailed and kicked. I was then trailed out of my cell, and during the course of my being dragged and hauled from the wing both my breasts were exposed to the jeering and mocking eyes of all the screws, there must have been about twenty of them. While being carried, I was also abused with punches to the back of my head and my stomach. I was eventually carried into the governor, my breasts were still exposed. While I was held by the screws the governor carried out the adjudication, and I was then trailed back and thrown into a cell.[3]

Sexual harassment by state forces has been a systematic complaint during the last twenty years that reappears in informal conversations with women, as well as in their narratives of encounters with security forces.[4] For the prisoners, the assault was as much a political attempt to discipline through punishment as a humiliating assertion of male dominance. Moreover, at the time of the assault, there was a lot of pain, grief, and anger among women prisoners. In addition to health problems and increasing petty harassment, a high percentage of women lost close relatives in shootings by Loyalist paramilitaries or the British army during their time in jail. The devastating emotions of mourning were repressed to preserve collective morale and inner strength, as well as to avoid special targeting from guards. The assault and enforced lock-up in the cells provoked a strong response. Shortly after the beginning of the protest, Mairead Farrell, leader of the women prisoners, described their situation in a letter smuggled out of jail:

> The stench of urine and excrement clings to the cells and our bodies. No longer can we empty the pots of urine and excrement out the window, as the male screws [guards] have boarded them up. Little light or air penetrates the thick boarding. The electric light has to be kept constantly on in the cells; the other option is to sit in the dark. Regardless of day or night, the cells are dark. Now we can't even see out the window; our only view is the wall of excreta. The spy holes are locked so they can only be open by the screws to look in. Sanitary towels are thrown into us without wrapping. We are not permitted paper bags or such like so they lie in the dirt until used. For twenty three hours a day we lie in these cells.[5]

The Dirty Protest was, by any standard of political culture, and certainly by that of Ireland, an unusual political action. The British national press, upon visiting Long Kesh for the first time, called it "the most bizarre protest by prisoners in revolt against their gaolers" and "self-inflicted degradation" (*Guardian* and *Daily Telegraph*, March 16, 1979). It was as incomprehensible to the general public as it was to prison officers and government

---

3. *Republican News*, February 16, 1980; McCafferty (1981); Women Against Imperialism (1980). The sexual overtones of the assault were confirmed by personal interview.

4. In relation to colonialism and sexuality, see Chatterjee (1989), Kelly (1991), Sangari and Vaid (1990), and Stoler (1991), among others.

5. *Republican News*, February 23, 1980; Report by Women Against Imperialism, April 9, 1980, p. 27.

administration. In the Catholic communities, widespread support for the prisoners was not forthcoming, for instance, until the end of the Dirty Protest and the beginning of the hunger strikes. The Dirty Protest provoked an inexpressible horror and a rising spiral of violence inside and outside the jails. If the men's Dirty Protest was incomprehensible, the women's was unthinkable, generating in many men, even among the ranks of supporting Republicans, reactions of denial. It was, no doubt, a form of warfare, a violent contest of power, as Feldman (1991) has noted. But why this form and not another?

Humiliation and Violence: The Deep Play of Subjectivity

Feces are a primordial symbol of revulsion as well as a primary mechanism for aggression and the assertion of will to power. As we know from Freud, they become especially significant in childhood during the period of sphincter training, an early systematic discipline applied on the body and a crucial step in socialization. The disciplines and ritual punishments enacted in jail were deliberately aimed at socializing the prisoners into the new social order of the prison. To that end, the identity of the prisoner as a political militant had to be destroyed. The random beatings, scarce diet, constant visibility, body searches, and denial of control over their excretory functions were directed at defeating the will of autonomous individuals and transforming them into dependent infantilized subjects through physical pain and humiliating practices. This divestment of individual identity is, in more or less drastic forms, characteristic of what Goffman (1959) called "total institutions." Once the power battle was displaced to the psychological arena of childhood, and the prisoners were left in a state of absolute powerlessness with nothing but their bodies to resist institutional assault, they resorted to the primordial mechanism of feces, at once a weapon and a symbol of utter rejection. Thus, an ex-prison officer admitted to anthropologist Allen Feldman that "[h]umiliation was a big weapon. Prisoners were constantly propelled into an infantile role. You could see the Dirty Protest as virtually resistance to toilet training in a bizarre way" (Feldman 1991:192). That is to say, the Dirty Protest can be interpreted as simultaneously literal and symbolic resistance to prison socialization and the accompanying moral system that legitimized it. Feldman has suggested that the prisoners carried out this resistance by utilizing the excretory functions as a detached weapon (1991:178). The use of excreta as a weapon of resistance was not, however, the only bodily weapon available to the prisoners. The hunger strike, to which the prisoners resorted later on, was a more likely and socially understandable form of political resistance. Neither was the Dirty Protest very effective in attracting international sympathy. Amnesty International, for example, concluded upon examination of the case that the prisoners' conditions were self-inflicted.[6] Any socialization process implies an emotional dynamic that Feldman does not analyze. After a year of close contact, an IRA ex-prisoner man openly

---

6. Amnesty International Report on Long-Kesh (1977).

admitted the turmoil of emotions provoked by our lengthy conversation on the Dirty Protest:

> I feel funny now, my emotions are mixed. You suffer a lot in jail, some people more than others. Some people remember the good things about jail, the laughs. You don't want to remember the times you felt like crying . . . It was just strange. You are on your own, you worry sick no matter how much you laugh or share, you have irrational fears. People cry in jail. A lot of strange things happen to you.

I would like to suggest that far from being a detached weapon, the Dirty Protest entailed a deep personal involvement, a process that was tremendously painful psychologically and physically.

Physical pain, insufficient diet, and constant humiliation evoked in the prisoners, in acute and extreme form, the vulnerability and powerlessness of childhood. The sense of permanent physical insecurity produced, as is frequently the case in these situations, anxieties about disfigurement (Goffman 1959: 21; Scarry 1985: 40–41). Fantasies of dismemberment, dislocation, and mutilation accompanied any venture outside the cells and were particularly present during body searches, forced baths and wing shifts.[7] In a personal interview, an IRA ex-prisoner recalled the terror experienced at being suspended in the air held spread-eagle by four officers who were pulling his arms and legs during a body search, while another inspected his anus: "It was very, very frightening because there were times when you thought you were going to tear apart." Forced baths entailed heavy scrubbing with rough brushes that left the body bruised and scarred. They also involved forced shaving of beard and hair with the frequent result of skin cuts. Not only physical pain but the images of mutilation triggered by the hostility of warders made the baths terrifying experiences:

> They used scrubbing brushes to wash you. The whole thing was very violent, a terrifying experience. After they finished they dragged me to the zinc and one cut my head with a razor and they cut my head in a whole lot of places while all the time they were making fun of me. Then they threw me to the floor, spread eagle. I had massive dark bruises all over my ribs and they painted them with a white stuff, I don't know what it was and they painted my face too.

The terror was augmented by the association of cleaning and death in other contexts. For example, another ex-prisoner of the same affiliation commented apropos of the situation: "it just reminded me of the Jews in the concentration camps because every man in the [visiting] room was bald and we were all very thin and frightened" (see also Feldman 1991).

---

7. These images are characteristic of childhood aggressivity and the formation of the image of one's body. They belong to the repertoire of the unconscious and thus appear frequently in dreams, myth, art, and so on. They are, however, easily triggered under special physical or psychological duress. See Lacan (1977: 10–11).

The prison dynamic of punishment and humiliation fueled feelings of hate and anger that threatened to overcome the psychological integrity of the prisoners. The following quotes from two prisoners interviewed by Feldman illustrate best the force of these feelings: "I hated the screws [prison officers]. I used to live for the day that I got out. I would have taken three day before a killed a screw. I was wrapped up in the hatred thing, and it wasn't political motivation at all" (1991: 196–97).

> The hate, I found out what hatred was. I used to talk about hate on the outside, but it was superstitious, it was depersonalized. There were wee people you didn't like. But it was in jail that I came face to face with the naked hatred. It frighten the life out of me when I seen it for what it was. When you thought of getting your own back on the screw, how much you would enjoy it, it really frighten you. You just blacked those thoughts out of your mind. At the end of the day I knew I was smarter than the screws. But I knew the road of black hatred. I just got a glimpse of it. It scared the balls clean out of me (1991: 197).

The Dirty Protest was simultaneously a sign of rejection and an instrument of power, but one that constituted also the symbolic articulation of dangerous feelings that could not be expressed in other forms without risking madness or serious physical injury. The feces constituted not so much the instrument of mimetic violence, as Feldman has suggested, but the crystallization of a conflict between the desire of mimetic violence against prison officers, and the need for restraint to preserve some physical and psychological integrity. In this sense, the feces appear as a compromise formation, a symptom in the Freudian sense of the term. However, unlike the hysterical symptom, the Dirty Protest had conscious meaning and political intentionality for the prisoners. Its significance was elaborated by them in the idiom of Republican resistance, which is part of Northern Ireland's Nationalist culture. The prisoners' political beliefs arise out of a shared social experience of the working-class ghettos and are essential to the protest in that they provide its rationale and moral legitimation, as the ethnographies of Burton (1978) and Sluka (1989) have well shown. In other words, the prisoners knew why they were smearing their cells with excrement and under which conditions they would cease to do so. They were also aware that their political language made sense to an audience outside the jail, even when their action remained largely uncomprehended. Thus, if we consider the Dirty Protest as an emotionally loaded compromise formation meaningful to the actors yet not to the larger society, we can read it as a symptom of profound alienation midway between the elusive hysterical symptom and the graspable cultural symbol. Here is where Obeyesekere's concept of personal symbols (1981, 1990) becomes useful. Obeyesekere has defined personal symbols as symbols that have meaning at the personal and cultural levels. Yet while Obeyesekere's personal symbols arise out of unconscious motivation, the feces as symptom-symbol arise out of a situation of violent political conflict capable of triggering powerful unconscious associations. Republican consciousness, then, is crucial in understanding the experience of the Dirty Protest, yet it does not exhaust it. To understand the Dirty Protest we need to look beyond what is experienced "subjectively" by the individuals (Lacan

1977: 55; Scott 1991). This requires a deeper probing into the kind of relation in which prisoners and guards were engaged, and the larger discourses in which such relation was embedded.

The prison experience since 1976 evoked for Republicans, in extreme form, the historical experience of neglect and the desire for social recognition that characterized the lives of working-class Catholics in Northern Ireland. The claim to political status was so important to them precisely because it implied a deep existential recognition, the acknowledgement that one's being-in-the-world mattered. Recognition can only come from an "other." At the closest level the significant "other" was represented by the Loyalist guards with whom prisoners interacted daily. Although in terms of profession, the guards occupied the lower ranks of the social structure, as Protestants, they occupied a position of social superiority vis-à-vis Catholics. Thus, the relation between prisoners and guards was mediated by a relation of social inequality larger and historically more significant than that existing in the prison universe. At a more removed level, however, the position of the "other" was occupied by the British government, which became the embodiment of the "Law of the Father." Britain became the absent presence whose law threatened to erase the prisoners by eliminating their political identity. The desire of recognition from Britain was implicit in the prisoners' and supporters' representation of the protest as a battle between Ireland and Britain. The prison disciplines, with their uniformity, the substitution of names for numbers, and extreme forms of humiliation, constituted an ultimate form of erasure.

If existential recognition was essential to the prisoners—literally a matter of life and death—the Dirty Protest must be understood as a violent attempt to force such recognition without succumbing to physical elimination, which could ultimately happen—as it did happen in 1981—with a hunger strike. In this context, which links prison power relations with larger social-political arenas, the feces of the Dirty Protest tap into a whole new domain of meaning. They are not just a symbolic and material weapon against the prison regime, and a symptom of the alienation of the prisoners qua prisoners, but also a social symptom that must be understood in historical perspective.

The symptom appears initially as a trace, as a return of a repressed history. In the words of Slavoj Žižek: "In working through the symptom we are precisely bringing about the past, producing the symbolic reality of the past" (1989: 57). In the case of the Dirty Protest, what we have is the reelaboration of Anglo-Irish history. The excreta on the walls of the cells made visible the hidden history of prison violence; furthermore, it appeared to the world as a record of Irish history. The Catholic Primate of Ireland, Archbishop Tomas O'Fiaich, upon visiting the Long Kesh jail, declared publicly that the situation of the prisoners was inhuman. He denounced the inflexibility of the British government that was violating the personal dignity of the prisoners and voiced concern about beatings and ill-treatment of the prisoners (*Times* and *Guardian*, August 2, 1978). Archbishop O'Fiaich's press declaration unleashed a polemic storm. The British government emphatically denied any liability for the protest as well as any mistreatment of the prisoners: "These criminals are totally responsible for the situation in which they find themselves . . . There is no truth in those allegations [of mistreatment]" (*Times*, August 2, 1978). While Unionists and conservatives accused O'Fiaich of IRA sympathy (*Times*, August 3, 1978), Nationalist parties supported the Arbishop's concern. The Presbyterian Church, on the other hand, attacked O'Fiaich for his "grave moral confusion" (*Guardian* and *Times*, August 5, 1978). The prison violence came to occupy an important place in public political discussions in Ireland and England, attracting also the attention of the international media. The connection between prison and colonial violence was drawn during the years of the Dirty Protest not only by the prisoners and their Republican supporters. The *Washington Post* compared the inflexibility of the British government with the "iron-fisted rule of Oliver Cromwell" (quoted in the *Times*, November 22, 1978). Even the European Court of Human Rights, while ruling that the prisoners were not entitled to political status, expressed its concern "at the inflexible approach of the State authorities which has been concerned more to punish offenders against prison discipline than to explore ways of resolving such a serious deadlock" (European Law Centre 1981: 201).

The rigidity of the British government, which held onto the banner of "The Law" with an intransigence highly evocative of paternal authority, as well as the refusal by prison officers to acknowledge any responsibility in the emergence of the Dirty Protest, echoed the historical denial of British responsibility in the dynamics of violence in Ireland.

Historical amnesia, though common enough, is never trivial or accidental (De Certeau 1988). Such emphatic negation of any relation to the dirty prisoners, coupled with the inability to end the protest, reveals perhaps a stumbling block in the history of Britain and Ireland that remains to be explained. In this context the power of feces as a symptom of the political (dis)order of Northern Ireland may lie not so much in what it signified, but precisely in that which resisted symbolization: its capacity to tap into unconscious fears, desires, and fantasies that had come to form part of ethnic violence in Ireland through a colonial discourse of dirtiness. That discourse provided yet another arena, or another field of power, if you will, in which the Dirty Protest acquired a new set of cultural resonances appearing as a materialization of the buried "shit" of British colonization, a de-metaphorization of the "savage, dirty Irish."

Excrement and the Fiction of Civilization

Dirtiness has been a metaphor of barbarism in British anti-Irish discourse for centuries. From Elizabethan writings to Victorian accounts of Ireland there have been recurrent descriptions of the dirtiness, misery, and primitiveness of the country and its people. "Irish" and "primitive" soon implicated each other, and the image of the dirty, primitive Irish became familiar to the English imagination through jokes, cartoons, and other popular forms of representation. Such images have proliferated at times of political turmoil in Ireland, with the Irish frequently depicted with simian or pig-like features (Curtis 1971; Darby: 1983b). After the partition of Ireland, "dirty" continued to be a favorite epithet to debase Catholics in Northern Ireland. My Nationalist informants were acutely aware of the operativity of this discourse and many, like this middle-aged woman, recalled growing up hearing that they were dirty: "You would hear people saying that Catholics were dirty, and live like rats, and had too many children . . . and you suddenly realized that was you and your family."

The investment of excrement and dirt with intense feelings of disgust, which are then associated with aggression and fear of racial contamination, is well known and need not be underscored here. Notions of dirt and purity are crucial, as Mary Douglas (1966) noted, in organizing ideas of savagery and civilization highly significant in establishing social boundaries and cultural differentiations. For many people in England and Ireland, the prisoners living amid their own excreta constituted the image par excellence of the uncivilized, the erasure of categorical distinctions that structure human society, the regression to a presocial state, with its concomitant power of pollution and contagion. In the women's prison of Armagh, officers wore masks, insulating suits, and rubber boots that shielded them from the polluting conditions of the prisoners' wing. Prisoners noted that the guards did not like to touch anything belonging to the prisoners even though they used gloves. Prison officers felt defiled coming in contact with the prisoners. As the women looked increasingly dirty, the guards tried to counteract defilement by increasing their care in making themselves up and having their hair done. Similarly, in Long Kesh physical contact with the prisoners was abhorrent for guards.

The images of the prisoners surrounded by excreta seemed to reinforce stereotypes of Irish barbarism, yet the inability of government and administrators to handle the situation reveals other effects. Thus, I would argue that the fantasies of savagery projected onto Catholics were appropriated, literalized, and enacted by the prisoners. This materialization inevitably confronted the officers in an inescapable physical form with their own aggressive fantasies, which produced shock, horror, and the futile attempt to erase them by increasing violence, forced baths, and periodic steam cleaning of cells—acts of cleansing that, like the dirtying of the prisoners, were both literal and symbolic (Feldman 1991: 185). The "Dirty Irish" had became *really* shitty. In so doing, they were transforming the closed universe of prison into an overflowing cloaca, exposing in the process a Boschian vision of the world, a scathing critique of Britain and, by association, of civilization. One cannot help but find a parallel of this critique in the writings of that polemic Irishman, Jonathan Swift.

Swift utilized the excretory function as a satiric weapon against the pretentiousness and self-righteousness of English civilization. His "excremental vision" (Norman Brown 1959: 179) is sharply displayed in part four of *Gulliver's Travels*. In "A Voyage to the Country of the Houyhnhnms," Gulliver encounters the Yahoo. Although Yahoos possess a human form, they are filthy and nasty, have a strong smell and bad eating habits, and use excrement as an instrument of self-expression and aggression (Swift [1726] 1967: 270, 313). Immediately after their encounter, the Yahoos shoot feces at Gulliver, who tries failingly to stay clear of them. If the Yahoo represents the archetype of human savagery, its juxtaposition with Gulliver's narrative of English life soon makes clear that the civilized human is nastier than the savage Yahoo. In other words, Swift made excremental aggression the hidden core of civilization, an insight hard to swallow.

In the context of the Anglo-Irish colonial relation in which it emerged, the Dirty Protest, like the Yahoo, acted as a mirror of colonial barbarism that reflected back to prison officers and British public an obscured image of themselves that challenged their identity as a civilized nation. This excremental image literally entered the center of gravity of British civilization when two supporters of the prisoners hurled horse dung to the startled members of parliament (*Guardian*, July 7, 1978).

Guards and government alike responded to this image with absolute denial, voiced in the argument that the prisoners' condition was "self-inflicted." Yet the guards' rising brutality reproduced on the incarcerated bodies the same barbarity attributed to the prisoners. Such mimesis seems inherent to the colonial production of reality, which frequently uses the fiction of the savage (or the terrorist) to create a culture of terror (Bhaba 1984; Taussig 1987). In Northern Ireland, the fiction of criminality of Republican prisoners ultimately exposed and reproduced the savagery of state policies. Inside Long Kesh, positions had been reversed: from objects of a defiling power, the prisoners had come to be the subjects that controlled it (Feldman 1991). Yet the prisoners were inescapably locked in a political impasse characterized by a vicious cycle of projection-reflection that spilled the violence from the prison onto the wider society.[8] While the men's Dirty Protest was locked in its own violence, the women's provoked a movement of social transformation. The impulse of such transformation came from the articulation of menstrual blood as a symbol of sexual difference with ongoing feminist discourse.

Dirt and Blood: The Meaning of Sexual Difference

Inside the walls of Armagh prison, filthiness was tainted with menstrual blood. An additional set of meanings resonated there. Journalist Tim Coogan, who visited the jail at that time, wrote:

> I was taken to inspect 'A' wing where the Dirty Protest is in full swing. This was sickening and appalling. Tissues, slops, consisting of tea and urine, some faeces, and clots of blood—obviously the detritus of menstruation—lay in the corridor between the two rows of cells . . . I found the smell in the girls' cells far worse than at Long-Kesh, and several times found myself having to control feelings of nausea (1980b: 215–16).

What can make thirty dirty women more revolting than four hundred dirty men, if not the exposure of menstrual blood—an element that cannot contribute much to the fetid odors of urine and feces but can turn the stomach? What Coogan expresses with his body—it literally makes him sick—is the horror and repulsion triggered by the sight of

---

8. As the violence inside the prison augmented, so did IRA and Loyalist assassinations and military repression. The brutalization of the warders had a direct effect in isolating them from their own communities and increasing conflicts in their domestic life. See Coogan (1980b) and Feldman (1991).

"that" which constitutes a linguistic and optic taboo, a horror that he cannot articulate linguistically. Through his own body, Coogan also inscribes a crucial difference between men and women prisoners. Ironically, it was this difference that Armagh women were trying to eradicate by joining the Dirty Protest.

Women did not belong to prison in popular consciousness, even though they had participated in armed operations and had been imprisoned in rising numbers since 1972. Most Nationalists perceived women's presence in jail as a product of an idealistic youth and the freedom from family commitments. Through the course of my fieldwork, some women ex-prisoners acknowledged that Republican men still assumed that, after marriage, women would abandon political activities that entail a risk of death or imprisonment. Although this frequently happens, it is by no means always the case. On the other hand, the image of male prisoners did not have an age reference. Although the majority of male prisoners were young, it was not rare for them to be married and have children. In contrast to male prisoners, female prisoners were permanently thought of as girls. Their cultural space was in this sense liminal. Neither men nor completely women, they were perceived at a general social level as gender neutral.

The women themselves did not consider gender a significant element of differentiation either. Female members of the IRA had fought to be part of this organization rather than part of its feminine counterpart, Cumman na mBan. Thus, they had consciously rejected gender as a differential factor in political militancy. To prove that gender was irrelevant to military performance in a male organization entailed, de facto, downplaying women's difference and interiorizing men's standards. At the level of consciousness, gender difference was at the beginning of the Dirty Protest completely accidental to its meaning. From the point of view of Armagh women, their Dirty Protest was not different from that of the men's: it was the same struggle undertaken by equal comrades for political recognition. The emphatic reassertion of the sameness of prisoners' identity, regardless of gender, must be understood as an attempt to counteract the overshadowing of women prisoners under the focus of attention given to male prisoners. Such eclipse was partly a consequence of the fact that women were not required to use prison uniforms, and thus were not subjected to the dramatic conditions that the men were. That fact asserted from the start a gender difference that worked against their political visibility. At this level, the Dirty Protest was, for Armagh women, an attempt to erase that gender difference introduced by the penal institution and to thus reassert their political visibility. Yet, unintentionally, the menstrual blood brought to the surface the contradictions involved in this process, shifting the meaning of the protest. It objectified a difference that women had carefully obliterated in other dimensions of their political life. That is, while their political identity as members of the IRA entailed at one level a cultural desexualization, and the Dirty Protest a personal defeminization, at a deeper level, the exposure of menstrual blood subverted this process by radically transforming the asexual bodies of "girls" into the sexualized bodies of women. In so doing, the menstrual blood became a symbol through which gender identity was reflected upon, bringing to the surface what had been otherwise erased.

Menstruation as an elemental sign of womanhood marks also women's social vulnerability. At the level of representation, it is a metonym linking sex and motherhood, a sign of the dangerously uncontrolled nature of women's flesh in Catholic ideology from which only the mother of God escaped (Warner 1983); a tabooed and polluting substance that must be hidden from discourse as it is from sight. In the context of arrest it is a sabotage of the body. The meaning of this sabotage has been forcefully expressed by Northern Ireland writer and Republican ex-prisoner, Brenda Murphy, in a short story entitled "A Curse." An arrested young woman gets her period in between interrogation shifts and is forced to talk about it to a male officer:

> "I've taken my period" she said simply. "I need some sanitary napkins and a wash." He looked at her with disgust. "Have you no shame? I've been married twenty years and my wife wouldn't mention things like that." What is the color of shame? All she could see was red as it trickled down her legs (1989: 226–27).

When it comes to women, impotence and shame has color, not name. Mary Cardinal, in the superb fictional account of her own madness (1983), calls the permanent flow of her menstrual blood "the thing." Her cure entailed a process of inscribing meaning in language, of finding "The Words To Say It." In choosing the theme of menstruation to talk about the experience of arrest, Brenda Murphy—who participated in the Dirty Protest—broke a taboo of silence that made Nationalist women's personal and political experience invisible. One can read her story as a commentary on the Armagh Dirty Protest. Indeed, on her release, Maureen Gibson, one of the protesting prisoners, said: "I do get the impression that people outside [the prison] don't fully realize that there are actually women in Armagh. They don't understand what the women are going through both physically and psychologically. You go through a lot with your menstrual cycle" (*Republican News*, September 27, 1980).

The shocking character of the imagery that the words of released prisoners evoked was recalled to me by Mary, a middle-aged Republican woman:

> I remember one rally in which a girl released from Armagh spoke about what it was for them during their periods. It was very hard for her to talk about menstruation, to say that even during that time they could not get a change of clothes, could not get washed. And some people, including Republican men, were saying "How can she talk about that?" They did not want to hear that women were being mistreated in Armagh jail during their menstruation. And so, the Republican movement did not talk about it. They only talked about the men, but they did not want to hear about girls. Some people just could not cope with that.

What the Nationalist community did not understand, and could not cope with, was *women's* pain. Not a mother's suffering, which ultimately roused the emotions of Nationalist people in support of the prisoners. Nor the suffering of incarcerated young men, whose image, naked and beaten, resembled that of Jesus Christ. Unintentionally, the women prisoners in Armagh brought to the fore a different kind of suffering, one systematically obscured in social life and in cultural constructions, devalued in Catholic religion and Nationalist ideologies: that women's pain of which menstruation is a sign and a symbol.

If the men's Dirty Protest represented the rejection of the civilizing mission of British colonialism, the Armagh women permeated that rejection with gender politics. At one level, it encapsulated the negation of dominant models of femininity embedded in the idealized asexual Catholic mother and elaborated in Nationalist discourse around the image of Mother Ireland. This model provokes high ambivalence in many Nationalist women for whom motherhood is at once a source of comfort and support, and a restrictive social role.[9] On the other hand, the women's Dirty Protest represented also a rejection of male violence fused, as noted below, with political dominance in colonial discourse and practice. In the prison context, the visibility of menstrual blood can be read as a curse redirected from the bodies of women to the male "body politic" of colonialism.[10]

As symptom, symbol, and weapon, the Dirty Protest involved an enormous suffering. The young women in Armagh, like the men in Long Kesh, conceptualized their physical and psychological pain within the parameters of a religious ethic of salvation acting in the political arena. At the level of conscious purpose it was for them a necessary requisite to save Ireland from colonization and re-establish a just and equal society in a reunited Irish land. This ethic of salvation acted as an interpretative language for pain that would otherwise be meaningless. Yet if a religious-political frame can provide meaning to the prisoners' pain, it cannot express it. Their suffering eludes language. Republican women could narrate the events of the Dirty Protest, but the emotional experience was encountered with painful silence and the explicit admission of lacking words to describe it.

For Elaine Scarry (1985), inexpressibility is what characterizes pain, which needs to be objectified in order to be comprehended. But pain does not operate in the same way for women and men. In Armagh jail, the prisoners' suffering became objectified in the menstrual blood; a complex symbol which inscribed their suffering inside the symbolic contours of what Gayatri Spivak has called "the space of what can only happen to a woman" (1988b: 184). As this space had been actively silenced in the cultural logic of nationalism, tensions were bound to arise on the different shades of the political horizon.

---

9. This ambivalence emerged in recurrent comments made by Nationalist women during my fieldwork. Particularly important were the discussions following the screening, in the Nationalist districts of Belfast and Derry, of the documentary *Mother Ireland*, directed by Anne Crilly and produced by the Derry Film and Video Company, and of the play about the Armagh women, *Now and at the Hour of Our Death*, produced by the theater group Trouble and Strife.

10. In this sense, the Armagh women's Dirty Protest is reminiscent of the kind of symbolic warfare enacted by women in some parts of Africa. Ardener and Ifeka-Moller have documented women's exposure of genitals as a powerful sexual insult used against men violating their dignity and rights. This display publicly states disrespect, denial of dominance, and nonrecognition of authority. See Ardener (1975) and Ifeka-Moller (1975).

Mimesis or the Power of Transgression: The Feminist Debate

The feminist movement in Ireland grew bitterly divided as the Dirty Protest went on.[11] Mainstream feminists were sharply critical of the male-dominated Republican movement, whose use of violence, they argued, divided women. At the head of these feminists was the Northern Ireland Women's Rights Movement (NIWRM), a broadly defined organization founded in 1975 and very hostile to nationalism in general, and Republicanism in particular. The NIWRM refused any support to Armagh prisoners on the grounds that they were aping their male comrades. Other women's groups, such as the Socialist Women's Group and the Belfast Women's Collective, quite literally agonized over the meaning and degree of support to the prisoners. The Republican movement, on the other hand, was no less hostile to feminism, which it easily dismissed as being pro-British. Preoccupied with the large number of male prisoners, Republicans had largely ignored the existence of women in jail, seeing them at best as an appendix to the men's protest. Was the Armagh women's protest a mimetic enactment? I think so, but one that had important political implications. Drucilla Cornell has argued that mimesis constitutes not a simple repetition, but a reappropriation entailing a process of refiguration (1991: 182). It is in this light that we must interpret the Armagh protest.

When the Armagh women demanded to be part of the IRA, rejecting its feminine branch, they were criticizing a genderized system that set them in the position of political subsidiaries. This critique already modified the terms of the system. Similarly, by mimetically reappropriating the Dirty Protest, the Armagh women at first negated gender difference, stating that their struggle was the same as that of the men. Yet this attempt to transcend a genderized context, by negating the feminine, was negated in turn by the objectification of sexual difference that the menstrual blood represented. Thus, the mimetic appropriation of the Dirty Protest entailed a process of rewriting a (hi)story of resistance that specified the feminine in its most transgressive form. But it also entailed a refiguration of the feminine inasmuch as it was affirmed not as a shared essence, but as existentially inseparable from class and ethnic positions.

The rising tensions exploded publicly when Nell McCafferty, a journalist from Derry City, wrote in the pages of the *Irish Times*: "There is menstrual blood on the walls of Armagh prison in Northern Ireland."[12] McCafferty shouted aloud in the main Irish newspaper what most people had been refusing to hear; that there was a specific women's pain, and that in Northern Ireland it was inextricably linked, but not reduced, to colonial oppression. Such a link was encapsulated in menstrual blood as a symbol of an existence, of a being-in-the world that could not be represented by dominant feminist and Nationalist discourses, even less by the discourse of the *law*. The menstrual blood stood as a symbol of that reality excluded from language. In so doing, it acted as a catalyst of cultural

---

11. In relation to the history and composition of the feminist movement in Northern Ireland, see Evason (1991), Loughran (1986), Ward (1987, 1991).

12. Nell McCafferty, "It is my belief that Armagh is a feminist issue," *Irish Times*, June 17, 1980.

change, a vehicle of reflection and discussion about the meanings of gender difference in Northern Ireland. The most public manifestation of such—often bitter—debate was McCafferty's article. As time went on, Armagh prisoners began to inscribe their differ-ence in language, translating the dirt and menstrual blood into a critique of a ready-made feminist subject that failed to represent them. In a letter published in the *Irish Times* in 1980, Armagh prisoners answered the NIWRM, which had contended that the predicament of the prisoners did not concern feminists, with a demand for redefinition of feminism:

> It is our belief that not only is our plight a feminist issue, but a very fundamental social and human issue. It is a feminist issue in so far as we are women, and the network of this jail is completely geared to male domination. The governor, the assistant governor, and the doc-tor are all males. We are subject to physical and mental abuse from male guards who patrol our wing daily, continually peeping into our cells... If this is not a feminist issue then we feel that the word feminist needs to be redefined (quoted in Loughran 1986: 64).

The articulation of the symbol of menstrual blood with ongoing political and feminist discourses forced a discussion among Nationalists and feminists alike on the exclusionary politics of the very categories of feminism and nationalism, which had a social effect.

By the end of 1980, a policy document on women's rights was approved for the first time in the Republican movement. Two years later, in 1982, a Women's Center was opened also for the first time in the working-class Nationalist ghetto of Falls Road. It set to work amid the discomfort and protest of many Nationalist men. Women flowed in with a hitherto muted knowledge. A Republican woman recalled that, "there were battered women, incest, rape, appalling poverty. We had been too busy with the war and didn't realize until the Women's Center that all those problems were there too." Another kind of shit had surfaced. As it gained social visibility, the stinking reality of male violence against women disputed both Catholic models of gender and Nationalist heroic epics. Since then, the Nationalist community, and Republicanism in particular, have not been able to ignore easily gender politics. Neither have Irish feminists been able to ignore Nationalist politics. Yet the problem of defining a Nationalist-feminist subject is fraught with difficulties as Irish nationalism—like other post-colonial nationalisms—continues to use gender discourse to advance political claims. Nationalist-feminists have to contend in Northern Ireland with a permanent split between anti-imperialist positions and feminist positions that both exclude them. It is precisely this self-conscious, split political identity that has opened the political field in Northern Ireland to new critical possibilities.

Conclusion

I have attempted to show that a Foucaudian critique of power as force relations is not incompatible with an interpretative anthropology sensitive to the "deep play" of subjectiv-ity. Departing from the premise that the Dirty Protest was a violent contest of power, I have tried to elucidate the dynamics that organized it in that form and not others, as well as its social and political consequences in a shared universe of meaning. I have conceptualized the feces and blood characterizing the protest as primordial symbols. These symbols are invested with political power; contrary to Mary Douglas, though, they are not just an expression of the social order. Neither are they locked in unconscious motivation. They partake of both domains and are simultaneously instrumental in that, like speech acts, they have a performative character. The excreta and menstrual blood arose out of a situation of violent political conflict that became overdetermined by tapping into the interconnected domains of prison violence, colonial history, unconscious motivation (infantile fantasies, fears and desires) and gender discourse, *all* of which constituted the political field at the particular historical moment of the Dirty Protest. It was precisely this overdetermination that gave the protest its shocking power, simultaneously allowing the prisoners to endure its suffering by crystallizing inexpressible and contradictory emotions. The meanings of the Dirty Protest were not fixed, but shifted with each domain of experience into which they tapped, acting simultaneously as weapon, symbol, and symptom. In so doing, they also revealed the gender organization of power.

I regard gender not just as a dimension of violence but as an intrinsic component of it, crucial to the understanding of its meanings, deployments, and ends. My analysis suggests that political violence performed on, and from, the body cannot escape the meaning of sexual difference. Despite the shared political consciousness and goals of men and women prisoners, their protests had different significance. While the men's protest was articulated through an intense dynamic of violence, the women's protest was crystallized around the meaning of sexual difference. Armagh women provoked, albeit unintentionally, a reformulation of feminine subjectivity. Inasmuch as sexual difference is, in Ireland as everywhere else, inseparable from class, ethnic, and even political positions, such reformulation in turn sparked a transformation of dominant discourses of feminism and nationalism.

I have suggested in this article that ethnic and political violence predicated on the bodies of women cannot be considered as an addendum to violence performed on men's bodies. As I have shown, it might have disparate meanings and effects that are crucial to both the construction of sexual difference and the construction of ethnic identity.

CHAPTER 3

What the Border Hides: Partition and the Gender Politics of Irish Nationalism[1]

On September 23, 1989, I drove my old car from Belfast to Dublin, crossing the border that separates Northern Ireland from the Irish Republic. Traveling with me were four women from the Belfast working-class Catholic district of Falls Road, well known as a stronghold of the Irish Republican Army (IRA). As we approached the border at the town of Newry, we held our breath and rode into its military fortress with the barbed wire, the observation post, the gray corrugated iron, the fully armed soldiers of the British army dressed in their combat fatigues, and the no-less-armed Royal Ulster Constabulary (RUC), the Northern Ireland police, imposing in their black uniforms and bulletproof vests.

Now that the Berlin wall has disappeared, the Irish border has possibly become the most militarized and surveyed frontier in Western Europe. It has been the scene of some of the worst political violence deployed by the security forces, loyalist paramilitary groups, and the IRA. The countryside around Newry is strongly Republican. Tightly knit rural communities, a difficult topography, and continuing violence have earned the area around Newry the name of "bandit country." The locals chuckle, half ironically, half proudly, at the name which echoes the folklore of the heroic Irish bandit. Pushed beyond the pale into the arid terrain of bogs and forests of the north-west of the island by the forces of British colonization, the image of the dispossessed Irish was reconfigured into the dangerous figure of the kern and highway robber, an incarnation of the wild Irish for colonial authorities and of heroic resistance in the imagination of Irish folklore (Óh Ógáin 1985). The image of the heroic Irish bandit recreated through ballads and stories redefined the remote and wild woods, where the native Irish had been confined by the "civilizing" forces of British colonization, as a stage of rebellion. Much of the heroic folklore of the Irish bandit is

1. Originally published in *Social Analysis* 42.1 (1998): 16–32. I am indebted to Gautam Ghosh for his editorial skill and his insightful comments on this article. I am also grateful to Michael Roberts and Kamala Visweswaran for their detailed suggestions. The research for this article was funded by grants from the Social Sciences Research Council, the MacArthur Foundation, and a Milton faculty research grant from Harvard University. Above all, I am grateful to the Northern Ireland women who figure in this paper and who provided much insight into the interlocking of gender and nationalism. Their names have been modified to preserve anonymity.

bestowed upon the contemporary IRA guerrilla through the same expressive culture of songs and storytelling (McCann 1985). For the authorities of Northern Ireland, the specter of surprise attacks by the IRA and the obsession to maintain the contested boundary between those variously "imagined communities" of the North and the Republic, of Protestant and Catholic, of colonial and postcolonial, has subjected the area around the Irish border to heavy militarization and intense surveillance. The border itself, with its paraphernalia of barbed wire and watchtowers, is a spectacle of state control, a ritualization of authority that betrays a profound lack of legitimacy. The border is the site where normality, the everyday order of things, is arrested into a state of subjection, a state of emergency that reveals the national order as one of "terror as usual" (Taussig 1992). The Irish border, I will argue in this article, is the site of troubled and troubling national imaginings.

Nationalists feel utterly vulnerable when they are stopped at the border.[2] At best they expect to be subjected to questioning and scrutiny; at worst they can be harassed, arrested, or even killed. Border "incidents" are part of everyday life for Nationalists, the people who cross the border regularly. Unionists rarely go into the Irish Republic, which they consider a permanent threat to their existence as Protestants and members of the United Kingdom. For Unionists, the border functions as a reminder of a permanent danger posed by the existence of the Irish Republic. For Nationalists, the border is a reminder of the incompletion of the Irish nation and the unfinished business of colonization. Because the border is an unrecognized national boundary for Nationalists, and because of the actual danger of crossing it, crossing the border becomes an act of defiance, filled at once with excitement and dread. Crossing the border is an act of transgression because, in its back and forth movement, it shows the porosity of the national frontier, its inherent instability. And in so doing, the back and forth movement of Nationalists across the Irish border also questions its very existence and lays a national claim over the whole island, north and south. For if nation-states come to be formed through artifices like maps and national borders, then it is at those sites that nations are not only imagined but also challenged. No wonder, then, that crossing the border trigger anxieties of different kinds for Nationalists and the Unionist security forces that guard it.

My friends and I were lucky. After a few questions about our identities and the purpose of our trip, we were allowed into the Republic. We were not so lucky, however, when we returned to Northern Ireland, later that same day, already into the night. It was 11:00 p.m. and it had been a nasty drive through a rainstorm. We were tired from a long day of political discussions. Immediately after crossing the border, as we were deciding whether to stop for a cup of coffee, I brushed against a car poorly parked in front of a

---

2. I use the term Nationalist in this article to refer to an ethnic identity more than a political one, irrespective of individual ascription to the various Nationalist political parties and agendas. In this sense, the term Nationalist could be (and sometimes is) interchanged with the term the Catholic in this article. Both terms are used in the literature of Northern Ireland to denote an imagined community that defines itself as Irish, and would prefer the national framework of a united Ireland rather than of the United Kingdom.

pub on a narrow street of Newry. We stopped. Out of nowhere several male police offi-cers materialized beside our car. They started questioning us, wanting to know what we were doing there. One of them asked for my driver's license. British soldiers came too, suspiciously poking their faces through the car windows while circling the car with machine guns in their hands.

The officer who asked for my license wrote down my personal data, then asked for the names of my passengers. We were now surrounded by RUC officers and British sol-diers asking the same questions over and over. A policeman said that we would have to go to the police station for a body search; the car had to be searched as well. Maura, the oldest woman in our group, asked why. "You are under suspicion of carrying drugs," the police officer responded. There was little in our appearance that could have been asso-ciated with drugs. Clothes, speech, and body management betray my friends as "ordi-nary women," as people say in Ireland to talk about working-class women, some of them with grown children. Furthermore, the drug charge appeared to the women traveling with me as a pretext, since there is very little consumption of drugs in Northern Ireland—with the exception of course of alcohol, cigarettes, and prescribed tranquilizers—that could jus-tify such an alarm. Drugs do play little part, indeed, in the public discourse of Northern Ireland.

Few things are more threatening to Catholic women in Northern Ireland than body searches in police stations. Women find them deeply humiliating, and there is a long his-tory of using body and strip searches as a form of intimidation and punishment of women in police stations and prison. My friends, all seasoned community activists, refused to go to the station or move from the car. An RUC female officer was brought to the scene and she repeated that they had to conduct a body search. If we did not col-laborate they would arrest us.

Policewoman: "You have the choice, we can search you here or at the police station."

Una: "Is this a joke? It's late and we have kids to go to."

Mary: "Listen, we brushed against a car and did the right thing, pulled up the car and waited until it is investigated. *That* is what you should be doing."

Policewoman: "We can investigate that too, but now I'm being required to do a body search."

Maura (angrily): "You mean we have to be searched in the middle of the street, at night, for no reason at all!?"

Una (angrily): "There is no reason for it! This is sheer harassment."

Policewoman: "We are not into harassment. You get out or we'll take the car to the police station."

There was a moment of tense silence inside the car. "I don't want to go to the police station," said Roisin, who, like me, had remained silent until then. "Let's get done with this here," said Maura, opening the door of the passenger's side. "This is ridiculous!" said Una as we got out of the car.

We stood in the middle of the deserted street, in a single line, each of us waiting her turn to be searched. It was freezing. While several British soldiers and policemen searched my car, the RUC woman went through our line of bodies. She looked into our handbags, clothes, pockets, seams, folded sleeves, and jackets. Her hands, then, rubbed our bodies one by one, front, back, legs, hair, and palms. I realized that, like my friends searched before me, I too was refusing to collaborate, not opening my jacket or legs, looking with a poker face into the distance, enacting that kind of resistance that is a parody of conformity (Butler 1993: 122). This kind of resistance, David Lloyd (n.d.) has noted, stages subjection as the condition of subjecthood, the parody of compliance underwriting authority as arbitrary ritual performance. As the search of my body was finishing, my eyes met Una's. We had been friends for a while now, but this was the first time we had experienced together the overpowering performance of the armed forces. When the policewoman released me, Una gave me a hug. No words spoken, no words seemed necessary. Nothing incriminating was found in the car or on our bodies and we were freed an hour after our detention, but the good humored chatty mood that had prevailed earlier in the car had changed to a restrained, angry silence.

National borders might be historical products of a particular kind of territorial imagination, as Benedict Anderson (1983) has suggested, but precisely because of that, borders are also the space where national imaginings are rendered unstable. What happens, for example, when national borders do not correspond with the outline of the imagined nation? What happens to national identity when an unimagined border forces a redefinition of the nation? The border might become then a space of instability, a space signifying what is lost, or left out of the imagined nation; a haunting presence that cannot be contained within the discourse of the existing nation-state but questions it by virtue of its presence. A national border of this kind—unimagined and forced by violence—becomes then a space of excess, the repository of what is denied or inarticulate in the discourse of the nation. In Ireland, such excess manifests itself in the hyper-visibility and hyper-vigilance of (Northern) state violence. Such visibility of violence iconized in the military paraphernalia that envelops the Irish border, mirrors the violence of the civil war that accompanied the birth of the Irish nation-state and which became the glaring absence in the discourse of official nationalism after partition. Once in place, borders are not inert, they have a ghostly existence capable of producing concrete effects. They configure the lives of people circumscribed by their contours and give rise to particular subjectivities and identities. Things happened to people not only in those border zones, but also as a consequence of borders. If borders have the power to affect people, so too do they affect the lives and identities of the nations they circumscribe. In other words, borders give rise to social and political imaginaries filled with dreads and desire. I want to insist on this because I think that it is the affective underpinnings of nationalism, its unconscious life if you wish, that Benedict Anderson's felicitous notion of imagined communities presumes, but leaves unelaborated. Anderson's notion of the nation as an imagined community has directed our attention toward the discursive production of the nation, but this focus has obscured the affective dynamics of nationalism that are inchoate, phantasmatic, capable of triggering the affective power of nationalism, yet not articulated into the symbolic order of discourse. Such processes belong to what Lacan has called the imaginary. Lacan's notion of the imaginary is not disconnected from the common notion of imagination inasmuch as it is characterized by images (rather than symbols or signifiers) and affects attached to those images. But, unlike imagination, which is placed largely in the arena of consciousness, the imaginary is largely unconscious. We could say that the notion of the nation as imagined community implies, yet obliterates, the imaginary of nationalism. By focusing on conscious processes of imagining the nation, it leaves behind those processes, images, and practices that phantasmatically complicate such imaginings. I think that a theory of nationalism must go beyond the discursive production of nationalism to explore its political imaginaries. We need to understand how particular political imaginaries articulate with the symbolic universe of nationalism in order to account for its affective power. Anderson has noted that this affective power stems from nationalism's skillful use of gender and familial metaphors. The power of metaphor to create affective states resides in the labor of condensation that taps into unconscious motivation to bring together different domains of experience (Fernandez 1986: 3–27), that of romantic and filial love and political action, for example. It is this unconscious mechanism that permits the forms of identification and projection that often accompany Nationalist discourse. In other words, the affective power of nationalism resides in its unconscious connection to formations of desire, in what it is absent from its discourse yet crucial to its formation. The shifting constructions of gender and sexuality, and their entanglement with the tortuous and tortured process of identity formation, constitutes the absent dimension of Irish nationalism, a dimension that is, however, central to the formation of the Irish nation. The Irish border is the site where such absent presences are crystallized in structures of feelings.

The search at the border was a deeply humiliating experience for my friends, a humiliation loaded with a history of repetition. Harassment by the security forces is an everyday practice in the Catholic areas of Belfast. The feeling of being overpowered experienced by working-class Catholics in Northern Ireland was inscribed at the border in the bodies of these women who felt poked and searched, manipulated and surveyed, and deprived of autonomy—just like the streets where they live were surveyed and controlled by the continuous occupation of the police and British army. And just as their bodies were appropriated by the security forces, these Nationalist women also felt that the Irish nation—still under British control in the political imaginary of Nationalists—was deprived of autonomy and held hostage within its own boundaries. This association between the body of women and the alienated space of nation was encapsulated by Maura as we got into the car to leave, "that you have to be treated like this . . . in your own country!" This association is not made in a representational vacuum; rather, it resonates with a long history in Irish Nationalist iconography, art, and literary production within which women have figured as allegories of the nation (Aretxaga 1997). Indeed, the inscription of the moral discourse of the nation in the body of women is common to Nationalist discourse more generally and particularly post-colonial nationalist discourse (Chatterjee 1989, 1993; Mani 1990; Mosse 1985). For Maura, the momentary dispossession of her body enacted the dispossession of the nation, a nation that the border materializes as an entity that simultaneously is and is not.

The whole episode at the border was for me a nasty experience that reminded me of similar forms of intimidation I had experienced at the hands of the Spanish police during the last years of Franco's dictatorship. But beyond the echoes of my own political experience, there was the rage, impotence, and humiliation contained in Maura's voice; feelings sedimented through a collective history of exclusion from the Irish nation and of exclusion from the political structures of Northern Ireland, feelings unintelligible outside of that history. For Maura, as for the other women in my car, the search in Newry materialized the exclusions of nationhood at the very level of the feeling, gendered body. It marked the contours of a difference iconized in a border that makes the north the absence of the Irish nation, that which being part of the Irish nation as an imagined community is nevertheless excluded from it; a border which makes Northern Ireland the negation of the Irish nation, and paradoxically its very condition of possibility. The incident of the search brings into relief the border as the imaginary site and material place where the Nationalist master narrative of the Irish nation is problematized through the operations of gender and sexual difference.

That Nation That Is Not One

The search that I have described speaks of the effect of the border in configuring Catholic identities through practices of intimidation and violence, as well as in producing particular structures of feelings. In Northern Ireland, unlike in the south, one can be searched or harassed for being Catholic (that is, Nationalist). The meaning of Catholic identity is not pre-established; rather, it is produced by discursive formations and histories of violence that have differed on both sides of the border. The politics of Catholic identity in the Free State and later on in the Republic are inscribed within the hegemonic discourse of state nationalism and the political dominance of the Catholic Church. In Northern Ireland, however, the politics of Catholic identity are inscribed within the political dominance of the Protestant state that excluded Catholics from power structures. This difference in the politics of Catholic identity is also the difference between the meaning of ethnic identity and nationalism north or south of the border. Such difference within ethnic identity (Irishness) delineates two different forms of existence, and arises not from the overt contours of identity—being Irish—but from what is obliterated, eclipsed in the common definition of Irishness on either side of the border. In other words, the border constituted Irishness as a split identity, the product of simultaneous recognition and disavowal of the violence of partition by the emergent Irish state. For while the Irish state could only function by the recognition of the border as a national frontier, the official discourse of nationalism denied its legitimacy by claiming sovereignty over the whole of the island. This process reinforced the link between Irish identity and Irish nationalism inasmuch as the Irish nation was an unfinished project. In so doing, the border constituted the difference in the meaning of Irish identity, North and South, as a residue of a proclaimed sameness of identity. And yet, that residue, that space of recognized and disavowed difference opened by the slippage in the meaning of nationalism north and south of the Irish border became precisely the kernel of identity, configuring it as permanently split and uncertain. What eludes identity in the formation of Irishness is precisely what conforms it.[3]

If the search at the border "speaks" of the aporetic configuration of Irish identity, it speaks also of the problematization of gender identity, and of the different realities that the border created for Irish women in the north and south. Difference among women, or if you will, difference within gender identity, has been the vexing question of feminist theory and politics. In Ireland, the question of difference within gender identity has been inextricably linked to the border and the unresolved issues of colonialism and nationalism that the border both manifests and hides.[4] It was precisely the interrogation of this difference in being a woman north and south of the border that had led us to Dublin that September day.

The aim of the trip was a meeting among left-wing feminists, all working-class community activists from Dublin and Belfast. Disenchanted with liberal mainstream feminism, this group of women had been trying to articulate an "anti-imperialist" politics from within the arena of feminism. In using the term "anti-imperialist," they linked patriarchal oppression in Ireland to the lingering effects of British colonialism, and the neo-colonialism of multinational enterprises in Ireland. Any struggle for women's rights, from this perspective, had to tackle the unfinished business of colonialism.

The ineludible question for a feminist project critical of colonialism (or neo-colonialist policies), and the central axis of the discussion in the Dublin meeting, was the meaning and consequences of nationalism (which was to say colonialism) for women north and south of the border. This had been historically a thorny issue among feminists and there was a clear tension and unstated line drawn between northerners and southerners. At that meeting, the border was not just an issue of debate, it was embodied by the women present, materialized by social histories and structures of feelings that traced an invisible space between northerners and southerners, and that hung there in the meeting room as a testament to inconmensurability. The aporetic issue of Irish nationalism was at the center of that space.

Northern activists defined themselves as Republicans (radical nationalists). Although none belonged to a political party like Sinn Fein, they supported—if critically—the armed struggle of the IRA to attain a united republic of Ireland. Southern feminists, on the other hand, had been overtly critical of Republican nationalism since second wave feminism

---

3. Hence the vexing question about identity in Ireland, what some critics have seen as an Irish obsession with identity (Herr 1991), an aporetic question that is, therefore, unresolvable.

4. See, for example, Coulter (1990), Marron (1989), and Meaney (1991).

began to make a dent in Irish politics more than a decade earlier. Such criticism was not surprising since, after independence, Republican nationalism in its most conservative form had become the state's official ideology and had drastically restricted the rights of women in the name of the Irish nation (O'Dowd 1987). Progressively, but inexorably, the new Free State of Ireland, formed in 1922, had constricted the social and political space of women, relegating them to second-class citizens while accentuating their position as allegories of an eternal and bucolic Ireland. The constitution of the new independent Ireland (1937) was the corollary to this process. It confined women to the home and defined motherhood as their social role: "The state shall endeavor to ensure that mothers shall not be obliged by economic necessity to engage in labor to the neglect of their duties in the home" (Article 41.2). This provision was accompanied by legislation that banned divorce, prohibited contraception, and severely restricted salaried work for married women, thus leaving them in a position of stark structural inequality.[5]

In the northern semi-state, however, under the grip of Protestant dominance and British authority, Republicanism was not the hegemonic discourse of the state, but a radical ideology of an embattled and disadvantaged minority kept at bay since partition by a heavy security apparatus. However, Republican ideology had been conservative, historically, in the north in relation to women. Most feminists (north and south) perceived northern Republicanism as a male movement and Republican women as subordinated to the directions of its male leadership. At the beginning of the 1980s, after an intense discussion about "the question of women," the Republican movement had approved an agenda for achieving gender equality (Aretxaga 1997). For those feminists sympathetic to the Republican movement, the locus of women's oppression was in a British colonialism that had given rise to a conservative state in the south and a sectarian one in the north. Inexorably, the discussion about women's rights and feminist strategies at the Dublin meeting was entangled in a debate about the status of Ireland, and such debate revolved around the ineludible fact of the Irish border that had created different forms of national identity and different forms of gender oppression in the north and the south.

What was clear to all the participants was that, to evoke Luce Irigaray, Ireland was this nation *that was not one*, that is, a nation that cannot be encompassed by ontological definitions of identity as unified self-representation. Ireland's division in two parts destabilized unified representations of the Irish nation, producing a discourse of Irish identity that the border symptomatizes as still dependent on British colonialism. Nationalists had imagined Ireland as the whole territory of the island, yet its materialization as a nation rested on the exclusion of one part. The Irish nation-state came into being on the condition of losing the six counties that form Northern Ireland. From within the discourse of Irish nationalism, partition meant that the Irish nation came into being as a nation-state on con-

---

5. See the speech by Eamon De Valera on St. Patrick's Day 1943, where he outlines his vision of Ireland as "a land whose countryside would be bright with cozy homesteads, whose fields and villages will be joyous with the sounds of industry, with the romping of sturdy children, the contests of athletic youth and the laughter of comely maidens." "The Undeserted Village Ireland" in Seamus Deane (1991: 748).

dition of negating its self-identity as nation. The official nationalism produced in the Free State after partition drew consistency from an act of silence (which was also an act of violence) about the fact that the Irish nation was *what it was not*; an act of silence about the fact that the identity of the emergent Irish nation was predicated on an absence (that of the north) which—like a fetish—had to be simultaneously recognized and disavowed. And it was—it is—this simultaneous disavowal and recognition that formed the core of national identity as fundamentally ambivalent and split, haunted, as Lloyd (n.d.) has put it, by the specter of its incompletion. Specters, Avery Gordon has noted, are real inasmuch as they produce social effects. They represent a reality that is hidden, that is not supposed to be there, yet makes the surface of things waver with its forceful presence (Gordon 1997). The specter of the border undermines a sense of separate identity for Ireland by reminding the nation of a history of intimacy with England and, furthermore, of the continuing presence of that intimacy.

The uncertainty and ambivalence of national identity, triggered by the border, manifested in Ireland as anxiety about gender and sexuality. The link between nationalism and sexuality is not particular to Ireland. As Mosse (1985) has indicated in his study of nationalism and respectability in Europe, one of the characteristics of nationalism is its capacity to produce normative ideas about sexuality and gender. Benedict Anderson has also noted the importance of gender and romantic imagery to the emotional underpinnings of nationalism. Indeed, romance has been the foundational genre of emergent nations in many parts of the world. The nation spills into libidinal economies in ways that are both consistent and unpredictable (Parker et al. 1992: 5). In Ireland the political imaginary of nationhood is marked by a history of intimacy with England that was cast in sexual and gender terms.

I turn next to this discourse of sexuality through which the Irish nation was envisioned, because it is essential to understand the control of gender and sexuality that accompanied the emergence of the Irish nation after partition, and that had a profound effect on both the lives of the nation and its women.

Does the Nation Have a Sex?

"Before we can do any work, any men's work, we must first realize ourselves as men. What ever comes to Ireland she needs men. And we of this generation are not in any real sense men, for we suffer things that men do not suffer, and we seek to redress grievances by means which men do not employ" (Pearse [1913] 1992: 557–58). With these words, Patrick Pearse linked gender to nationhood reminding his compatriots, three years before the Easter uprising of 1916, that masculinity was a necessary prerequisite to achieving national independence. Pearse, a writer and a leader of the rebellion of 1916—immortalized in Republican history as the heroic event that led to the war of independence—was a most influential producer of a radical cultural nationalism, in which masculinity and armed struggle went hand in hand. For Pearse, political agency was a concomitant of sexual potency: "[b]efore we can do any work [of liberation], any men's work." Political/sexual potency was located in a clearly defined masculinity that Pearse found lacking in Ireland: "we are not in any real sense men." The problem, he intimates, is not only the emasculation of men—"we suffer things that men do not suffer"—not just to use a popular metaphor that men do not have balls, but that they do not even realize it. For Pearse this lack of consciousness is more problematic than the actual lack of manliness, for if men do not know what they lack, how are they going to redress their situation? This lack of consciousness blurs gender distinctions, and it is this gender confusion that, for Pearse, compromises the potency of the nation. For without men how would the nation—imagined as a female object of love—ever be engendered? For Pearse, then, gender confusion needed to be dispelled if the nation was to be realized.

Pearse's national and sexual anxieties[6] can only be fully understood within the context of a colonial history wrapped in a rhetoric that had constructed Irish identity and Anglo-Irish relations within shifting categories of gender and sexuality. If early colonialist writers, like Spenser, saw Ireland as unruly, disorganized, and feminine (Jones and Stallybrass 1992), the polemicists and politicians of the eighteenth century represented Ireland as a tearful lover abandoned by masculine England or as prostrate daughter to be rescued by the noble hand of Anglo-Irish ascendancy.[7] The most influential texts in the colonial construction of Irish Identity were the studies in Celtic culture initiated by Ernest Renan and followed by Matthew Arnold. Drawing on the emergent sciences of philology, ethnology, and anthropology as well as on the positivist discourse on sexuality, the intellectuals of the nineteenth century would argue that the Irish were "an essentially feminine race" (Cairns and Richard 1988: 46) characterized by political incapacity and emotional instability. This feminine nature made the Irish—like women—incapable of government, legitimizing English political dominance. Political unrest during the nineteenth century in Ireland complicated, however, neat gender definitions of Irish identity. Anti-Irish political discourse and cartoons brought the language of racialized savagery to bear on representations of the Irish, who were often portrayed in a Caliban guise, with simian features and violent gestures, threatening an Ireland represented as a helpless maiden (Curtis 1971; Foster 1993). Needless to say, those representations played an important part in justifying the "civilizing" intervention of British force to save the feminine country from the unruly violence of Irish (male) bodies.

The emergence of an anti-colonial nationalist discourse rested in Ireland—as in other parts of the world—on the negation of colonial stereotypes of identity. For the intellectuals of turn-of-century Ireland actively involved in the political and cultural production of the Irish nation, the feminization of the Irish was deeply problematic inasmuch as it rendered Irish men politically impotent. Nationalists writers, such as Pearse and W.B. Yeats, felt an urgency to "restore manhood to a race that has been deprived of it" (Pearse [1916]

---

6. For an excellent biography of Patrick Pearse, see Edwards (1977).

7. See, for example, Swift ([1746] 1905), and Grattan ([1782] 1991).

1992). They counteracted the subservient position derived from the association of the Irish people with Victorian femininity by creating a heroic tradition of Gaelic warriors, and displacing feminine traits of character into the imported follies of urban modernity. In this way, they reappropriated the virile potency of Caliban versions of Irishness into the knightly violence of unequivocal masculinity. The creation of virile representations of the national subject had its correlate in an image of Ireland as beautiful maiden or idealized mother—the object of romantic desire and/or of religious devotion.[8] These representations enabled the association of Nationalist historical subjects with the heroic warriors and martyrs of Gaelic and Catholic mythologies. The fusion of sexual and political potency was thus reorganized in ways that were useful to the unfolding Nationalist project. Excluded in both colonialist, as well as Nationalist, arguments about the gender identity of the nation's people were women who, of course, featured only as allegories. Although women did participate in the struggle for national liberation, in the Nationalist imaginary the historical subjects were men. Indeed, within this political imaginary, manhood was supposed to be achieved in the process of asserting national sovereignty, its culminating moment arising with the proclamation of the nation. This moment was, then, charged with a symbolic and phantasmatic weight that requires some consideration.

After three years of generalized guerrilla warfare, the British government and the leaders of the IRA signed a treaty in 1921 that conferred partial independence to twenty-six counties of Ireland—henceforth to be known as the Free State of Ireland—and severed from the national project the six counties from the northeast that became Northern Ireland. Partition was the condition set by the British to agree on the formation of an Irish state—the Free State—that was to remain, however, within the British commonwealth until 1935. The Free State was not, however, the independent republic imagined by Irish nationalists, and, for those who opposed the treaty, it could only doubtfully be called a nation without the north.

The IRA divided over the signing of the treaty, and the country divided in a civil war. The violence of the civil war and the extreme political repression that characterized the following decade became the great silence upon which the Nationalist historical narrative of the Free State was founded; so did violent riots mark, too, the birth of Northern Ireland.

The border was supposed to be provisional. Article 12 of the treaty left the door open to a renegotiation of territorial boundaries by a commission formed by three members appointed respectively by the Irish government, the government of Northern Ireland and the British government: "The boundary of Northern Ireland shall be such as might be determined by such commission" (Article 12 of the Agreement for a Treaty between Great Britain and Ireland, December 6, 1921). This provision convinced the pro-treaty side that partition was a provisional measure that would disappear once the Free State

---

8. See Patrick Pearse's poem, "A Mother Speaks," and W.B. Yeats' play *Cathleen Ni Houlihan* for paradigmatic examples.

became a reality. The border commission was established in 1924 yet in 1925, in the face of unresolvable disagreement, the commission considered the boundaries of the border fixed.

As historian Terence Brown has put it, the permanence of the border was "a drastic shock to nationalist aspirations . . . a crippling blow to nationalist hopes" (1985: 38). A crippling blow indeed. In the context of the gender and sexual anxieties that had permeated the discussions of Irish national identity, the severance of Northern Ireland can be read as a symbolic castration that questioned the potency of the nation at the very moment of its inception. Such questioning is, for example, subtly represented in the acclaimed film, *Michael Collins*, at the crucial moment when the Irish flag is finally to be raised over the Dublin Castle, the bastion of English rule in Ireland. Michael Collins, a national hero and head of the revolutionary forces now transformed into the army of the new nation, as well as the chief negotiator of the treaty, has to preside at the historical event that would inscribe symbolically the birth of the Irish nation in the annals of history.

The troops are in formation, the flag ready, and the political authorities prepared and anxiously looking at their watches—only Michael Collins is missing. He arrives in a frenzy, disturbing the still choreography of the military formation. "You are seven minutes late," scolds the president of the recently constituted government, dressed for the occasion with an elaborate hat with white tassels. Collins looks at him, hastily composing his tall body into an appropriate military pose, and says, "We waited seven hundred years; you can have your seven minutes." The British flag begins to descend from the pole where the Irish flag is going to fly now. The music and military formation signifies the solemn moment. Everybody is standing to attention respectfully. Collins says, "So that is what caused all the bother . . . now what?" Then he breaks the solemnity of the occasion by cracking a joke, "Do I get to wear that hat?" he asks laughing. The country is on the brink of a civil war; his best fried and former right-hand man has joined the anti-treaty side. Read against this background of fratricide that the raising of the Irish flag over the Dublin Castle implies, Collins' lack of composure reveals a profound ambivalence about the status of the nation and renders its birth a self-conscious farce. Such ambivalence cannot be erased by recourse to a fraternal imagined community because the national community is divided. The birth of the Irish nation was not marked by the celebration of a fraternal community, but by the anxieties of fratricide, not by the proclamation of sovereignty, but by the acceptance of allegiance to the British crown that made the Free State politically dependent on England for its first fifteen years.

The masculinity of the nation, linked to the independence of the whole island in the nationalist imaginary, was ironically the price that the new Irish nation had to pay for its existence as a political body. No wonder then that partition would generate a great deal of anxiety about national identity that would be expressed in the following decades as anxiety about sexuality. The regulation of sexuality became a central concern of the new Irish state, and a major, if often veiled, theme in the literature of post-colonial Ireland (Cairns and Richards 1988). The new state was characterized by social conservatism and the repressive morality of the Catholic Church.[9] The new government passed restrictive legislation in matters of sexuality and family law: divorce legislation was banned in 1925, censorship of films and publications was introduced in 1923 and 1929, contraceptives were made illegal in 1935, and salaried work for married women was seriously restricted after 1937. The image of an idealized rural family, with women firmly situated in the role of mothers, served as the metaphor of social cohesion that attempted to transcend the bleak divisions of partition and civil war. Thus posed as central metaphor of the new nation and as the space of the unspeakable, this model of the family had the effect of silencing both violence within the family and violence within the nation. This double silence is precisely the suppressed meaning of the border. We can read the border, then, as a compromise formation in both the political and Freudian senses, as a symptom in the body of the nation that contains an excess of signification. For the border both enables and negates the nation; what is suppressed is an economy of sexual difference that locks women into allegory to hide precisely what the border as a sign manifests: that the nation is not one.

In his poem "An Open Letter" (1983), Seamus Heaney represents partition as an act of rape by Britain—"still imperially male"—that rendered the Irish parliament a cuckold. The poem expresses the phantasmatic content of partition that nationalist discourse leaves inarticulate, that is, that partition emasculated the Irish at the very moment of achieving manhood. Within this poetic space of sexual violence and disavowal, the restoration of manhood was predicated on the control of women's bodies. "Mother Ireland" emerged as the allegory of a nation that did not want to know its own violence. The cost of this silence has been represented by contemporary artists and writers who have attempted to subvert the image of Mother Ireland from within. The poet Maighread Medbh, for example, goes back to the image of Ireland as a woman in her poem "Easter 1991" (1993). Easter commemorates the Irish rebellion of 1916 and is the day of nationalist celebration. But the Ireland that Maighread Medbh invokes is one tired of the silence covering the gendered violence within the nation:

> I am Ireland and I am silenced.
> I cannot tell my abortions,
> my divorces,
> my years of slavery,
> my fights for freedom

The painter Michel Farrell portrayed "Madonna Ireland" as a whore, and subtitled the work "the first real Irish political picture." The painting, according to the author, was intended to make "every possible statement on the Irish situation" (Herr 1991: 11). If the

---

9. See Brown (1985), MacDonagh (1983), O'Dowd (1987), and Ward (1983).

hegemonic discourse of the Irish nation has been contested through female representations, so too has the challenge to nationalist representations (Boland 1989); and this, in turn, through a re-figuring of the politics of partition.

Irish nationalism sought to transcend the ambivalence of partition by representing the nation through female allegory, while controlling the lives of individual women. As allegories, women had been trapped within a discourse that foreclosed the space to the representation of a reality and a discourse of their own. Within dominant representations, women could only speak through the patriarchal language of nationalism; that is, through a language that was not theirs. But the discourse of Irish nationalism did not represent the nation either. Inasmuch as the nation was not one, the hegemonic discourse of the nation was in Ireland "an-Other's" discourse. This left women in Ireland to be the phantasmatic embodiment of an absence, rather than an allegory of presence. Any attempt at opening spaces of representation for women had to engage that absence. At the Dublin meeting, a woman from the north said in this respect, "We know what we are not, but not so well what we are." "The Irish language," she said, "is becoming important in helping us define who we are." By referring to the Irish language as a vehicle of identity within a discussion about the different meanings of being a woman in Ireland, this woman was linking "who we are"—as women—to "who we are" as Irish, making gender and Irish identity inseparable. The uncertainty of identity at both gender and ethnic levels stems from an existence of difference within (gender and ethnic) identity that has been disavowed in the discourse of Irish nationalism.

Writing about the link between the exploitation of women and Indian nationalism, Gayatri Spivak has said that, "in the decolonized national context the strategic deployment of subaltern heterogeneity can make visible the phantasmatic nature of a merely hegemonic nationalism" (1992: 99). This statement can well be applied to Ireland where the different realities of women created by the border, bring into relief the phantasmatic nature of both a hegemonic Irish nationalism and a hegemonic gender identity. The body search that we—northerners—underwent at the border was indeed an indication that what it meant to be an Irish woman was marked by different, if interdependent, kinds of violence north and south of the border.

CHAPTER 4

Does the Nation Have a Sex? Gender and Nation in the Political Rhetoric of Ireland[1]

Introduction

In a 1988 newspaper interview, Peter Robinson, a member of the British parliament and the deputy leader of the Democratic Unionist Party that defended the unity of Northern Ireland with Great Britain, harshly criticized the so-called "Anglo-Irish Agreement." Signed in 1985, this agreement gave the Irish government, if not exactly a decision-making capacity, at least the right to express an opinion about matters related to Northern Ireland before the British government. Despite the minimal possibility of the Irish government intervening politically in the development of Northern Ireland, it incurred the wrath of Unionists, for whom the mere proximity of the Irish Republic to the British "province" of Northern Ireland has always provoked a defensive political reaction.[2] Peter Robinson's criticism, one among many others circulated by Unionists in recent years, is not, then, surprising in itself. Instead, what makes it interesting and relevant for the theme under discussion here is its form, or metaphorical style. For in his attempt to convince those listening, Peter Robinson used the following words: "If a man has a row with his wife, it won't be resolved if the in-laws get together and work out a solution" (Whitney 1988). Robinson was thus framing a political conflict in kinship terms. For those unfamiliar with the stormy history of Anglo-Irish relations and the conflict in Northern Ireland, it might have been unclear who was who in this familial comparison. Yet for the above-mentioned political forces in Northern Ireland, as well as the British and Irish public as a whole, there was absolutely no doubt. For the mere idea, as suggested by a Unionist politician repre-

---

1. Originally published as, "¿Tiene sexo la nación? Nación y género en la retórica política sobre Irlanda," in *Arenal* (julio–diciembre 1996): 199–216. English translation by Cameron J. Watson. An earlier version of this article was presented at the *XII Semana Galega de Filosofía*, organized by the Aula Castelao, Pontevedra, Spain, in April 1995.

2. The very nomenclature used to define Northern Ireland highlights the conflictive status of this part of the island. While Unionists tend to use the terms "province" or 'Ulster' (the region of Ireland that was historically composed of nine counties, but was reduced to six with the partition of the island in 1921) to refer to Northern Ireland, Nationalists typically say "the six counties" or the 'north of Ireland' to emphasize belonging to the political unit of Ireland and not Great Britain. I have, therefore, deliberately used the word "province" when referring to Unionists to highlight their specific political position and national vision, which differs greatly from that maintained by Nationalists.

senting a Protestant population of which he is a prominent member, that he may be in the role of wife lacks meaning. And it does so because the familial metaphor is based on a central assumption of the Protestant community's political superiority over their Catholic neighbors.[3] This political supremacy was, in fact, the foundational premise of Northern Ireland, encapsulated in the phrase that launched its first parliament—"a Protestant government for a Protestant people"—and rooted in a socio-political structure aimed at systematically discriminating against the Catholic population there (Farrell 1976; Cameron Report 1969; Darby 1983a). Thus, from the vantage point of knowing this political context, it is quite clear that Peter Robinson imagined the Protestant community in the role of husband, while situating the Catholic one in that of wife. Even so, one might still argue that these marital positions do not necessarily represent an inequality of power. However, the political inequality between Catholics and Protestants, together with the highly patriarchal social and ideological structure characterizing Irish society in both north and south, leaves little doubt as to the meaning of the inequality of power referred to in the metaphor under discussion here. Far from being a casual observation, Peter Robinson's comments legitimized the unequal political relationship between Protestants and Catholics in Northern Ireland, in that they represented this political relationship as one of natural inequality between men and women. Furthermore, in situating the political conflict within the domestic sphere, he disguised the unequal relationship that both groups had with the nation-state, creating the illusion that this relationship has been cemented, not through the political economics of British imperialism, but through the "natural economy" of family relationships.[4]

Peter Robinson's comment was not, of course, an isolated one within the context of Ireland, but just a recent example of a long history of political debates codified in gender terms that have taken place since the eighteenth century. One might say, then, that the use of gender as a political metaphor gained momentum together with the emergence of the nation as a modern political construct.

In the last decade, a growing number of observers have highlighted the importance of the category of gender in the construction and legitimization of sexual, ethnic, and class differences in colonial and nationalist discourse. The sociologist Ashis Nandy (1983), for example, has demonstrated eloquently how the British colonization project in India was represented as one of masculine penetration, in which reason had to prevail over the effeminate, emotional, and unstable Indian population. Similarly, the scramble for Africa was accompanied by a rhetoric of gender in which the African landscape itself appeared as a female body, whose mysteries awaited, inert and passive, to be discovered and pen-

---

3. I refer here to Protestants and Catholics as ethnic communities more than in strict confessional terms. In Northern Ireland, these identifying categories are used, by both academics and the general public, in interchangeable fashion with those of the more political categories of Unionist and Nationalist.

4. Geraldine Meaney (1991) highlights this point in stressing the recurring use of marital metaphors in Unionist discourse.

etrated.[5] Such colonial discourse was, however, not free of ambivalence. For, as the critic Edward Said (1978) has pointed out, by exotically feminizing the whole population, imperialism transformed it not only into an object of appropriation and supremacy, but also an object of desire.

Veiled or openly sexual metaphors abound in different nineteenth-century colonial discourses, leading to a rich literary production in which sexual violence functioned as a powerful metaphor of colonial conquest. And Ireland, as we will see later, was, in this sense, no exception. The metaphorical use of sexual violence to represent the political violence of Ireland's colonial relationship appears over and over again, and in its most recent expression can be seen in the work of the Nobel Prize-winning Irish poet, Seamus Heaney.[6] The representation of colonial relationships through the rape metaphor reveals the unequal power relationship between colonizers and the colonized, but at the same time it also preserves this relationship within the strict confines of a heterosexual relationship. As Sara Suleri (1992) has argued, this obscures the fact that behind the facade of a submissive femininity there lays a male relationship—a relationship characterized by a hierarchical component between colonizer and colonized.

If the colonial project was conceived in sexual and gender terms, one might ask in what terms the national liberation project would be devised, and indeed, what would be the nature of the nation itself. Does the post-colonial nation have a sex? And is this sex the same as that of its people? These questions are important in understanding the reformulation of gender relations accompanying the creation of new nations, a reformulation that has often converted women into repositories of the new national tradition[7] or symbols of national identity, thereby restricting their own autonomy and frequently making them objects of political violence.[8] Before attempting to analyze more fully the mutual dependence of nationalist formulations and gender, one must define what is understood by the term nation.

What is a Nation? Essence? Pathology? Cultural Construction?

"What is a nation?" asked Ernest Renan in an 1882 lecture at the Sorbonne. After rejecting racial, geographic, economic, and linguistic dimensions as constituent elements, Renan answered, "The nation is a soul, a spiritual principle" (Renan, quoted in Bhabha 1990: 19). A century later, in an interview about the future of Europe, Julia Kristeva (1992) defined nationalism as pathology, a narcissistic and impossible nostalgia for primordial

---

5. See, for example, Comaroff and Comaroff (1991).

6. See, for example, Seamus Heaney (1980, 1983). In these works, Northern Ireland is represented as a woman raped by an "imperially macho" England, while the Republic of Ireland is represented as a dishonored husband. The consequence of this simultaneously sexual and political violence is a dual form of decadence on the part of Northern Ireland.

7. See, for example, Lata Mani (1990).

8. One recent example of this, in both Algeria and the former Yugoslavia, has been the transformation of the female body into a battlefield itself.

origins. In spite of the historical distance that separates these two French intellectuals, and despite the diametrically opposed positions they retain as regards nationalism, Renan and Kristeva do, however, coincide in conceiving both the nation and nationalism in essentialist terms. Consequently, for them, whether fundamental principle or psychological aberration, the nation seems to reside beyond historical or cultural processes. The positions of these two authors represent a basic ambivalence provoked by nationalism that, as Tom Nairn (1977) has pointed out, tends to simultaneously perceive it as both an object of desire and an object of fear. Intellectuals who, twenty years ago, celebrated the liberating project of minority and anti-colonial nationalisms, are horrified now at the apparently irrational violence that such nationalisms can unleash. Their response tends toward demonizing nationalism, which itself contributes to a reification of the phenomenon, and obscures the complex dynamics that encourage it and the tremendous differences that characterize it.

During the last decade there has been a dramatic increase in the number of studies of nationalism by anthropologists, historians, political scientists, and all kinds of critics, both western and non-western. These studies have attempted to unravel the mysteries of this modern formation we term the nation and that social phenomenon we call nationalism. Yet the conceptual confusion that has characterized the theorization of nationalism is due, in great part, to the contested meanings of the concept itself of nation.

Etymologically, the word "nation" derives from the Latin *nationem*, which originally referred more to a racial group than a political formation (Williams 1976). This was the principal meaning of the word during the Middle Ages. However, originally, the concept of race—no less problematic or ambiguous than that of nation—did not imply the vast difference it acquired in the nineteenth century, with the emergence of scientific discourse. On the contrary, its limits were flexible and variable, which in turn allowed for a great mobility between racial groups. As a result, during the Middle Ages the nation was a variable, essentially porous phenomenon, without fixed limits and without any necessary relation to the apparatus of state. And the concept of nationality, which became more widespread at the end of the seventeenth century, did not acquire a political meaning until the end of the eighteenth and beginning of the nineteenth centuries. There is, then, a constant, yet shifting, superposition of two meanings—racial (or ethnic) group and political formation—in the concepts of nation and nationalism, which means that they simultaneously have both positive and negative connotations. However, nationalism has not always been associated with a "racial" formation. As Raymond Williams observes, in countries under colonial rule, nationalism has formed the basis of political movements that embrace various languages and ethnic groups, as well as in regions where it is more closely associated with one ethnic or linguistic group. The concept of nation (and one could say the same for that of nationalism) is, then, a complex one whose opposing meanings have coexisted and changed historically to such an extent that it is difficult to reduce it to just one definition. This is so in spite of the fact that, paradoxically, nationalist movements, in the same way as their critics, tend toward a reductionist essentializing of themselves.

Within the long list of recent theorizations on the subject, one of the most influential and thought-provoking works has been that of political scientist Benedict Anderson. In his *Imagined Communities: Reflections on the Origin and Spread of Nationalism*, Anderson shifts the discussion of the nation from the world of essences to the terrain of cultural constructions (Anderson 1983). For Anderson, nationalism is not so much an ideology with a capital "N," like Liberalism or Fascism, but rather an artifact or cultural product, like kinship, for example. In order to understand the phenomena of nation and nationalism one must analyze how their meaning developed and changed historically over time, together with their capacity to generate a profound emotional legitimacy (Ibid.: 4). From this perspective, Anderson defines the nation as an "imagined political community, imagined as inherently limited and sovereign" (Ibid.: 6). It is imagined, he contends, because members of even the smallest nation will never personally know the great majority of their compatriots, yet they all share the idea of a national community. The nation must thus be imagined in order to exist.

According to the anthropologist Ernest Gellner, nationalism is precisely the formulation of this particular imagination: the nation does not give rise to nationalism as an expression of national consciousness. Rather, nationalism invents nations where previously they did not exist. For Gellner, there is an inherent deception in nations that, despite being recent inventions, invoke an immemorial past. Yet, for Anderson, the fact of being imagined does not imply a somehow false or inauthentic condition, given that ultimately all communities are imagined or thought of in a certain way. What distinguishes some communities from others, then, is not so much the criterion of authenticity but more a question of style, that is, the style in which they are imagined. Anderson sees three basic characteristics that define the nation as an imagined community. First, the nation is imagined as limited, that is, with more or less flexible boundaries beyond which there are other nations; secondly, it is conceived as sovereign, and its sovereignty is legitimized by its very existence, more than as a result of divine will or dynastic machination. Finally, the nation is conceived as a community in itself because, despite any inequalities it may have, the national community is represented as one of horizontal comradeship, or a community of citizens. However, this constitutive sketch of the nation does not explain its extraordinary emotive capacity. In order to comprehend this, one must examine the narratives and metaphors that make up the body of the nation, making it appear as a natural immemorial formation more than a specific historic and cultural product. For the nation is constructed as a historical subject and basic reference point through such metaphors and narrative plots, within which different national subjects concurrently construct their own history. Metaphor, as James Fernandez (1986) has argued, has the role of uniting two fields of experience within one single dimension, thereby creating not only new meanings, but also affective states. Metaphor thus generates a simultaneous cognitive and emotional movement that always takes place within a social and political context that imparts it meaning. Metaphorical analysis is thus a useful way of understanding the formation of the nation as an imagined community.

The contradiction between its recent invention and its appeal to an immemorial past has characterized the nation, since its conception (in the dual sense of both origin and idea), as an essentially ambivalent formation.[9] It is hardly surprising, then, that the nation attempts to resolve this ambivalence through appeals to other constructions, conceived as natural and fixed, such as the family or gender difference, both favorite tropes for the nation in its multiple versions. However, while Anderson discusses the family metaphor extensively, surprisingly he does not dedicate even a sentence to gender.

The persistence of the gender metaphor in the construction of the nation as an ontological reality is more problematic than one might imagine. On the one hand, gender is one of those cultural constructs conceived as a parameter of all things natural and fixed, and therefore an ideal metaphor to legitimize and impart the nation with a natural quality. On the other, gender, like the nation, is an essentially contradictory category, with multiple and even opposing meanings, subject not only to cultural variation but also historical change. The nation, in order to affirm its essential identity, has attempted, in essentialist terms, to stabilize and define the gender category, on which it has relied since its inception, and on whose fictitious certainty it depends. This alliance has continuously had unpredictable results. On the one hand, the link between gender and colonial and national projects has irredeemably politicized gender relations, at the same time as it has sexualized colonial and national relations. This interrelation has made it impossible to separate gender constructions from these political projects. On the other hand, the inherently contradictory nature of femininity in European cultural production from the eighteenth century onwards, as a national allegory and impure materiality, as an object of desire and fear, and as an object of reverence and conquest, would have a frequently contrary effect to that desired, intensifying the inherent ambivalence of the nation more than resolving it.

I will now return to the example of Ireland in order to illustrate the functioning of this ambivalence in the mutual construction of the nation and gender. Ireland is an especially interesting case because it is both a European and a post-colonial nation. This dual marginality, as Geraldine Meaney (1991) has termed it, confers on Irish national identity a liminal, ambiguous and undefined nature. Being both European and post-colonial, Ireland is neither one thing nor the other. Moreover, if one takes into account the fact that one part of the island, Northern Ireland, continues under British rule, Ireland is also an incomplete nation. One might argue, following Luce Irigaray (1991), that Ireland is "that nation that is not one." This instability over its personality is reflected in the never-ending debate about national identity that dominates historical and cultural discussion in contemporary Ireland, and that translates in parallel and uniform fashion to the debate of Irish women over their identity as women and as feminists, between the West and the third world.

---

9. It is precisely such ambivalence that imparts nationalism a twin face, capable of arousing both noble and altruistic sentiments, as well as pernicious and oppressive emotions.

A superficial analysis of the definition of Ireland in nationalist rhetoric swiftly demonstrates the intimate relationship between nationalist conceptions of Ireland and its representation in different colonial discourses. Indeed, both in colonial and in nationalist rhetoric gender metaphors emerge as a core notion shaping the political relationship between England and Ireland.

"An Essentially Feminine Race": Sexual and Gender Metaphors in the Colonial Discourse on Ireland in the Eighteenth and Nineteenth Centuries

The representation of Ireland in female terms appears frequently in colonial discourse, although not just with one meaning. On the contrary, the femininity of Ireland, revealing the very ambiguity of gender itself, appears as especially malleable material for the arguments of different political opinions. The great Irish author and satirist, Jonathan Swift, a member of the Anglo-Irish elite that maintained political and economic control of the country until well into the twentieth century, used gender and sexual metaphors as a political weapon. In one of his most celebrated satirical works, "The Story of an Injured Lady," Swift represented Ireland as a mistress abandoned by her lover (England) for another (Scotland).[10] In this story, the woman complains of her lover's ingratitude on being abandoned after a loyal period of service. One should immediately note here that this satire on political relations is based on the unquestionable assumption of male dominance. However, this dominance does not presuppose an arbitrary or tyrannical attitude such as that demonstrated by the lover (England), which confers some legitimacy on Ireland's historical lament. In spite of the sympathy that such a lament might arouse in the hypothetical reader, one should remember that Ireland is here represented, not as a wife, but as a lover, with the obvious implication that the despair of the country is the logical result of its political prostitution.

In what might be viewed as a perfect patriarchal sequence, the fallen woman is rescued by a noble gentleman. The gentleman, Henry Grattan, is, of course, an illustrious member of the Anglo-Irish elite. A late eighteenth-century politician who led Ireland during a brief period in which the country enjoyed a measure of legislative autonomy, Henry Grattan inaugurated the new Irish parliament in 1782 with the following words: "I found Ireland on her knees, I watched over her with a paternal solicitude. I have traced her progress from injuries to arms and from arms to liberty . . . She is no longer a wretched colony, returning thanks to her governor for his rapine, and to her King for his oppression" (Grattan [1782] 1991: 919).

In his speech, Grattan represented Ireland as a woman, but from his position as a noble liberator, the woman could not occupy the role of prostitute. Nor could his class-based, elite position allow him to represent the country as free. On assuming the role of

---

10. The allusion was to the 1707 Act of Union between England and Scotland. See Swift ([1746] 1905).

patriarch ("I watched over her with a paternal solicitude"), Grattan, in one single metaphorical movement, represented Ireland in a doubly dependent role: as a young woman who had not yet reached adulthood.

Whether as abandoned lover or stricken daughter, in the late eighteenth-century political imagination, Ireland appeared in both a passive and dependent role, awaiting rescue by, or the compassion of, a political structure whose power was precisely represented in masculine terms. This representation of Ireland really has little in common with other European national female allegories. For example, in Great Britain the figure of Britannia is, much like the goddess Athena, frequently armed, thus appearing strong and dignified. In France, Marianne appears at the forefront of the revolutionary barricades, her breasts exposed, in a defiant gesture as she addresses peasants and artisans. The Irish Hibernia, however, typically appears weak and tearful, threatened by the barbaric masses of Irish nationalism and reliant on the protection of Britannia's military wing.

In the nineteenth century, the gender rhetoric permeating political relations between England and Ireland acquired new dimensions. In nineteenth-century discourse, gender did not occupy a merely rhetorical role. Instead, it came to form part of a scientific discourse that conferred a fixed nature, not only on sexual differences, but also on ethnic or (to use a typically Victorian term) racial distinctions. The new sciences of ethnology and philology played an especially important role in configuring a new gender discourse about the Irish that would, in turn, have an extremely important influence on later nationalist discourse. In other words, the concept of femininity would be expanded from framing Ireland as a colonial body to defining the Irish as a "race." Ernest Renan ([1896] 1970), for example, argued in his essay on Celtic poetry that, "if it be permitted us to assign sex to nations as to individuals we should have to say, without hesitance, that the Celtic race . . . is an essentially feminine race."

What Renan understood by the term "feminine race" was a series of characteristics that, in the nineteenth century, came to define the intrinsic nature of women; and these, once established, were used as basic parameters to define entire peoples. At the same time, these very peoples also came to think of themselves in the terms of the dominant racial discourse of the time which had been popularized by the new science of ethnology. This confluence of gender and racial discourse thus allowed for the organization of human diversity into a hierarchical scale that classified different peoples, not only according to physiological, but also characterological, differences. The Celts were, then, for Renan, sensitive, poetic, emotional, and spiritual—in sum, feminine. However for this French writer and lover of bardic poetry, attributing a feminine status did not necessarily imply a position of subsidiarity. On the contrary, in his opinion it implied a spiritual superiority that offered an ideal complement to the rational and warlike (that is, masculine) nature of the Anglo-Saxons. Renan believed that, if the Irish did not dominate in the socio-political sphere, they did so in the spiritual one. This would have been of little consolation to a country that had just lost 800,000 people as a consequence of the famine, and a million more to emigration as a result of the misery that destroyed the country in the mid nineteenth century.

If Renan attempted to value the Irish by attributing them with a superior feminine spirituality, this was a double-edged argument, given the inherently contradictory and ambivalent character of femininity in the nineteenth-century Victorian mind. Drawing on the same gender discourse as that of Renan, one contemporary, the English poet, critic, and philologist Matthew Arnold, underscored the necessity of political dependence for the Irish people. Basing his arguments on the female idiosyncrasy of the Celts, Arnold stressed not so much their creative or spiritual dimension, but rather their emotional instability and "nervous exaltation": "No doubt, the sensibility of the Celtic nature, its nervous exaltation, have something feminine in them, and the Celt is particularly disposed to feel the spell of the feminine idiosyncracy; he has an affinity to it" (Arnold, quoted in Cairns and Richards 1988: 48).

This Anglo-Saxon discourse put forth an argument disguised in the language of natural rights to maintain the colonial domination of Ireland and legitimize the repression of different movements that emerged to fight British administration of the country during the nineteenth century.[11] The Irish, like women and in the same way as savages or primitive peoples, appeared in colonial discourse as incapable of government; something to which the English, with their rational (masculine) nature, were perfectly suited. It was no coincidence that similar gender discourses were also deployed in India and other British colonies. Characterizing these colonies as feminine meant dispossessing them of their capacity for self-determination, and allowing for the adoption of a multiplicity of political positions from paternalism to repression.

If in colonial discourse political power was linked to a notion of masculinity, the formulation of its anti-colonial nationalist counterpart would also embrace a counter-discourse based on gender. In the Irish case, those previously described scenarios, in which Ireland appeared as a mistreated maiden or defenseless daughter, always referred to gentlemen of English extraction, whether aggressors or saviors. In either case, Irish men did not appear in the scenario, and were relegated to an impotent status—an impotence which, given the romantic nature of these scenarios, was, at the same time, both sexual and political. This impotence was doubly reinforced by their supposed feminine identity. As a result, Irish men, on being defined by their feminine nature, appeared to be endowed with a defective or inadequate masculinity. The political effects of such associations did not escape intellectuals involved with an emergent Irish nationalism, who responded to the subordinate nature of this racialized femininity by emphasizing the masculine aspects of the Irish character.

Instead of questioning the paradigm of a political hierarchy based on a rigid construction and dichotomy of sexual differences, nationalist intellectuals simply inverted their

---

11. See, for example, Lewis P. Curtis (1968), and Cairns and Richards (1988).

putative sexual identity. If the capacity to govern depended on masculine qualities, they needed to masculinize the "race." Both the great Irish poet William Butler Yeats and the writer Patrick Pearse (among others) turned to the bardic sagas studied by Renan and Arnold, although this time in search of warrior heroes that might serve as national role models. The nation as a political allegory thus continued to be embodied as a woman in the imagination of these intellectuals, but the task of rescuing her from the yoke of repression had to fall, not to a foreign savior, but to the fraternal community of Irish manhood. In order to awaken necessary political passions, this community had to imagine itself as one of sons and lovers, and therefore it had to change sex. In several of his works, Patrick Pearse left no doubt as to the fact that the fundamental task of Irish nationalism was the recuperation of a lost masculinity: "A new education system in Ireland has to do more than restore a national culture. It has to restore manhood to a race that has been deprived of it" (Pearse [1916] 1992: 292–93). The nation personified as a grieving woman needed masculine heroes ready to redeem her of her oppression. As opposed to the Ireland of colonial discourse, the Ireland of this growing, early twentieth-century nationalism was represented, at the same time, as both an object and a subject of national liberation.

As an allegory, the nation itself needed a more noble position than that of an abandoned lover or adopted daughter. In a series of romantic cultural productions, the architects of this new nationalism imagined the nation as an erotic object, simultaneously tangible and unattainable. One of the most enduringly successful images, and one that has dominated the imagination of the Irish nation up to the present, is that of *Cathleen Ni Houlihan*, the play written by W.B. Yeats at the beginning of the twentieth century with a specifically nationalist purpose. This drama represents Ireland as an old woman transformed into a beautiful maiden when the men of her country go off to fight for her. This was an incredibly popular work in Dublin. Ireland had finally found its role. Dignified, yet eroticized, the image of Cathleen ni Houlihan seemed capable of rescuing the country from its impotence—both sexual and political—and inspiring a heroic national passion. Such passion was obvious in the poetry of nationalists like Joseph Plunkett, who was executed (together with Patrick Pearse) for his part in the 1916 Easter Rising that led to the war of independence (Plunkett 1916):

> And we two lovers, long but one in mind,
> and soul, are made one only flesh at length;
> praise god if this my blood fulfills the doom,
> when you, dark rose, shall redden into bloom.

This romanticized image of Ireland as a young maiden was not, however, the only way it was portrayed, for next to that image, there was also Ireland as mother. This was capable of awakening a different form of fervor, something more akin to religious, rather than romantic, passion, but no less emotive. In his poem, "A Mother Speaks," for example, Pearse identified his mother as the Virgin Mary, while reserving for himself the sacrificial role of Christ. Whatever the context, whether maiden or mother, early twentieth-century nationalist intellectuals imagined Ireland as a passive woman, while at the same time affirming the masculinity of the Irish people in heroic acts of individual sacrifice. However, women remained excluded from the national project in this narrative. Despite the active participation of Irish women in the national independence struggle, the new nation was imagined and framed as a male community. Furthermore, the redemption of the nation's idealized body would be preached through the progressive control of the body of women.[12]

Nationalism, Domesticity, and Gender

In 1921, with the signing of an agreement between the British government and the leaders of the Irish war of independence, the Irish Free State was created. It enjoyed widespread political autonomy but was still subject to the limitations of being within the British Commonwealth. During the first fifteen years of its existence, the Irish government, which passed universal suffrage for those aged twenty-one and over (1923), also introduced a number of legislative measures designed to progressively restrict the social role of women.[13] Divorce was made illegal in 1925, as was the use of contraceptives in 1935. The 1937 Irish Constitution, that declared the country an independent republic, also confined women to the domestic sphere and defined motherhood as their social role. This provision was accompanied by legislation that restricted severely any possibilities of finding a salaried job for married women, leaving women in a position of severe structural inequality. The masculinity of the nation had been strengthened at the cost of the subordination of women, who had participated actively in its construction.[14]

One should also point out that the exclusion of women from the Irish national project was linked to the partition of the country into the Irish Free State and Northern Ireland. In 1921, after three years of guerrilla warfare more or less throughout Ireland, the British government sat down to negotiate, not national sovereignty but autonomy within the state. Ireland thus acquired the status of "Free State" within the British Commonwealth, as a transitory step toward national independence. Within this context the British government placed one non-negotiable condition: the separation of Northern Ireland (the most industrialized part of the country) to be retained under British rule. The Irish leaders negotiating the treaty were divided, and as a result, the Irish people were also divided. The majority accepted the treaty as a pragmatic solution in the context of a war that

---

12. On the participation of women in Irish nationalism, see Ward (1983).

13. The concession of the vote to women in 1923 was, without any doubt, the result of the struggle by the Irish Suffragist Movement. But it was also an opportunist measure designed to defeat the Republican sector that had opposed the division of the country in the referendum reaffirming the peace treaty with Great Britain in 1923.

14. Any nation that relegates half its population to a Manichean division somewhere between, at best, a symbolic position and, at worst, one of exclusion cannot hope to avoid some instability. In recent decades, Irish feminists have started, in no uncertain terms, to redefine the nation. The question is, from what political or imaginative space is such a redefinition possible. In this regard, see Coulter (1993), Boland (1989), and Hackett (1995).

was considered unsustainable. For this sector, a limited sovereignty represented a more advantageous option than the possibility of achieving nothing. For the other sector, more influenced by a transcendent vision of the nation than state-based pragmatism, national sovereignty was not a question of degree that could be measured on a scale; you either had it or you didn't. A sovereignty that excluded one part of the national territory was not sovereign and was, therefore, unacceptable. These different positions represented, to a great extent, the inherent tension within the idea of the nation as a modern concept. For, at the same time, it projects itself as an essentialist and transcendent identity, yet also uses state-based pragmatism in its search for power. This tension would give rise to a civil war that remained a silenced, dark chapter in the heroic narrative which subsequently came to form part of the official history of Ireland. Precisely because of the silence, this absence was the principal source of an uncertain Irish national identity during the coming decades.

In 1937, when Ireland declared itself an independent nation, it did so with the acute awareness that part of it was missing.[15] Within the context of debates about the sexual identity of the nation, the partition of Northern Ireland might be read as a symbolic castration that called into question the potency of the Irish nation at the very moment of its birth. The masculinity of the nation, which early twentieth-century nationalists had argued so forcibly, was precisely the price of its existence as a body politic. Further still, the birth of the nation was marked, not by the fraternity of a male community, but by fratricide; not by the airy proclamation of national sovereignty, but by an under-age child that remained dependent, during the first fifteen years of its life, within the British Commonwealth. If the narrative style in which nationalist intellectuals imagined the Irish nation was historical tragedy, the style which marked its birth and subsequent development was farce. If the nation, as Benedict Anderson contends, is defined as a fraternal, sovereign community with territorial limits, the Irish nation was created as a narrative displacement. Indeed, it even went against its own self-definition, given that, as a nation, Ireland had always been represented as a territorial whole. And equally, its sovereignty extended imaginatively over all Irish people, not only those of the Republic of Ireland. As a fraternal community, then, the Irish nation has been defined by not only the traumatic division of the civil war, but also by that other, more problematic divide between north and south, and further, between Protestants and Catholics. The national identity of Ireland has, like the sexual identity that shaped it, remained split, ambivalent, shifting, and unresolved.

The problem of national identity has been a central theme in Irish literary and academic production. And unsurprisingly, this predicament has frequently been elaborated through making sexual identity itself problematic. Irish literature since the late 1920s is full of authoritarian, sexually inadequate men and unsatisfied, frustrated women. This anxiety about sexual identity and efficiency permeating contemporary Irish literature operates as a metaphor of the problematic and ambivalent national identity of Ireland.

---

15. The 1937 Constitution claimed the right of national sovereignty over the whole territory of the island, north and south.

And the theme of sexuality leads directly to that of the family as the other great metaphor of the nation.

In Ireland, the family metaphor, as prominent as in other nationalisms, was not so dominant until the creation of the Irish Free State and the partition of the island. Previously, sexual and gender metaphors had actually occupied a more prominent space. As I mentioned before, the new nation would progressively reduce the social and autonomous space of women through restrictive legislation in questions of reproduction, family, and labor rights (O'Dowd 1987). With the national community violently divided by the civil war, the family as a metaphor of the nation emerged as simultaneously problematic and necessary in the process of constructing the nation. Basing their arguments on Catholic ideology, successive Irish governments promoted a family metaphor centered on the image of the mother, the only member of the family that retained a certain credibility within the national historical narrative. The mother, an image that already formed one of the principal allegories of the nation, was thus transformed, within the new national discourse, into the guardian of the national tradition. And the family therefore became central in the new national legislative policies. In effect, the family was constituted, not in terms of marital or fraternal relations, but as a father-son relationship—the relationship that most adequately represented the authoritarian nature of the new national state. On placing the family at the heart of the nation, and even within both private and public time and space, it would acquire an essentialist and fixed nature in the national discourse. The family was thus framed as a unit outside the historical dynamic, frozen in time, and a metaphor of the national essence. As a national essence the family would function as a space that, being so central, escaped any political debate. Therefore it was constituted as something that, precisely because it was so central to the nation, was never questioned; and that, precisely because of its conscious presence, was actually excluded from the discursive center.

The ability of nationalist leaders to establish an identity-based relationship between the family and the nation would allow them to relegate the tricky problem of the civil war, and its accompanying violence, from the terrain of public debate to the family environment, where it would remain outside language, hidden behind a veil of domestic isolation. In this way, the violence of the civil war acquired the status of domestic violence—something that everyone knows is taking place, but never talks about. Conversely, sexual or "domestic" violence would eventually become the great silence of the nation. This silence, that brought together both political and domestic violence in the national discourse, would transform the family into a metaphor of national paralysis. Significantly, questioning this national discourse in the 1970s led, in parallel fashion, to a questioning of the family as a national institution by the feminist movement. And the explosion of violence in Northern Ireland in 1971 also contributed to a critical examination of the political consequences of the family metaphor in the Republic of Ireland.

The relevance of the feminist movement in reshaping the definition of the nation in Ireland is important and leads one directly to the question of the woman as a historical subject. Specifically, from what cultural and discursive space could women participate politically in a national context? This question would become central in the late 1970s in Northern Ireland, when a group of women attempted to reconcile a national and feminist project.

A large part of the 1970s feminist movement contemplated any Nationalist position with some reticence, varying from suspicion to outright opposition. However, operating from outside the nation is not as easy in a country where the nation represents not only a relationship of sexual oppression, but also liberation from a long and devastating colonial oppression. This ambivalence was much more pronounced in the case of women as a historical subject than in that of men. For Irish women, the nation not only represented the crystallization of an oppressive politics of sex and gender, but also the manifestation of a colonial liberation struggle.

Both in Northern Ireland and the Republic of Ireland feminists from different political positions have arrived at the conclusion that any attempt to reform family policy and gender relations in Ireland must, necessarily, confront the history of the nation (which also means confronting its colonial past), given that both gender and national identity have been mutually constructed in one historical process. Indeed, the social and cultural meaning of the terms "woman," "man," "masculinity," "femininity," and "sexuality" are inextricably tied to those of "colonialism," "nationality," "class," and "ethnicity." What it means to be a woman in Ireland does not depend on any universal ontological identity; rather, such meaning has been constructed through the intersection of various discourses and political practices that accompany them. The awareness of this intersection has given rise to a collective debate between Republican feminists from both north and south, about the ways in which the different development of nationalism in both places has led to different meanings of gender. These debates, born out of the necessity of confronting political differences within the Irish feminist movement, have consequently resulted in the beginning of a reworking of the concepts of both gender and nation, in such a way that the nation might accommodate a plurality of identities and positions. For this to occur, it is necessary that both concepts are understood, not in a dichotomous or essentialist way, but rather in fluid, heterogeneous, and plural fashion.

CHAPTER 5

The Sexual Games of the Body Politic: Fantasy and State Violence in Northern Ireland[1]

> Though the rain had made the colours run,
> the message it was plain,
> women are being strip-searched in Armagh jail
>
> Christy Moore (singer) "On the Bridge."
>
> Waking from a bad dream does not necessarily console you. It
> can also make you fully aware of the horror you just dreamed
> and even of the truth residing in that horror.
>
> Bernhard Schlink, *The Reader.*

On March 2, 1992 an extraordinary event took place in the high security prison of Maghaberry in Northern Ireland, which houses IRA female prisoners—an event that disrupted the crafted monotony of prison routines, inflicting a political and psychological wound on the body of IRA female prisoners. Out of this wound flowed questions about the functioning of technologies of control, about the fictions that legitimize these technologies as rational necessities, about the fantasies that animate technologies of control and which manifest themselves in an excess for which no amount of rational purposive action can adequately account. Out of the body of these prisoners emerged questions too

1. Originally published in *Culture, Medicine and Psychiatry* 25 (2001): 1–27. A different version of this article appears as "Engendering Violence: Strip Searching of Women in Northern Ireland," in *History in Person: Enduring Struggles, Contentious Practice, Intimate Identities*, edited by Dorothy Holland and Jean Leave (Santa Fe, NM: School of American Research Press, 2001), 37–61. A slightly modified version of the article was also delivered at the University of Massachusetts, Amherst, November 13, 1997, as the *Annual Distinguished Lecture in European Anthropology.* I am indebted to Jacqueline Urla for her invitation to deliver the lecture and her insightful comments. I am grateful for comments and critical readings of various versions of this article, to Byron Good, Mary-Jo DelVecchio Good, Arthur Kleinman, Stanley Tambiah, Kenneth George, Michael Herzfeld, Geeta Patel, Steven Gregory, Liisa Malkki, Kay Warren, Paul Willis, Dorothy Holland, Jean Lavi, Michael Kerney. My major debt is to the women in Northern Ireland who spoke to me about strip-searches. Research was made possible by grants from the Social Sciences Research Council, MacArthur Foundation, and Tozzer grant from Harvard University.

about the institutional production of sexually differentiated bodies, about the mechanism through which sexual difference structures state violence, about the permutations of gender in performances of authority, about the mingling of power and desire. The event I am about to analyze was a mass strip search of women prisoners which lasted the whole day, from morning to night, and was conducted in the midst of screams, insults and physical violence. Nothing threatening the security of the prison was found in this search. Although the governor of the prison called the search a routine "security procedure," the extent and violence of this strip search was unprecedented and triggered a strong reaction of repulsion by human rights organizations in Belfast. This form of violence was not only unprecedented but had a Dantesque excess that I want to take as the kernel of this essay. Out of this excess, I attempt to unravel the interweaving threads of changing technologies of power, structures of sexual difference and the production of political identities. If the search of 1992 was unprecedented in its form, strip searches, however, were not new as a punishing mechanism. Indeed, strip searches were one of the first things I heard about during my first visit to Belfast in the summer of 1987. I had gone to the Falls Road to talk to Con, an older woman whose name had been given to me by a colleague as somebody who knew about "Nationalist women." My interest triggered in Con a long and intense diatribe about women's suffering, a suffering that went unrecognized despite their being "the backbone of the struggle," as she put it. It was in the middle of the conversation that she jumped from the suffering of mothers, weekly visiting the prisons to see their relatives, to the imprisoned young women who had to endure strip searches: "Those girls, I don't know how they go through it, I couldn't!" she said.

She sent me to the women's center across the street, an old Victorian two-story terrace house, with a door painted royal blue, which was accidentally blown up the following year by the IRA. The building was derelict, the narrow stairs opened to a room with some toys in the corner. A battered couch and few chairs constituted all the furniture. A small room functioned as an advice office. Christine, the young woman who ran the center, was busy talking to somebody. Sitting on the couch were a middle-aged and an older woman. When I said I was interested in writing a book about women's experience of violence in Northern Ireland, the older woman explained that her daughter was in jail. She said that, "Nobody knows what these girls are going through with the strip searches, it's very degrading and they can happen at any moment. It is very difficult for a mother to know that your daughter is degraded in this way." When I finally talked to Christine, the woman running the center, she too mentioned strip searches as a form of violence that affected women very deeply. She gave me the name of an ex-prisoner who was in charge of the campaign against strip searches and invited me out. It was time to close. She herself, I would later know, was an ex-prisoner, one of the Armagh Women who went on the Dirty Protest, using their body as political weapon, smearing their cells with excrement and menstrual blood, to gain recognition as political prisoners against the official labeling of them as criminals (Aretxaga 1995, 1997). The following year, when I returned to Belfast for a longer stay, she was already gone. I never met her again.

However recurrent the theme of strip searches was during my first visit to Belfast, they fell out of my attention during the following year, when I was living for sixteen months in the Falls Road. Strip searches became marginal to my research, even though in retrospect they never ceased to emerge into the flow of social discourse. More like a nagging disruption than a central statement, strip searches would suddenly erupt within the tenor of everyday life in the form of the odd song in a nightly repertoire of rebel songs at the local social club;[2] as an argument among different feminist organizations;[3] or as a site of political resentment and personal shame emerging unexpectedly in a conversation and hanging there awkwardly in a silence that echoed a local graffiti which said, "For those who know no explanation is necessary." Perhaps my reluctance to deal with the issue of strip searches is part of a widespread reaction of simultaneous fascination and resistance in the face of sexualized political violence; a resistance which makes it a somewhat intractable phenomenon from which analysts tend to distance themselves, either through sheer rationalization or striking mutism; a conspicuous absence hovering over studies of political violence like a stumbling block, in its articulate inarticulateness.

In January 1995, I returned to Belfast to research how Republican women were interpreting the recently opened peace process. Yet strip searches emerged again onto the surface of the everyday order of things preoccupied then with the peace talks, disrupting it like a symptom of some other, ungraspable reality. I was in the Falls Road Women's Center waiting for my friend Una when one of the workers began to tell me a harrowing story about a mass strip search conducted in Maghaberry prison in 1992. The worker was the sister of one of the prisoners who had been stripped that day. She was working on a dossier that the prisoners were putting together to sue the governor of the prison. The story was substantially different from any other I had heard before. Not only was the occurrence of this strip search unprecedented in the form in which it was conducted, unprecedented too was the response of the prisoners who, for the first time, were suing the governor of the prison for sexual abuse. The arbitrary and excessive quality of the violence that was deployed that day in Maghaberry prison—there was not a riot or even a conflictive situation that could justify it—could be read, taking a cue from Jaqueline Rose (1996), as a symptom of the state, a sign of an excess which, being intrinsic to the reality of the state, cannot be contained by its symbolics of purposeful rationality.

In writing about the symptom in his later work, *Moses and Monotheism*, Freud resorted to a political analogy to describe it. Symptoms, he said, "are as a state within the state, an

---

2. The Irish folk singer, Christy Moore, wrote a song about strip searches which became popular in the social clubs of Nationalist areas in Belfast. The song was actually the only song about women in the usual repertoire of rebel songs that celebrate male heroism. See Christy Moore, "On the Bridge," in *Unfinished Revolution*, LP, audiocassette, CD, 1987.

3. The issue of strip searches was a charged point of conflict among feminist groups of differing political persuasions. Republican women often accused mainstream feminists of not responding to this institutionalized form of violence against women whenever the latter attacked the Republican movement for their use of political violence of which, main-stream feminists argued, women were the main victims. See Aretxaga (1997).

inaccessible party, useless for the commonwealth; yet they can succeed in overcoming the other so-called normal component and in forcing it into their service" (Freud [1939] 1964: 76). Reversing Freud's analogy, Jaqueline Rose suggests that the modern state too can be read as a symptom, as a social construction which contains an ungraspable excess and which relies on fantasy for an authority it cannot fully justify. Following Weber, she argues that the power of the state relies on the subjective meanings that people attach to it, on the hopes and fear of the magical power people attribute to it (1996: 8). The subjective foundations of the state have been noted by a number of social theorists who have seen the state as the reification of an idea (Abrams 1988), as powerful fetish (Taussig 1992, 1997) or as the effect of modern technologies of power (Foucault 1979). In either case, this reified idea constitutes itself as an omnipotent reality whose power relies on something that reason cannot fully account for and which alerts us to what Judith Butler has called "the psychic life of power" (1997). Fantasy, then, appears as a major component of political life and a key structuring factor of power relations. I understand fantasy here in its Freudian sense, not as a purely illusory construction but as a form of reality in its own right, a scene whose structure traverses the boundary between the conscious and the unconscious (Laplanche and Pontalis 1989). Fantasy in this sense belongs to what Žižek has called "the objectively subjective" (1997: 119). It is not opposed to social reality but constitutes what Rose calls its "psychic glue" (1996: 3).[4]

Evoking the figurative meaning of "being in a state" as loss of control, Rose goes on to suggest that a recalcitrant excess, at odds with and often taking over rational functionality, characterizes the modern state as a social reality. One could further say that the being of the state is, as it were, one of recurrently being *in a state*, of being a symptom. If the symptom is a stage setting of fantasy (Žižek 1989), can we not say that the state, too, is a privileged setting for the staging of political fantasy in the modern world? In this article, I am interested in analyzing one such moment of excess, when the state falls into a *state* betraying the phantasmatic foundations that articulate seemingly rational technologies of control. In a seminal article, Maria Torok (1959) defined fantasy as, "a fleeting, imaginary representation intruding upon the ego's activities and being in that context [in the context of the rational ego] a total misfit" (1959: 30). Torok's notion of fantasy as an imaginative intrusion that throws the rational ego out of control, revealing thus the force of another (repressed) reality, can be helpful in understanding those instances when the rationality of the state is taken over by an inexplicable excess such as the mass strip searches analyzed in this article. Indeed, what I will argue is that this case of strip searches constitutes an eruption of fantasy that questions the ideology of rational control, which

---

4. Freud ([1939] 1964), following Nietzsche (1956), links the origin of the state, social law and morality to the fantasy of a primordial crime, the death of a powerful and authoritarian father in the prehistory of humanity. The guilt generated in the work of mourning for this fantasized crime is, for Freud and for Nietzsche, what constitutes the psychic glue that binds people to the state and sustains morality. For a terrific book that explores the relation of mourning to national identity see Santner (1990).

legitimizes power relations in the prison, revealing in so doing the unconscious, phantasmatic substrate of power relations.[5]

If the state is a symptom, then a symptom of what? Both Freud and Kafka, in their different ways, saw statehood as symptom of the modern world. How does this notion of the state relate to a Foucauldian theory of the state as the effect of discourses, technologies and micropractices of power?[6] Nowhere is Foucault's theory of the state clearer than in his study of the prison as modern form of punishment. Foucault argued that modern forms of punishment belong to a political technology of the body aimed at the formation and transformation of "souls," that is, of subjectivities. What is important in the new modern style of punishment emerging during the eighteenth century, he says, is the binding of subjects to the state; not through fear of spectacular punishment, but through the production of particular states of mind, inclinations, disposition, feelings; that is, through the interiorization of the Law. To this aim, punishment is regulated by an economic rationality attendant to the effects that it will produce on the social body, as well as on the prisoner. And this, Foucault says, because now "What has to be analyzed and calculated are the return effects of punishment on the punishing authority and the power that it claims to exercise" (1979: 91). Through these delicate calculations punishment becomes "an art of effects" (1979: 93). This art of effects is nothing other than a political art of tactical and strategic use of technologies of power (forms of knowledge, procedures and disciplines) applied on the body, which becomes a field of power relations, invested with the power of the state. Foucault's account of the prison and the function of punishment in general is the account of a political rationality without a subject, of a Machiavellian economy of tactics and effects without a Prince. Yet could we not say that this careful economy of production of modern subjecthood rests on a fantasy of social control, in which subjects do not even know what the nature of their subjugation is, nor even that their desires and inclinations are already, before they became subjects of will, somewhat formed through subtle operations of a diffuse power? And isn't there, in Foucault's account itself, a certain horror fantasy of body shackling by the modern technologists of the soul? "The soul is the effect and instrument of political anatomy; the soul is the prison of the body" (1979: 30).

My point in this essay is not that Foucault's anatomy of power is wrong, but that it can only function through a fantasy support. Indeed, that the technologies themselves might constitute a fantasy screen of detached objectivity in the management of bodies that masks a desire for total control, a *jouissance* that wildly exceeds the calculated rationality of punishment. After all, the technologies of the body used in prison bring into intimate

---

5. In social contexts, one does not always have access to the verbalization of fantasy that Torok finds particularly operative in psychoanalytic therapy. Yet fantasy might be nevertheless plainly at work in what Žižek has called "material externality" (things, conduct, ritualized performances, and so on) (1997: 3). What seems important for social analysis is Torok's emphasis on the temporal overthrowing of rational control which provides a point of entry to the repressed of social and political reality.

6. See in this respect Wendy Brown (1995).

contact warders and prisoners, those who punish and those punished, an intimate contact arising indeed out of a body field. Foucault notes this intimacy:

> The training of behavior by a full time-table, the acquisition of habits, the constraints of the body, imply a very special relation between the individual who is punished and the individual who punishes him. It is a relation that not only renders the dimension of the [public] spectacle useless; it excludes it. The agent of punishment must exercise total power, which no third party can disturb; the individual to be corrected must be entirely enveloped in the power that is being exercised over him. Secrecy is imperative, and so too is autonomy, at least in relation to these techniques of punishment (1979: 129).

The binding intimacy implied in this passage threatens from within to compromise the whole strategy of the modern reform of punishment, "the power that applied the penalties now threatens to be as arbitrary, as despotic, as the power that once decided them" (1979: 129).

This threat from within, this fantasy of total control over others, this arbitrariness of violence, is not just an ironic effect, a tactical miscalculation, but an intrinsic part of the functioning of the prison and, by extension, of the state. Isn't this threat to the rationality of the modern penal system not so much an external threat, but the symptom of its craziness, an index of the fact that the domain of Law (and the state) is not one of neutral and formal adjudication but is "permeated with obscene enjoyment" (Žižek 1997: 11)? As Garland (1990) has noted, neither punishment nor penal history can be wholly understood in terms of rationality. In this article, I discuss the importance of unconscious fantasies to the operationality of technologies of control, and to the political understanding of "what takes place in the dark" (Cornell 1993) of state institutions.[7]

Elsewhere I have analyzed strip searches as part of a colonial history which produced the Irish body as an ethnized, feminized, inferior body (Aretxaga 2001). Here I focus on the convergence of fantasy and technology in inscribing the body (of politically rebellious women) with the meanings of sexual subjugation through a form of violence that phantasmatically replicates the scenario of rape. For the body of violence, the body of the state as well as the body of its subjects is not a neutral body, but a body already invested with the meanings of sexual difference and ethnic domination.[8] Such difference not only gives

---

7. On the psychoanalytic notion of Fantasy, see Laplanche and Pontalis (1989). For critical uses of the notion of fantasy in political analysis see Žižek (1997) and Rose (1997).

8. When I write of ethnic identity here, I refer to Catholic and Protestant identities. In the political culture of Northern Ireland the terms Catholic and Protestant not only refer to religious ascription but function as powerful signifiers of ethnic identity and difference. Recent scholarship on ethnic violence has approached this phantasmatic dimension that pervades ethnic, racial and other forms of violence as a form of mythification that follows the attempt to establish categorical identity distinctions through the violent inscription of the body of the Other (Appadurai 1998; Feldman 1991; Hayden 1996; Malkki 1995; Tambiah 1997; Taussig 1987). These scholars have emphasized a semantics of the body as a map of social and moral worlds, and as a field of struggle. Yet such recourse to the symbolic significance of the ethnic body leaves unexplained an intimate relation that violence simultaneously both tries to eliminate and establishes between perpetrators and targets of violence (Appadurai 1998; Tambiah 1998; Taussig 1987). Most of these studies also fail to draw the link between sexual and ethnic violence, treating the body often as an undifferentiated construct.

signifying valence to bodies categorized as male and female, but also produces different effects within the structures of political violence as a whole (Cornell 1993; Peteet 1994; Das 1995, 1996a). It is this sexually differentiated body that is obliterated in Foucault's account of the prison, in which the body appears as an abstract entity, a passive surface of inscription through which power operates. But as Grosz (1994) has noted, such an abstract universal body is, de facto, a male body. What is missing is the way in which the intimacy of power relations in the prison operates on, and through, the bodies of women to produce specific (female) subjectivities. Not only are the technologies of control often different when applied to women's and men's bodies, but the same technology might produce different effects on sexually differentiated bodies, as I have argued elsewhere (Aretxaga 1995). This lack of sexual specificity of "the body" subject to ethnic, racial or state violence, is also absent in a great deal of otherwise excellent scholarship on political violence, including Feldman's (1991) analysis of the body and political terror in Northern Ireland. Yet, one does not need to go to the recent dramatic examples of the mass rapes of women in Bosnia, or the assassinations of unveiled women by radical Muslims in Algeria, to notice the complicit and inextricable relation between sexual difference, political violence and state formation. Let me start my analysis with a brief history of strip searches as penal practice in Northern Ireland.

Strip Searches: A Technique of Punishment

Strip searches began to be used randomly in Armagh women's prison in 1982, after a dramatic hunger strike ended a prolonged conflict in the prisons. Before this time, women were strip searched when they first came into jail as part of the ritual of committal that also included a bath. The usual procedure when women left the prison was a routine rub-down search accompanied by a metal detector. In October 1982, two remand prisoners (prisoners awaiting trial) were found in possession of two keys which, apparently, they had picked up in the court house and brought with them into prison (NCCL 1986: 7). This incident was the single justification adduced by the Secretary of State and the prison governor for a change of policy that instituted random strip-searches. The rationale was the maintenance of security at the prison. Yet women prisoners had rarely surpassed forty in number, and in 1985 the ratio of prison officers to prisoners in Armagh was as high as two to one.

The form and frequency with which strip searches were conducted since November 1982 did not follow a consistent pattern. Initially, women were strip searched every time they went in and out of jail, whether it was for parole or to attend a court hearing. For women awaiting trial, strip searching was a frequent occurrence, as they were required to report to the judge weekly, even though prisoners were constantly within the confines of police officers when visiting the court. Strip searches could also be conducted before and after visits with relatives or friends.

In March 1983, the prison administration dramatically increased the number of strip searches carried out on women prisoners. The searches also changed from a relatively stable to a random pattern and concentrated especially on non-sentenced prisoners, namely those most vulnerable to institutional pressure. Prisoners could be called for a strip search at any moment, even when they had not abandoned the prison building or had no scheduled visits. This arbitrariness triggered in the prisoners a great sense of uncertainty about their safety. It also attracted a wide range of condemnation by political, feminist and community organizations that considered the searches deeply damaging psychologically and totally unnecessary for the security of the prison (Community for Justice 1987; NCCL 1986; Stryker 1998).

In 1986, women prisoners were transferred to the newly built high security prison of Maghaberry, and the old Victorian prison of Armagh was closed. Maghaberry was equipped with state of the art surveillance technology that made any breach of security practically impossible. There was no justification for frequent strip searches. However, despite the prison's panoptic surveillance and its advanced technology of control, strip searches continued to be performed in Maghaberry, although they seemed to become less random. Neither in modern Maghaberry nor in the former decaying prison of Armagh was anything that could compromise the security at the prison ever found in a strip search.

In 1992, a period of relative tranquility in the prisons but rising ethnic tension in Northern Ireland, IRA women prisoners were the object of a violent assault in the form of an unexpected mass strip search that left them terrified and with a deep sense of distress but produced also new forms of political subjectivity. What was at stake in this search, I will argue, was a disciplinary measure aimed, as Foucault has put it, at the transformation of souls—an attempt to transform committed political prisoners into docile inmates through a series of techniques. But the rationale of this technology of power was complicated by two factors. One, that the technologies of power were applied on bodies marked by ethnic and sexual difference; and two, that such technology of power was supported by a fantasy of sexual violence. The material for the analysis that follows comes primarily from the narratives handwritten by the prisoners after the attack, from interviews with prisoners released from jail after 1992, as well as prisoners experiencing strip searches prior to that date.[9] Let me turn now to the events of March 1992, that I will describe through extensive quotations from the prisoners.

Women's Narratives

Theresa

I woke at 8:00 a.m. as usual to the signs of screws [this is how prison officers are called by prisoners] coming on to the wing which signals the morning unlock of cells. There

---

9. I have also consulted a variety of communiqués and other documentation published since 1982 on the issue of strip searches.

seemed to be a longer delay than usual. I glanced at my watch that marked 8:20 a.m. and I thought that the unlock was getting later every morning. Just then I heard footsteps and the sound of jingling keys, however the screws passed my cell and stop next door at Rosie's cell. I heard them telling her that we would not be unlocked that morning due to a search being conducted throughout the jail. Just as I was settling down to write some letters a shout from Rosie told us that something was wrong. She explained that one of the PO [prison officers] had informed her that as each cell was being searched individually so too would the occupants be subjected to a "full search," that is a strip search.

Bernie

Around 10:00 a.m. I heard that they were going to strip all of us. I couldn't believe it because we had jail searches before but they never involved us being stripped. Then I saw the search team coming in with full riot gear and I heard one of the men screws singing "happy days are here again."

Carol

They came into the wing, a lot of screws, both male and female, all dressed in black, with shields, helmets, visors in the helmets, padding in elbows and knees, you couldn't distinguish men from women, they were carrying dogs.

Anne Marie

I saw a stream of screws in full riot gear entering the front gate of the jail and advance towards our wing. They were all dressed in navy-blue, boiler suit type of outfits with helmets and carried shields and batons, I don't know if they were all females as it was difficult to see their faces. I felt bewildered and frightened. I couldn't understand why the riot squad had been brought in since we had just awakened and all prisoners were still in their cells. Within a few minutes someone shouted, "What is going on?" and the reply came, "The riot squad is in with Theresa, they are stripping her." I felt totally shocked and horrified. It was difficult to believe that they were going to strip me in my cell. When someone shouted that they were barricading themselves in I did the same by pushing my bed against the door. Another team of screws arrived and I heard them working on the outside of the doors taking the frame off so that the doors would open out onto the landing. Then I realized that my barricade was no longer any use.

All prisoners were struck by the riot apparel, which seemed to serve more the purpose of striking terror than that of protecting the officers. Since prisoners were assaulted one by one in the small space of a cell, the paraphernalia of military dress, batons, shields, dark visors and dogs was clearly unnecessary. Unnecessary too for the purpose of security was the presence of men. Yet the riot dress had the important effect of blurring gender lines. Men and women officers appeared indistinguishable from afar, thus creating the impression that all of them could be men, adding a particular edge to the fear of violence.

Women prisoners say that they constantly worried that male officers were present while they were being forcefully stripped. The fear triggered by this indistinguishable gender identity was intensified by the fact that officers used numbers rather than names to call themselves, thus accentuating the anonymity, hierarchical distance and antagonism between prisoners on the one hand, and officers (both male and female) on the other: prisoners were the ones stripped, officers the strippers. The isolation in their cells, and the reliance on hearing and fragmentary seeing for knowledge of the situation, undermined women's sense of control and constructed a phantasmatic realm of military terror.

The forced strip searching of women began at approximately 10:30 a.m. and lasted until 9:00 p.m. in the evening with two breaks for lunch and dinner (an incongruent fiction of routine). I continue with the narratives:

Ailish

The riot squad entered the cell of Marie. I could hear a lot of commotion and Marie shouting at them to leave her alone. This went on for quite some time before they moved on to Louise in the cell next door. Again there came the sound of things being knocked over and Louise screaming. Everything went quiet for a few minutes and the only sound was made by Louise gasping for breath.

Karen

All day long these screams of anguish came from the cells and I had to sit and listen to what the women were going through and helpless to do anything about it. The male screws stood laughing and taunting the women and were in the wing while these women were being raped. It was nerve-wracking waiting and knowing that they would eventually get to me.

Shaureen

During most of the attacks I saw and heard both male and female screws laughing and jeering while women were being pinned down and stripped naked. At one stage I watched a male screw making sick and disgusting sexual remarks. I cannot describe what it is really like to watch women being trailed off the window bars to be sexually assaulted and to listen to their cries and screams—it's a nightmare.

This Dantesque quality was evoked by all the prisoners, who insisted that hearing the screams of other women being assaulted produced a feeling of impotence and anxious waiting that was almost worst than the assault itself.[10] Many women described officers

---

10. Crapanzano (1986) has written insightfully on the meaning of waiting as a situation that erases historical time and that is thoroughly predicated on anguish. See also Veena Das and Ashis Nandi (1985). Scarry (1985) has also elaborated on the power of sounds to create terror. See Feldman (1991) and Aretxaga (1995) for semantics of sound in Northern Ireland prisons.

(men and women) laughing with each other. Carol, for example, heard male officers outside her cell laughing and coaching the woman officers that were stripping her. Ailish described how "when the screams of women began, male officers in the wing laughed and shouted, held up their middle fingers and stuck out and wiggled their tongues." Another prisoner heard a male officer saying "We are going to fuck you all." In addition, several prisoners reported that sexual remarks were interspersed with anti-Catholic abuse.

The waiting time—filled with screams and cries of women, laughter and sexual joking of officers, barking of dogs and shouting by everybody—produced a heightened state of terror among women locked in their cells, associated with the threat of rape. Carol, one of the released prisoners I interviewed, expressed this association when, apropos of describing the atmosphere in the jail that day, she said suddenly, "The worst nightmare of any woman is being sexually abused, and . . . it was terrifying!"

The prisoners did not attend passively to this assault. They barricaded themselves, pushing their beds against the door. The officers responded by unhinging the doors out of their frames. Prisoners hung on to the bars of windows and kicked the prison officers when they could. They also shouted encouragement to each other. In the process of being immobilized, prisoners were bruised and injured in more or less severe forms. The actual strip search to which I turn now followed a ritualized pattern of militarized sexual assault. The prisoners were reduced by force to the floor or the bed. The officers (sometimes women, sometimes men and women) held the prisoners on painful locks that were changed at command. The operations on the body of women followed military codes such as "change lock" or "lock 4" or "reverse position." This use of codes is particularly jarring, as prison officers coexist closely with prisoners and are known by first name. One can think, thus, of a deliberate attempt to produce a defamiliarization and sense of estrangement within the established parameters of the prison universe. Four officers (sometimes five) immobilized the body of each woman while two undressed her and searched her clothes. They began by the shoes working their way up the body and finishing with the bra. After the strip, the officers left or stood by watching while the prisoner gathered her clothes. In some cases, they dressed the prisoners when the latter refused to do it themselves. Let me quote some narratives:

Mary

Throughout the day I listened as one woman after another was attacked in her cell; I can still clearly hear the screams and shouts. When the riot squad entered our cell Theresa and I [these are two sisters who share a cell] sought to protect ourselves the best we could. Ten screws entered the cell dressed in riot gear complete with shields helmets and batons. We held on to each other and at the same time clung to the bars on the window. I was aware of the sound of the other women in our wing shouting at the screws to leave us alone. One screw was hammering at my fingers on the bars with a baton while the rest were pulling at my legs and one grabbed me by the hair and pulled my head back. On my right hand side I could see Theresa being roughly dragged out and she was screaming to the screws to leave me alone. I am not exactly sure at which point we became separated but I could constantly feel screws pulling and clapping at me. When my head was pulled back by the hair one screw was digging her baton into my neck and the next thing I was being thrown to the floor, my face pushed into the corner, arms twisted up my back and a screw standing on the joints at the back of my knees. As I was lying on the floor I could hear Theresa calling my name from the cell they had taken her to. One screw was pulling at my track shoes, she took off my socks also before proceeding to take off my track bottoms, leggings and my panties. When I was naked from the waist down with screws twisting my arms and legs my jumper, tee-shirt and then my bra was removed.

The narrative of Mary's sister Theresa is the same until the point when they became separated by guards:

Theresa

They were kicking at my legs and had my arms behind my back in a painful lock as they dragged me towards the door of the cell. Once outside the cell I was ordered to lie down on the floor, as I was refusing to do so I was slammed face down on to the wing where I was held by at least four screws. The screw pressing my face on to the floor yelled at me to bend my legs and for one moment I thought I was going to be strip searched on the wing [there were male officers on the wing]. I was panic-stricken and struggled even harder. After a few minutes of violent struggle the screws managed to carry me into an empty cell. Once in the cell I was again slammed face down onto the floor and held there for ten minutes before the sexual assault on me began. During this time and in between my own screams I could hear the assault on Mary going on in the other cell. After a seemingly endless wait, the attack began. My shoes and socks were removed first, then my leggings. At this point a sheet folded into a ridiculously small shape was thrown across the lower half of my body. I still don't know why this was done because once my panties were removed it was lifted. Once I was naked from the waist down a screw sat on my legs while the others ease their grip slightly to remove the clothes from the top half of my body. When I was totally naked they told me to get dressed as they left me lying on the floor. I then insisted that they dress me. The four screws who had held me down and the two who had stripped me re-entered the cell and stood looking everywhere but at me. The same two screws who had torn the clothes from my body seconds earlier now stood fumbling and avoiding my angry stare as they gathered my clothes which were all over the floor and put them on my body.

For Carol, one of the prisoners with whom I talked, the feelings of violation and humiliation produced by the violent assault were compounded by the fact that she was having her period:

Carol

They came into my cell and threw me to the floor, they held me between four screws and two other removed my clothes forcefully. I was taking my period. They took the sanitary towel and threw it to a corner as if I was shit! They had the door open and the male screws were outside, I don't know how much they could see. They were coaching the female screws and could hear everything.[11]

Traumatic Effects

The forced appropriation and visibility not only of the surface of the body but also its most intimate physiological functions produced a feeling of humiliation, impotence and personal shame, a feeling of being treated like "shit" in the words of Carol, against which all women prisoners had to struggle. Ann said, "One screw was watching me while I started to dress. I have never felt more humiliated and degraded in my life." Geraldine wrote, "They all left the cell leaving me lying on the floor with no clothes while the screws laughed. It was very humiliating." The humiliation was deepened by the seeming enjoyment of the officers, who were laughing and joking. "They laughed and looked at me, enjoying every minute of it," wrote Maureen.

Prisoners were left deeply shaken and terrified after the strip search. They wrote the reports of what happened after the assault, but to talk about it was still difficult two years later. Ann Marie, for example, became visibly distressed when she was telling me how they came into her cell, having to struggle to repress tears. Many prisoners could not talk about what happened to family and significant others. Speaking about the assault entails, of course, a process of reliving it that brings the pain back to the surface and betrays a deep emotional effect on the prisoners, behind a facade of strength.[12] It is as if the absence of speech signals a domain of embodied injury that the proliferation of written testimony attempts to counteract politically. Many prisoners prefer to express their feelings about strip searches in poetry rather than ordinary discourse (Harlow 1992). Louise, a vital and outgoing woman, successfully avoided all my attempts at discussing her experience during the 1992 search. She said that it was all written down in her "statement" and insisted on giving me a copy of the prisoners' reports. Instead she talked about the poems written in jail, including those about strip searches, as if her ability to speak about this traumatic event required the distancing of writing and the mediation of poetry.

---

11. I have analyzed elsewhere the deep feelings of vulnerability and shame produced by the forced disclosure of menstruation, especially in a situation of utter powerlessness such as incarceration or interrogation. For most young women in Northern Ireland, as in many other places, it is embarrassing to talk about menstruation in public and deeply distressing to have the blood exposed, more so to people known to be hostile and in a position of control. Police authorities know this and frequently use menstruation and sexual harassment as a psychological weapon against women detainees during interrogation (Aretxaga 1995, 1997).

12. See Olujic (1995) on the traumatic effect of recounting the violence of rape for Croatian women. See also Draculic (1993) on women's refusal to talk about rapes in Bosnia. Also on the violence of gathering testimonial evidence in cases of rape, see Nordstrom (1996), and Winkler and Hanke (1995).

Sleeplessness and nightmares were common symptoms among the prisoners who suffered the assault as were fear, nervousness and depression. Louise said that women inside Maghaberry jail were still terrified that it might happen again: "A small disruption of routine, a delay in serving a meal or opening a door is very upsetting," she said, "because you think that they are up to something." Fear is thus encapsulated in the anxiety triggered by any deviation from institutional rule; trauma acting as a form of institutionalization. There have not been strip searches of this kind since 1992, but nothing guarantees that there might not be one again.

The assault left prisoners with a sense of profound uncertainty about their safety. Women prisoners had long complained about strip searches as a distressing invasion of privacy.[13] But this was the first time that they had openly spoken of a strip search as rape and sexual abuse. In the working class culture of Catholic Belfast, rape and sexual violence fall into the space of the unspeakable, evoking feelings of deep vulnerability and shame. Thus, their inscription into discourse constitutes an important shift that can be linked to a discursive space opened by feminism and the social recognition of sexual harassment as a specific form of power against women. In talking of strip searches as rape, Republican women were challenging legal definitions of rape that ignore institutional forms of violation of the body as well as their political character "as an attack on the core constructions of identity and ontological security in its most personal and profound sense" (Nordstrom 1996: 151). The testimonial genre under which all prisoners' narratives fall raises a question about the status of the narratives, a question about a possible narrative formalization of violent events for the purposes of political propaganda.

Narratives of collective violence tend to be formalized within local systems of social and political referentiality (Feldman 1991; Malkki 1995), which are instrumental in the creation and recreation of forms of consciousness. Yet, I have no reason to doubt the veracity of the accounts of strip searches produced by the prisoners. Nor do I have a reason to suspect a devious political motivation. Sinn Fein did not encourage women prisoners to sue the governor after the assault, nor did they understand why women resisted the order of stripping. The mostly male constituency of Sinn Fein resisted hearing anything about sexualized violence against women. Some prisoners' boyfriends and male relatives questioned women's will to resist strip searches as unnecessarily endangering themselves (Stryker 1998). The political genre in which these reports were coded was, however, a subject of confrontation between prisoners and civil rights organizations contesting strip searches. However, this confrontation was not about the sexual nature of the assault, but rather about the political identities as "prisoners of war" adopted by prisoners in their descriptions. The prisoners' claim of strip searches being like rape was not called into question by civil rights activists who agreed that strip searches were rape without pene-

---

13. Women have systematically complained since the early years of the conflict about sexual harassment by British soldiers and Royal Ulster Constabulary (RUC) officers (McVeigh 1994). Women prisoners at Maghaberry jail had also experienced sexual harassment during interrogation. Verbal abuse and threats of sexual violence are common in this situation along with some form of physical violence (Aretxaga 1997).

tration (Stryker 1998). The ability to recognize and name the 1992 strip searches as rape must be connected not only to the discursive space of feminist politics, but also to a fundamental change in the practices of institutional power. Let me explore next the changing battleground that characterized these practices.

The Theater of Domination: A Changing Battleground

Strip searches had been conducted since their introduction, in 1982, in a special room with cubicles. Women were supposed to undress in the cubicles, hand the items of clothing to the officers for inspection and put on a sheet. Once every piece of clothing had been inspected, the officers turned to open the sheet and visually inspect the bodies of the women, first in a comprehensive form, then in detail: hair, hands and soles of feet, armpits, bringing what Feldman has called "optics of domination" to its maximum expression (1991: 156). It is not difficult to see how such practices reify prisoners by transforming them into objects of scrutiny. Through the examining gaze of the guards, prisoners are stripped not only of clothes but of personhood. This sense of objectification was conveyed by Carol, an ex-prisoner who, in describing a strip search, said that it felt like "you are cattle in a market." Not surprisingly, strip searches provoke deep feelings of humiliation and impotence. Brenda, another ex-prisoner, preferred to be beaten than stripped: "You feel so vulnerable when you are naked," she said. "You don't feel like fighting back when you are naked because you expose yourself in every way. You were nearly crying when you knew you were going to be strip searched. It made you very angry and very violent too." Brenda's vulnerability reveals the character of strip searches as a technique of domination that questions its instrumental rationalization as security regulation.

When strip searches intensified as a punitive technique through augmented frequency and randomness, women prisoners decided to physically resist them. What happened then was in the words of Brenda that "they literally had to pull the clothes off you. That was embarrassing because you were kicking and struggling and they were ripping the clothes completely off you and you feel . . . I cannot describe the way I used to feel. You felt as if you were nothing, you feel degraded. It's like a rape of some kind. They are ripping the bra and the panties off you [sigh] you felt like crying, you felt like rolling back in a ball and getting into the corner and never coming out of there again!" Jennifer, the leader of women prisoners in 1989, told me that physical resistance was taking an enormous psychological toll on the prisoners; it gave them a sense of agency but at a great cost. Not only was it deeply distressing to be forcefully undressed and injured in the process, but prisoners were punished afterwards for disobedience with loss of remission and solitary confinement.

As the frequency and randomness of strip searches diminished after a prolonged campaign against them by civic and religious organizations, prisoners' tactics also changed. From 1984, they stripped in their cubicles but refused to put on a sheet, remaining naked and silent. Not answering the remarks that they say the guards often passed about their bodies and looking directly into their eyes with a sardonic smile. "We often said to [the guards]," said Brenda, "'Would you do this to your daughter? Are you getting a kick out of this? Why are you doing this? We've got nothing,' they got more angry then." These gestures were aimed at turning the embarrassment and humiliation from the prisoner to the guards, thus switching the field of confrontation. They bring to the surface forms of enjoyment that the technologies of control are supposed to disguise. Although strip searches clearly engage the subjectivity of guards and prisoners, they are surrounded by an appearance of impersonality, neutrality and sanitary distance: the cubicles, the sheet, the ritualized sequencing of the search. Such sanitary distance cloaks the appropriation of the body of the prisoners in the detached procedure of an institutional rule. This disassociation between, on the one hand, the intersubjective dynamic of hostility, humiliation and control that pervades and indeed constitutes the strip search as mechanism of punishment, and, on the other hand, its institutional rationalization as aseptic and necessary procedure, permits prison officers to negate the actual power relation in which they are engaging by shielding themselves under the cover of professional duty. After all, as Foucault has noted, "power is tolerable on condition that it masks a substantial part of itself" (1980: 86). This negation is particularly injuring to the prisoners that are thus stripped not only of their clothes but also of their experience of violation with its concomitant feelings of humiliation and powerlessness.

Prisoners have tried to break this disassociation in several forms. First they refused to strip, obligating prison officers to engage physically with the violence of stripping. Then, they engaged in tactics of passive resistance such as refusing to use the sheet. This refusal is highly significant because the sheet functions in this context as a masquerade of propriety. It is there not to cover but to be opened, constituting a second act of forced disclosure, a double strip that masks the visual invasion of the body with the aseptic meanings of the medical examination.[14] Women refused to collaborate in this fiction of power by remaining naked, while looking silently at the officers in the eye and smiling sardonically; that is, by doing what Judith Butler has called "a parodic inhabiting of conformity that subtly calls into question the legitimacy of the command" (1993: 122). Not so subtly in this case, the parody of conformity countered the sanitation of strip searches by addressing directly the persons shielded behind uniforms and forcing them to confront their own engagement in a power relation. It is as if the very nakedness of the naked body also left naked the phantasmatics of domination intrinsic to strip searches. According to an investigation conducted by the National Council for Civil Liberties some prison officers found the prisoners' attitude disturbing (NCCL 1986: 12).

Performative Gender and Sexual Difference

The 1992 strip searches departed remarkably from the semblance of aseptic professionalism in which prison authorities had attempted to wrap them. The pretension of institu-

---

14. See also Feldman (1991) on use of medical metaphors during interrogation and in the subculture of violence of some paramilitary groups.

tional regulation was not totally eliminated. For example, women were ritually asked if they would conform with the prison regulation of stripping, and in some cases a sheet was thrown upon the half naked body of an immobilized woman. However, the fiction of disciplinary routine was reduced to the minimum during the search, only to be reasserted afterwards in the act of charging women with disorderly behavior. All of them were sentenced to punishment cells, loss of recreation and several other disciplinary measures for disobeying prison orders. Rather than constituting punishment for disorderly behavior, these sentences acted as the legitimating force for the guards' assault. In other words, the sentences applied to women prisoners were not a response to an existing act of insubordination subject to ensuing adjudication, but rather the fabrication of such an act needed the sentences. They produced the "act of rebellion" rather than resulting from it, in the same way in which perpetrators of sexual violence often rationalize their violence as a response to some previous act of the victim.

Contrary to the appearance of institutional routine that these sentences attempted to create *a fortiori*, the long lasting strip searches were orchestrated as a ritualized display of military power that was deployed within the arena of sexuality; a deployment that was aimed at producing a maximum effect of terror. For Foucault, sexuality is not so much a property as "an especially dense transfer point for relations of power." Sexuality, he says, "is not the most intractable element in power relations but rather one of those endowed with the greater instrumentality: useful for the greatest number of maneuvers and capable of serving as a point of support, a lynchpin for the most varied strategies" (1980: 103). Sexuality was, in this case, the support point for a strategy of submission whereby the penetration of the prisoners' bodies enacted the penetration of their political identities, thus enabling the governor to control the carceral space. The control of prisoners' bodies appears, then, not so much as a show of force, but rather as an attempt to reconfigure the prisoners' subjectivity—from political to conforming prisoners, but also, and equally important, from rebellious to subordinate women. This much was clearly understood by the prisoners, who claimed that sexuality was being used as a political weapon against them. Theresa, for example, said that "just as rape can only be described as an act of violence to gain power over women, so too can strip searches only be described in this way."

Prisoners were also careful, however, to note that what happened in 1992 could not be understood *only* from a feminist perspective as an attempt to subordinate women. Carol, in response to the attention that the case attracted from feminist and civil liberties organizations, insisted that the attack was also aimed at weakening their identity as Republican political prisoners. Their identity as women and members of the IRA appeared to prisoners indissoluble. Indeed, at the time of the assault, there were in Maghaberry jail twenty-one female prisoners and three hundred male prisoners. Women had retained their political identity as members of the IRA, maintaining their own organizational structure, while men had renounced their political identity and conformed fully with prison regulations. For the governor of the prison, women were the only obstacle to full political control of the institution. The subjection of their political autonomy was

organized as a re-inscription of identity, within the normative bounds of a hierarchical gender system, which attempted to transform the body of the militant into the sexualized
body of the subjugated woman. This transformation was performed through a violation
of the political body of the prisoner by the male body politic, represented by the governor
and prison officers. Inasmuch as the body of women prisoners is marked with the signs
of ethnic subordination and colonial history, and inasmuch as the body politic is represented by British authorities, the subordination of women has the extended meanings of
dominating the Catholic/Nationalist community. And it is inscribed within a history of
political representations in which Anglo-Irish colonial relations have been often cast in the
idiom of sexual violence.[15]

I suggest that the strip searches of 1992 constituted a *mise en scène* of military mass
rape, one in which female officers acted as an extension of the male body. Let me elaborate. First of all, there were male guards alongside women conducting the search. While
the threatening presence of military men was accentuated by carrying with them barking
dogs and shouting sexual abuse, gender markers of women guards were erased. They
were erased, on the one hand, by the use of military uniforms including helmets and visors
that made it difficult to distinguish the gender of officers unless they were very close. On
the other hand, gender was blurred by the apparent participation of female officers in the
laughter and sexual joking of male guards. Last, but not less important, gender distinctions between male and female officers were obliterated in the forced undressing of prisoners, a kind of violence that women prisoners identified with male violence.

The conflation of gender distinctions between officers appeared particularly poignant
to one of the prisoners, Maureen, who felt disgusted at these "so-called women" who do
what another prisoner called plainly "rape." In this context, women officers, in performing like men, appeared to women prisoners no different from them. Here, gender ceases
to be predicated upon biological matter to be dependent on performance, as Judith Butler
has suggested. "Consider gender," Butler says, "as a *corporeal style*, an 'act', as it were, which
is both intentional and performative, where '*performative*' suggests a dramatic and contingent construction of meaning" (1990: 139). We can see how effective this 'gender act' can
be in prisoners' responses to it. Indeed, when I asked prisoners if the fact of being forcefully undressed by women made their feeling of violation less real, they all responded neg-
atively. Their response suggests that women officers "acted" as men in performing a fantasy of collective rape that could not have taken place, in its legal definition, without
costing the prison governor his career.

As I said at the beginning of this article, fantasy constitutes its own form of reality. In
writing about a fantasy of collective rape, therefore, I do not mean that it was not real.
Indeed, the sexualized violation of the body was real and so were its psychological and
emotional effects. I do not mean either that women who abuse other women are not "real"

---

15. See for example Aretxaga (1997), Herr (1990), Nash (1993), Kilfeather (1989), Cairns and Richards (1988), and
Heaney (1983).

women. What I mean is that unlike previous strip searches, the one taking place in 1992 was a violent "act" in Butler's sense of being both intentional and performative; an "act" animated by the phantasmatics of heterosexual mass rape. In performing this "act," the guards de facto—psychologically and politically, if not legally—carried out a rape that was heterosexual and ethnically marked. Carol's comment, that men were coaching woman officers while she was being stripped, would confirm this interpretation, as do the descriptions by other prisoners. It is precisely this sliding between the reality of legal definitions of rape and the actual experience of sexual violation, which permits the exercise of forms of rape under the cover of institutional rule.

The collective violation of the prisoners in 1992 was enabled by a realignment of gender positions that was not contiguous with sexual difference. For Lacan (1977: 281–92) it is not biology that determines sexual difference, but the position of the signifier that matters in the creation of sexual difference within a symbolic order. How, then, is sexual difference produced within this theater of domination? The erasure of gender difference between men and women officers allowed, and was a condition for, the establishment of a choreography of sexual difference inscribed within a gender hierarchy, according to which women prisoners were forced into the subordinate position of women, while officers (women and men alike) were reaffirmed in the controlling position of men; and not just men, but ethnically dominating men.

So much for gender bending of woman officers. How about the *body politic*? Inasmuch as the governor and officers represent the *body politic*, this apparently neutral body is revealed as thoroughly sexualized while its sexual operations, the assaults on women's bodies, are thoroughly invested with the political power of *the State*. Sexual and political relations of power become, in the case of strip searches, not just interdependent, but inextricably fused through the operations of fantasy and technology of control. Such fusion reaches full expression through the simultaneous violation of the prisoner's body and her only private space: the cell. The stripping of women prisoners in their own cells, instead of in the usual space of the cubicle, represented a double violation that deprived women of a secure psychological space. There is nowhere to go after the assault; the cell is transformed into an estranged space that acts as a constant reminder of their vulnerability.

The violent excess of the strip searches of 1992 questions the rational instrumentality that justifies it. If the strip searches conducted in Northern Ireland are not about utilitarian purpose, nor is the power relationship that defines them a neutral one, between "prisoners" and "officers." On the contrary, such a power relationship occurs within the space of a cultural and personal imaginary marked by ethnic difference, and it plays upon sexualized and genderized fantasies populating it. It is uncertain, given their silence, how much guards were affected by the fantasy scenario that animated the strip searches of 1992. One could only speculate that they were affected at some level, since women officers were provided with counseling after the event. Prisoners' requests for independent counseling were denied. They were offered only the services of the prison counselor, which they refused on the grounds that the counselor was part of the prison structure that had assaulted them. Carol said that some officers continued to sexually harass them at vulnerable moments such as family visits.

Final Remarks: Trauma and the Formation of Subjectivity

Maghaberry women prisoners have sued the prison governor for sexual harassment, a collective measure as unprecedented as the type of strip search orchestrated by the governor.[16] Ex-prisoners talked about the terrifying effects of the forced strip, but they were also adamant that they had become "more political" as a consequence of it. What women like Carol and Ann Marie meant by this, was that the violence had made them think more deeply about the connections between different forms of domination. Many of these women had become involved in the IRA as a gut reaction to the militarized repression of Nationalist communities. For them, this new political consciousness meant an understanding of how domination was structurally organized to subdue them as both women and Catholic-Nationalists. For these prisoners, being a woman took a politicized dimension that it did not have before. What became problematized by this politicization was, to echo Denise Reiley's question, what being a woman meant.

For the prisoners, femininity was linked to political subjecthood, their active involvement in a nationalist struggle against the British government. This politicized subjectivity, of which the prisoners became particularly aware after the stripping, was an obstacle to the male governor's total control of the prison. It was also a challenge to socially dominant norms of femininity that have long seen "terrorist" women as exceptions in the best of cases or gender deviations in the worst—in either case, as not quite women (Elshtain 1987; Rolston 1989). The strip search can be understood as the use of bodily violence to subdue the prisoners, not only into the norms of the prison but also into the ethnic hierarchy of Northern Ireland, within which Catholics had to be put in their (subjugated) place. Yet in Northern Ireland, strip searches are not just another kind of violence, but one specifically targeted at women. It is not just violence, but the form that violence takes, that matters in the formation of subjectivities and political discourse, as Das and Nandi (1985) astutely noted.[17] Inasmuch as resisting prisoners were women, the violence of strip searches was simultaneously aimed at subduing women into the norms of passive femininity by

---

16. The individual reports of what happened that March 2 were written primarily as testimonies for the judicial case and are thus intrinsically political. For this reason, some people may question the truth value of the reports. However, my interviews with some of the prisoners and the reading of all the individual handwritten reports, leaves me no reason to doubt the veridicality of the stories. I perceived no inconsistencies or disingenuity either in the written or verbal recounting of the event. To my knowledge, women in Northern Ireland do not easily verbalize experiences of sexual harassment, whether these are linked to the security forces or not. It seems extremely unlikely to me that the accounts of the strip search of 1992 were produced to attract political attention, finding more reasonable the prisoners' argument that it was the collective experience of excessive institutional abuse that led them to contest it in court.

17. See also Das (1995, 1996a) and Taylor (1997) on the way in which violence on the bodies of women can reconfigure political discourse.

transforming an autonomous female political subject into a male dependent one, stripped, so to say, of political agency.

Modern mechanisms of punishment, Foucault (1979) observed, are aimed at transforming subjectivities, at reconfiguring identity. Yet such transformation is a tricky process. Subject itself to the contingency of collective and personal histories, to phantasmatic intimacies and fantasies, the transformation of "souls" is unpredictable and often backfiring. The attempt at bending the politically radical Republican identity of women prisoners by sexualizing their bodies into "possessable" femininity did not produce tamed subjects, but new definitions of femininity linked to radicalized political identity; and yet their bodies were also inscribed with the signs of institutionalization, the marks of new vulnerabilities. In the process, what seemed challenged were both hegemonic constructions of gender identity and the ideological foundations of state power. Gender emerged as unfixed and performative, capable of accommodating itself to different structures of power. State power lost the neutral, rational mantle that legitimizes it to reveal a thoroughly sexualized, symptomatic body politic.

Part II

States of Terror: Nationalist Youth and the Political Imaginary in the Basque Country

CHAPTER 6

INTRODUCTION

I: States of Terror: Displacements[1]

I don't remember the first time the word terrorism entered my consciousness as a powerful and mysterious reality of a dubious character. Dubious because its density seemed to be different from that which organized the everyday real of my childhood—different from the reality of the corner grocery store, down the windy alleyway called familiarly "the tunnel," where La Carmen, the voluminous owner, kept a credit tab for our meager purchases. My life revolved around the materiality of this windy uphill tunnel, with its blind spots that, for years, terrified me whenever I had to go through it at night to take the garbage down the main road, or walk up home from school in the evening. The tunnel was a terrifying space of threat and potential violence, where bad men could hide for all sorts of scary purposes. Adults would warn you against staying in the tunnel at night; "come home quickly" they would admonish, following with a tale of some scabrous event having taken place there.

There was a symbolic geography to the tunnel, at once enclosed by its walls and open by closed doors and passages to a multiplicity of spaces outside it. But the tunnel was more than a symbolic space; its materiality organized spatially my immediate existence. La Carmen was at the bottom of the tunnel; the clinic, with its little garden of pansies and its lush trees, where I played all kinds of childhood games, was at its top. There were signs in the façade of the clinic and in the pansy garden that required silence and we, neighborhood kids playing around its grounds, were always in fear of running into trouble. But the clinic fascinated me, with its off-limits presence, where strangers came and left speaking in soft voices, looking unwell. These were mysterious lives I could only touch for a moment with an intent and brief gaze, a seemingly distracted look that interrupted the intimacy of playing with a whiff of the unknown. The clinic became, in my childhood, a refuge of sorts. I was taken there quickly when I cut my heel with a broken piece of glass while jumping over the traditional bonfire on St. John's night, June 21. All that I remem-

1. Unpublished manuscript.

ber of that first visit to *la clínica* was the kind voice and smile of the nurse who bandaged my foot. The cut was so deep that I couldn't go to school for days and that night, as I lay on my parents' bed with my newly-bandaged foot, I saw the last episode of a terror mystery on television, not the sort we kids were allowed to see in those days, and which I pulled off only as a side benefit to being in my parents' bedroom where our first black-and-white television was, and where I had been allowed as a source of post-traumatic comfort. In that episode, which I have remembered with unfading clarity to this day, a kind of Dr. Jekyll figure, a harmless-looking English gentleman, killed a young woman with a knife-like device hidden in his perfectly folded, perfectly respectable black umbrella, the kind you would see every man in my home town carrying around on a rainy day, the kind that seemed to cut the space in half with a gigantic black wave that moved tightly through the streets like a tide fencing against the leaking sky. So ubiquitous was that umbrella in my rainy region, so common, so familiar, so invested in everyday intimacy, that the idea that such a comforting object could hide such a deadly threat filled me with terror.

I intuitively learned then that terror is not the effect of an outside source, like the violence perpetrated by a foreign agent radically different from one's world, as with the subversive of the Francoist state: always linked in state propaganda to that seemingly endless gold that came from Moscow to fund the criminal and terrorist activities of all sorts of dissenters. Terror, I understood, was not a force one could set aside, outside the confines of the socially intimate from which one can separate, defend against—at least not always. Terror, I understood, was not the product of estrangement but of familiarity, not a force but a state of being, one deeply immersed in the everyday order of things. Jacques Lacan articulated conceptually the inexpressible terror I experienced when I realized the threatening violence that lurked in the materiality and space of the quotidian. He called it the Real (with a capital R). Cultural critic Slavoj Žižek has defined the Lacanian Real as reality devoid of the ideology that makes it cohesive and bereft of the fantasy that makes it palatable. The Real is, then, an irruption within the symbolic system that gives sense to our everyday world; it is a tear in the fabric of everyday life, an incongruence in the tale that we tell ourselves about life. Such a rupture forces us to see a dimension of the real that we do not generally see and which seems intolerable and inexpressible, unsymbolizable and which therefore has a shocking effect. Susan Stewart sees the shock of the Real as bonded to death, to the brush with death, its sight or touch—a sensual encounter with death in any case. But what might be traumatic of such encounters with the Real might well be the unbearable lucidity of being. Suddenly, a series of pieces which did not have shape before, come together in a single picture; one which one both instantly understands and does not comprehend at all.

It was this Real, which Freud might have called the uncanny, that erupted into my life that fateful night I cut my heel in the form of a scene, a terror scene, leaving an indelible print that has shaped both my intellectual pursuits and my existential anxieties ever since. If I bring up that scene here it is not because I have a burning desire to talk about my life, but because it exemplifies the ordinary, intimate and hidden terror that characterized everyday life under the Franco regime. It is this very ordinariness, its overwhelming presence and eclipsed reality that made both the Francoist state and life under Francosim, a state of terror, one so intimate, so familiar, so institutionalized as reality, that the state of terror became the normal state of being. I believe this terror scene articulated for me what I must have been perceiving all along through the whispers and fragmented conversations that, in spite of their sotto voce, reached my child's ear. Such fragments spoke of a frightening reality never quite spelled out, not entirely material yet as real and present as the air one breathes. At some level, I realized that the terrorists of whom the press and the television spoke might not be such monsters as they were made out to be, and that the Generalissimo might not be such a benevolent figure as the *Noticiero Español*, the official newsreel of the state, presented him.

I don't remember when I began to have the suspicion that there was more to the reality of terrorism than we were told, but I do remember the day when the word *terrorists*, printed on the front page of the local newspaper, *La Voz de España*, in bold red letters, struck me as a strange charade. I don't remember the event that gave rise to that headline, nor even the headline itself, or the situation or the time of year. All I remember is the word "terrorists," strangely charged, invested with a mysterious quality tinted in red, and the distinctive sense of inhabiting a deceptive reality. Perhaps that was the moment when the ideological fantasy of a happy, industrious nation which sustained a quotidian regime of terror in Francoist Spain ruptured for me, leaving a disturbing gap not yet filled with meaning. The familiar landscape oozed danger. Reality was penetrated by an absence that could not be apprehended.

I have always pondered why the arrest of the Dr. Jekyll of my childhood, which followed the killing of his last victim in the television series, did not assuage the terror triggered by the scene of the killing. The terror that persisted for years was not just the result of inchoate childhood terrors. Rather, that childhood terror was overdetermined by the invisible but palpable terror of the political regime hidden under the smiling face of Franco's appearance on television, and accommodated by then into a dissociated normality in which violence was a public secret and life itself revolved around its dirty center. But there was more, because this terror had to do with the violence of the Spanish Civil War; with the intimate knowledge, rancor, desires, envy, and fears that split neighbors and even families in different war camps in towns and villages, leaving a long unspoken trail of resentment and bitterness. Intimacy itself was traversed by danger and violence. The nearly forty years of Francoist dictatorship were characterized by a timeless time filled with the silence of massive violence, a silence that structured the terror of the regime as a permanent absent presence. Silence was a crucial part in the normalization of a state terror.

Some years after the fateful scene of the fictional killing so impacted my childhood, Spanish film director Victor Erice represented the unspoken terror of the new regime through the figure of a famous monster. *The Spirit of the Beehive* begins with an itinerant film company arriving at a small Spanish village soon after the end of the war, to show a film, announced by a poster as *Dr. Frankenstein, the Maker of the Monster*. The whole village, kids included, gather in the town hall for the entertainment. Ana, a little girl, becomes fascinated with the monster and deeply intrigued by the key scene of the movie where the monster kills a little girl who has befriended him, and is in turn killed by villagers. Ana is deeply impacted by this sequence of events, unlike other kids in the audience who watch the scene with their eyes half-covered; Ana is glued to the screen with wide-open eyes, impressed yet puzzled. "Why does the monster kill the girl and why is he killed afterwards?" she asks her older sister, Isabel. "They don't kill him," Isabel says. "In the movies everything is a lie; besides," she adds, "I have seen him, he only comes out at night, he is a spirit." Ana becomes obsessed with the monster/spirit with whom she tries to communicate. One day after school, she goes to an abandoned house inhabited by the monster/spirit, according to her sister Isabel. In the abandoned house she discovers a wounded soldier. In an earlier scene, we have seen the soldier jumping off the train in the middle of the night with the clear suggestion that he is a Republican soldier on the run. Ana fuses the soldier and the monster/spirit with whom she seeks to connect, and brings the wounded soldier clothes and food, befriending him. There is a shooting in the middle of the night and the body of the now-dead soldier is seen in the headquarters of the Civil Guard (the military police who dominated rural areas). The next day, Ana goes to the abandoned house, but there is nobody there. The scene is one of desolation which is accompanied by Republican music. She finds the remnants of a bullet and understands that her friend has been killed. Horrified, she runs into the forest and gets lost. She sees the image of Frankenstein's monster dead in the river. He comes out of the river and the monster and the girl look at each other, face to face. The girl is finally discovered lying on the ground by her father and a group of villagers. She is in shock, cannot eat, doesn't speak, and the light bothers her. At the end, a now-recovered Ana tries to communicate with the monster/spirit, now mixed with the memory of the soldier.

I have described the film at length because it is one of the first to tackle the terror of the regime and the silence sustaining it—the surreality of a violence at once all-pervasive and exiled from language, the ghostliness of a terror that functioned as a state of being rather than as event, that was in itself a producer of mad states, to follow Jacqueline Rose (1996). In *The Spirit of the Beehive*, the state of disconnection that characterizes events and social life in the village is mirrored in the domestic universe of Ana. Communication between the parents is practically absent, their relationship dominated by silence. The house itself is covered in shadows, projecting a somber mood broken only by the two sisters playing. Ana's mother is preoccupied with an absent, enigmatic other from whom she was separated during the war and to whom she writes letters which are always returned. In one of these letters, Ana's mother writes, "Sometimes, when I look around and see so many absences, so many things destroyed and at the same time so much sadness, something tells me that maybe with those things went also our capacity to really feel life." Without the feeling of life, what remains is an incessant activity, such as that characterizing the beehive that Ana's father attends, and which seems to him a *triste espanto* (sad ghost).

We quickly realize that, in this social universe of the postwar dictatorship, it is not presence but absence that dominates social life, transforming life itself into present absence, ghostliness. There are the unnamable absent presence of the defeated, those Republicans killed, exiled, or hidden—like the enigmatic figure that so preoccupies Ana's mother, condemned to non-existence by a ban from social life, and even from language. There is also the absent presence of a life before it was crushed, the remnants of which hang onto the matter of things and buildings, like ghosts. Social life in the Spanish postwar era is, in sum, the absent presence of life itself banned from language. Life outside language, suggests Giorgio Agamben (2000a), is not life; yet it is not necessarily death either, it is living death or undead life as Eric Santner (2001) prefers to call it—like the monster in the movie that so much fascinates Ana. Indeed, in the film, the monster allegorizes this undead life and the enigma that surrounds it. It condenses everything that has been banned from language and which is read by the little girl Ana as charged enigma, as the undecipherable knot of domestic and social life. Who is the figure that haunts Ana's mother? Who is the soldier killed by the Civil Guard? Who really is the father who spends his nights writing? There is no answer to these questions, only the fragmented gaze of the camera on a collection of photographs, which reveals the existence of a former time now condemned to silence. These questions allegorize the central enigma of life in the postwar dictatorship, as a state of terror, and of the violence of the Civil War travestied into glorious crusade. It is an enigma of this sort, Laplanche (1999) suggests, that constitutes the unconscious and constitutes the subject as a self around an enigmatic Other. It is not surprising that it is Ana, a little girl, who symptomatizes this state of estrangement. For she senses this displaced life and reads its enigma but cannot decipher it. The monster condenses all that is condemned to non-existence in social life, iconizing the latter as truly monstrous. Ana's desire to befriend the monster is a desire for connection, a desire for an intimacy that can restore life to life, and presence to the self, estranged now from itself by a history of violence rendered secret. Befriending the monster, then, holds the promise of an answer to the enigma of political, social and domestic estrangement; it holds the promise to presence, to a life reconnected to itself.

Ever since I saw *The Spirit of the Beehive,* I have felt a sense of kinship with Ana and a sense of recognition in her character. Growing up during the dictatorship was growing up with mysterious fragments of life, things said in whispers, bits of information here and there, leaflets too dangerous to be picked up, graffiti suddenly appearing on unexpected walls, and then the official discourse about terrorism, Basque terrorism. There was an incongruence between the official characterization of the terrorists by the regime as monsters paid by the "Moscow gold" and the sense of jubilation I could sense from those adults close to me. It was a silent satisfaction, only betrayed in a whisper or a gesture made within the intimacy of friends, but as a child I could sense it. Both gesture and sense are important as configuring, articulating, and indeed constituting the political as a subjective experience. It was at the level of the senses that the fundamental conflicts and faults underlying the apparently smooth surface of political life could be articulated. While the regime worked on the visual representation of an idealized political community embodied by the *Caudillo*, Franco, people used other senses to articulate a far more ghostly and sinister reality. Thus, for example, the secret police was not so much "seen" as "smelled"; one could smell them everywhere.[2] Years later, when I was doing the research for this book I encountered this sensual apprehension of the political in the stories told by young radical activists. As we will see later, this heightened sensibility articulates an intangibility, a reality triggered by symbolic rupture, the Lacanian Real. Such sensual configuration, which is intrinsic to the political (its spectral dimension perhaps), takes form and concreteness in the gesture. For Giorgio Agamben, the gesture is pure mediality and politics the sphere of absolute gesturality: "The gesture is essentially always a gesture of not being able to figure something out in language; it is always a gap in the proper meaning of the term meant to compensate for a loss of memory or an inability to speak" (2000b: 58). This *sense* of a political otherness charged with feelings of disguised joy or official outrage, constituted my political self as one inhabiting a field of displacement.

Displacements

To write about displacement is to write about relations of contiguity; it is to write about the logic of metonymic operations that animates the symbolic universe of culture. How is such logic deployed in a political space to dynamically constitute a specific political culture? To explore this question, I would consider political culture to be analogous to a dream. In doing so, I am following a cue from Gananath Obeyesekere's "work of culture" (1990). For Obeyesekere, culture is produced in a dynamic and changing form in ways similar to those that produce the dream as an interpretable reality. According to Freud, the key to the interpretation of the dream is the operation of condensation and displacement, that is, the relations of substitution and continuity which characterize not only the unconscious but symbolization itself. In language, these operations characterize the logic of metaphor and metonymy. The meaning of culture is, like the meaning of the dream, never exhausted and, like the dream, culture contains an unsymbolizable kernel which Lacan called the Real.[3]

Although I analyze relations of metaphoric substitution as they play in the political field of the Basque Country, I give greater attention to the less explored logic of metonymic displacement. Displacement allows us to follow a train of connections between disparate things, events, ideas, which may be hidden in political discourse. I will follow the movement of displacement to track, for instance, the unfolding figure of the *cipayo*, the pejorative and charged insult given to a newly formed Basque police force. Through the

---

2. Michael Taussig (1993, 1997) has elaborated on the power of the senses to configure the political.

3. Jacques Lacan's interpretation of Freud placed condensation and displacement within the field of structural linguistics, emphasized metaphor and metonymy as the operations of the unconscious. James Fernandez (1986) followed Lacan, rather than Freud, in articulating a vision of culture delineated by the operations of metaphoric predication.

logic of displacement, I will try to unfold not only the formation of a discourse, but the formation of certain passions associated with this figure, and with those political entities associated with it: nation, state and sovereignty. The displaced moves by which *cipayo* takes density, form, space and affect in Basque political culture will permit us to see not only how ideology works, but the fantasy (and its affective content) that supports this ideological construction.[4] I will come back to the centrality of fantasy to the political later.

There is a way in which my own dis-placement colors my analysis and perhaps even determines it. As a Basque academic working and living in the U.S., my writing on the troubled politics of the Basque Country feels profoundly intimate, yet also the product of a spatial remove, a self-chosen impossible distance. Such dis-placement entails not only an estrangement from place, but an estrangement from emotional location. This position of estrangement from both place of origin and place of residence does not mean that there is no emotional attachment to place, but rather that such attachment is complicated by a position of dis-centeredness. My position as a Basque woman engaged in American academics makes me an insider/outsider and places me in an undetermined location from where my discourse emanates. Despite its ambiguities, such a position has had at least one clear advantage in conducting my research in a deadlocked and polarized political culture. I found myself going back to a Basque Country where people who were friends, when I left in 1985, had been torn apart by political violence and were not speaking to each other anymore. Had I remained in the Basque Country, I too would most likely have been forced to take sides, but being away I found I still had friends on opposing political sides. Talking with people who were not talking to each other and to whom I was linked by friendship ties was both illuminating and emotionally taxing.

Furthermore, my relation to the Basque Country through former friends was also mediated by a past of political activism. From my adolescent years, when I was in high school, to until shortly before coming to the U.S., I had been involved in a number of social movements and political organizations. These began to emerge at the end of the Franco dictatorship, in clandestine form, and exploded within the public space during the effervescent early years of the democratic transition. In particular, I was part, from their inception, of the student, feminist and anti-nuclear movements. These movements formed a network of political activity with links to each other, so that there was nothing unusual about my multi-affiliation. Political associationism was, and continues to be, intensively dense. I was also a member of a small radical nationalist party which disappeared in the political competition that followed the first democratic elections. In coming back to the Basque Country, my person was often located within this political map of the past. Of course for many young activists—who were the object of my research—this activist past remained vague and distant, but it afforded me a point of entry and often helped to dis-

---

4. In relation to the work of fantasy as ideological support, see Žižek (1997) and Rose (1996), for a discussion of the work of fantasy as animating political belief and action: "Fantasy is not therefore antagonistic to social reality; it is its precondition or psychic glue" (Rose 1996: 3).

pel the reticence and suspicion which was so pervasive during the late 1990s among radical nationalist youth. Politics, however, was not my only location. I could also be publicly
identified by my writing; and some friends introduced me to young activists by referring
to me as the author of my first book-essay on the political funerals of ETA members
assassinated by the government-organized death squads, GAL. That essay was generally liked and provided legitimacy for further writing on radical nationalism. During 1997,
when I was conducting this research, social scientists were under enormous suspicion and
attack, as many activists believed that they were at the service of the government. In any
event, the Foucaudian relation of power/knowledge seemed to these young activists self-
evident and pervasive, and they were therefore disinclined to collaborate with any kind of
research. My position, therefore, was characterized by a displacement from militancy by
academic writing and a displacement from academic writing by past militancy. My contemporary relation to both was displaced by spatial and temporal distance. In trying to
understand the political culture of this so seemingly puzzling new generation of activists,
I often found myself trying to remember my own thoughts and feelings when I was their
age. In a way, the preparation of this book implied a passage through memory for me,
a reckoning with a time and a place I had left behind some seventeen years earlier during which I was busy getting my Ph.D. and making my life in another country. In some
ways, then, this book is also the product of personal, social and political displacement and,
in complicated ways, it re-articulates a relation to that displacement.

Mourning and the Production of the Nation

> Death is a problem, not because we cannot surmount its loss or imagine our own death, but
> because it forces us to acknowledge that what belongs to us most intimately is also a
> stranger or enemy, a type of foreign body in the mind.
>
> Jacqueline Rose, *Why War?*

One of my first vivid political memories is that of a state of exception declared by Franco in the (then) Basque provinces, during 1975.[5] What might a state of exception have
meant, I wonder now, in the context of an already existing State of exception. For that is
how we can consider the lengthy dictatorial regime of Franco, which arrested the country
from the contingencies of social and political time and condemned three generations to life
in the hellish ever-present of Francoist social imaginary. I would say that the state of
exception declared in 1974 entailed the suspension of civil liberties and the enactment of
military and police powers. But such powers were already in place during the Franco

---

5. "State of exception" ("*estado de excepción*") was the name used by the regime when it declared an extra-ordinary state
of emergency, as it did several times during the late 1960s and early 1970s. Carl Schmitt ([1922] 1985) and Giorgio Agamben (1998) after him focus on the state of exception as the ideal place for an investigation of the question of sovereignty
in modernity, which entails necessarily a reflection on the nature of Law and the State.

regime, and there were no civil liberties to suspend. The Francoist "state of exception" was a visible materialization of what was there all the time, in more or less disguised form; so habitual, that it had become invisible. In this sense, it might be considered an "outing" of the regime, as it were, from its public representation of paternal benevolence embodied in the image of "*el abuelo*" (Franco as grandfather), to its true military nature. The state of exception was the visible enactment of the regime's foundation of terror, which Benjamin's everyday "state of emergency" brought into relief.[6] The 1974 state of exception was, then, an interruption of the habitus of the regime that revealed—if such revelation was necessary—its character as pure force, disturbing thus the deadening forms of accommodation promoted by the same regime.[7]

For me, the memory of the state of exception is condensed in images filled with the force of feeling. I remember the empty streets in the evening, heavy with a silence so dense it seemed to form a natural continuum with the Nordic fog. Plastered on the walls there were half torn posters in support of Txiki and Otaegi, the now-legendary ETA members condemned to the death penalty and soon to be executed, despite international protests. I remember people scurrying home avoiding potential trouble, and the patrolling of police armored vehicles watching the deadness of streets for signs of protest. I remember the dim light of the rainy autumn and the fear hanging in the air; and a few young people like myself, then fifteen years old, moving surreptitiously through back streets, communicating in a grieving sotto voce the latest information about the impending execution and about a quick demonstration—nothing more than the shouting of a few slogans of protest before the presence of the police would break the gathering and send everybody running for cover—small gestures amounting, perhaps, to no more than a tear in the seamless fabric of silence and fear imposed by the regime. But perhaps the newspapers would mention it the following day, if only in a distorted way, writing of "paid provocateurs" attempting to disrupt the public order. Since that day, political violence comes to me dressed in a grey color, just as political resistance seems to be associated with the rage and impotence of grieving. However, on closer look, death, the labor of death, as opposed to the labor of mourning, stands out in the production of Basque nationalist consciousness and political rebellion.

Since the early 1970s, the political landscape in the Basque Country has been punctuated by posters, graffiti, banners, murals and memorials denouncing the death of nationalist militants and constructing a memory of absence constituting the repository of national presence; a locus for national identification. Such public landscape is often continuous with an intimate one where dead militants are remembered through posters or other memorial objects displayed at home. During the 1970s, it was common practice to

---

6. Walter Benjamin argues that the "state of emergency" characterizing the rise of fascism is not an exception in the progression of political time but the rule: "It is our task to bring about a real state of emergency, and this will improve our position in the struggle against fascism (1968: 257)." (1968: 257).

7. See Santner (2001) for a discussing of deadening by power.

issue memorial cards (*recordatorios*) with the photograph of the dead militant, which, in turn, would be carried in one's wallet or posted on the wall of one's bedroom or living room.

Death, of course, has long occupied a privileged place in the nationalist imagination, mostly in the form of glorious death in the pursuit of national liberation or national defense.[8] Yet in the Basque case, the death made visible on the walls of towns and cities by virtue of plastered posters is not death inflicted on others in a demonstration of sacrifice and military might, nor the death of battle, but that resulting from the unjust violence of an abusive power: the state.[9] Death is publicly represented by radical Basque nationalism as loss, but this is neither the melancholic loss of nation in a bygone primordial or political past,[10] nor heroic death in battle. Rather, death has here the quality of the uncanny, unclear death, as in the activist killed by death squads or the prisoner found hanging in his cell. These are deaths that point to uncanny agencies. Fran Aldanondo's was one such death.

Fran Aldanondo, or "Ondarru," had just left prison when I met him back in 1977. I was seventeen then and deeply involved in activism on behalf of political prisoners. Aldanondo was an unusual man as political prisoners go. Unlike most political prisoners, he had joined a struggle undertaken by fellow prisoners charged with non-political offenses, termed at the time "common prisoners." This was the first struggle in Spain for prisoners' rights and improvement of prison conditions. Foucault was actively involved in similar kinds of campaigns in France. The fight was rough and, as Foucault theorized, played right on the field of the body. Prisoners ingested pieces of silverware and cut themselves with razors to make their points. Aldanondo was the first Basque political prisoner to identify with the struggle of "common prisoners" and join their ranks in solidarity, erasing thus the very distinction between common and political prisoner, a distinction until then firmly marked by prisoners charged with political offenses. In retrospect, this is not so surprising for Aldanondo was a member of *Comandos Autónomos* (Autonomous Commandos), a small armed revolutionary group of anarchist ideology which operated in the Basque Country during the late 1970s. His anarchist ideology must have contributed to the challenge of long-standing hierarchies and boundaries within the prison population. Yet the source of Aldanondo's solidarity was profoundly personal. I first met Aldanondo at a meeting between representatives of prisoners and political and grass roots organiza-

---

8. See in this respect Benedict Anderson's now classic *Imagined Communities* (1983, 1991). There is now a vast literature on nationalist capitalization of the death.

9. Unlike the IRA, ETA has never represented itself in a military guise in murals or posters. When rebellion is depicted, this has a popular character rather than a military one.

10. See in this respect Marilyn Ivy (1997). Some scholars in the Basque Country, namely the sociologist Alfonso Pérez-Agote (2004), have argued that ETA is caught in the melancholic mourning for the political time of the dictatorship, when a sense of national unity was possible and they could be celebrated as antifascist heroes. The refusal of radical nationalists to admit that anything substantial has changed since 1975 would have its explanation in melancholic paralysis. Along these lines, although referring to a melancholic attachment to a primordial Basque past, there is also the explanation of Spanish essayist, Jon Juaristi (1997).

tions. The meeting was summoned to organize a public campaign in support of the struggle unleashed in the prisons. He was a tall, broad-shouldered and handsome man, and rather unassuming. I remember being impressed by his softness and kindness which, through time, I learned was genuine. What had led Aldanondo to armed struggle was a profound humanist concern with the suffering of fellow human beings and an equally profound dislike of capitalism.

We learned of his assassination in 1979 through the local newspapers, which published a photograph of his torn and bloodied body lying on the slopes of a local mountain. Aldanondo was one of those killed militants whose death was not claimed by any group. When Basque militants were killed, their death was often claimed by one right-wing group or another and, through the years, there had been a succession of them in the Basque Country. Basque armed groups, similarly, had a pattern of claiming their assassinations. This was not only a form of political propaganda, it created a cosmological map of political struggle, an ideological order where death could be re-located as political agency. Yet, there were also those unclaimed political deaths, uncanny because they could not be located. Those deaths, such as Aldanondo's, created terror and political confusion showing, in fact, the fragility of political categories. Was Aldanondo killed by the extreme right or was he killed by competing Basque militants? Both possibilities were plausible; and it was this plausibility that rendered the field of political struggle ethically ambiguous, while also making his death uncanny. Ultimately, his death was never claimed, becoming the object of ongoing speculation, memorialized as was the practice in those days in a little *recordatorio*, an in-memory card with a photograph of a smiling young Aldanondo. The political uncanny in the form of death has haunted Basque political culture since the 1970s up to this day.

When I arrived in the Basque Country in February 1997 to conduct research for the present book, I was greeted few days later with the scandal of the death of a political prisoner, Jose Mari Aranzamendi, who appeared hanged in his cell, his hands and feet bound with a rope. Prison authorities said he had committed suicide. This death unleashed a chain of protests, as well as banners, posters and other kinds of graphic representations accusing the state of Aranzamendi's death, depicting the image of his inert body. Thus displayed, this kind of death becomes a scene where national identifications are made possible through operations of intimate and sensual exchange between the body of the dead militant and the body of the nation,[11] an exchange which simultaneously intensifies and negates the loss. I will argue that, in this scene of death and through the prostrate body of the victim, the nation is fetishized as a hyper-present absence subjected to the uncanny forces of a powerful, ghostly state. This fetishization is not confined to the dead, but also to prisoners, whose sequestered bodies are also the object of obscure, arbitrary violence. Thus, in this book, I am less concerned with the production of bodies through terrorist attacks

---

11. Michael Taussig's description of the reburial of Simón Bolívar captures this kind of sensual exchange (1997).

as a form of actualizing power (Feldman 1991), as I am with the production of bodies through uncanny agencies to configure a political culture wherein death functions as the exchange currency for transactions in national sovereignty, statehood and the law.

Sovereignty

When I was growing up in the 1960s, the discourse on national sovereignty came mostly from the dictatorial regime of Francisco Franco. *La Soberanía Nacional* seemed to inhabit almost all official discourse, including all new broadcasts of the official newsreel of the regime, *El No-Do*. Indeed, the very existence of the regime appeared to rest on the sacrosanct task of safeguarding national sovereignty, by which term the regime referred to Spanish unity and singularity. So much emphasis on national sovereignty could not but betray its contested state by internal and external forces. Not only was the country filled with American military bases at that time, but there was also a more or less silent opposition to Franco and his Spanish nationalism in different regions of Spain—especially in the Basque Country and Catalonia, which had a well-developed nationalist consciousness and had enjoyed, during the brief time that preceded Franco's victory in 1939, advanced forms of self-government. Thus if the rhetoric of the regime was punctuated by the cadences of "national sovereignty," it was also being contested in the Basque Country and Catalonia by the echoes of regional nationalism, the echoes of a different kind of national sovereignty: one linked to democracy and the free association of regions. But the term "national sovereignty" was also tinted with the topsy-turvy realities of Francoist life, and so it was not widely used during the 1960s and 1970s by nationalist movements. Instead, terms such as *askatasuna* (freedom), *independentzia* (independence) and *autodeterminazioa* (self determination), were central to the rhetoric of Basque nationalism. A growing influence of socialism and working class ideologies during the 1970s, as well as the recognition of other regional minorities within the Spanish State, also led to the nuancing of an early opposition between "Spain" and "Euskadi" (the Basque Country). The discourse of radical nationalism, well in place by 1974, was anchored on terms such as "*pueblos del estado español*" ("peoples of the Spanish State") instead of a blanket "Spain." "*Estado Español*" recognized the nationalistic character of the state but denied any legitimation to its nationalist claims. It was not anymore a case of Basques versus Spanish, but of different nationalities and peoples (Basques, Catalans, Galicians, Andalusians, and so on) against a nationalistic and totalitarian state. This discourse, evocative of internal solidarity and challenging of a Spanish identity, changed during the late 1980s and 1990s with the emergence of a new generation of radical nationalists.

During the 1990s in particular, the new nationalist discourse produced by radical nationalists was organized around a polarized opposition between "*España*" and "*Euskalherria*" (the Basque Country), between Basques and Spaniards, and the context for solidarity shifted from within, to outside, the Spanish State. The European Union became the locus of a politics of minority nationalisms. Radical nationalists envisioned Basque National Sovereignty as the first goal to be articulated in the context of a "Europe of the Peoples" or a Europe constituted by the free association of independent regions. During the 1990s, the discourse of sovereignty has been accentuated and alongside it, so has the discourse of citizenship. "Basque citizens" has become a major term in the discourse of national sovereignty and the tactics have been to, de facto, act as if there were a Basque state in place. Some of these practices have been mostly symbolic, such as, for example, the production of a Basque national identity card and passport, while others amount to the organization of parallel structures of government, such as an assembly of nationalist mayors and town councilors. There are yet other practices of statehood with a phantasmatic character, such as the appropriation of policing functions (by virtue of policing and punishing if appropriate) the politics of ordinary people. These practices of statehood have not been devoid of contradiction, as we shall see later on, because if statehood had become in the 1990s an intense object of desire then it was also charged with all that was dreaded and feared. Such ambivalence has traversed and dominated the politics of radical nationalism for over a decade and will be the object of detailed ethnographic attention. The question is, then, why should sovereignty and statehood be such an urgent desire in a globalized world in which states seem to be less and less independent? And why, moreover, in the Basque Country, where an independent state seems unviable? And why should this demand for a Basque state appeal to a new generation of youth socialized not only in Basque culture, but also in the transnational youth culture that is found all over the world? The emphasis of the current radical nationalist movement in the Basque Country on sovereignty and statehood opens a reflection on the aporias and paradoxes of what Agamben (1998) has called "the logic of sovereignty."

II: Content of the Book: Historical Background and Theoretical Significance

With the peace process in Northern Ireland well underway, the Basque Country remains the only region in Western Europe still dominated by a violent nationalist conflict. In spite of growing social opposition, nationalist violence has become more virulent in recent years, intensifying tensions and deeply dividing the social fabric in towns and cities. A crucial factor in the intensification of this conflict is the emergence of a new generation of radical nationalists who have become increasingly involved, during the late 1990s, in practices of intimidation against opposing parties and in practices of urban warfare against "the (Spanish) State." Under the rubric of *kale borroka* or street fighting, this radicalized youth have deployed a new style of violence characterized by aggressive rioting against the Basque police, burning of public property such as municipal buses and garbage containers, attacks on public buildings (such as law courts and government offices) and ATM machines with homemade petrol bombs, and violent intimidation of those opposing violence. Although not easily classifiable as "terrorism," this nationalist youth violence has risen to unparalleled levels of social anxiety, partly because of its capacity to attract hundreds of young people, and partly because they are perceived as the future recruits of a hardened and more politically intransigent ETA (the terrorist organization). Paradoxically, the demands for legal control of these youth gave them a central place in the political discourse and transformed them, during the second half of the 1990s, from an aside to the violence of ETA into the stars of the political scene. This project focuses on this new phenomenon of youth violence in order to understand why and how a violent nationalism has continued to exist, in spite of growing opposition within the Spanish democratic regime. I am interested in the political culture and the social dynamics that have made possible the emergence of a new generation of violent activists and that have shaped their political interventions.

I focus on this new kind of youth violence rather than on the more established and researched terrorism of ETA for two reasons. In the first place, this generation, unlike previous generations of Basque radicals, was born in a democratic regime. Thus their political motivations and historical attachments to radical nationalism might be significantly different from those of previous generations whose commitment to violence sprang out of a direct experience with a totalitarian regime. Many of these youth have a kinship connection with radical nationalism, being themselves the sons and daughters of radical nationalists with direct experience of an imprisoned relative. This experience raises the question of affect and emotional loyalty as direct motivations of violent politics. While theories of nationalism have noticed the importance of kinship metaphors in creating a sense of belonging and attachment to the idea of nation, the nature of the relation of family loyalty to nationalist political violence remains widely under-researched.

The second reason for my focus is that youth violence remains incomprehensible for most people, triggering unparalleled levels of civic anxiety and civil confrontation. Two sociological studies commissioned by the Basque government testify to the political anxiety generated by the violence of this movement (Various Authors 1994; Elzo 1995). Yet, with the exception of these governmental studies, both of them of a quantitative character, nationalist youth violence remains practically under-researched. While they have been often likened to neo-Nazi youth cultures in the official discourse of politicians and government officials, my research indicates that youth violence is inscribed within a heterogeneous, anti-authoritarian culture which borrows from transnational youth culture, while simultaneously being deeply entrenched in Basque local sociality and rigid ideology of nationhood. Several studies, carried in the late 1980s and early 1990s on Basque youth culture, already pointed to this transnational connection (Ramírez Goicoechea 1991; Lahusen 1993; Urla 1995). My research indicates that the nationalist youth movement is a highly contradictory formation, at once deeply anti-authoritarian and rigidly dogmatic in its nationalist ideology, borrowing from transnational culture and deeply entrenched in local networks.

These tensions are expressed in the organizational relations that the nationalist youth organization, Jarrai, has with other groups within the youth movement. While the latter tend to support radical nationalism, they often resent Jarrai's domineering nationalism. Similarly, groups within the radical nationalist movement have often opposed the youngsters' sabotage tactics. The latest example of this conflict came during the ETA ceasefire (1998–99), when the leadership of the radical nationalist movement unsuccessfully asked nationalist youth to stop their violence in favor of the peace effort. During the period of the peace process, however, more than 370 attacks were carried out by nationalist youth. Despite how crucial these tensions are in shaping political practice, no research to date has explored their manifestations at the level of everyday political culture.

Alongside this local/transnational dimension in the formation of nationalist youth culture, another crucial area of research is that of the discourses of "terrorism" and the 'state'. Because nationalist youth is associated with the violent nationalism of ETA (which these youngsters support), and because their actions are legitimized as a struggle against the (Spanish) state and in favor of a (Basque) state, it is imperative to understand both the complex forms in which discourses and practices of statehood and terrorism have shaped the field of violence, and the very political subjectivities of Basque nationalist youth. For example, during the ceasefire, when terrorist violence had stopped, the Spanish ministry of the interior referred to youth violence as "low intensity terrorism," using it as an argument to withhold negotiations. The question is not only how nationalist youth perceive and react against a state who opposes their own desire for a Basque state; but also how the perception and fear of these youngsters by state officials (as actual or potential terrorists) delineates state forms of violent intervention that reinforce and often encourage youth violence. My study, then, approaches youth violence as shaped by a political culture over-determined by the complex terms of "terrorism" and the "state," studying the ways in which these terms are socially imagined and experienced in everyday life as powerful agents. In this sense, it is also an ethnographic study of the social construction of the state which explores the double valence of the state as an object of fear and desire for radical nationalists. At issue is how the state, seemingly weakened by contemporary processes of globalization, is imagined and experienced as a powerful object of threat and desire by new generations of ethnonationalists all over the world; and how this experience of the state is articulated with a fantasized ethnic nation. I use fantasy here to emphasize those subjective processes of identification and attachment that form the affective glue of nationalist movements, and which have proved so powerful in drawing Basque youth to nationalist violence. I agree with Jacqueline Rose (1996) that the notion of fantasy is a productive heuristic tool to understand the irrational and excessive dimensions of the political. I am interested here in how fantasies of state and nationhood articulate with local and personal realities, so as to produce violent confrontations and states of terror. The book thus approaches the new phenomenon of youth violence within the context of the intersecting histories of the youth movement, the radical nationalist movement and state violence in the Basque Country.

Beyond the Basque case, this book has important implications for understanding the local social dynamic undergirding and reproducing ethnonationalist conflicts in the contemporary world. One of the paradoxical effects of global economic, political and informational interconnection has been an upsurge in ethnonationalist conflicts that have often taken the form of terrorist violence. In some cases, these conflicts emerged as a concomitant effect of the demise of the socialist states and the end of the Cold War. Yet in others, they seem to be an effect of the opposed process of supranational unification, such as the formation of the European Union. In the latter case, the erasure of frontiers among member states has not curtailed national aspirations held by minority groups such as Basques, but rather bolstered them. What seems at stake is a renewed and often violent investment in creating ethnically defined nation-states at a moment when the model of the state itself seems to be eroding. What remains poorly understood are the forms that these nationalist investments take at the local level. The volatility and troublesome character of peace processes set in place in various regions afflicted by ethnonationalist conflicts, such as Israel/Palestine, Northern Ireland and recently the Basque Country, attest to the necessity of re-approaching the place held by the nation-state in the collective political imagination, the ways in which the state and nation are not only imagined (Anderson 1983) but fantasized, that is, held as objects of fear and desire.

The role of youth cultures in formulating radical nationalist (both right and left wing) ideologies and identities is posing an increasing challenge to democratic discourse and practices, yet this is a phenomenon poorly understood and under-researched in the scholarship of nationalism. In the Basque Country, there is little doubt that the new generation of radicalized youth is currently feeding the ranks of ETA. Yet the dynamics of this recruitment are far from clear. Although the nationalist youth organization, Jarrai, and ETA are part of the ensemble of organizations that compose the radical nationalist movement in the Basque Country, there is not a direct organizational relationship between the leadership of ETA and youth violence. Youth violence is a very flexible phenomenon, rooted in the micro-socialities and political dynamics of particular localities, and transcending the boundaries of a single organization. There are, however, informal relations between the leadership of ETA and youth violence, the nature of which have changed through time. The continuation of youth violence during the ETA ceasefire, in spite of its counterproductive effects, seem to indicate a level of autonomy not subordinated to the political discipline of ETA, and sometimes even at odds with it.

The breakup of the peace process in 1999, after fifteen months during which the only nationalist violence was of this youth variety, makes it all the more urgent to understand the political culture of this new generation for establishing and sustaining a peace process that can put an end to the violence in the Basque Country. Similarly, understanding the role of the state in the production of terrorism, through the deployment of illegal violence against nationalists, is a crucial task in maintaining a sustainable peace. My hope is to contribute new forms of thinking about ethnonationalist conflict and the state, while at the same time providing a better understanding of the social and cultural dynamic of violence in the Basque Country, which may ultimately help to establish a lasting peace process in the region.

The death of General Francisco Franco in 1975 marked, in Spain, the end of the dictatorship and the beginning of a transition toward a democratic regime. The development of Basque autonomous institutions (such as the Basque Government and Parliament) was a central part of this democratic reform, which needed to address the long-standing demand for autonomy in this, and other, regions of Spain. The most dramatic manifestation of such nationalist demands was the terrorist violence of ETA. However, in spite of a steady development of Basque autonomy that included (in 1985) the formation of a Basque police force, the violence of ETA did not stop until 1998, when a ceasefire was declared by this organization, pending the opening of political negotiations with the Spanish government. However, that ceasefire collapsed in December 1999, and radical nationalist youth continued to carry out sabotage attacks against public property and state institutions.

During the last two decades of the democratic regime, both Basque nationalist violence and the violence of the state has, in fact, intensified and diversified into new forms, being today the most important single problem in the Basque Country. Yet the "problem of terrorism" is complicated by the fact that it does not denote a particular kind of violence, as much as it constitutes, as Basque scholars have noted, an over-determined discursive and performative site (Zulaika and Douglass 1996; Arriaga Landeta 1997; Beriain and Fernandez 1999); a field that condenses a variety of social anxieties, such as the redefinition of Basque identity and the Basque nation within the global system, the definition of the state in a country of autonomous ethnic regions, and the status of democracy vis-à-vis the persistence of illegal state violence such as torture and paramilitary assassinations.

Throughout the 1990s, the intensification of rioting and arsonist violence carried out by radical nationalist youth has made these social anxieties more acute, bringing to the surface deep fault lines within Basque society which have threatened the very core of an imagined national community (Anderson 1983, 1991). This new form of youth violence emerged in conjunction with two political and technological developments: first, there was the disclosure of the involvement of the Spanish government, socialist party and security forces in the assassination of Basque separatists under the cover of a paramilitary group called GAL (Grupos Antiterroristas de Liberación, Antiterrorist Liberation Groups). This operation became known in the mass-media as the state's "dirty war." The judicial cases against politicians and military officers involved in this operation are still underway, triggering deeply emotional political reactions. The second development concerned the emergence of a Basque police force and their use of new technologies of control, such as street video surveillance. These surveillance technologies were accompanied by technologies of disguise, best signified in the figure of the secret police who young nationalists believed was infiltrating public spaces such as bars and hang-outs, and in the police use of hoods to hide personal identity. In turn, nationalist youth resorted to alternative information technology to create autonomous spaces of discourse and action such as pirate radios (Urla 1995) and internet networks from which to combat what they perceived as suffocating state control. They also resorted to mimetic forms of disguise, such as the use of hoods, and practices of rioting Basque police and petrol-bombing police vehicles.

During the late 1990s, such technologies of control and autonomy transformed political culture into a ghostly space in which the state and youth violence were/are at once all-pervasive and impossible to locate in a single structure, organization or site. If the police could appear unexpected anywhere, taking names and arresting people, so could a group of youngsters unexpectedly emerge to petrol-bomb a police vehicle and then disappear. The use of such surveillance techniques made the Basque police the latest embodiment of uncontrollable terror in the eyes of Basque policemen/women. Mirroring stories about violence flourished on both sides and circulated through different social channels, creating a social reality of fear where the boundary between the real and the fantasy was impossible to locate.

Complicated by its multiple associations, terrorism and the state are in the Basque Country terms that condense a mirroring political dynamic, wherein reality appears dislocated and political fantasy flourishes. It seems that this dynamic framed the ceasefire in the Basque Country, leading ultimately to the erosion of a peace process. A quick look at the political reactions and public commentary following the breakdown of the ceasefire seems to indicate a preoccupation with a rift in perception of reality between radical nationalists and the rest of society, but also between the Spanish and Basque governments.

This book investigates the experience of reality among radical nationalists by focusing on discursive practices about terrorism in its incarnations as both state and eth-nonationalist violence, that have dominated the political culture in the Basque Country of Spain during the 1990s. It closely examines key events charged with symbolic and political significance. Some of these events include the state's "dirty war" against Basque activists; ETA's assassination of local politician, Miguel Ángel Blanco; and the killing of two Basque policemen by a Basque nationalist youth in a lapse of consciousness. It also examines ritualized practices of rioting, sabotage and police technologies of control. In a close examination of these events and the discourses produced around them, I provide ethnographic accounts of the subjective experience of state and nationhood among radical nationalists.

Recent anthropological scholarship on ethnic conflict has insisted on the culturally encoded nature of political violence, emphasizing process of signification that structure violence at both local and state levels (Warren 1993, 1998; Nordstrom and Martin 1992; Tambiah 1997; Appadurai 1998; Feldman 1991; Malkki 1995; Zulaika and Douglass 1996; Taussig 1986, 1997; Aretxaga 1997; Das 1995). How people experience and conceptualize violence is, from this perspective, not just another dimension of violence but crucial to its structure, operation and effects. In this body of work, the narrative of violence is not just expressive, it has a structuring and constitutive power (Geertz 1973; Foucault

1975; Hayden White 1978; Bhabha 1990; Fernandez 1986; Herzfeld 1987). In the form of official political discourse, the discourse of the mass media, political ephemera and informal everyday conversations, narratives about political violence are a pervasive component of the political culture in the Basque Country (Spain). Whether they are about police torture, the assassinations perpetrated by the terrorist organization ETA, or the novel phenomenon of sabotage and riotous destruction of property by radical nationalist youth, stories of political violence intensified during the 1990s, generating a climate of social tension in towns and city neighborhoods that materialized in public clashes between social intimates (neighbors, friends, relatives) who found themselves on opposing sides of the political divide marked by ethnonationalist violence. The result has been a sense of fear (generated by social estrangement) and distrust that had as its effect the construction of reality as a phantasmatic universe in need of constant interpretation, where recurrent practices of state and terrorist violence signal the presence of an occult real which dominated the everyday order of things. The constitution of such a phantasmatic universe at the everyday level is the less studied dimension of political violence.

This book investigates this everyday political culture, wherein stories about violence proliferate and organize the practices of state and terrorist violence in an intimate and mirroring relationship. In current ethnographies of violence, the narrative of violent events (real or imagined) has emerged as a privileged site for the structuring of identity and political claims (Malkki 1995; Brass 1997; Appadurai 1998; Nelson 1999; Diana Taylor 1997). While some scholars have focused on the importance of the narrative of violence to establish categorical ethnic distinctions between self and other (Malkki 1995; Appadurai 1998), others have emphasized the use of narrative to articulate a culture of terror (Taussig 1987; Suarez-Orozco 1992; Tambiah 1997; Warren 1993) or structure collective memory and mythical histories (Aretxaga 1997; Feldman 1991; Hayden 1996). In either case, ethnographers have noted an intricate and constitutive relationship between events (of violence) and their narrative elaboration (see also Foucault 1975).

Such a relationship becomes particularly clear in the political scandal of the "dirty war" against Basque nationalists. The scandal was triggered in 1994 by the confessions of high-ranking police officers about the assassination of Basque nationalists from 1983 to 1987. The detailed narratives furnished by the implicated officers triggered a web of horror stories that involved Spain and the Basque region in the most serious political crisis since a failed coup d'état in 1981 threatened the democratic reform. This expanding narrative web had the effect of creating in the Basque Country a phantasmatic universe where the state was perceived, through the prism of the horror story, as a ghostly all-pervasive power. Basque scholars have suggested that nationalist violence cannot be understood outside the myths and social rituals of local culture (Zulaika 1988; Pérez-Agote 1984, 1987; Arriaga Landeta 1997; Beriain and Fernandez 1999). I suggest that Basque nationalist violence cannot be understood either outside the narrative and practices of statehood that have constituted the Spanish state in the Basque Country during the transition to a parliamentary democracy. In this sense, a study of youth violence entails a study of the manifestations of the state.

More generally, a number of scholars in anthropology and social sciences have recently began to question the conceptualization of the state as a unified, coherent structure or apparatus separated from civil society (Mitchell 1991; Gupta 1995; Wendy Brown 1995; Navaro-Yashin 1998; Taussig 1997; Nelson 1999; Coronil 1997; Hammoudi 1997; Herzfeld 1992, 1997; James Scott 1998). Following Foucault's studies on governmentality, some of these scholars (for example, Mitchell 1991; Gupta 1995) have argued that the notion of a self-willed, autonomous state is an effect of the new techniques of disciplinary power that accompanied modernity; an illusion produced by disseminated and contradictory practices of power (Abrams 1988; Wendy Brown 1995). Yet the question is how the illusion of a single agency called the state has so much power. How does it maintain its hold in people's imagination? How does it reproduce itself? Recent scholarship has begun to productively explore these questions by conceptualizing the state as a fetish—a dreaded object invested with power—and looking at the social practices and discourses that speak about the state, both to understand how it operates in social life and what kind of affective states it triggers (Taussig 1992, 1997; Nelson 1999; Navaro-Yashin 1997; Rose 1996; Wendy Brown 1995; Aretxaga 2000a; Siegel 1998).

In the Basque Country, the state appears as a recurrent presence in the constant "talk" that circulates in the public sphere (bars, cafes, streets, newspapers, radios) about security, terrorism, police harassment, youth riots, and so on. It manifests itself in the signs and images that inscribe the urban landscape (murals, political posters, graffiti and memorializations of killed activists). These signs and discourses shape what I call, following political theorist Cornelius Castoriadis (1997), a radical political imaginary (see also Anderson 1983, 1991; Norval 1996), a nationalist cultural universe wherein the nationalist community and the Basque nation are perceived to be under the threat of a powerful agent/object called the state.

In an intimate relationship with this symbolic universe, ritualized political performances constitute another arena wherein the state is reified and invested with power. Such rituals include riots between police and radical youth, as well as sabotage performed by radical youth against what they perceive as embodiments of the state such as Law Courts, police vehicles, bank buildings, and political parties headquarters, to mention only a few. My project takes these social sites of confrontation as areas of violent articulation and reproduction of fetishized notions of the state and terrorism. Examining how notions of the state and terrorism are produced and articulated with each other in the Basque case has important implications for understanding the spreading circle of violence between ethnonationalisms and states that has accompanied the rapidly growing discourse of international terrorism during the last decade (Zulaika and Douglass 1996).

CHAPTER 7

The Death of Yoyes: Cultural Discourses of Gender and Politics in the Basque Country[1]

This paper is an attempt to understand a puzzling event, an unusual political assassination. This act must be considered in the context of the current socio-political life of the Basque Country, which is defined to a great extent by the nationalist issue.[2] My concern in this paper is not so much to give a clear answer to the question of why Yoyes was killed, which seems to me an impossible task; neither is it to pursue the socio-political and symbolic implications of her assassination, for it is too early to assess these precisely. My guiding question concerns, instead, the conditions of possibility: how is it that this death could happen? In answering this question, I explore different overlapping domains of experience, which, together, form the larger context of Yoyes' death, but which also offer diverse angles and layers of meaning for interpreting it. In exploring these personal, historico-political and cultural domains I present various plausible readings of the death, while at the same time I show how seemingly distinct discourses are interwoven. I attempt to see the forms in which cultural constructions, particularly of gender, weave with political and personal action within a particular historical context.

Yoyes' death has provoked multiple interpretations in the Basque Country. These interpretations both express and constitute a struggle for meaning that plays deeply into the political field. I do not claim for my interpretation a special authority outside that arena.

In September 1986 a political event shocked the Basque Country, creating a general mood of reflection and heated debate among Basque nationalist people. A commando

---

1. Originally published in *Violence, Feminism, and the History of Sexuality*, a special issue of *Critical Matrix* 4.1 (Women's Studies Program, Princeton University, March 31, 1988): 83–113. A short version of this paper was presented at the Fourth Annual Graduate Women's Studies Conference, *Feminism and its Translations*. I want to express my gratitude to the organizer of the panel, Agnes Lugo-Oritiz, and to Barbara Corbett who translated the original paper from Spanish. Throughout the process of writing this paper I enjoyed the assistance, encouragement and intellectual stimulation of a great number of people: Mark Whitaker, Penny Schwartz, Madeleine Brainerd, and Professors Hildred Geertz, Kay B. Warren, James W. Fernandez, and Ernestine Friedl. My major debt is to the people in the Basque Country who shared their time and knowledge in talking about a difficult topic.

2. The history of Basque nationalism is too long and complex to be encapsulated here. For a good source, see Corcuera Atienza (1979).

from the armed Basque nationalist organization ETA military[3] killed Maria Dolores Gon-
zalez Catarain, an ex-militant woman in this organization, popularly known as "Yoyes."
For the first time in the history of Basque nationalism, a woman was accused of treason
and executed. ETA(m) (the specifically military wing of the organization) accused Yoyes
of "betrayal to the Basque Country and herself"[4] for returning to the Basque Country
after years of exile, thus morally legitimating the policy of the Spanish government
against ETA. From ETA(m)'s perspective, Yoyes' return presupposed an acceptance of the
Spanish government's "social reinsertion plan" for those members of ETA who wished to
abandon the armed fight.

This plan, initiated in 1982, and carried out with the mediation of the conservative
and moderate leftist nationalist parties, Partido Nacionalista Vasco (PNV) and
Euskadiko Ezkerra (EE), implied the release from prison and the return from exile of former members of ETA who—recognizing the democratic character of the Spanish
state—laid down their arms. This policy, accepted by the recently dissolved ETA(pm) (the
politico-military wing of the organization) and used by the majority of its members, was
strongly rejected by ETA(m), who saw in it a way of eroding the morale of its militants
and supporters.

ETA(m) began a virulent ideological struggle against this plan, defining as traitors
and repenters the militants who used it. The polemic on the reinsertion was at its peak
during these early years (1982–83) and deeply divided the nationalist community into
opposing sides. By 1985, when Yoyes came back to the Basque Country, the debate had
already calmed down. More than three hundred ex-militants of ETA, mainly (but not
exclusively) from the politico-military wing, had used the reinsertion plan, and members
broadly know as "terrorists" were calmly walking the streets of their own towns. The radical nationalists supporting ETA(m) had come to see reinsertion as a fact to live with.

Yoyes, like many before her, was called a traitor and accused of collaboration, yet
her assassination in September 1986 was most striking. When put in relation to the
"repentance" of other nationalists, the shooting did not make sense. After more than three
hundred "traitors," what was the political advantage of killing this one? More than at any
other time, confusion among radical nationalists was complete, so much so that before
the killing was claimed by ETA(m), many people thought it to be a work of right wing
fascist groups. The elected representative of Herri Batasuna[5] to the European Parliament

---

3. The nationalist organization Euskadi Ta Askatasuna (ETA, Basque Country and Freedom) was born in 1959 as a
response to Franco's repression of Basque identity. In 1974, ETA split into two branches: ETA(m) (military) undertaking
exclusively military actions, and ETA(pm) (politico-military) whose tasks, besides military attacks, also involved agitation,
raising of consciousness and political organization. ETA(pm) dissolved completely in 1981. Both wings defined themselves
as socialist. In this paper, ETA will refer to both branches when unspecified. For more information about ETA, see Jáuregui
Bereciartu (1981) and Garmendia (1979). The bibliography concerning Basque issues is broad; one excellent source is Bilbao (1970–1976).

4. Public statement of ETA(m), published in the Basque journal *Punto y Hora de Euskal-Herria* 444 (September 18–25,
1986).

5. Herri Batasuna (HB) is the main radical nationalist political party. It was born in 1977 as an electoral coalition and
maintains ideological affinities with ETA(m).

said in an interview in June 1987, "I still do not know why she was killed. I cannot dispel the mystery of this death."[6] Some people saw a warning in Yoyes' death, a threat against the possibility of further "repentance." Accurate as it might be, the explanation does not resolve the puzzle. Why was Yoyes—someone retired from political activity for more than six years—the chosen victim for this warning? Why were none of the other repenters chosen? Why did the killing have to be performed at this particular moment and not years before, when the issue of the reinsertion was at its height? In sum, was Yoyes' "treason" worse than that of the other ex-militants? And if so, why?

Yoyes' death could be read, in a sense, against the screen of a classical tragedy: the outcome of a conjuncture of circumstances woven together by an intermingling of cultural models, historical events and Yoyes' own actions. Her death is at once an exceptional and a paradigmatic event. It is an event that encapsulates the paradoxes and ironies of Basque politics, showing them brutally in a single act and, in so doing, forcing the audience—that interpretative community of Yoyes' death that is the nationalist world—to reflect on these paradoxes. It is only by unraveling the conditions that allowed Yoyes' murder to happen, that this death becomes meaningful. That is the aim toward which this paper now turns.

Yoyes' Political History[7]

Yoyes was born on May 14, 1954 in the small industrial town of Ordizia, a center of gravity for the rural villages scattered along the Goiherri valley, famous in Franco's time as an ETA stronghold. Yoyes was the second of eight children in the family Gonzalez-Catarain. The Gonzalez-Catarain family represented the meeting of two quite different and contradictory socio-cultural experiences that have molded the modern history of the Basque Country. Yoyes' mother came from a tradition of Basque-speaking farmers with a strong Basque identity and nationalist political orientation. Her father, raised in a family of Castilian immigrants, considered himself Spanish rather than Basque and held a respectful attitude toward the Spanish political establishment. Because of potential conflicts and because of the repressive Francoist policy toward ethnic expression, it is easy to imagine that political issues remained absent from Yoyes' family life. Unlike other militants coming from nationalist backgrounds, Yoyes discovered a Basque identity outside of her immediate family relationships.

Yoyes first heard about Basque ethnicity and Franco's repression in covert conversations with other students at school. By 1971, she was mixing with nationalist people and was involved with an underground political discussion group, while at the same time reading Marxist theory and essays on Basque nationalism. While her nationalist consciousness was growing, this process was not without conflicts: as her diary testifies, Yoyes was, in 1970, a practicing Catholic. Her religious beliefs led her, and many others at the time,

---

6. Quoted in *Interviú* 12.580 (June 24–30, 1987).

7. Data about Yoyes' life came from various sources: first hand information, Yoyes' personal diary, as well as political and journalistic documents.

to consider social issues such as poverty, freedom and political inequality. At the same time, she was becoming more aware of the Francoist dictatorship and the political struggle for Basque expression. With these preoccupations, Yoyes felt the need for social action; she did not yet know, however, in what direction to pursue that need. She deliberated between going far away to be a missionary and staying to fight for her people. The radical nationalist ideology of ETA, with its revolutionary tones, appealed to her but their use of violence posed a deep problem.[8] The socio-political ambience of the time was decisive in resolving Yoyes' ideological struggle. In December 1970, several members of ETA were tried and received capital punishment sentences in the highly controversial Trial of Burgos. This trial was hotly contested, with the largest public demonstrations in the Basque Country since the beginning of Franco's regime. The Trial of Burgos had international echoes; Sartre and other intellectuals wrote manifestos against it. The sympathy for ETA rose rapidly in areas like the Goiherri, where Yoyes lived.

In 1972, when Yoyes moved to San Sebastián to study education, she had already joined ETA. In December 1973, knowing that the police were looking for her, she escaped to the French Basque Country (a traditional refuge for Basque political refugees), beginning an exile that lasted twelve years. During her exile in France, she remained active in ETA. In 1974, when ETA split into its politico-military and the military branches, Yoyes aligned herself with the military wing. In subsequent years, she became the only woman known to have high-ranking responsibilities in ETA(m). December 1978 saw an important event in Yoyes' career. Jose Maria Benaran Ordenana, or "Argala," a member of the ETA(m) leadership with whom Yoyes shared political views, was murdered by fascist paramilitary forces, and Yoyes was asked to occupy his position in ETA(m). Yoyes accepted, but a month later, in January 1979, she handed over her responsibilities and began to distance herself from the organization. After the death of Argala, the dominant line in the leadership of ETA(m) opposed participation in the political structures of the Spanish state and favored a hard offensive of military actions. Yoyes disagreed strongly with this line. Some months later, she announced to the organization her decision to drop out and move to Mexico, where she fled in December 1979. ETA(m) asked Yoyes to maintain a silence about her decision, and, thus, her break with the organization remained secret.

Silence is important. From ETA(m)'s point of view, since Yoyes was a well-known, almost mythical figure, her desertion, if publicly broadcast, would be demoralizing for ETA(m)'s sympathizers. From Yoyes' point of view, silence also made sense. Although in disagreement with its increasingly militaristic tactics, she still believed that the political conditions in Spain were not democratic enough to delegitimize the existence of ETA. By that time, she had brothers and sisters involved in radical nationalist groups sympathetic to

---

8. The Catholic Church in the Basque Country, especially the low clergy, has historically been sympathetic to Basque nationalism. Toward the end of Franco's dictatorship, in the late 1960s, some priests became politically involved with ETA. Yet this political support was not without ambivalences and contradictions, since Catholic values and Catholic institutions opposed violence. Hence, Yoyes' conflict was by no means exceptional.

ETA(m) and close friends in the organization itself. Publicity was probably an unthinkable option for Yoyes.

Despite Yoyes' efforts to stay in the shadows, however, the media associated her on several occasions with terrorist activities. She was accused in Spanish newspapers of performing several attacks in Spain between 1980 and 1981, when she was already in Mexico. In 1982, Mexican newspapers named her as an ETA militant who was collecting money in Mexico. Being silent about her political status put Yoyes in a complicated situation. She remained part of the Basque nationalist political story and considered herself to face a difficult dilemma:

> My immediate future is at stake because now that I have finished by B.A. I would like to go back to France and for that matter it is convenient to leave things very clear with the police, as well as with ETA, about my complete withdrawal years ago from the political world. But it seems that ETA does not want to acknowledge it. They are like a husband left by his wife, who as long as nobody knows it still maintains hope of her return. Meanwhile, the Spanish police plays with this fact to annoy me and provoke a reaction which they can use politically in the issue of the reinsertion. I am in a very delicate situation, caught between two fires. On the one hand, the police accuse me of being a terrorist and with that excuse they could kill me as I step into France; and the others [ETA] scream to heaven if I deny it and go back (Garmendia Lasa et al. 1987: 166–67).

On the one hand, the Spanish government, accusing her of terrorist activities, could hope to provoke a response from Yoyes that would wrest popularity from ETA. On the other hand, by speaking about her "terrorist actions," the Spanish government reinforced the mythical image she held in nationalist circles, allowing people to believe she was active in ETA(m). Furthermore, publicity about her could make Yoyes vulnerable to an attack from fascist paramilitary groups. Indeed, there had already been an attempt on her life in France in 1979, and it had failed. Yoyes interpreted the manipulation of her name as a provocation.

She decided to ignore the threats, hoping that time would divert attention away from her. In June 1984, however, when Yoyes thought everybody had forgotten about her, the news hit her again. *El País*, the main Spanish newspaper, published:

> M[aria] Dolores Gonzalez Catarain, Yoyes, 30 years old and one of the three women with documents of political refuge in France, was, during 1979 and 1980, one of the leaders of ETA. Although she has lived in Mexico in 198[1 and 1982?] after leaving her responsibilities in ETA, the Spanish police think she is now in France where she has taken up again, since 1983, her tasks as a leader of the organization (Garmendia Lasa et al. 1987: 196).

Some days later, her husband, who lived in the Basque Country, sent a letter to *El País* saying that Yoyes had been separated from ETA(m) since 1979. Yoyes then got a notice from a militant member of ETA(m) blaming her for publicizing her break. The letter made clear how little ETA(m) had accepted her resignation.

The year 1982 was one of both political and personal transition for Yoyes. At the political level, the policy of the reinsertion, which opened the door for exiled ETA members to return to Spain, made this option worth considering. That same year, she also gave birth to a son. For Yoyes, having a child seems to have represented a clear and irrevocable turn in her life, the proof of her break with her former political activities. It was also a decisive factor in her returning to the Basque Country, since Yoyes' husband was working and living there, and her family life was becoming increasingly difficult.

In 1984, Yoyes thought of moving to Paris where she could be near the Basque Country while continuing her studies. In June 1985, she fled to Paris with her son, hoping to get a grant to study for a Ph.D. in sociology. The financial support was not granted, however, and without any job opportunities in Paris, she decided to investigate the conditions under which she might return to the Spanish Basque Country. She wrote in a personal letter: "It was very clear to me that I would not accept any conditions of condemnation of what had been at one time my political life, and that neither would I make any political statement about my present position."[9] She says in her diary that the Spanish government put no conditions whatsoever on her return. Yoyes did not have to ask for a personal pardon, because there was no proof of her activities after 1977, the year in which a general political amnesty that included her was granted in Spain. She was thus assured that she did not have anything to fear from the Spanish government. This is not difficult to believe since, given the mythical image built around her, a return would be a political victory for the Spanish government against ETA(m). Yoyes wanted to check the situation with ETA(m) and to clarify possible misinterpretations of her position. She arranged a meeting with some members of the organization and told them about her return. Leaders of ETA(m) let her know the group's position against the reinsertion policy and they suggested to her that she either join them or keep out of the Basque Country. Yoyes then reaffirmed her decision to return, but made it clear that she would not use the reinsertion channel; she would use neither the mediation of PNV nor of EE, both political opponents of ETA(m).

Yoyes crossed the French-Spanish frontier in October 1985. Her presence in the Basque Country created uneasiness and was soundly denounced in radical nationalist circles. In fact, the return of Yoyes, whose political estrangement was never publicly evident, was a serious blow to the more radical nationalist sectors. They interpreted it as a great moral boost to the repressive policies of the Spanish government, which had been especially marked in recent years. Accusations of treason appeared on the walls of Yoyes' hometown, where years ago she had been painted as a hero. This interpretation was reinforced by those who, from a very different angle, saw her as a repentant ETA leader. The most obvious instance occurred in January 1986, when a Spanish pro-government political magazine, *Cambio 16*, published an issue with the front page title, "The Return of the

---

9. *El País.* June 21, 1984. All translations from Spanish in this paper are my own.

[la] ETA leader." To treat Yoyes as a leader of ETA was to underpin radical nationalist perceptions of her as traitor.

Yoyes feared that the situation would mount to more than angry words and social dismissal. "It is as if everybody wanted to kill me," she wrote in her diary, referring to the mutually reinforcing interpretations of nationalists and anti-nationalists. In November 1985, she wrote:

> I am not the ETA's opponent. Not to be on their side does not mean to be with their ene-
> mies . . . I always tried to prevent the image of me built from different positions [terror-
> ist/hero] from influencing my decisions about my life. Today the struggle is the same, pro-
> tecting myself from the new image projected on me [repenter/traitor]. I did not consider
> myself in the past a hero, I cannot consider myself now an anti-hero. The fact of not being
> one now does not make me automatically in favor of the political establishment.[10]

Yoyes responded once again with silence and, in contrast to many other ex-militants who joined the social-democratic nationalist party, Euskadiko Ezkerra, she kept herself free from any political alignment. But these steps aimed to break the circle of her entrap-ment were to narrow it more tightly.

Yoyes was killed on September 10, 1986 in the midst of the annual festival of her hometown, Ordizia. Her murder has the flavor of a death foretold. According to some informants, the possibility of Yoyes' execution had been envisioned among radical nation-alists but was rapidly discarded as a senseless idea. It had been difficult to conceive of the reality of Yoyes' death because it contradicted the basic premises among radical nation-alists that define the very existence of ETA as freedom-fighters representing the people's will. By definition, support for ETA and membership in it are freely given and cannot be militarily imposed. Her killing would also contradict that implicit knowledge[11] which makes ethical and political distinctions possible: in this case, the knowledge that allowed people to differentiate between their real enemy (the Spanish armed forces and the Spanish gov-ernment) and their political rivals, such as PNV and EE, and to justify deadly attacks against the former while ruling out such attacks against the latter.[12] That many nation-alists thought Yoyes' death to be the work of a fascist attack, before authorship was claimed, indicates how much these usual political distinctions were confused in this case.

When Yoyes' death and ETA(m)'s responsibility in it became public knowledge, the reactions among radical nationalists were mixed. Their ambivalence was the expression of a conflict between loyalty to the struggle as represented by the performers of the act—ETA(m)—and the nationalists' ethical convictions which profoundly condemned the act. In order to resolve this conflict, some nationalists projected responsibility for the action onto the Spanish government for its having offered reinsertion, and also onto Yoyes

---

10. Ibid., 206.

11. See Taussig (1987) for an elaboration on this notion.

12. The fact that the mere idea of Yoyes' murder could appear raises questions about the ambiguous and paradoxi-cal character of such knowledge. But this problem surpasses the scope of this paper.

herself for returning at a moment of intense repression of her former organization. Many others remained silent, refusing or avoiding the topic. The tension of such a conflict remains, however, and the topic comes up persistently in bitter private conversations. Why did ETA do it? Why did they have to do it? These are puzzling questions upon which people still speculate.

To understand why Yoyes' murder could first be imagined, and then become real, we must consider briefly the political moment within which it was embedded. It is to ETA's angle we turn now.

The Political Context

The armed struggle of ETA strongly marked the Basque political dynamic since the early 1960s. Their resolutions concerning the new political process that appeared in Spain after Franco's death in 1975 were decisive for the political development of the Basque Country. ETA(pm) changed their tactics to adapt the struggle for Basque independence to the new political conjunction, creating a political party, Euskadiko Ezkerra (EE), which took on the political direction of the struggle. ETA(pm) remained as a military organization under the direction of EE.

The post-Franco government called elections in 1977. The political forces subsequently elected were to write a democratic constitution and to begin a period of political reform in place of Franco's dictatorship. On the Basque nationalist left, EE, with the support of ETA(pm), decided to run in the elections while ETA(m) proposed to boycott them. For ETA(m) the elections could not be truly democratic as long as political prisoners remained in jail, and as long as the state's apparatus was still in the hands of Franco's heirs. Since there had not been a disassembling of the Francoist state, participation in the election would only legitimate a process seen as a mere reform of Francoism. For EE and ETA(pm), on the other hand, participation in the elections and the new political institutions was considered a means by which to achieve a truly democratic change. Although the Spanish government granted a general amnesty shortly before the elections, it was too late for ETA(m) to articulate a way of participating in them. A real rupture with Francoism was and still is, in ETA(m)'s view, a precondition for a legitimate democracy.

In 1978, while the text of the new constitution was being negotiated in Madrid, the government of Adolfo Suárez approved an anti-terrorist law, which, in practice, turned the Basque Country into a police state. In addition to harassment by police, fascist paramilitary groups began attacking not only ETA members but also citizens in towns and villages for their nationalism. In December 1978, the constitution was submitted to a referendum. The constitution was rejected by all nationalist groups and the majority of the population in the Basque Country, but approved in the rest of the Spanish state. For nationalists from a range of ideological positions, the constitution was unacceptable because, by underscoring the unity of Spain and the primacy of the Spanish language over other national languages, it did not recognize the right of Basque people to self-government or to a separate political identity. Under these conditions, any possible autonomy for the Basque Country could not go beyond decentralization. Although the Basque parliament was granted control of primary education, local taxes and other provincial services, the main political institutions—legislation, administration of justice, higher education, the police and international economic decisions—remained under the Spanish government. These severe limitations delegitimized, in the radical nationalist view, any political institutions born in the shade of the constitution.

In March 1979, general elections were called to form the first Spanish parliament of the democracy. Radical nationalist parties with ideological affinities to ETA(m) decided to form a coalition called Herri Batasuna (HB) to run the electoral campaign with the aim of showing their political strength, but without the intention of participating in the new parliament, which they did not recognize. The elections were a success for HB.

In October 1979, the first statute of autonomy for the Basque Country since 1936 was approved in a referendum with the support of conservative PNV and social-democratic EE nationalists and despite the opposition of HB and ETA(m). Some months later, when the first autonomous elections were held, HB showed itself to be the third strongest political force in the Basque Country (after PNV and Partido Socialista Obrero Espanol, PSOE, the Spanish socialist party), with eleven deputies elected to a parliament of sixty. Taking into account that HB had openly expressed the illegitimacy of the Basque parliament and, consequently, its intention of not participating in that parliament after the election, their strong showing in the election revealed a powerful minority who did not believe in the legality of the newly elected institution. Refusing to participate in the official political institutions meant that radical nationalist positions were expressed outside the legal channels provided by the state machinery. Radical nationalism was limited to an extra-parliamentary political program which had, as a central motif, opposition to police repression. Support for radical nationalism was, in my view, effectively underpinned by the Spanish government's repressive policy toward radical nationalism.

"Anti-terrorist" policies rendered the democratic discourse of the centrist government quite unbelievable, at the same time giving ETA a reason to maintain activism. From December 1978 to December 1979, 652 persons were detained for their supposed connections with ETA. The Basque provinces, with 3.5 percent of Spain's territory and 7 percent of its populations, were the object of 17 percent of its military's attempts to keep the public order (Clark 1984). The overwhelming presence of the hated Civil Guard and police, in turn, deepened the feeling of occupation and kept alive the anti-repressive consciousness generated under Franco, a consciousness that was being capitalized on politically by ETA(m) and used to legitimate their military offensive. The cycle is well known: ETA actions provoke repression against common citizens who, angered at this, support more ETA actions.

The government's repressive policies were also the consequence of the inherent contradictions of a "democratic" regime born from the structures of a dictatorial state. For instance, the commanding positions in the army, administration and national police were still in the hands of noted supporters of Franco. Accustomed to running the country, the army could not easily allow any demonstration of radicalism and threatened to resolve things for itself, if the government would not. These contradictions, inherent to the officially sanctioned "democratic reform," were enacted constantly.[13] A dramatic instance occurred when Joseba Arregi, a member of ETA(m), was tortured to death on February 13, 1981, while under detention in the central police station of Madrid. The Basque Country responded to the assassination with a general strike. On February 23, to make things worse, a coup d'état led by Colonel Antonio Tejero of the Civil Guard kept the whole Spanish state in suspense for twelve hours. As a result, ETA(pm) decided to lay down their arms, fearing a political regression to the former dictatorial regime. Armed struggle, for the members of ETA(pm), had become counterproductive. For ETA(m), on the other hand, the coup d'etat was the best evidence of the anti-democratic character of the new regime, and they felt themselves further entitled to maintain a violent offensive.

In 1982, the social democratic party, the PSOE, won the second general election in Spain and took over the government. In response to Basque violence, the PSOE government combined an intensification of repression with the offer of a political way out for ETA members: personal pardons or "the reinsertion" as it was generally known. The repression included international negotiations to extradite Basque political refugees in France. From the beginning of 1984 through July 1986, thirty-six prisoners were deported from France to countries other than Spain and eight were extradited to Spain. This is a process that has not yet ended. Along with these deportations, the Spanish government started what became known in the nationalist world as the "dirty war." The dirty war was a plan worked out by the security services of the Spanish state against Basque political refugees living in the French Basque Country. This plan was carried out in the disguise of a new paramilitary fascist group, Grupos Antiterroristas de Liberación (Antiterrorist Liberation Groups, or GAL). The task of GAL was the physical elimination of Basque refugees, some of whom were ETA members. The overall goal of the government was to create a state of disorganization and psychological pressure and, through intimidation, to lessen ETA(m)'s political control. Since 1983, ETA(m)'s strength had been damaged significantly by the assassination of its leading militants at the hands of paramilitary groups, by the growing numbers of extraditions of political refugees, and by the increasing detention of its sympathizers. From December 1983 to February 1986, ETA(m) had suffered, at the hands of the GAL, twenty-two deaths, the disappearance of two members and the wounding of fifteen. When added to this ongoing physical and psychological pressure, the plan for reinsertion resulted in the complete abandonment of the armed struggle by ETA(pm) and the subsequent return of its militants to Euskadi, the Basque Country.

Reinsertion entailed explicit declarations of the senselessness and inadequacy of armed struggle in the political situation. For ETA(m) this was a difficult blow. As we have seen, since 1977, Spain had experienced an important process of change that affected

---

13. For further information see Agustín Ramos (1985).

Basque politics: a new constitution was approved as well as a Basque autonomy statute, and the Spanish and Basque parliaments became key political institutions for Basque people. The elected social democratic government obliged Basque, as well as Spanish, left-wing groups to readjust their political approach. The reinsertion policy led one former 'terrorist' organization, ETA(pm), to publicly reject armed struggle, at the same time that international negotiations were greatly damaging the remaining armed organization, ETA(m), and the political reform was, by 1985, too strongly planted to be overthrown by the activity of ETA(m). Despite its inherent contradictions, the Spanish social democratic government was not Franco's dictatorship. Not to realize this was to miss completely the fact that a struggle against the new state required new directions and new methods. Yet ETA(m) was using the same political analysis and tactics that it had used in 1977.

ETA(m) was not effectively counteracting the government's offensive; instead, the group resorted to an increasingly mythologized discourse and ritualized activities, such as funerals, to maintain popular support. The organizational and political situation of ETA(m) upon the return of Yoyes was especially difficult. From the radical nationalist point of view, Yoyes had no right to return at a time when members of her previous organization were being extradited and murdered. Her death can thus be interpreted, in this sense, as the result of a particular historical conjuncture: as a radical solution to what ETA(m) considered a new threat that weakened and undermined the faith and cohesion of its militants and sympathizers. It remains to be explained, however, why Yoyes was considered more dangerous than the many militants of ETA(pm) who had returned from exile before her—in fact, why she was perceived as menacing at all. If, according to ETA(m), it was the use of personal pardons that made former militants into repenters, then Yoyes was less a repenter than the other returnees. If the denouncement of the armed struggle made former members of ETA traitors, then Yoyes was all but a traitor. What, then, was the meaning of her 'treason'?

Looking for Cultural Meanings

Yoyes' death was commemorated about a month after the murder in a funerary homage celebrated in her hometown of Ordizia. Funeral homages are important political rituals within the nationalist realm. Ironically, this homage was planned and carried out in a way similar to those organized for the members of ETA(m) murdered by the repressive forces of the Spanish state. As in the case of ETA(m)'s funerary homages, Yoyes' was held in the social center of the village: the main plaza. Similarly, there were singers, *bertsolariak* (troubadours), poetry readings and speakers. The political discourse present in these funerals is not one articulated in a programmatic way, but one formed with images taken as much from the traditional Basque rural culture as from the historical past.[14] In the case

---

14. Fernandez (1972) has elaborated the notion of "the argument of images" as a crucial element in the organization of human experience and the role of iconic symbolism in cultural representations and ritual action.

of ETA(m) members, this discourse counters the image of the terrorist, diffused by the Spanish government, with that of the martyr-hero; in the case of Yoyes, the image of the martyr was opposed to the image of the traitor presented by ETA(m). Hero, traitor, martyr—Yoyes was everything that, from the cultural premises embedded in nationalist practice, a woman could not be. Moreover, Yoyes was a mother. In the nationalist context, the models of hero, traitor or martyr and the model of the mother are mutually exclusive. It is precisely, I believe, the synthesis of these models in the person of Yoyes which made her "treason" much more unbearable than that of other ex-militants. The cultural models and images which permeate the activity of Basque radical nationalism are unequivocally delineated in its funeral homages. In order to understand the exceptional character of Yoyes' case, it is necessary briefly to examine these models.

The heroic model in radical nationalism is constructed around the idea of the redeemer death, learned from the Catholic Church. In the funeral context, the death of a militant parallels the death of Jesus Christ; that is, the militant gives his life for the freedom of Euskadi just as Christ gave his for the salvation of humankind.[15] It is precisely his death which elevates the militant to the category of martyr-hero. At the same time, the martyr-hero is not a remote figure, but one who is inscribed within the framework of symbolic familial relationships. In Basque nationalist discourse, the militant is a son of *amaberria* or *aberria*, the Basque motherland,[16] and thus becomes, in the ritual context, a brother of his nationalist companions present at the funeral. He is the ideal brother who sacrifices himself for Basque freedom; that is, for each and every one of his Basque fellows. This framework of symbolic familiar relationships allows the participants in the funeral ritual to identify with the dead militant as someone who is both categorically superior and equal to his followers. This identification is strengthened by the presence in the ritual of the real family of the militant—especially the mother—but also brothers, sisters, and children.[17]

The story of the martyr-hero is elaborated in the funeral against a cultural background in which religious models and family conceptions have a central role. Edward M. Bruner (1986) has suggested that culturally central "stories give meaning to the present and enable us to see that present as a part of a set of relationships involving a constituted past and future." In Basque nationalist funerals, the story of the dead militant embodies a historical construction which helps us to understand both radical nationalism and women's role in it. In the Basque Country, the death of a political militant only acquires meaning when it is placed within a historical vision that denies that there has

---

15. The importance of religious models in Basque political nationalism has been frequently suggested. Indeed, the role of seminaries and parochial groups in maintaining consciousness of ethnic identity and generating nationalist militants has been enormous. For more information, see Pérez-Agote (1984) and Zulaika (1982).

16. The centrality of *ama*, mother, in Basque culture has been frequently pointed out by local scholars. This centrality is also reflected in the political domain. *Ama* has been identified in the nationalist rhetoric with *aberria* (motherland), *Euskadi* (Basque nation), and *Euskara* (Basque language). In this nationalist ideology, those entities transcend human interests.

17. It is interesting to note that the figure of the father is symbolically irrelevant. This significant absence certainly needs further study.

been substantial change in the Spanish political system. Faced with the political rhetoric of the current Spanish government, which centers on the idea of "change,"[18] the discourse of radical nationalism is articulated in terms of the opposite idea: the continuation of the Francoist state behind a democratic disguise. This discourse, which might seem completely untenable to an outsider, is convincing for those who have experienced the continuation of repressive practices (detentions, torture, assassinations, disappearances and restrictions of civil liberties) as a part of everyday life. These practices legitimate the armed struggle of ETA(m) and make it meaningful for a wide portion of the Basque population.

Together with this, let's say, "external continuity" of the political system, the funeral ritual also creates an internal sense of continuity: that of the permanent struggle of the Basques for the liberty of their motherland. Michael Taussig (1987) has called attention to the interplay of history and memory in rendering significant political events meaningful. In the case of radical nationalist ideology, the use of the past to explain the tensions of the present also plays an important role in maintaining political distinctions and in making political violence understandable in the context of a formal democracy. For instance, in the last 150 years, the Basque Country has fought three wars on the losers' side. With the loss of each war, a piece of political autonomy was also lost.[19] Perhaps the most relevant of these events is the last one: the war of 1936–39 in defense of the Spanish Republic against the military uprising of Franco. In the nationalist view, the fight was not so much in defense of the Republic, but in defense of Basque freedom symbolized by its recently achieved autonomy. Current members of ETA are publicly projected as the genuine successors of the nationalist fighters of 1936. And the images that this rhetoric evokes allow radical nationalists to interpret the current armed struggle of ETA(m) in terms of historical memory and ethical obligation. For this conceptualization of history, the symbol of the mother is central.

In nationalist funeral rituals, the figure of the mother expresses the idea of historical continuity. The mother is the link in a generational chain, the means of continuity through her children. Within this ritualized framework, the mother is a bridge between two times situated outside the present—the past and the future—two moments of a single struggle, which is seen as a continuum. The role of mediation embedded in the symbolism of the mother, however, transcends the recreation of history to become a sacramental type of mediation between the son (martyr-hero) and the audience. This type of sacramental symbolism is best expressed in the religious context. In Basque religious imagery, the *Amabirgina*, or virgin mother, is the sacramental figure par excellence. In this Marian tradition, the essential mediation between the faithful and God does not occur through the "Son" to "God the Father"; rather, it is the mother, *Amabirgina*, who mediates between the faithful and her "Son," Jesus Christ. It is the virgin, in the Basque religious context, who furnish-

---

18. The word *Cambio* (change) has been used by the successive governments to encapsulate the image of the "Spanish Political Reform."

19. For more information, see Larrañaga (1984).

es a model of omnipotent mediation, while Jesus Christ provides the object of religious identification, offering the model of an exemplary life and sacrificial death.

The profound anchoring of these models in radical nationalism was especially evident in the 1950s and 1960s, when clandestine political activity was inseparable from religious beliefs among militant nationalists. During the late 1970s, religious rhetoric was replaced by a political discourse strongly influenced by Marxism and anti-imperialist movements of national liberation. In the 1980s, in light of the general crises of the political models of the Left and under severe political and military pressure from the Spanish state, ETA(m) is resorting to an increasingly sacramental and mythological discourse and to ever more rit-ualized activities. The nationalist funerals, now more symbolically charged than they had been in the past, constitute a privileged framework within which to reenact traditional reli-gious models. And the government's policy of physical elimination of Basque refugees has contributed greatly to the capacity of these funerals to evoke emotional responses.

In this new context, the figure of redeemer-hero, which had been validated by the church years before, is now legitimized through the figure of the mother. Symbolically, she is beyond any moral reproach. By being present in the ritual and accepting the death of her son and its meaning, the mother also accepts his life, thereby validating the struggle for which her son has died. Her presence transforms the distant image of the under-ground militant into a closer and familiar one. But, as we have said, the militant is, in the context of the funeral, more than the concrete son of a concrete mother. He is also sym-bolically a son of *aberria*, who receives the death of "her militant son" as his real mother does. In the ritual context, a chain of associations makes the symbolic equation of *Ama* (mother) and *Aberria* (motherland) possible. The mother, now identified with the super-ordi-nary category of the motherland, symbolically becomes the mother of all those present, who are themselves identified with the militant son. The mother not only makes the iden-tification of the public with the dead militant possible, but also makes that identification an emotionally powerful one, transforming a disrupting event—the death of a mili-tant—into a politically integrative one.

How are women affected by these cultural models which permeate the nationalist struggle? The redeemer-hero ethic, proposed as a form of activism, poses problems in terms of female identification because the martyr-hero is (in the symbolic languages of religion and kinship) son and brother. Militant women can only identify with this model of an active fighter by denying themselves as female. The actual existence of activist women performing actions culturally defined as masculine does not make the model of the martyr-hero any less male. Indeed, these women are recognized as being politically or militarily valid at the cost of not being women; they become instead "exceptions." Indeed, popular language defines well this idea when it depicts courageous women as "women with balls." They are perceived not only as embodying masculine attributes, but as pos-sessing that one which defines the essence of masculinity. The redeemer-hero model of radical nationalism, then, can be alienating for women if they cannot recognize themselves in it.

The other possibility for women is to identify with the image of the mother, assuming the mediating role. In Basque radical politics, this role is not only symbolically important, but is also of vital practical importance. Women organize protest campaigns, look after the needs of prisoners and refugees, and provide necessary contact between the inner worlds of the prison and of political exile and the outer world. The acceptance of this mediating role implies that women organize their lives in terms of the needs of others. If the role of the militant man in radical nationalism is to transcend himself in the act of fighting for a superior ideal, that of the woman is to support, to bridge gaps and contradictions; to mediate, in a word, between different worlds and generations.

Although the mediation and the moral support that the women provide are essential to the nationalist struggle, the ramifications of this have not been seriously explored. Even less explored are the psychological and emotional implications of the mediational role for women. The importance of these women (mothers, girlfriends, sisters, and *compañeras* or partners) to the moral and psychological care of political prisoners has been pointed out by the prisoners themselves on various occasions. These "bus women," so called because of the long and arduous journeys they make each week to jails at the opposite end of the Spanish peninsula, have no male counterparts. An informant and friend, who is a radical nationalist and former political prisoner herself, expressed it clearly: "There are men who go regularly to see their girlfriends, but they are minimal, very few." Although there are women political prisoners in the popular imagination "bus men" do not exist, while "bus women" are an institution.

It is easy to see now that Yoyes was an anomaly in the radical nationalist world, as much in terms of the political role she assumed as in terms of the images that were projected onto her. Yoyes was treated as a hero and as a traitor, but she was a mother at the same time. A mother by definition cannot be a hero or a traitor in the cultural context of radical nationalism; she is beyond these categories. Yoyes collapsed gender differentiations at a moment when ETA(m) needed them more rigidly than ever. As a woman who made her way through a masculine organization, she became a hero but also an exception with respect to other women. The conflicts inherent in this process were expressed by Yoyes in her diary:

> The hope of imposing myself in a world of men [ETA] pushed me; I felt strong, full of life and enthusiasm. And when I did it, it was already late, the struggle had exhausted me. First I understood that it was something individual that did not translate into more respect or solidarity for other women, and second that "victory" was the defeat of my struggle as a woman in the near future (Garmendia Lasa et al. 1987: 160).

Yoyes' decision to become a mother radically contradicted her heroic image. She understood her pregnancy as the mark of a break with her former political role: "When I realized that I would no longer be involved with my former political life, I decided to have Akaitz [her son]" (Ibid: 205). Having a child was not mediating a political continuity, but performing a non-reversible rupture with her former nationalist comrades. Yet Yoyes remained outside of the party (EE) to which "repented" ex-militants of ETA belonged. By staying independent, she blurred the firmly established lines of political demarcation and the polarized political distinctions so essential to the struggle of ETA(m).

Had Yoyes spoken out against ETA(m) and joined a political party as the other "repenters" did, she would not have been politically alone, and most probably she would not have been killed. In this hypothetical case, Yoyes would have behaved like a traitor, according to ETA(m) definitions, but she would not have questioned the polarized political distinctions of ETA(m). Ironically, because Yoyes did not behave like a repenter and a traitor, but lived "normally" in the Basque Country, her presence contradicted ETA(m)'s discourse of historical continuity and generated, from their viewpoint, an unbearable ambiguity. As a woman, Yoyes could have been a political exception, but then she could not be a dissident, much less an unclassifiable one. In a nationalist context in which women must play roles of unconditional support and mediation, a woman dissident is more unbearable than a man would be. Yoyes' "treason" was in this sense a greater fault than others' since from the radical point of view she had been allowed to be what did not correspond to her. Steps which theoretically separated Yoyes from other "traitors" and "repenters" in practice worked against her, making possible her murder.

CHAPTER 8

The Intimacy of Violence[1]

Joseba Zulaika begins his article, "The Anthropologist as Terrorist," by recounting the story of how his anthropological vocation led him, during the initial stages of his research in Basque political violence, to the inappropriate and dangerous situation of wanting to join ETA, temporarily at least. The thought was not related to any political reasons, personal loyalty or heroic aspirations, but rather due to simple intellectual curiosity. "Unexpectedly," recalls Zulaika, "I too had fallen under the spell that 'the truths we respect are those born of affliction.'" (Sontag 1978: 49–50, quoted in Zulaika 1995: 208). Fortunately for Zulaika, and for all of us who enthusiastically follow his intellectual production, ETA wisely decided to deny him entrance, thereby saving him from the affliction that would surely have come his way had he achieved his wish. If Zulaika's anthropological passion might seem, at first sight, excessive, his drive to participate intimately in the lives of those he tries to understand should come as no surprise at all. In fact, such intense intersubjective relations form the maxim of anthropological understanding. Nor should it come as any surprise to hear of the risk he took in almost becoming involved in a dangerous situation in the course of his anthropological work. For anthropological literature is full of examples of anthropologists involved in all types of conflicts, frequently against their wishes or knowledge. Often, these situations of profound intimacy with the lives of the people one studies have given rise to excellent ethnographies. Several examples spring to mind, of which I will cite two I especially admire: One is the classic work, *Deadly Words: Witchcraft in the Bocage* by the anthropologist Jeanne Favret-Saada (1980), where she recalls how, unwillingly, she became involved in the intersubjective relations and violence intrinsic to the structure of witchcraft in the French village she was studying. Remaining outside this structure was simply impossible because there was no external point of contact to this witchcraft phenomenon, which permeated all social relations in the village. Consequently, placing herself outside this was, in fact, adopting a position within its structure. Denying all contact with witchcraft and those suspected of practicing it was in fact a tacit affirmation of the existence of a witchlike identity. Edward Evans-Pritchard found himself in

1. Originally published as, "La intimidad de la violencia," Epilogue, in Joseba Zulaika, *Enemigos, no hay enemigo (Polémicas, imposturas, confesiones post-ETA)* (Donostia: Erein, 1999), 231–53. English translation by Cameron J. Watson.

a similar situation in his study on witchcraft among the Azande, concluding that the phenomenon went beyond a mere question of ideology and ritual practice, forming its own epistemological system that differed considerably from its western counterpart, but not at all lacking in rationality. The other example is a recent ethnography by Philippe Bourgois (1995) about the world of drugs (and in particular crack) in a Puerto Rican neighborhood of New York. In the book, *In Search of Respect,* Bourgois demonstrates, through his participation in the intimate world of drug dealers in East Harlem, the profound humanity of subjects trapped in the violence of an ongoing struggle against the degradation of poverty and racism. The subjects in Bourgois' ethnography are victims of a structural violence as brutal as it is invisible, and at the same time seen as perpetrating violence against others. This situation, namely that of being simultaneously victim and victimizer, poses important moral dilemmas in regard to the violence about which Bourgois writes. From which vantage point that isn't already, in one way or another, that of accomplice, can one judge this violence? None. For there is no external position—now that God and Reason have been replaced as guides of universal values—that functions as a moral guarantee and redeems us from the personal burden of moral responsibility. Bourgois' inevitable involvement with his subjects' criminal behavior is in no way at odds with the professional ethics of being an anthropologist. For such ethics oblige him to not harm the people with whom he works, and to stay loyal to the sociocultural reality he reveals in his research. In this sense, the ethics of anthropology differ little from those of journalism or psychology, professions that depend on intersubjective relations; as such, the anthropologist's obligation is to analyze sociocultural reality, not judge it. However, this does not mean that such anthropological work should lead one to falling into what Zygmunt Bauman terms "a moral relativism in its embodiment of distant indifference" (1992: xxiv). In his or her intellectual quest, the anthropologist faces, necessarily, a whole range of ethical dilemmas, and especially so when confronted by violent situations. In such circumstances, the anthropologist cannot avoid the responsibility of confronting such dilemmas and making what he or she believes to be the most appropriate decisions. Yet it would be ingenuous (or perhaps not so ingenuous) to think that one can free oneself of this personal moral responsibility by adopting a position beyond the realm of good and bad, a position from which it would be possible to establish universal moral truths and judgments. Ultimately, the ethical and moral dilemmas confronted by the anthropologist are no different in nature to those confronted by our informants.

Unfortunately for those of us in anthropology who examine politically sensitive and socially complex subjects like violence, the very lack of a position guaranteeing moral purity is a constant source of discomfort and uneasiness. Fortunately, such unease is a good antidote against the temptation to adopt an overbearing attitude of moral and intellectual superiority that once characterized colonial anthropology; and that, surprisingly (or perhaps not), still tends to surface now and again from the most diverse collection of individuals and institutions, especially when the conclusions drawn by ethnographic research contravene dominant social stereotypes or political interests. At such moments, accusations of moral ambiguity are added to those of political irresponsibility, and can easily turn into threats and even punishment. A friend of mine, a Greek anthropologist who works in the United States, received countless threats, each more coarse and ugly than the last, in addition to public accusations, for the mere fact of writing an ethnography about Macedonian ethnicity that annoyed the dominant nationalist sensibilities of the Greek political landscape. The audacity of writing a book that questioned certain sacrosanct truths in the Greek nation-state had more specific consequences, beyond the unpleasant experience of continually receiving threats. The prestigious publishing house that had agreed to publish the work (already in its final stages of going to press) cancelled the agreement, on the pretext that doing so was potentially dangerous for their company, thereby sanctioning the violence of prior censorship. Is there any doubt that this is also a form of complicity, this time with the interests of state? The story, fortunately, ended on a happy note, and my friend finally published her work with a more prestigious publishing house than the previous one.

Zulaika knows, from personal experience, the sometimes subtle and sometimes not so subtle effects of censorship, for he has also been accused of political irresponsibility and moral ambiguity. And, together with co-author William A. Douglass, he has also experienced the rejection (after being initially accepted) of a publisher for a book they wrote on terrorism, based on a combination of political reasons, when the Oklahoma City bombing transformed their study of terrorism into an inopportune text. The prevailing tone in the United States after the bombing did not permit reflection on, nuance about, or historicizing of that phenomenon known as "terrorism," but rather, favored the consolidating writing-in-stone of a stereotyped enemy that could be easily identified, isolated, and eliminated. In this case, a prestigious publishing house yielded to the dominant ideology without any problem.

Both cases illustrate the increasingly typical and, therefore, more worrying experience of censorship that those who write about the controversial subjects of ethnicity, nationalism, and violence from critical perspectives employ to question the dominant "truths" (disguised as universal values) of the nation-state. To be sure, much of the moral discourse emanating from governmental institutions and media sources that flourishes when dealing with the subject of terrorism and nationalist or ethnic violence, is not differentiated from what we term "politics"; that is, linked to interests, arguments, and power struggles that have little to do with morality. My argument here is that regarding nationalism and violence, there is no position that remains "uncontaminated"; in other words, that does not take part, consciously or unconsciously, in the power games that the discourse of terrorism itself has demarcated beforehand.

As regards the Basque case, to recognize that all positions are *already* implicated in the relations between forces in a political conflict opens up the possibility of dialogue and the resolution of violence. Maintaining a "moral" truth at all costs against an enemy that is the source of all evil implies situating oneself in a monolithic, stationary position where any resolution will only take place after defeating one participant in the conflict. If such a defeat is not feasible—as in the Basque case—this strategy is disastrous because it deepens and extends the political conflict, while at the same time threatening to break the entire social structure. For, in the case of ETA, this is not a group of crazy individuals disconnected from the rest of society, but a whole social framework sufficiently large and complex to represent almost twenty percent of the population.

The problem of "terrorism" in the Basque Country is, precisely, that the "terrorists" and the social environment surrounding them are not socially marginalized or pathological characters, nor abstract and distant external enemies who can be portrayed as the personification of evil without feeling like such a portrayal is a sham. This distancing encouraged by a stereotyped image of the terrorist in the mass media might work in the United States and perhaps also in the rest of the Spanish state, but not in the Basque Country, for the simple reason that the "terrorists" turn out to be one's neighbors, acquaintances, or family members—people who are too close and whose lives we know, and who we cannot disregard so easily because they form part of the intimate social framework. To blind oneself by maintaining a "terrorist" enemy that is simply the embodiment of all evil and who one merely has to defeat, is to deny the obvious: that the assassinations and destruction provoked by nationalist violence are rooted in the everyday sociocultural reality that constitutes and articulates social life in the towns and neighborhoods of the Basque Country. Such a position, then, is not only short-sighted, but also tremendously counter-productive, resulting in the fact that, the more one denies the social reality in which ETA's violence takes place, the more violent and destructive it seems.

Two basic themes underpin Joseba Zulaika's essays. The first is defined by a heartfelt preoccupation for the social intimacy into which ETA's violence is inscribed. The second is a deconstruction of the antiterrorist discourse that makes up, without doubt, the other side of the social intimacy of violence. For those used to discussing the "Basque problem" in purely instrumental terms, the subject of intimacy might seem trivial. However, in my opinion, the question of intimacy, far from being irrelevant, constitutes a key, and insufficiently studied, dimension of the reality and resolution of violence. I will concentrate here on a discussion of three aspects of what might be termed "the intimacy of violence." The first is what the anthropologist Michael Herzfeld calls "cultural intimacy." Herzfeld defines this notion as a set of known and shared practices and life-forms that define a sense of group belonging and, likewise, for which the group is stereotyped and condemned from positions outside the group. In other words, this sense of cultural intimacy is made up of a mutual self-recognition and non-recognition by those outside. This intimacy shapes, according to Herzfeld, the necessary substratum of the nation-state; what the political scientist Benedict Anderson terms its affective glue.[2]

---

2. See Herzfeld (1997) and Anderson ([1983] 1991).

Cultural Intimacy

In the everyday life of towns and neighborhoods, the stereotyped image of the "terrorist" coined by the media erases the reality of people with names and experiences that do not differ greatly from the rest of the population. The "terrorist" is, then, a next-door neighbor, your high-school friend's brother, an acquaintance with whom you've had a drink on several occasions, or that guy from your college class. In the letters I receive from the Basque Country, political news is rarely narrated from an abstract or impersonal perspective. On the contrary, any information about an assassination or arrest is always accompanied by the recalling of some meeting or personal connection ("I know him because we were both on the same vacation together"); biographical notes that locate the "terrorist" at the intersection of a complex network of life stories of which the person relating the news is also a part. The "terrorist" thus stops being just an anonymous name or face in the newspaper and becomes a person in one's same social framework. "It's a small world in Euskadi [the Basque Country]," a friend told me after establishing a series of links to an arrested ETA member whose photograph had just been published in the newspapers. In the story at the beginning of this article, the ETA members with whom Zulaika talked about the possibility of joining the group were not unknown to him. The meeting was possible thanks to a friendship network, through an old friend close to the leadership of ETA. Such closeness was not the result of the author's moral perversity, but rather the sociality structure in the Basque Country: "I knew personally some of the young boys who had accepted the call to patriotic martyrdom and ended up killing innocent people. They were simply my neighbors" (Zulaika 1995: 206).

Many sociological studies have emphasized the importance of informal associational relations in Euskadi. The spatial framework of social relations formed by, for example, public squares, bars, and all kinds of associations and groups, meant that towns and neighborhoods acquired a strong sense of community articulated by this dense social network.[3] Such face-to-face contact makes the demonization of ETA sympathizers difficult, not only because of the shared social space and collective life experiences, but also because this communal sociability or *habitus* means that people perceive such "violent" individuals beyond the mere terms of political sympathies or antipathies. That is, ETA sympathizers are also people: a work colleague, your nephew's schoolteacher, the local storekeeper, and so on. At the same time, this social intimacy can be a source of social dislocation and estrangement, as we will see a little later. The isolation of left-wing *abertzale* or nationalist circles under the pretext of an antiterrorist discourse has resulted in the erosion of the social framework at a local level, with all the cultural and emotional consequences that this entails. In this sense, the most brutal violence has been the result of political confrontation between inhabitants of the same towns or neighborhoods. This is due to the

---

3. See Pérez-Agote (1984), Ramírez Goicoechea (1991), and Arriaga Landeta (1997).

failure of the Ajuria Enea Pact,[4] which has produced an intensification of the violence and has almost broken the social structure at the local level. Such social pressure and political isolation have only served to intensify the emotional links making Herri Batasuna not just a political phenomenon, but what Mikel Arriaga Landeta (1997) terms a "community of feeling." The cultural intimacy characterizing sociability in the Basque Country has been intensified in the case of Herri Batasuna as a result of the appearance of a common enemy and the shared experience of victimization that is expressed as a continuous suffering and fear.

Herri Batasuna is not merely a political group. It is also a way of life composed of relational practices and associational spaces. With its own bars, social events and rituals, associations and groups, Herri Batasuna has responded to the social and political pressure by becoming an ever more intense social microcosm and thereby perceiving itself as a metonym for the Basque nation—the model of the imagined national community.

This intense intimacy characterizing interpersonal relations within Herri Batasuna is aided and exploited by the party itself, in its articulation of a systematic strategy of repression against it.[5] Such repression is not just reduced to terms defined by abstract, and scandalously high, figures of harsh treatment at the hands of the state. Rather, it is personified by known individuals: family members, friends, neighbors, and so on. The physical and emotional communion surrounding the traumatic experience of everyday violence—both by the state and by ETA, whose violent actions likewise provoke a traumatic social ostracism—compresses and deepens the intense intimacy that characterizes radical Basque nationalism. This communion of grief produces both emotion and empathy that, as Zulaika points out, leads many people into the armed struggle and a loyalty that makes positions of distension and distance seem like personal and patriotic betrayal.[6] In good measure, radical nationalist identification is produced through the personification of violence. For radical nationalism, the Basque nation is embodied by its dead, injured, tortured and imprisoned militants. It is within this conquered body that the Basque nation is simultaneously literalized and allegorized (Aretxaga 1987). The tortured body of the political prisoner thus becomes, for the left wing nationalist movement, the tortured body of the nation. Letters published by prisoners in *Egin* (a now defunct newspaper sympathetic to radical nationalist positions), posters with the photographs of prisoners on the walls of towns and neighborhoods, and demonstrations by relatives all construct the Basque nation as one of absence and the body of the nation as a tortured, imprisoned, and

---

4. A pact signed in 1988 by all Basque political parties, with the exception of the radical nationalist Herri Batasuna (HB), that committed the Basque government to mobilizing its resources in favor of a social reaction against, and isolation of, individuals and groups suspected of supporting "terrorism."

5. In 1985, forty-one percent of HB sympathizers had had problems with the police and feared becoming targets of harassment for their political sympathies. See Arriaga Landeta (1997: 127n64). Other sources estimate that, during the Spanish transition to democracy (1975 onwards), fourteen thousand Basques have been arrested for political reasons and eighty-five percent of those detained have suffered varying degrees of rough treatment. See Zulaika and Douglass (1996: 204–205).

6. Cf. Arriaga Landeta (1997).

repressed one. The nation is, consequently, made sacred and maintained through the image of this tortured body. Such identification with the suffering of the nation, personified in the kidnapped bodies of male and female prisoners, thus becomes one of the most potent political motivations for radical nationalism. Indeed, no other subject is capable of unleashing such strong emotions. One of the most persistent responses to the reasons behind the *kale borroka* (literally "urban violence," or vandalism, depending on who is talking) during my fieldwork in 1997 was, precisely, the suffering of prisoners. As such, the multitudinous 1999 demonstration in Bilbao in support of the prisoners highlights the sensitivity of this issue. The dispersion of prisoners, the persistence of torture and the violence of the state literally construct the national community as one of suffering, to which one is linked not just through emotional bonds but also through feelings of fear and panic.

The intimacy of these social relations is the cement that binds the abstract concept of the Basque nation with the more concrete reality of day-to-day life. This intimacy of social practices and spaces, of the communion of loss, and of political rituals, is what shapes the imaginary nation as a community of feeling and purpose; and what explains one of nationalism's most difficult aspects to grasp: namely, the affective weight it is capable of mobilizing.[7] Anderson reminds us that love is a basic ingredient of the nation's rhetoric. That this notion of love should be elaborated within the familiar language of romance or kinship not only reveals the nature of patriotic love but also, and perhaps more interestingly, it demonstrates the impossibility of imagining the nation outside an affective space. Yet the production of the nation—as both an object of desire and a space of intimacy—requires something more than just rhetoric. The nation is constructed discursively by its current intellectuals, but at a more popular level it is imagined by people through existent spaces of social intimacy, such as friends and family. As an imagined community, the nation is constructed from the bottom up as a projection of these social spaces. At the same time the sacred nature of the nation radiates out over these other (and also imagined) communities of feeling, such as the local, political, and familial communities. These communities are, in turn, invested with a fraternal feeling that is heightened the more secret or perilous they are.

The Birth of the Moral

This social intimacy that recognizes a familiar face as a "terrorist" sympathizer, and that converts this category into a highly problematic one in the Basque Country, can at the same time also lead to a feeling of social dislocation or cultural shock. This is especially true when the familiar face or someone previously close carries out morally or culturally unacceptable acts of violence, such as threats and actions against members of the same community, for political reasons. In these cases, closeness turns into estrangement and

---

7. Neither social change nor historical circumstance can, in themselves, explain the affective attachment that people feel towards the nation—a recently invented notion, observes Anderson, who wonders "why people are ready to die for these inventions" ([1983] 1991: 141).

lack of recognition, leading to the question with which Zulaika begins his story of the tragedy of Carlos: "But how can that be?"[8] It is precisely this social intimacy that makes the political rupture among Basque nationalists, heightened during the last decade, appear as a break in social reality and felt as a falling out among close friends. This explains the words of one radical leader, Jon Idigoras, during the 1999 cross-party demonstration in Bilbao in favor of political prisoners, when he expressed his delight at the reunion of different nationalist sectors. This also explains the fact that the broken friendships and even family ties that have often accompanied political divisions or violent activity are remembered in such traumatic ways. A friend of mine, whose brother was assassinated by ETA, told me of just how traumatic it was for her when she met an old friend from her town in a bar—a Herri Batasuna member with whom she had shared the intimate social practice of *txikiteo* (bar hopping) and to whom she had sent books when he was in prison—celebrating her brother's death with champagne. For her, this act of personal betrayal came to symbolize the violence against her brother, also understood as an act of betrayal among neighbors, that is, close friends.

The lament of the women from Zulaika's natal village of Itziar with which he begins his ethnography of the violence—but how can that be?—demonstrates the excess of this violence among close friends. An excess that occurs in such a brutal and indescribable way forces us to confront the dark varieties of intimacy itself, with its unrecognized ambivalence and violence, by way of that unknown dimension that for Freud formed the very nucleus of psychic life and that Lacan terms the Real.[9] The Real that punches us in the face and leaves us unable to offer any reply is the consequence of a repressed terror that emerges unexpectedly, upsetting the social order of reality itself; the Real is the trauma of a violence among close friends in which the completely incomprehensible and the incredibly mundane come together. Indeed, Freud ([1930] 1989) located, in an original violence among close friends, the very rise of moral conscience, so the mythical moment in which sons kill their father in the original horde constitutes the birth of law and culture.

The unspeakable assassination of Carlos and its traumatic effect stemmed not from the fact of being unimaginable, but rather from the ambiguity of being simultaneously imaginable and unimaginable. The unimaginable nature of Carlos' death was not the assassination itself, which, logically, given the political context of the time, anyone could have imagined. Rather, it was the fact that such an image (unimaginable at an existential

---

8. Zulaika (1985), later revised and reprinted as chapter 4, "History as Tragedy," in Zulaika (1988: 74–101). Here Zulaika recounts the story of two men from his natal village of Itziar, Carlos and Martin. As babies, both had been nursed by Carlos' mother, after Martin's mother had died, and as they grew up, they became close friends. Yet Carlos was from a family that sided with the Franco uprising during the Spanish Civil War, while Martin came from an anti-Franco Basque nationalist family. While Carlos was viewed, then, as supportive of the subsequent Franco regime, Martin was involved in clandestine political activity against it. Because Martin kept this a closely guarded secret, when Carlos later found out about the activity, he felt betrayed by his childhood friend, Martin. After 1960 these men increasingly came to represent two different and adversarial factions in the local community. In the summer of 1975 Carlos, the alleged police informer of the village, was assassinated by ETA, with bewildered neighbors asking, "But how can that be?"

9. See Freud ([1899] 1985) and Lacan (1981).

level) became reality and thus changed, in this way, the meaning of reality itself, making it sinister—that is, both familiar and strange at the same time,[10] as if everyday life had been ripped apart, allowing us to catch a glimpse of a hidden side of the Real. The unspeakable element here is the sudden appearance of a crude reality that clashes shockingly with the inscrutability and solidity of the matter. The body of the murdered neighbor or the torturer's gleaming boots (Zulaika and Douglass 1996: 191–226) materialize an unspeakable excess or "radical alterity" (Cornell 1998: 141) of violence, something beyond (or beside) the system of meanings that constitutes reality itself (Žižek 1989: 163). Carlos' death allows one a glimpse of the inherent ambivalence and ambiguity in an intimate social relationship—an ambivalence that goes against the cultural imperatives that condemn all animosity among neighbors; an ambiguity fed on assumptions: the assumption by Carlos of the affective betrayal of Martin and the assumption on the part of villagers of Carlos' political betrayal. The objective of the violence in this case, just as in others, resulted in the elimination of this social ambiguity that posited Carlos as both neighbor and traitor, and the restoration of an unambiguous moral-political order. The act of violence also created, however, new ambiguities.

The "but how can that be?," that questioning of the radical alterity of violence, was not about Carlos' death per se, but rather the potentiality of violence among close friends, a violence that threatens the moral limits of the community. In this sense, the existential question, "but how can that be?," is also a moral query that casts doubt on the validity of a (national) community formed on the basis of the violent exclusion of some of its members. And the intimate stage on which Carlos' death took place made this event a tragedy and paradigm for other forms of violence.[11]

The third dimension of the intimacy of violence that I will highlight is the phantasmic connection between those two subjects of impossible definition: the state and terrorism. This phantasmic relationship has led the state to undertaking forms of violence that reflect, in spectacular fashion, the terrorism it seeks to combat.

Terrorism: That Obscure Object of Desire

The problem with antiterrorist discourse is not only its logical incoherence and the heuristic malnourishment of the category—terrorism—that confuses more than it clarifies and

---

10. See Freud ([1925] 1955). One might also interpret this assassination, following the theory of the scapegoat by René Girard (1979), as an attempt to destroy Carlos' ambiguity—at the same time, a well-known and liked member of the local community, milk-brother of Martin, and informant-traitor. The elimination of Carlos would thus have served to re-establish the political certainty and homogeneity questioned by his ambiguous presence. In a recent article, Arjun Appadurai (1998) suggests that, in many cases, brutal forms of ethnic violence are attempts to re-establish, in an unequivocal way, the identity of mostly similar people who, for whatever reason, have come to occupy ambiguous or uncertain positions.

11. Although various literary treatments of this intimacy of violence spring to mind, I will highlight just two. Both Ariel Dorfman ([1991] 1994)) and Jacobo Timerman (1981) explore the link between torturer and victim. The case of the former high-ranking ETA member, Yoyes, gunned down on the orders of her former friends after she had left the organization, gone into exile, and then returned to the Basque Country, is another example of the unspeakable burden of intimacy in which the death of the victim is an attempt to erase the ambiguity of an independent position where one is neither friend nor foe.

offers illusory solutions to complex problems.[12] Nor is it just that the ideological nature of the discourse that has come to replace the nuclear threat of the Cold War with that of terrorism. It is also that terrorism has become a social specter capable of producing undefined fears and desires, of organizing both discursive terrain and practical politics in a highly authoritarian way. Evoking portraits of the nineteenth-century "savage," terrorism encourages both terror and fascination in those who encounter the phenomenon solely as a collective representation by the media. Zulaika and Douglass point out and document the impossibility of any sufficiently coherent reality capable of grouping together such disparate phenomena under the sole rubric of the terrorism category, without falling immediately into complete epistemological confusion. What is termed terrorism, in both media ideology and academic discourse within the growing field of terrorism studies, is a more and more disparate collection of social realities that have little or nothing in common with one another, except their use of violence. Terrorism, as an ontological concern, is a specter that, frequently, is used to cover up democratic deficiencies and justify political authoritarianism. The erosion of civil liberties, together with the violation of human rights and international frontiers, is often justified by the need to respond to a terrorist threat. Within the dominant world order terrorism is the "other" of capitalist democracy, and democracy the entrance ticket into the global market.

In the Spanish state, terrorism has been transformed into the oversimplified explanation for all democracy's problems, as well as the legitimizing document of state. Within this democracy-terrorism polarity, democracy tends to stop being a governmental system in which those in power are responsible for their actions before the citizenry, and becomes instead a reified or essentialist notion of a static state that must defend itself to the death, whatever the cost. In this mission to save democracy from the dangers of terrorism, democracy itself has been compromised, often falling into what Baudrillard (1997) has recently termed "democratic despotism." The defense, at all costs, of democracy has led to an endless succession of antiterrorist laws, the violation of human rights, and the use of torture and assassination by the state security forces. This series of security measures and police saturation in the Basque Country has not only not managed to defeat "terrorism" but has actually worsened the situation, leading to new and even more intolerable forms of violence. What should have been the defense of the democratic order has ended up becoming an obsession in which everything is justified in regard to defeating the "terrorists," even breaking the law. Without any doubt, in the current democratic situation there is no political justification for the violence of ETA. At the same time, there is, without doubt, no justification for the organization of paramilitary groups like the GAL,[13] the persistence of torture or the policy of dispersing Basque political prisoners. This is behavior more fitting of the previous Franco regime that, in great measure, reinforces the the-

---

12. On the history and evolution of terrorism discourse, see Zulaika and Douglass (1996).

13. An acronym for *Grupos Antiterroristas de Liberación* (Antiterrorist Liberation Groups), death squads organized and financed by Spain's socialist government that killed twenty-seven people between 1983 and 1987.

sis of radical Basque nationalism that there has been little change in the transformation of Spain from dictatorship to democracy. ETA has used state violence as its main legitimizing reference point, the justification for its existence and the often cited reason for its continuity. The state is thus transformed, through a violence personified in specific and well-known people, in the phantasmal, all-powerful, and highly threatening enemy that demands the cohesion and loyalty of all Basque nationalists, and especially those of the radical variety. The dominant war mentality within radical nationalism needs this external foe known as the state, and the state actively encourages its own imagining for nationalists as the arch enemy. Indeed, given its hatred for Basque terrorists, the state goes so far as to extend this dynamic to all Basques and nationalists in general, provoking an anti ethnic fervor that recalls the worst excesses of Spanish nationalism. The fact is that if ETA resorts to a war mentality against the state, so the state becomes trapped in a war mentality against Basque terrorism.

Clearly, there exist advantages for both parties in this situation. The state blames terrorism for all its deficiencies and channels the latent discontent among its citizens, as a result of economic inequalities and growing social insecurity, towards the enemy. ETA finds a political rationale to continue, legitimizing its decision in the violence of the state, and the vicious cycle can keep going ad infinitum. Yet the costs are high, with the greatest one being democracy itself, and this leads me to believe that the state-terrorism vicious cycle goes beyond mere instrumental interests. In fact, within this relationship there is a hint of an imaginary intimacy, a mutual obsession and fascination that dominates and defines the joint identity of these two politico-mythological actors. This fascination was particularly apparent in the emergence of the GAL, and especially in its kidnapping of Segundo Marey.[14] Here, this famous representative of the state not only planned a kidnapping, but decided to carry on with it, even when its operatives knew they had made a mistake. Indeed, they even went so far as to imitate terrorist behavior, sending communiqués, designing anagrams, and imposing their own revolutionary tax. This episode of imitating terrorism reveals an imaginary identification with the figure of the terrorist, whose power resides not in the law, but in its transgression.

ETA and the social group surrounding the political party Herri Batasuna are also obsessed with the idea of the legitimacy of state (a state with a capital *S*). One can see this in the activities that, in symbolic and imaginary terms, envisage a Basque state—from

---

14. Segundo Marey was the son of socialist parents from the Spanish Basque border town of Irún. In 1936, when he was four years old, the family fled the city after the outbreak of the Spanish Civil War. They settled in the French Basque border town of Hendaye, where Marey grew up and later worked as a furniture salesman, lived a quiet life with his wife and two daughters, and had no political affiliations. On December 4, 1983, he was kidnapped by the GAL in its first acknowledged operation, the balding fifty-one-year-old being mistaken for a thirty-seven-year-old ETA member. Following the capture of one of his kidnappers, the French police believed he had been taken across the border to Spain, but the Spanish authorities refused to investigate the case. In fact, Marey was, at the time, in the secret custody of the Spanish police, in a shepherd's hut in the province of Santander. On December 14, an anonymous phone call informed the French police that Marey had been left in a wooded area on the Franco-Spanish border. He never fully recovered from the ordeal. See Woodworth (2001: 81–83).

handing out symbolic Basque passports, through the policy of "constructing the nation"—whose ultimate expression can be seen in the name of the new political formation replacing Herri Batasuna: Euskal Herritarrok ("Basque Citizens"). In sum, "the state" and "terrorism" form part of the same political imaginary and their actors make up a phantasmic relationship that links them intimately together, with each one depending on the other for their own definition and legitimacy. It is for this reason that the success of any peace process will depend on the capacity to confront, face-to-face, our political phantoms.

The end of ETA's violence has opened up a necessary space for redefining the political situation. This redefinition depends, as Zulaika (1999) argues, on the abandoning of the terrorist enemy and the recognition of the social complexity in which ETA violence has been inscribed. It also depends on a more nuanced understanding of some basic concepts: about democracy, the historical process and different forms of government, as well as about the state. It is, however, discouraging, at such a key moment, to see the Spanish government responding by continuing to fight it out tooth and nail with the idea of terrorism. It is particularly disappointing that, at a time when ETA "terrorists" have laid down their arms, the government has found a new terrorist subject in what was previously termed "street violence," and is now branded "low intensity terrorism" (the aforementioned *kale borroka*). It is hardly surprising that the government, the principal opposition party and, most likely, high ranking members of the security forces feel ambivalent about the ceasefire, given that ETA has been a raison d'être for so long. And, perhaps for the same reason, there are also some people that feel the same sort of ambivalence within the ranks of radical nationalism. Yet the Spanish government should not place its political specters and interests above the resolution of a violent conflict. Such a resolution demands negotiation and a distancing from the war mentality that stresses a defeat of the "other." It demands recognition of the social and historical complexity of nationalist violence and state responsibility in maintaining such hostility. It demands recognition and an examination of the historical dynamic of democracy in the Spanish state, of its birth, sanctioned and controlled by the previous Franco regime and of the constitutional limits established by the power of a dictatorship that refused to completely disappear. During the years of the Spanish transition to democracy after 1975, democracy became a fetish, the entrance ticket into modernity and the economic success of the European community. Now that the Spanish state is an undeniable member of the European Union, it is time for democracy to become something more than just a fetish, or reification of an idea. It is ironic that, while Spain appears in the pages of the *New York Times* as a champion of democracy as a result of its warrant for the arrest of Chile's former dictator, General Pinochet, those responsible for the murders committed by the GAL have walked free.[15] Undoubtedly, ending the dispersion of Basque prisoners—one of the most emotive and politically sensitive issues in the Basque Country—will not destroy Spanish democracy; quite the contrary, for it can only reinforce it.

---

15. See the *New York Times Magazine*, January 17, 1999.

Redefining the Political

In the political field, Zulaika proposes a "politics of friendship" as a radical redefinition of the political (1999: 228–29). The advantage of such a redefinition is that it demands an abandoning of the notion of the "enemy" as a central organizing principle of political culture. A politics of friendship thus requires the transformation of Manichean structures that perceive everyone and everything that differs from one's own political postures as an enemy. This Manichean perspective has led, in the Basque Country, to truly unsustainable situations, most visible in the counter-demonstrations of pacifist groups and the main organization favoring an amnesty for Basque political prisoners, with the *Ertzaintza* (the Basque police force) forming a human wall to separate the two. It is physically and symbolically difficult to not comprehend such political demonstrations as symptomatic of the dominant social hysteria, as the source of a commitment expressing the inextricable nature of the conflict. In such a physical and frontal confrontation between "violent" and "peaceful" people, between "terrorists" and "democrats," a stereotyped vision of the "other" emerges. This in turn becomes a depository of pure negativity, the presence that in some absolute way denies one's very existence. In such a situation there is no mediation; one position is the mirror image of the other, and language ceases to have any meaning, becoming a circular exchange of the same tautological accusations: "You are violent, I am democratic; no, I'm democratic and you are violent." Friendship as a metaphor of political relations attempts to substitute this vicious cycle between two mirror-image positions by exchanging differences among more than just two poles.

The ending of ETA's armed activity is the necessary change that opens up the political space to multiple political scenarios. If democratic identity has been forged, in good measure, by its opposition to terrorism, the disappearance of the terrorist enemy necessarily forces a redefinition of democracy itself, as regards its own political identity. Such a redefinition should also incorporate a transformation of forms of identity based on resentment of an "other" framed in terms of the pure negativity of existence itself.[16] The "politics of friendship" proposed by Zulaika is an attempt to imagine democracy positively, that is, without an archetypal opponent. In essence, it represents a utopian, Habermassian scenario of democratic pluralism, where conflicts and disagreements among different political positions all have a place within different institutions of government. Although coinciding with this vision of democratic pluralism proposed by Zulaika, I cannot help but feel uncomfortable with the key notion of friendship as a metaphor for this new political subjectivity.

Friendship implies a mutual recognition that is, or should be, one of the components of any pluralist democracy, but within friendship, unlike politics, such recognition is the outcome of mutual trust and attachment. In politics, recognition of the other might be a question of pragmatism; in other words, one can recognize another's position without feeling any affection for it at all. Friendship demands a horizontal relationship that recognizes

---

16. On the importance of the Nietzschean idea of *resentement* in identity politics, see Wendy Brown (1995).

ideological differences but that positions itself outside said differences; in other words, friendship might be affected by politics but, in itself, it cannot form the political landscape, a terrain formed by power differences. Friendship, like love, cannot be forced through an act of will. Within politics, however, mutual recognition can, and often is, forced through an act of willpower. What does applying the metaphor of friendship to politics imply? At one ideal level, it implies introducing the Levinasian ethic of genuinely recognizing a different "other," before which we are all responsible in the field of politics. Such an imperative would have, as its consequence, the creation of a public sphere where said recognition would enable open and transparent political communication. Without any shadow of a doubt, this would constitute a radical change in political culture. Yet, on the other hand, would it not also imply a *tabula rasa* of these power relations that make up the very nature of politics? And what would one do with a history of relations scarred by violence? Is it really possible to eliminate such a history with a stroke of the pen for the sake of a new politics of friendship?

Personally, it would be difficult for me to make friends with people whose political views I find repugnant, or with those who might have tortured my daughter, or others that murdered my brother. My friend whose brother was killed by ETA might be able to recognize (identify, understand) the position of a friend in Herri Batasuna who, after her brother's death, was celebrating in a party as if nothing had happened. She might be able to recognize the position of someone who was once her friend and the need for establishing a means of mutual recognition that would allow an end to the violence, but their friendship has finished forever. In the same way, Zulaika's discussion of violence in his own village of Itziar implies a face-to-face dialogue, a recognition of difference, but not a relationship based on friendship. It is, precisely, the awareness of belonging to the same community and feeling free to not be "friends" with someone that, in my view, makes genuine dialogue about political differences possible. For, what would be left of friendship—that by definition cannot be forced—if we were to make it a political command? According to Zulaika, reinventing politics based on friendship requires, at the same time, abandoning the concept of sacramental friendship that demands absolute loyalties and politico-ideological identity. Recognizing a different "other" unites, then, in Zulaika's proposal, the spheres of friendship and politics. Even so, I ask myself whether politics based on friendship does not imply, to a certain extent, eliminating all political reason. Even for Emmanuel Levinas, this is different from ethical reason, despite the fact that both are necessarily entwined.[17] Whatever the case, in a country where the intimacy of personal relations constitutes the very fabric of politics, Zulaika's proposal, framing this bold collection of essays, can at the very least only serve as a source of inspiration at this historical juncture where political culture must, necessarily, reinvent itself.

---

17. See Zulaika (1991) and Zulaika and Douglass (1996: 191–226).

CHAPTER 9

Before the Law: The Narrative of the Unconscious in Basque Political Violence[1]

> *Law*: 1a. the body of rules, whether proceeding from formal enactment or custom, which a particular state or community recognizes as binding on its members or subjects (in this sense usually the law.) Also in early use a code or system of rules of this kind. 1b. Often viewed with more or less personification, as an agent uttering or enforcing the rules of which it consists. Hence (b) colloq., a policeman, the police.
>
> Oxford English Dicitonary.

> The exception is more interesting than the regular case . . . the general is thought about not with passion but only with comfortable superficiality. The exception on the other hand, thinks the general with intense passion.
>
> Carl Schmitt, *Politische Theologie*.

> The exception is the originary form of law.
>
> Giorgio Agamben, *Homo Sacer*.

The Event

In December 1995, an extraordinarily shocking assassination took place in a small rural town at the heart of the Basque Country. It was a crime that received heightened attention in the mass media and rippled Basque society with a wave of panic and anxiety. This is the event in brief: on December 10, 1995, Mikel Otegi, a twenty-three-year-old Basque youth, took a hunting gun hanging on the wall of his farmhouse, came outside, and shot two *ertzainas* (Basque policemen).[2] He then called the *Ertzaintza* (Basque police) and surrendered himself. In his deposition to the judge, Otegi could only remember that at some

---

1. Unpublished manuscript. Paper presented at the *School of American Research Advance Seminar*, April 27–May 2, 2002.

2. *Ertzaintza* is the name used in the Basque Country to refer to the Basque police force. *Ertzaina* is the name for an individual policeman or policewoman. Both terms will be used in this paper, alternating them with the English term Basque police for variation.

point he had "lost it." He said that he saw the two *ertzainas* on the side of the road, less than a mile from his farmhouse, when he was driving home early in the morning. When he arrived home he went to bed. Later, he heard the dogs barking, came out of the house to see what was happening and saw the two *ertzainas*, one of them near his car. According to his testimony, the *ertzainas* asked for his identity card. When he refused to give it to them, they asked Otegi to accompany them to the police station. Mikel Otegi told them to go away but the *ertzainas*, he said, ignored him. He then "lost it," went inside the house, grabbed the hunting gun, and could not remember what happened next (Forest 1997: 247–48).

This event became emblematic, within Basque society, of a certain state of violent lack of control, iconized in the figure of new radicalized youth. This violent state appeared to have intensified through 1995.[3] Some months prior to Otegi's double killing, in March 1995, a Basque police patrol van was attacked with Molotov cocktails by radical nationalist youth in the industrial town of Rentería. The van caught fire and the *ertzainas* suffered burns of various degrees, one of them severe. The image of their bodies in flames horrified the public.[4] That same year, an *ertzaina* was publicly beaten in Bilbao, and Gregorio Ordoñez, a member of the Spanish conservative party, the Partido Popular, and an elected representative on the city council of San Sebastián, was assassinated by the Basque separatist group, ETA (Euskadi Ta Askatasuna, Basque land and freedom). It was the first time that a local politician had been targeted by this group. Otegi's killings came at the end of a year of violence that seemed to challenge the moral premises bounding the sociality of the Basque community, representing the epitome of a state of lack of control that threatened to become the new order of things; a force that in negating the law so profoundly showed itself as what Benjamin has called a lawmaking force ([1921] 1987: 283–84). For Benjamin, "lawmaking is power making, and, to that extent, an immediate manifestation of violence" (Ibid: 295). But the lawmaking function of radical nationalist violence becomes almost literal as it manifests itself in a will for national sovereignty and statehood; a will that openly refuses the prevailing order of democratic law and the existing level of Basque self-government as constituting disguises of both an authoritarian and foreign rule. Thus, radical nationalist violence not only challenges the law in its function of preserving the instituted (democratic) order, it also challenges the imaginary Basque national community by splitting it from within into law preserving and lawmaking violences. Mikel Otegi's double murder was so shocking (and so interesting) because the case replicates this problematic of law in relation to a split national self, indeed enacts it and

---

3. In December 1994, the confessions of two policemen revealed that members of the Spanish government, the military, the police, and the secret services had been involved in the organization of paramilitary assassinations of Basque separatists during the 1980s. The scandal gave rise to an increment of youth violence in the Basque Country in the forms of rioting and arsonist attacks on objects, buildings, and persons associated with "the state."

4. See the local newspapers *El Diario Vasco* and *Egin* of March 25, 1995 and subsequent days for different views on the reactions to the attack. That same weekend, there were more than fifty arson attacks against public buildings, Basque police, and headquarters of political parties. The Chief Director of the Department of the Interior of the Basque government, Jose Maria Atutxa, declared that, "the situation was dramatic and incomprehensible." *El Diario Vasco*, March 26, 1995.

renders it visible if not comprehensible, opening the door—like a dream or a nightmare—to an endless narrative that in attempting to explain what happened also tries to contain the terror that it instills.

This essay is an attempt to make sense of this relation between violence, narrative, and the law that articulates a troubled national self in the Basque Country. I am concerned with the effect that new representations and materializations of "the law," made possible by the development of an autonomous, state-like administration in the Basque Country, have had on the production of violence. In the larger scheme of things, this case brings up the issue of how to think about emerging radicalized forms of ethnic nationalism within an increasingly unified Europe and increasingly globalized world. In the Basque Country, the politics of ethnic nationalism during the last twenty years have been overdetermined by the status of the law, partly because they challenge what is called in Spain the "Estado de Derecho," literally, State of Law—a state whose legitimacy comes from the law as opposed to the authority of a totalitarian ruler. In Spain, this State of Law signifies a break with the former regime of General Francisco Franco and inaugurates a new political form. On the other hand, this "Estado de Derecho" has been associated with forms of violence characteristic of the former regime (such as police abuse and paramilitary assassinations).[5] This state of law has legitimized state violence in the name of democracy and, in its materialization as repressive force, it has also legitimized nationalist violence; which in the form of riots, arson attacks, and terrorist assassinations continues to challenge the state of law in the struggle for an imaginary Basque sovereign state. In the post-Franco era, the law, which has become (not without some anxiety) an emblem of democratic identity in the rest of Spain, has come to signify for radical Basque nationalists an arbitrary and oppressive violence. In Benjaminian fashion, radical nationalists see the law as a ghostly force that is pure means aimed at the destruction of Basque identity.[6]

The association of the law with a threatening force, as I will elaborate later, is rooted in the experience of the dictatorial regime of Franco and his emphatic anti-Basque policies. What is puzzling, however, is that the young activists who have taken leadership of the movement for Basque independence have no personal experience of the dictatorship. They are the product of the democratic transition. Furthermore, contrary to general expectation, the development of Basque institutions, particularly an autonomous judicial apparatus and police force, have not counteracted the semantics of the law as both alien and arbitrary amongst radical nationalists. In fact, instead of curtailing nationalist violence, the autonomous embodiment of the law has had the effect of generating new forms of violence. This puzzle points to important questions concerning the relationship of violence to the law in small regions where the politics of (European) globalization underwrites

---

5. The organization of state terrorism in the form of a paramilitary organization called GAL (Grupos Antiterroristas de Liberación, Antiterrorist Liberation Groups) during the 1980s is the most clear example of this ambiguous character of the democratic state.

6. On the form of the law in modernity see Benjamin ([1921] 1978), Derrida (1991), Agamben (1998), Copjec (1996).

the political desire of ethnic nationalism. The murder case analyzed in this essay opens a space in which to investigate the "force of law" (Derrida 1991)—as it becomes ineluctably enmeshed in practices of statehood and fantasies of nationhood—and the political instabilities, social anxieties, and violent operations that it engenders.

I focus on the discursive production engendered by the murder (mainly in newspapers, interviews, and social commentary) to track the anxieties and unconscious operations that seem to articulate the violent politics of identity in the Basque Country.[7] As we will see, this articulation takes place in a sphere of thick social intimacy which overdetermines political anxieties and triggers uncanny effects.[8] In a way, political violence in the Basque Country is a familial affair, yet family here is not meant to figure as separated from the political but, rather, the very site where the political takes place and where nation is invested with affect. The narratives analyzed in this essay constitute also a field of struggle; a struggle for meanings and for power among various political movements and organizations. Ultimately, what the narratives articulate might be a kind of knowledge already spoken through the equivocal language of a speechless act, a murder—a knowledge that might have to do with the anxieties and aporias posed by the traumatic (dis)articulation of the uneasily joined terms nation-state. Not only is this peculiar political form—nation-state—not withering away in the face of the globalizing effect of millennial capitalism (Comaroff and Comaroff 2000a), but it is creating new nationalist desires for statehood. How the imaginary relation with a fantasized nation articulates with the powerful constraints and castrating effects of the absent presence of state remains to be seen. One thing is sure: that attempts at this disjointed joining take the form of traumatic violence. This essay on the law is part of a larger project that investigates just such traumatic violence. I have borrowed the title from Kafka's famous allegorical story "Before the Law" to evoke precisely the enigma and aporia of the experience of the law, as that which haunts us from within the national self. Before I turn to the murder case, let me provide a short background on the recent political history that might help situate the actors in this story.

Encapuchados, Ertzainas, and the Political Transition

The death of General Francisco Franco in 1975 marked the end of the dictatorship in Spain and the beginning of a transition toward a democratic regime. The development of Basque autonomous institutions (such as the Basque Government and Basque Parliament) was a central part of this democratic reform which needed to address the long-standing demand for autonomy in this, and other, regions of Spain. The most dramatic

---

7. During the last decade the scholarship on violence has grown considerably. For works that emphasize the role of narrative, see for example: Feldman (1991), Foucault (1975), Malkki (1995), Taylor (1997), Brass (1997), Tambiah (1997), Aretxaga (1997), Nordstrom and Martin (1992), Appadurai (1998), Zulaika and Douglass (1996), Taussig (1987), Das (1995), Warren (1993), and Nelson (1999).

8. For various elaborations on public intimacy see Berlant (1998). For more specific theorizing of public intimacy and nationalism, see Berlant (1997) and Herzfeld (1997).

manifestation of such nationalist demands was the violence of the separatist group, ETA. ETA was born in 1959 as a response to the fierce cultural and political repression suffered in the Basque Country under the Franco regime. Its armed actions did not commence, however, until 1969 with the killing of Melitón Manzanas, inspector of the infamous Francoist secret police and widely known as a vicious torturer.[9] The ultimate goal of ETA was the formation of an independent Basque nation, yet until the death of Franco in 1975, its targets were mostly members of the security forces. The negotiated democratic reform that followed the death of Franco was opposed by a significant number of Basques for leaving intact the structures of the former regime (the military, police, judiciary, and bureaucracy) and reaffirming the unity of Spain as a nation-state. The most important product of the democratic reform, the Spanish constitution, was rejected in the Basque Country for not acknowledging the right to self-determination for the ethnic regions of Spain (especially Catalunya and the Basque Country, which had strong nationalist movements). What the constitution included, however, was a process of increasing regional autonomy. During the following two decades the Basque Country developed, under a formal statute of autonomy, what could be considered the structural apparatus of a state. Although subordinated to the Spanish Constitution and legislation, the Basque Country now has a highly sophisticated administrative and political apparatus including a government, parliament, judicial and educational structures, its own police force, and even its own taxation system—the only region to enjoy such financial autonomy. In spite of this notable development of self-government, separatist violence has continued as a permanent feature of Basque political life. During the late 1980s, the violence of ETA intensified and in the 1990s, young arsonists began to target members of the newly-formed Basque police or *Ertzaintza*.[10] Here, I will elaborate on the *Ertzaintza* since they are main actors in the murder drama.

The Basque Country has long been troubled by the excessive force of police violence which has left an extensive record of assassinations, torture, and abuse of radical nationalists. Despite the democratic reform initiated after the death of Franco, the two Spanish police bodies—the national police and the Civil Guard—continued to practice illegal forms of violence against radical nationalists in the form of arrests, torture, assassinations, and beatings.[11] This shadowy violence made Spanish security forces an object of distrust for the majority of the Basque population. Precisely for this reason, the creation of a Basque police force became a central claim for Basque nationalists, an inseparable part of a grow-

---

9. Melitón Manzanas was recently honored by the Spanish government as a victim of ETA, in the midst of great controversy and the condemnation of Amnesty International.

10. During this period, popular support for radical nationalist politics (including violence) has varied, but has rarely descended below 15 percent.

11. In 1985, 41 percent of people voting for the radical nationalist political party Herri Batasuna (HB), had had problems with the police and were afraid of being mistreated because of their political allegiance (Arriaga Landeta 1997: 127n64). Other sources estimate that more than fourteen thousand Basques have been arrested for political reasons during the democratic period, and of those arrested 85 percent have complained of police mistreatment (Zulaika and Douglass 1996: 204–5).

ing process of autonomy for the region that culminated in the formation of a Basque autonomous parliament and government.

The *Ertzaintza* is a young police force. Its first year of graduating officers from the Basque police academy was 1988. It was intended to be the trusted civil police that the Basque Country never had, unburdened by the legacy of the Franco regime. Unlike the officers of the Spanish police forces who were born and raised in other parts of Spain and were in the Basque Country only for a transitory service period, the young officers of the Basque police were local men and women. Unlike the Spanish police forces who for the most part lived in their own headquarters on the outskirts of towns and villages, the *ertzainas* lived interspersed with the local population, had their families and friends within the Basque geography, and thought of themselves as an integral part of a local and (Basque) national community. The Spanish police forces identified as Spanish, the Basque police officers identified as Basque. As the new Basque police developed in numbers and complexity of functions, they also were called to the labor of riot control and anti-terrorist struggle. These more specialized interventions entailed the deployment of force against radical Basque nationalists, who are the main actors in political demonstrations, riots, and of course terrorist violence.

The intervention of the Basque police had a profound effect on reorganizing the "scene of violence" in the imaginary of radical nationalists. Until the introduction of the Basque police, radical nationalists conceptualized the scene of violence in the Basque Country as one of a liberation struggle that pitched Basques—as an ethnic minority—against the oppressive forces of the Spanish state. This transcendental national struggle was dramatized in the recurrent riots in which Basque activists confronted the Spanish police during the last years of the Franco regime and the subsequent transition. With the *Ertzaintza* assuming tasks formerly associated with the Spanish police, the scene of violence was complicated. The confrontation became one between Basques: radical nationalists versus Basque Government. This confrontation came to signify a split in the imagined national community and furthermore a split within Basque identity itself. On the one hand, this split within Basque identity (which had hitherto remained homogeneous in the discourse of radical nationalism) translated in the towns and villages into an everyday confrontation between neighbors, those Basques supporting the radical politics and violence of the separatist group ETA, and those supporting the Basque government against ETA and the violence of radical youth. On the other hand, this split within Basqueness was dramatized in the riots between young radicals, now called *encapuchados* (masked ones), and young *ertzainas*, also wearing masks. The conflict between the Spanish state and Basque radicalism did not disappear from the discourse of Basque radicals; rather it became mediated by a more intimate (and threatening) conflict among different kinds of Basques. But when did these *encapuchados* emerge into the political arena?

The *encapuchados* are the young protagonists of a new form of nationalist violence termed *kale borroka*, meaning "street fighting," but most appropriately translated now as urban warfare. The term *kale borroka* is not new, however. During the last years of Francoism and the first decade of the democratic transition, *kale borroka* referred to rioting with the police, which at that time was still the Spanish police force. It has the connotation of popular opposition to repressive police force and evokes the ideas of reactive resistance to a previous act of violence. For example, the rioting that broke out after the police charged violently on a peaceful demonstration—as happened almost daily during the late 1970s and early 1980s—was understood and referred to as *kale borroka*. In the 1990s, however, *kale borroka* took on new meanings. It came to signify not a defensive resistance against state violence, but rather an offensive attack. It also widened its content to include not just rioting with the police (predominantly now Basque police) but acts of sabotage (arson attacks on government buildings, headquarters of political parties, ATM machines, public buses, telephone booths, and, significantly, court buildings). *Kale borroka* has indeed become more like urban warfare and less like the street fighting of the old anti-Francoist type.[12]

To counteract the anti-authoritarian and revolutionary connotations contained in the term *kale borroka*, the government and the press often refer to this form of action as "*violencia callejera*" (urban violence) emphasizing the dimensions of arbitrariness and vandalism. The change in the content of the *kale borroka* came about after 1992, when the leadership of ETA was arrested in a widely publicized operation which was announced by the Spanish minister of the interior as the end of violence. With ETA seriously wounded, the radical nationalist movement found itself, in the words of an activist, "in a black hole," that is, in a state of demoralization and disorientation.[13] The lack of leadership, however, threw radical nationalist youth onto center stage of the political arena. To fill the vacuum left by the weakening (but not death) of ETA, they devised a tactic of sabotage and aggressive rioting against the police.[14] Although this new political intervention was incomprehensible for the general public, who puzzled about the reasons for everyday burning of public property and unprovoked rioting, it had the capacity to attract youngsters and heightened public attention. As these actions increased, the *Ertzaintza* (Basque police) began video-taping riots as a means of identifying participants. In response, young activists began to wear masks. Soon they were popularly addressed as *encapuchados* (masked ones).

By 1995, it had become a quotidian scene in towns and cities to see a group of up to forty youngsters, between fourteen and twenty years of age, coming into the central streets and plazas, their faces covered with hoods and kerchiefs and their hands full of

---

12. The techniques used in the *kale borroka* during the 1990s were borrowed from those used by the alternative movement in West Germany, and to a lesser extent from the lessons of the autonomy movement in Italy.

13. There is practically no published material on this movement of radical nationalists and very little material on the Basque youth movement more generally. On the latter, see Ramírez Goicoechea (1991), Lahusen (1993) and Urla (1995). A study commissioned by the Basque government contains general and not very accurate information, yet it was received with hostility by radical nationalist youth sectors and the leading researchers received violent threats. See Department of Culture of the Basque Government (Various Authors 1994). Most of my information comes from my own interviews with activists and archival primary research of documents and ephemera.

14. ETA was long held to be the leadership of the radical nationalist movement, which is comprised of an array of diverse sectorial organizations.

Molotov cocktails destined to burn public buses and telephone booths, attack courthouses, ATM machines, the headquarters of opposing political parties, police vehicles—permanently stationed in the centers of public space—and any other representation of an imagined State enemy. During 1995 and 1996, there were 408 and 440 such attacks, according to the provincial attorney's office, and they rose by 25 percent during 1997.[15] Volatile, unpredictable, and seemingly without limits, the violence of the *encapuchados* was, and continues to be, a source of anxiety and epistemological rupture; as my friend Juana, born and raised near Otegi's farm, put it, "*te rompe los esquemas mentales*" ("it shatters your mental schemes"). This apprehension and eerie feeling is triggered not so much by the actual actions of violence, as by their ghostly character; by the simultaneous feeling of close familiarity and utter estrangement evoked by the young *encapuchados* which produced an uncertainty as to what this violence was about and how to react to it. For many people, the problem of the *encapuchados* was one of positionality, of finding the proper perspective in relation to them. Were they to be considered troublesome boys or dangerous proto-terrorists? The boy next door or an alien presence? Was this violence a passing phase or did it announce an uncontrollable form of violence? Otegi's double murder occurred within this context and came to iconize all that was inchoate and uncanny in it.

Back to the Event

Two years after his arrest, Mikel Otegi testified at his trial that one of the policemen had drawn a gun in the course of the discussion; he became very frightened and went back to his house, got the hunting gun and came out again. It was at that point, when he and the policemen were facing each other, that he lost consciousness.[16] The scene is reminiscent of the film *High Noon*, when Gary Cooper (as the lawman) stands alone, facing a group of bandits threatening him with the imposition of another (criminal) law. It is at that scene of encounter, face-to-face with the law, that something happened, something outside Mikel Otegi's will and consciousness. It is as if the agency that carried out the double killing was not his own, but somebody else's. Some other agency manifested itself through the body of Otegi as if he was possessed. For what defines the possessed is precisely that s/he speaks with somebody else's voice (De Certeau 1988). One could possibly say that Otegi's double murder constituted a discourse of some kind originating outside himself. But if so, what is this agency acting through Otegi and what is the discourse that speaks through this act? What space does it occupy within the discourse of the law?

One factor that made this crime unusual within the catalog of killings in the Basque Country was its ambiguity. Otegi's double killing had an unclassifiable character that blurred the boundaries between political and merely personally motivated crime, between

---

15. Sabotage as a crime category does not figure in the records of the provincial attorney until 1995.
16. *El Diario Vasco*, February 25, 1997, 5.

sanity and madness, between accident and intent. The councilor of the interior of the Basque Government expressed this ambiguity when he said that the crime "was not an organized terrorist assassination but neither was it an ordinary crime."[17] This ambiguous quality of the crime had the effect of destabilizing epistemological certainties and unleashing a great deal of anxiety. Neither a terrorist act nor a common crime, this offense stood aside as a kind of "matter out of place" to use Mary Douglas' (1969) felicitous expression for categorical transgression; a matter that demanded definition, so that the political and social boundaries it transgressed could be safely reestablished. And yet it is this very "matter out of place" which, in threatening the boundaries of the social system—in this case the categories of identity—raises questions about the exclusions, anxieties, and tensions underlying the structures of social identity.[18]

More than anything, Otegi's crime brought to the surface something unsettling and unsettled in Basque nationalist identity, by showing, through the traumatic act of a "familial" kind of murder, a deep split; not just at the level of ideology and organization, but also at the level of fantasy and what counts as reality. It brought to the surface the unspeakable anxiety about political fratricide and civil confrontation lying at the core of the national community. For the judiciary who adjudicated the case, and for the larger public alike, the question of nationalist identity was mediated by the attempts to define a violence that defied established categories: was Otegi's crime intentional or an accident? Was it the inevitable product of a belligerent police or the feared sign of a violent nationalism out of control? Did it signal Otegi's troubled personality or a deep rift in the nationalist community? Defining the nature of this crime had implications on the state of national identity and the very nature of the "state" associated with it. As such, it became the urgent task of scientific experts, politicians, media commentators, the public in everyday street conversation, and of course those involved in the juridical case. Questions generated around the crime represented not only the point of confluence of a variety of discourses struggling for meaning and political hegemony, but also a battleground where the media and the various political parties took their positions. In this sense, Otegi's case reminds me of the famous case of parricide discussed by Foucault (1975) and his team of researchers.[19]

In the hands of Foucault and his colleagues, the parricide of Pierre Rivière became not only a battleground between competing discourses and institutions struggling for social hegemony through the definition of the event; it also opened a window onto a series of social and historical contexts, all of them bearing a relationship to the crime, yet not directly explaining it. Ultimately, the *truth* of the event in the case of Pierre Rivière, as in the case of Otegi, remains elusive, and thus it is not the primary object of this essay.

---

17. *El Diario Vasco*, December 12, 1995, 4.

18. In this respect see, for example, Douglas (1966), Kristeva (1982), and Stallybrass and White 1986).

19. For a very good analysis of political violence in India that leans on the model of Foucault (1986), see Paul Brass (1997).

My goal, then, is not to establish the truth about the killings, or to provide another authoritative discourse to add to those which entered the scene of the crime at the time. Rather, what intrigue me are the political anxieties filtered through the narratives generated by Otegi's killings. These anxieties constitute, I believe, the undercurrents of political and social life in the Basque Country, motivating its ebbs and flows in ways that are not always recognized. The different narratives of Otegi's double murder and their social contexts are like the different parts of a puzzle which fit together, yet yield no final picture. Unlike Pierre Rivière, who wrote his own memoir of the crime, Otegi has produced no text of his own, he has remained silent, like a ghostly presence, at the center of his own narrative, a remnant stubbornly embodying a political invisible (Derrida 1994). Unlike Pierre Rivière, Otegi is strangely absent from his own actions, having killed, literally, in a lapse of consciousness. Oddly enough, this absence becomes a presence in the narrative configuration of the crime and above all in the discourse of the Law. It is this absent presence that haunts the social imagination in the Basque Country and haunts me as well, for it seems to not only pervade the whole case (infusing it with phantasmagoric and uncanny qualities), but also the whole domain of political violence in the Basque Country. Thus, it is that lapse of consciousness, that gap, that other agency displacing the subject, which becomes the organizational center of my narrative. I take as a point of departure Lacan's definition of the unconscious as the discourse of the other (1977: 54), which emerges precisely in the gaps, in the blackouts, of personal and collective histories. If Otegi's double crime is the effect of an-Other agency produced in the gap of (political) consciousness, then we might say that what we are confronting here, in this speechless murder, is in fact a discourse; the discourse of the unconscious in the field of Basque politics. Something is being said through Otegi's double murder, but what is said and who is saying it? In this article, I take the double murder as a site of condensed meanings, a materialization of a discourse which does not find linguistic articulation but whose significance is best manifested in the proliferation of narratives it engendered. It is to these narratives that I turn now.

Otegi's Narrative

During the trial, two years after the killing, Mikel Otegi recounted the events leading to the crime.[20] He preceded the narrative by stating that what happened "was an unconscious act and I am very sorry for the families of the two *ertzainas*. I am sad." He then went on to his recollections of that fateful December 10, 1995.

He had returned the night before the crime from Germany, where he habitually traveled as part of his work as a truck driver. He spent the evening of the following day play-

---

20. I am following the report of the trial published by the newspaper *El Diario Vasco*, February 25, 1997. The following citations are taken from this edition (p.5). The trial testimony does not differ from the deposition made by Otegi after the killings.

ing cards with friends. He said he had a snack but did not eat supper. He had several drinks (rum and coke) while playing cards. At night, he and his friends went to the rock concert taking place in his town. He drank a lot of beer during the concert and that night he did not sleep. In the morning, he went with his eighteen-year-old niece to have breakfast at the local bar, Ibarre. He said that he had a fight with somebody in the bar, who he assumed was an *ertzaina*. He does not remember who began the incident but admitted that "it came to fists." He then started home, and near his farm house he saw an *Ertzaintza* patrol car stationed in its usual place. He did not pay attention to it, and when he got home he went directly to bed. Then he heard the dog barking, came out to look, and saw the two *ertzainas*:

> I didn't know what time it was, but I heard the dog barking and I got up as I do whenever the dog barks at unusual times. I came out [of the house] from the hayloft and saw the two *ertzainas*. At that moment a verbal fight ensued. The *ertzainas* told me to go with them, that I was under arrest. I told them to go away and leave me in peace. One of the *ertzainas* took out his gun and aimed at me; then I got scared and went into the house again.

He did not relate the presence of the *ertzainas* with the fight he had at the bar. When he went back into the house, he saw the hunting rifle and loaded it with three cartridges and came out again, rifle in hand, where he resumed the fight. "Then I don't know what happened. I saw only that the two *ertzainas* were on the ground. I don't remember shooting them." He said that after "what happened," he got into the police car and used the radio to alert the police station.

Mikel Otegi added to his testimony that for several years he had been constantly harassed by the Basque police. He said that he had been beaten by several *ertzainas* on New Year's Eve in 1994, when he came up to them with the aim of wishing them a happy new year. He said that, since that moment, he had been constantly stopped by them and searched during work and on the way home. It was because of this harassment that he changed jobs, from being a construction worker in his brother's business to becoming a truck driver. The psychiatrist expert for the defense testified that Otegi was afflicted by fantasies of persecution by the Basque police (Forest 1997: 81). The defense argued that the important point in the adjudication of Otegi's killings was not the reality of the harassment, but *the reality of the feeling of persecution* that "he experienced to such a degree that his personality could not tolerate it" (Forest 1997: 81). The prosecuting attorney asked Otegi if he considered himself mad. He answered, "No." He then asked, "Have you ever been in psychiatric treatment?" Otegi answered, "No." Between madness and reality, occupying an undefined and undefinable space, blurring the boundaries of both, stands this psychic reality, this fantasy of police persecution which was echoed by the whole radical nationalist movement and elevated to political fact.

Otegi's narrative is that of an absence. Unlike the case of Pierre Rivière, we find here no text, no description of motivations or thinking, no internal logic leading to the crime. His deposition to the judge and his later testimony in the trial contained only a short description of events before the crime. The vicissitudes of the event constitute an absence, indeed the event itself is defined by an absence, of consciousness, of subjecthood. Otegi's narrative communicates that the subject of the crime is in a very fundamental sense absent from the scene. The presence is the presence of fantasy.

The Reactions

Otegi's killings had the effect of a shock, posing an epistemological rupture articulated initially in the language of madness. "*Está loco*" ("he's mad") was the first thing my sister said. My friend Juana, who was born and raised in the same town as Otegi, also thought him crazy and linked his madness to hidden domestic violence. Juana said that,

> Everybody knew that guy; so did I, since I was a kid, because my father sold his family hay for the animals. His farmhouse is behind my house. His father was very authoritarian, one of those who beat the children quite often, and Mikel was among those who were in the front line of riots and he was always cursing the *Ertzaintza*. He hated the *Ertzaintza*. He was the kind that throws stones, breaks things, the kind that when something appeared broken in the town everybody suspected that Mikel had something to do with it. It seems that he was a bit crazy. A few years ago, he burned his mattress and almost burned the attic in the house. He apparently had a big problem with authority. I can understand that one has a moment of madness and kills somebody, but what I don't understand is that the same day there is a demonstration in my town of people demanding "*Mikel askatu*" ("free Mikel"), *that* is mentally shattering. You say . . . "But what is happening here?! Are we all crazy? Is this happening here? In my town?" Not in the USA or some remote place that you see on the television news, but my town!

In Juana's narrative, the discourse of madness is both asserted and problematized. For if Juana links Otegi's craziness to the intimacy of family violence, she also links political violence to a kind of collective madness, one which de-realizes reality all the more for occurring within the boundaries of the socially familiar. Thus in Juana's narrative, family violence and nationalist violence are linked by multiple associations. First, in the person of Otegi, who partakes of both; second, in the identification of the radical nationalist movement with Otegi's predicament; third, in the social intimacy that renders Otegi's killings and nationalist violence a shock—like a family murder. These associative links complicate the attribution of the crime to individual insanity. For if Otegi's madness could be understood, it was more difficult to understand the apparent madness of the people who identified with him and demanded his freedom—and more threatening, too. For Juana, individual madness does not threaten the premises of the social order; collective madness, however, blurs the very distinction between madness and sanity, and thus turns reality upside down. Juana's associations are significant because the family has been a recurrent metaphor of the Basque nation in the rhetoric of both radical and moderate nationalists—law abiding and law transgressing nationalists. If the intimacy of family is linked to the nation in both Juana's narrative, and in the rhetoric of nationalism, so is political violence tied to the intimacy of family in the discourses following Otegi's killings. For some reporters, as for Juana, the madness of Otegi is linked to the madness of national intimacy.

The Newspapers and the Narrative of Fratricide

A reading of the local newspapers reveals radically different interpretations of the event, and diametrically opposed political positions. *El Diario Vasco,* the local newspaper most read in the Basque province of Guipúzcoa (where the killings took place) began its reporting on the front page under a photograph of the farm house and Mikel Otegi. The headline read: "A youth kills two *ertzainas* by shooting them with a rifle in Itsasondo." The subheading followed: "Mikel Otegi, 23, thought the policemen had come to arrest him because of a fight he had had earlier with another policeman in a bar, and he shot them in the back."[21] The narrative elaborated that, at about 10:30 am, Mikel Otegi was having breakfast in the bar Ibarre when an off-duty *ertzaina* entered. Otegi made an insulting comment aimed at him, followed by several more insults outside the bar. Otegi then hit the *ertzaina* and also his car. Then he went home. He then saw the arrival of an *Ertzaintza* car patrolling the area as part of their routine and happened to be there at that moment. The report says that Otegi, suspecting the *ertzainas* were there to arrest him for the fight he had at the bar, took the rifle and shot them in the back. The *ertzainas*, who had been oblivious to the incident in the bar, had exited their patrol car and were surprised by Otegi, not having time to defend themselves.[22] A statement from the Basque Government's Department of the Interior said that Otegi had been arrested in January 1995 because of his participation in riots throughout the area. The report in *El Diario Vasco* said that Mikel Otegi was sympathetic to the radical nationalist organization Herri Batasuna and hung out with other radical youth.[23]

The radical Basque nationalist newspaper, *Egin,* had a very different headline on its front page: "Two *ertzainas* killed by shots in Itsasondo," along with the subheading, "Neighbors say that Mikel Otegi, arrested for the killings, had been harassed by the *Ertzaintza*."[24] Instead of a photograph of the scene of the crime, *Egin* had a photograph of the *Ertzaintza* closing the road to Otegi's house, with a caption reading, "Officers controlled the area surrounding the farm house." Inside, the newspaper emphasized that Mikel Otegi had been harassed for three years by the *Ertzaintza.* The source of this report were neighbors who, according to *Egin,* said that the *Ertzaintza* controlled all his movements and this was the reason he changed jobs and started driving a truck, "to be able to breathe," and the report insisted that the police harassed radicalized local youth, and the neighbors quoted by *Egin* insisted that they did not "think that Mikel thought that the *Ertzaintza* was going

---

21. *El Diario Vasco,* December 11, 1995, 1.
22. Ibid., 4.
23. Ibid., 5.
24. *Egin,* December 11, 1995, 1.

to arrest him, but rather he reached a situation in which he could not take it any more."[25] I suspect that the neighbors quoted by *Egin* were local youth, since they offered first-hand information about the rock concert, and only young people go to those concerts.

The larger Spanish newspapers emphasized the link between Otegi, radical nationalists, and pathology. *El País* opened with the headline: "A youth shoots two *ertzainas* in the back," above a subheading reading, "The killer has a record for rioting."[26] *El País* followed the version made public by the Department of the Interior of the Basque Government, and also published by *El Diario Vasco*, according to which Otegi had had a fight with an *ertzaina* in the bar Ibarre before he went home on the morning of the tenth. There were, however, some new details: "According to a witness, Otegi told the *ertzaina* who was buying some items in the bar, which is also a general store, 'Drink, drink, later we'll check your alcohol level.'" This sentence, also quoted by *El Diario Vasco,* sounds like a mockery of something a policeman might have told Otegi. "The *ertzaina* did not respond to Otegi and left the bar after paying for his shopping items. Afterwards, Otegi left the bar and slapped the *ertzaina* while insulting him." However, the most salient theme in the report published by *El País* was a connection made between the madness of Otegi and the madness of the radical nationalist movement. Under the headline "Fertile ground for paranoia," reporter José Luis Barbera affirmed that "the killings in Itsasondo suggest the existence of a relationship between the individual paranoia suffered by the killer and the paranoia collectively practiced by those who regularly incite attacks on the officers of the *Ertzaintza.*"[27]

El Mundo made the connection between radical nationalism and the death of the *ertzainas* more explicit than any other newspaper. It started its front page story with the headline, "Two *ertzainas* killed in the latest expression of radical violence in Euskadi [the Basque Country]." Above the headline, an underlined subheading condensed the story: "A radical nationalist youth shot them in the back when he thought they were going to arrest him." And the subheading below the main headline completed the tale: "The presumed assassin, who had been arrested as a result of a confrontation with the Basque police, had just had a conflict with an *ertzaina* whom he called *zipaio* [an insult signifying "betrayer," which radical nationalists use to address the *Ertzaintza*]. He is a member of Jarrai [the radical youth organization associated with the armed group ETA]."[28] In this narrative, the double crime was a sign of the ongoing opposition between radical youth and the *Ertzaintza,* or Basque police. It continued: "The event is the latest expression of the conflict that has pitted radical youth against the *Ertzaintza* since ETA (the nationalist armed group) made the *Ertzaintza* a target of its violence."[29] *El Mundo* established the crime as political in character. It was not the result of an individual act as much as the product of a political position, held not just by radicalized youth but by a terrorist organization. Furthermore, *El*

---

25. Ibid., 12.

26. *El País*, December 11, 1995, 1.

27. Ibid., 17.

28. *El Mundo*, December 11, 1995, 1.

29. Ibid., 1, 7.

Mundo focused on the insult *zipaio* as metonymic of this conflict between radical national-ists and Basque police.[30] In their report, Otegi receded from the scene of the crime. The subject of the killing was not so much him as a collective political subject: the different groups collected under the rubric of radical nationalism.

Fratricidal Anxiety

At the local level the killing at first appeared incomprehensible, an unreadable sign. All the newspapers referred to the puzzlement of the villagers who seemed at a loss for any explanation: According to *El Diario Vasco*, "He seemed a normal boy . . . He belonged to a normal family like any other . . . He sympathized with Herri Batasuna [the radical nationalist party], but that doesn't mean that he was violent. He was very normal, like any other youth of his age."[31] *El Mundo*, too, insisted on the apparent normalcy of Otegi. This newspaper reported that he was sympathetic to radical nationalism but that this was not unusual in his village, where the majority was in fact supportive of radical nationalist parties and the mayor himself was a radical nationalist. *El Mundo* preceded a column on the crime with a quote from a villager: "A normal boy, hardworking, nervous, one of those who throw stones [at the police] . . . The villagers say they do not understand what might have happened to make Otegi react by shooting the two *ertzainas*. The villagers acknowledge that relationships between the *Ertzaintza* and local youth were fraught with tension but 'not to the point of ending like that.'" And the conflict between the *Ertzaintza* and radical youth, which was perceived as the real agent of the crime a page earlier, appeared from the perspective of fellow villagers as routinized and ritualized social exchange: "Until 'the tragedy' yesterday the neighbors of this village looked with indifference at the ren-dezvous between youth and *Ertzaintza*."[32] In the narrative of the villagers reported by these newspapers, the crime was a tragic event, the result of an error, of something snapping out of place in the cultural habitus of political exchange.

The newspaper, *Egin*, reinforced this sense of tragedy, according to which a "normal boy" was arbitrarily struck by a fateful destiny not of his choosing. *Egin* quoted Otegi's friends, for whom the crime was the result of the tight surveillance of youth by the *Ertzaintza*, which anticipated a reaction: "There was a fear that something might happen."[33] For Otegi's friends the crime did not represent a broken habitus of confrontation, but the result of an unbearable feeling of suffocation: "The harassment suffered by Mikel in the last three years was driving him crazy," and, in *Egin*'s report of the friends' narrative, the suffocation felt by Otegi had risen: "He has a strong character that makes him snap quickly . . . the simple sight of an *ertzaina*'s uniform made him nervous . . . he said again

---

30. Ibid., 7.
31. *El Diario Vasco*, December 11, 1995, 5.
32. *El Mundo*, December 11, 1995, 8.
33. *Egin*, December 11, 1995, 11.

and again 'they are always on top of me.'"[34] According to these friends, Otegi said that he preferred to go to Germany rather than endure such control. And they also revealed that, upon returning from a trip to Germany, Otegi commented that the *Ertzaintza* had resumed their presence near his farm: "There they are again," he said. For Otegi's friends, the author of the crime was the *Ertzaintza* and Otegi was the tragic victim, an ordinary youth driven insane by the pressure of police surveillance. *El País* ironized about the narrative of normalcy which perceived an indication of collective paranoia:

> Contrary to what one might think, the presumed assassin of the *ertzainas* is considered a normal youth by his fellow villagers, who did not notice any signs of disequilibrium . . . some remember now that the presumed author of the killings charged against a bank with a backhoe in the course of a riot. His record situates him at the center of the collective paranoia of those who believe they are living in a war, but protest when their social havoc is repressed.[35]

Tragic victim or violent paranoid, Otegi emerges in these narratives as a metonym of something else, as a displaced sign.

The various interpretations surrounding the person of Otegi soon gave rise to political positionings around the event, producing a series of anxious interpretations that locked the incident into a discursive oscillation between madness and political monstrosity. The phantom of fratricide[36] came to haunt the reports, editorials, and articles published by *El Diario Vasco*, the most widely-read local newspaper. There was something eerie in the picture of a farm boy from an all Basque village—a privileged allegory of Basque identity for Basque nationalists—killing Basque policemen, the current embodiment of Basque autonomy, and thus the embodiment of an imagined Basque state. "We are killing ourselves," said the brothers of one of the policemen killed, referring to the Basques.[37] The authority of scientific experts came to sanction the specter of civil confrontation. Javier Elzo, a well-known sociologist, noted that "the crime points to two societies increasingly estranged from each other," fearing "the possibility of confrontation between two parts [of Basque society]." For a professor of psychiatry at the Basque University the killing expressed "a pathology of delirious ideas" [among radical nationalists].[38] Underlying the opinions and comments of scientific experts and political authorities there is an opposition between reason and madness—the reason of democratic coexistence against the madness of nationalist violence. The councilor of the interior of the Basque Government, for example, affirmed that the killing "has no explanation other than the madness of the youth in the radical movement, so fanatic that they have lost reason . . . but the truly guilty ones

---

34. *Egin*, December 12, 1995, 3.

35. *El País*, December 12, 1995, 20.

36. An editorial in *El Diario Vasco*, December 11, 1995, 3, explicitly invoked the phantom of fratricide: "The demonstrations in support of the aggressor accompanied by threats to the *Ertzaintza* brings to the surface how the cancer of fanaticism is weaving a fratricide strategy with very perverse effects on the future."

37. *El Diario Vasco*, December 13, 1995, 1.

38. Javier Elzo in *El Diario Vasco*, December 12, 1995.

are those who stand behind them instigating kids to that collective madness."[39] For political officials like the councilor of the interior and mainstream political leaders, the collective madness of radical nationalists was embodied in the individual madness of Otegi, as he became a metonym of a social movement and a symptom of its malady.

Political leaders accused Herri Batasuna, the radical nationalist party, of responsibility for the killings even though Mikel Otegi was not a member of that party.[40] It was as if Mikel Otegi was the embodiment of the evil side of nationalism, its monstrous face, with the civilized, rational side being represented by the Basque Government and symbolized by the *Ertzaintza*. The crime was also interpreted in the discourse of mainstream newspapers as the logical consequence of a climate of violence unleashed by Basque radical nationalists against the Basque police:

> The double assassination cannot be abstracted from the context of hostility against the *Ertzaintza* promoted by the current strategy of the MLNV [Movimiento de Liberación National Vasco, Basque Movement of National Liberation, an umbrella organization for radical nationalism] and it has devastating consequences for the peaceful and civilized civil coexistence. The danger is that this seed of hate, appealing to some psyches that then degenerate into paranoid pathology, will be justified by attributing to it a political motivation.[41]

The police, the Basque police, thus became another metonymic sign, that of the democratic, rational state and the civility which it is supposed to incarnate. In this discursive field, Otegi and the *Ertzaintza* were both metonymies, displaced signs, traces of something else, and phantasmatic characters in the scene of political violence. For radical nationalists, Otegi was also a symptom, a packed sign, but one speaking of a different and inverse reality than that conveyed by the mass media and the Basque Government.

The reality conveyed by radical nationalists emerged as the madness of the Basque police becoming increasingly violent against nationalist youth, and was materialized as nervousness and a sense of being harassed by the police. Jon Idigoras, a leader of Herri Batasuna, said, "Nobody should be surprised if in this situation [of growing police violence] we see more cases like Otegi. They are no more than the product of impotence and rage produced by the constant aggressions that we are suffering." Otegi was, thus, for radical nationalists a sign of collective impotence and rage, and a discourse of passion and suffering was attached to the crime. For radical nationalists it was the Basque Government and its councilor of the interior that created the conditions leading to the killing. In their discourse, Otegi became a victim of "civil nationalism," a victim of the state in its incarnation as Basque government and Basque police, thus questioning the civility of those institutions. And radical nationalists too used the language of madness to accuse the Basque authorities in charge of the Basque police: "They should be in the hands of a psychiatrist for sending seven thousand *cipayos* (a derogatory name for the *Ertzaintza*) to act

---

39. *El Diario Vasco*, December 12, 1995, 4.
40. Ibid.
41. *El Diario Vasco*, December 11, 1995, 3.

brutally"[42] In the discourse of radical nationalism, then, the rationality of the state was crazy.

In these two sets of political discourses, that of civil nationalism as state and radical nationalism as victim, the border between rationality and madness was blurred. Otegi was mad but rational. The state was rational but mad. In the days that followed the event, local newspapers constructed the meaning of the killings along incommensurable and speculative realities: a sign of an increasingly violent and "crazy" youth political culture and the result of an increasingly violent state embodied in a "crazy" (Basque) police. Mikel Otegi, the perpetrator, remained silent, like a ghost, the event itself inscrutable. The specter of fratricide violence hovered over the public sphere. It is this spectral reality seeping through the cracks of discursive statements that I am interested in tracking here. For the specter of fratricide violence is the manifestation of a deep and troubled anxiety about the meaning and boundaries of being Basque; that is, about the existence of difference within Basque national identity and the politics of such difference. What one might grasp through the discourse on Otegi's killings is a terrible fear, a panic, in the face of a split at the very core of Basque national identity; a split in the very being and imagining of the Basque nation; a split embodied in the emblematic figures of young *encapuchados* and young *ertzainas*. This strangeness at the heart of the familiar is precisely what Freud calls the uncanny. It produces a spectral reality, for the specter is none other than—like Otegi—the familiar stranger (Gordon 1997), the recurrent "visibility of the invisible" (Derrida 1997: 101), a kind of suppressed knowledge embodied in immaterial matter. It is to this uncanny sense, as it manifests in the rumors and stories of shadowy political violence, that I turn next.

The Political Uncanny

In the Basque Country, a traumatic political real surfaces as rumor-filled stories erupting suddenly in the density of public life, whispered from ear to ear, in kitchens and corners, in bars and streets, in a public space filled with the dense materiality of words and images, murals, posters, leaflets, banners and all sort of signs. I first heard about Otegi in the course of one such whispering conversation held in 1997, as I walked through the bars and streets of Bilbao, invested with the political intimacy of a secret knowledge that can turn dangerous in the ears of the wrong person.[43]

As we walked through the labyrinthine, narrow streets and plazas of the old part of Bilbao, Jesús, a soft-spoken and soft-mannered man in his early twenties, began to talk about the *Ertzaintza*, the Basque police, as if prompted by memories sprouting out of the urban landscape. "The *Ertzaintza* are crazy," he said:

---

42. *Egin*, December 16, 1995.

43. In the world of Basque political radicalism, *talk* is dangerous, invested with the threat of informers and the violence of the state. For this same reason, *talk* is also invested with the intimacy of trust and fear.

They are ready to repress anything that goes out of their control. The other day, for example, the unemployed were in this plaza having a meeting, as they do every week, and the police came all of a sudden with their vans and their sirens all dressed in riot gear and told them to disperse in two minutes. For no reason! They had always met there. They are increasingly belligerent and aggressive.

I heard many stories about the "craziness" of the Basque police in the following months. "The way the Basque police are acting is excessive," said Jesús. "I think they are doing experiments with some towns, like Hernani and Rentería" (both well known as radical towns). Itziar, a girl from Hernani, told me on another occasion that they used to laugh at the Basque police, but "now we don't laugh anymore. We are frightened. With the national police or the Civil Guard you always knew what they were up to, they either beat you or they didn't, but with the Basque police you never know . . . you can be doing nothing and they come and beat the hell out of you; they are crazy."

Jesús and the rest of us had come into one of the bars dotting the old part of the city and were sitting at a table eating lunch. There were very few people in the bar and indeed out in the streets, but Jesús was whispering and looking down, and over his shoulder from time to time, as if to make sure nobody else was listening. "They broke my arm after a demonstration. There wasn't even a riot or anything, and suddenly this *ertzaina* throws me to the ground shouting "*puto vasco de mierda*" (damned shitty Basque) and started beating me with his wooden baton. And they're Basque! I haven't gone to a demonstration since then. I'm too scared." His friend said that he has also been followed by the police. "For three months," said Jesús. "You got into the car and it was you and three other cars behind. You could go through a check point with no problem, they'd see the police cars behind you and let you pass. There were constantly several plainclothes policemen behind me, no matter where I went. It creates a lot of panic," he said, "and paranoia. It's very frightening and it's difficult to stay calm. Some people react violently and just go and get a gun" [meaning, enroll in the armed organization ETA]. This is when I heard about Otegi for the first time, along with Anuk, a young member of ETA who claimed to have been abducted by the *Ertzaintza*. Jesús continued, "This poor guy, Otegi, who shot two *ertzainas* . . . it could have happened to anybody . . . it's terrible that there are two people dead but it's not strange. The presence of the *Ertzaintza* is so suffocating."

I remembered the flow of talk the night before in one of the radical bars in the old part of Bilbao. Somebody entered the bar with a story about the *Ertzaintza* waiting for some high-school students at the door of their houses, intimidating them with threats of violence if they continued with their radical activities. The story provoked the outrage of all those present and generated a string of similar tales. "That's what they're doing now," said Marga, "and they've taken to strip searching women detainees, that's how they terrorize the girls." "People don't know about this," said Jesús, "because you don't see it, it's never reported; the mass media is distorting reality. They're manipulating what's happening. What happened to this guy, for example—what was his name, Anuk?—was terrible." "What happened?" I asked. Jesús replied:

He was kidnapped by the Basque police and they did all sort of things to him, experiment-
ed with him giving him drugs, and using psychological techniques. Then they let him go but
they were following him all the time. He managed to send a letter to the leadership of
ETA—you see, he was a militant—in which he told about what was happening. He appeared
a few days later with a toy gun in his hand in front of an old garage and almost immediately the *Ertzaintza* and the Spanish police came on the scene and fought among themselves
to arrest him. It was clear that they were waiting for him, that this was something prepared. And then the national police took him to their station and obviously he couldn't take
it anymore and threw himself out of the window.

For the young *encapuchados* involved in defacing the state with Molotov cocktails, the
Ertzaintza had become, alongside the Spanish police or the Civil Guard, the embodiment of
a powerful and ghostly state. This ghostliness becomes materialized in the black mask
that *ertzainas* wear underneath their helmets; a mask that they call *verdugillo*, or little exe-
cutioner. For Tasio—a vocal Basque policeman—the use of masks is defeating because he
thinks it conveys policemen's fear and iconically blurs the line between terrorism and policing, between the terror of Law and the law of terror: "When you see the images of the
police with masks and the terrorists without them you realize that the police have failed
as such." The masked police evoke an image of the state as outlaw. Yet for Tasio, police
failure does not reside in the self-attribution of a sovereign power it does not have, but
rather in the public acknowledgment of the arbitrary nature of the police force. Hidden
under the mask, disguised by the *verdugillo*, individual policemen are not easily accountable.
For Tasio, the *verdugillo* promotes what he called "the psychology of impunity." The reasoning accompanying this psychological dynamic is that if the *encapuchados* can attack the
ertzainas under cover of their masks so can the masked *ertzainas* get back at the *encapuchados*. "There is a lot of play between the *encapuchados* and the *ertzainas*," said Tasio. The
Ertzaintza thus becomes for radical nationalists an object of fear and resentment, a powerful shadow that is and isn't; a familiar figure turned stranger, a betrayer. These rumor-
filled stories of familiar and unpredictable violence circulate freely in the dense public
sphere of Basque politics, in bars and streets, in commentaries and informal chats, constituting the political imaginary of radical nationalists, a social universe bound by fear of
a strangeness within.

The Inverted Double

The uncanny feeling of the familiar strange is not, however, the monopoly of radical
nationalists. On the other side of the political looking-glass, the *ertzainas'* reality seems
deeply affected by their encounters with the *encapuchados* who are the embodiment of the
familiar strange. They, too, are the object of all sorts of rumors about their identity. Jayone, head of an *Ertzaintza* patrol, follows the same routes through the streets every day.
She thinks that the *encapuchados* are manipulated by older radical nationalists. "Some of
those people are dogmatic, they are like a sect and you cannot talk to them because they
don't listen or think by themselves," she said. She thinks that some are idealists and oth-

ers are hired to create trouble. "A fellow officer told me," she said, "that his sister was caught in a riot and she took refuge in the hall of an apartment building along with a group of young guys; and an older man entered the building, took his wallet out of his pocket and gave 5,000 pesetas [around $40] to each of them. The sister of this officer, afraid of being discovered as an outside presence, took the money and left." Jayone uses this example to claim that some *encapuchados* are paid, and to lend force to her claim, adds that most *ertzainas* think so too.

As Jayone talked, I remembered the story told by my neighbor, a woman in her fifties who like many of her generation does not approve of the sabotage and arbitrary rioting, even though she sympathizes with radical nationalists. She, too, wondered about the identity of the *encapuchados* and thought that some of them might be paid by the "state" to act as provocateurs and create bad press for radical nationalists. "They are not our people," she said. And her story followed the same plot as that of Jayone, only the paying agent was different. My neighbor assured me that, after a riot in the old city, she herself once saw an old man give 5,000 pesetas to a young fellow. She said she told them they had no shame and they both lowered their heads, and this is how she knew that this was payment for stirring trouble. Rumors of secret agents and paid provocateurs are common in contexts of political violence.[44] Juan, a savvy cultural activist, laughs at the story when I ask him what he thinks about the rumors of paid *encapuchados*. "Oh sure, I too have heard them, all the stories have the same plot," he says, and he repeats it to me down to the 5,000 pesetas. "So you, too, have heard them?" I ask. "Of course, it's part of the political folklore," he replies.

Yet to me this mirroring conspiracy theory seems an attempt to give form to, and thus exercise a certain amount of control over, a fearful, ghostly reality of violence. Jayone said that there is no doubt that the *encapuchados* are organized in a secret structure that she calls "commandos Y." "We [the *ertzainas*] believe that they [the commandos Y] are organized in the following way: a group with a leader that only knows the leader of another group that in turn only knows the leader of another group, etc. That is the structure that we think they have." Her friend, however, thinks that the *encapuchados* are local youth who do not have anything better to do. He said that, even when wearing masks, he can tell who they are by such things as the way they walk, because they are local youths and everybody knows them. Both familiar and strange, the *encapuchados* seem to organize the experience of being a Basque police officer as one dominated by fear. Indeed, fear seems so omnipresent that, like the *encapuchados*, *ertzainas* were willing to talk with me only after many reassurances and mediation by trusted intermediaries. Still, Jayone does not want to be recorded, and as we talked in her living room, she said with a nervous voice that I could take notes but not a recording:

> The central experience as patrolling *ertzainas* is fear. The *encapuchados* are a source of fear. With the *encapuchados* you have a sense of helplessness, a sense that you can be attacked at

---

44. See for example Tambiah (1997), Feldman (2000), and Spencer (2000).

any moment and you cannot do anything, because they are the ones who throw stones or flares or Molotov cocktails at you. And you are in there, trapped in the small space of a van or a car and are just an easy target. And if you hit somebody you can be punished for it. You feel very impotent and vulnerable, particularly in the face of the judicial system because they are ready to find a culprit and the penalties are higher for us than the ones they give to these youths.

She also told how the *Ertzaintza* was called one night to a small town,

Because somebody had set a trash container on fire. A van went and it turned out to be an ambush. More than a hundred *encapuchados* emerged suddenly, throwing stones, and the *Ertzaintza* started shooting rubber bullets and somebody hit one of the *encapuchados* in the eye. There was a whole investigation until they found the officer who had hit the guy in the eye, which is something very difficult to know because there are several people shooting at once and all of them are wearing masks.

Jayone told the story of the ambush as an illustration of the vulnerability that the *Ertzaintza* feels in the face of the *encapuchados*, and in the face of the Law which she herself embodies as a policewoman. In her story, the Basque police appear as a particularly alienated body: at once an agent of the Law and a subject who fears the Law; a split subject being the Law and looking at it from the outside. The police as Law are an agent of violence and itself subjected to the all encompassing violence of the Law. The police thus appear, in stories like that told by Jayone, not so much as a subject capable of transgressing the Law, as the Law's abject side; a side without which the order of the Law cannot exist yet one which remains outside its domain of recognition: its phantasm.

Jayone's story is a remarkable mirror of those rumored by young radicals. Like the latter, the *Ertzaintza* experiences the *encapuchados* as spectral subjects of violence, a reality governing their lives yet un-apprehensible. And, like the *encapuchados*, such spectral violence that can erupt unexpectedly at any moment works through the production of fear, which then circulates within a strange cultural economy spawning a universe of mimetic practices between the young radical *encapuchados* and the Basque police, the other *encapuchados*, a ritualized *fort-da* play[45] that futilely attempts to master the absent presence of the other. So, too, the *ertzainas* resent and distrust the Law, which in the shape of the judicial apparatus can turn against them. As with the young radicals, for the police, the production of a culprit is an arbitrary process that renders the space of the Law a space of vulnerability. There is a measure of arbitrariness in the detention and charge of radical youngsters. Since the activists are covered by a hood and the arrested youth generally have their faces uncovered at the moment of being arrested, there is no way of telling who was doing what. Jayone's description of the production of a culprit after a young man was shot with a rubber bullet echoes the same situation. This sense of defenselessness that the police feel

---

45. A game invented by Freud's grandson, that he interpreted as the child's attempt to assert mastery through play.

in the face of the Law reached the level of paroxysm with the outcome of Mikel Otegi's trial.

In a shocking verdict, a popular jury found Otegi not guilty, heeding the defense's argument that Otegi's killings were the consequence of a heightened feeling of persecution that translated into a moment of mad rage. Otegi was set free. "That was *very, very* hard," said Jayone. She continued,

> It hurt very deeply because you felt totally vulnerable and impotent, totally at their mercy, it is like they [the Law] had given them [radical nationalists] impunity to do anything. There are two people dead and he is *free*! He is not in a psychiatric hospital or anything like that, he is free. And the next day you are on the street on duty and see a demonstration of young radicals shouting, "Mikel *askatua*" [Mikel Free] and applauding, and you have to be there listening to it and you cannot do anything because they are not doing anything illegal, they are just shouting! I saw fellow officers cry with anger.

The Sentence

On March 6, 1997 Mikel Otegi stood before the Law for the second time. The doors of the justice court had closed at the request of the jury, composed of eight women and one man. The jury found the defendant not guilty of the charge of assassination pursued by the prosecution. The jury considered that Otegi was temporarily alienated from himself at the moment of the crime. He was not in control of his will and thus "not responsible for his acts when he killed two *ertzainas*."[46] Mikel Otegi left the prison at 8:10 a.m. His freedom triggered shocked reactions of anger and disbelief among the relatives of the two policemen killed and the members of the Basque police. The father of one of the *ertzainas* killed resorted to the language of madness to express his shock: "It [the verdict] is crazy." The result of the trial appeared to have triggered the same de-realization of reality as the killings themselves. The verdict also affected the institution of the law itself. The prosecution accused the presiding judge of not properly advising the jury and manifested their decision to appeal the sentence. The judge answered that neither the defense nor the prosecution had objected to his instructions.[47] There was no formal misconduct. The case was brought to the Supreme Justice Court of the Basque Country with an appeal to overturn the sentence. The institution of the jury, introduced in Spain in 1996 as a major symbol of democratic reform, came under question. The state prosecutor, for example, challenged the appropriateness of popular juries in the Basque Country when it came to politicized cases such as that of Mikel Otegi. For him, the political tension and climate of intimidation dominant in the Basque Country impaired the impartial judgment of the members of the jury.[48] While the Supreme Court of the Basque Country studied the appeal of

---

46. *El Diario Vasco*, March 7, 1997, 1.

47. See, for example, *El Diario Vasco*, March 7, 1997; *El Mundo*, March 22, 1997 and June 9, 1997; and *Egin*, April 29, 1997.

48. See Interview with Luís Navajas, Chief Prosecutor of the Provincial Court. *El País*, June 9, 1997, 21.

Otegi's sentence, several minor suits were filed. The *ertzaina* with whom Mikel Otegi had a fight the morning of the killing, filed a suit against Otegi for aggression to authority. In turn, Otegi filed a suit against the *ertzainas* who arrested him after the crime, alleging mistreatment. Because of the pending accusation against him, Otegi is deprived of his passport by judicial order. Yet on June 7, 1997 the passport was returned to Otegi after the court found the retention unwarranted.[49]

Otegi remained as silent, after he was set free, as he had been during the time that lapsed from the killings to the trial. In the face of the polemic adjudication and the controversy that followed, he remained a ghostly figure. He had been before the Law for the second time and for the second time the result of this encounter was shock. What happened the second time is not any clearer than what happened the first time he came up before the Law. If the killings were the effect of an unconscious agency, an absent presence, Otegi's liberation had the effect of a state of indecision and doubt, an impossibility to know. It was this doubt, in relation to Otegi's agency, that the jurors invoked to absolve him from all charges. This space of dubitation, undecidability and absence of consciousness seem to point to a ghostly, uncanny presence, to an-Other agency at the heart of political violence in the Basque Country. I have been arguing that such a presence, capable of throwing into disarray the actors in this scene—the Law and the radicals who defy it—such a presence might indeed be the negated, unacknowledged presence of the other within. The presence of the state, as the enemy of radical nationalists, is no longer outside but inside the national self, a self that they must now identify with and fight against. The terror of fratricide that hovered over the shocked public in the Basque Country might be also the terror of self-destruction. For what is really terrifying is that the boundary that separated Otegi and the policemen he killed is blurred in the nationalist imaginary. What Otegi faced that fateful morning might, then, be just a mirror image of himself, a law of the father whose punishing authority is all the more threatening because it is inside oneself. As in Kafka's short story, Otegi's law was made just for him. Yet Otegi would not be important were he not an emblem, indeed an allegory of an instability, a certain state of lack (or out) of control inherent in the model of the nation-state itself. It is, indeed, that diminutive, taken-for-granted hyphen, that tiny gap between nation and state that is the site of a traumatic constitution of the nation, where the *jouissance* of national identification encounters the ruthlessness of violent difference.

Postscript: The Supreme Court of the Basque Country annulled the sentence that had declared Mikel Otegi not guilty.[50] By then, Mikel Otegi had disappeared, banished, becoming—literally—a famous ghost.

---

49. See *Egin*, June 7, 1997.

50. See Sentencia del Tribunal Superior de Justicia del País Vasco. Sala de lo Civil y Penal, June 26, 1997. Ponente: Sr. Zorrilla Ruiz.

CHAPTER 10

Of Hens, Hoods, and Other Political Beasts: What Metaphoric Performances Hide[1]

Meanings and Passions

One of the things that drew me to James Fernandez's work at the beginning of my anthropological career was his careful attention to the play of affect in culture. I was then looking for a way to think about that mysterious state that Fernandez calls "the inchoate" and which I saw as the driving force of intense political experience. Not that I knew about it at the time. I was twenty-five years old then and in a theoretically inchoate state myself, puzzling about what it is that moves people to passionate nationalist sentiment and how was that moving affect accomplished. I knew then that no conventional theory of nationalism could account for the depth of feeling that drove people to risk their lives and to commit violence for the Basque nation. Fernandez's theory of tropes proved particularly illuminating. For, lurking behind and running throughout Fernandez's theory of tropes, there was a theory of the play of affect in culture, a theory that spoke of culture as a space where meanings were indeterminate and shifting, subject to the permanent play of ambiguity, ambivalence and paradox in people's experience, a theory of shifting affects whose mastery by way of metaphoric predication was temporary and fragile.

When I arrived at the bucolic retreat of Princeton University by the kind hand of Jim Fernandez, I had two suitcases and a carry-on bag filled with the turbulent political experience of more than a decade of political activism. I had witnessed first-hand the political effervescence of the end of a dictatorship, the flourishing of the political imagination, the explosion of social debate, the emergence of all sorts of social movements, the energy and the will to shape the future. I had marched countless times in political demonstrations, confronted heavily-armed police with little more than political conviction and two legs on which to run. I knew friends who had been injured in such demonstrations and killed by paramilitary squads. I saw the formation of an autonomous Basque Government and the

1. Unpublished manuscript. Paper presented for the panel, "Movements of Moral Imagination: The An-trope-ology of James Fernandez," at the *Annual Meeting of the American Anthropological Association*, Chicago, November 17–21, 1999.

fissuring of long-standing friendships over the definition of Basque nationhood. Life in the Basque Country, where I was born and lived until I moved to Princeton, was vertiginous and intensely passionate. And nationalist passions filled the moral imagination of the emergent Spanish democracy. Nationalist passions in the Basque Country not only generated a great deal of social liveliness, they also engendered a great deal of violence that led to disillusion and traumatic wounds. This political experience was my historical baggage that I intended to sort out when I came to Princeton University.

The question of nationalist passion continues to vex theorists of nationalism. Part of the problem has been a tendency to privilege representation as transparent locus of nationalist affect. Thus, for example Benedict Anderson (1983) links the production of love for the nation to the use of familial and kinship metaphors in nationalist rhetoric. But, just as surely, such metaphors must also trigger feelings of hostility, loss, ambivalence and rivalry—so much a part of that complex reality we call family.[2] While the nation is surely imagined and thus constituted in and through narrative (Bhabha 1990), and while the complexities of its internal differences are delicately negotiated through the allegories of romantic and filial love (Mosse 1985; Parker et al. 1992; Sommer 1990), such images also execute complex operations of erasure. James Siegel (1998) has recently argued that in using the family as metaphoric predication for the emerging Indonesian nation, the state triggered not only nationalist fervor, but also a displacement of authority from the family to the nation. The moral authority that was formerly invested in parents was now appropriated by the nation, while families became morally suspect. This displacement of feeling and moral authority from the family to the nation turned the family into a discursive locus for the disallowed violence of the state. The national family became "the dark at the bottom of the stairs," to use a rich Fernandezian trope, the site of something frightening that remains displaced, ghostly.

What is often erased in the metaphorics of the nation (and yet contained by it) is precisely the complications of history, the contingencies of hostility, power, loss and ambivalence that come to form part of the national being as haunting phantoms.[3] Such phantomatic presences produce a sliding in the metaphoric association of nation and family, a sliding that opens a space of indeterminacy of meaning precisely at the very moment when meaning is fixed by virtue of metaphoric predication. This space of indeterminacy is what makes metaphoric performance both powerful and fleeting.

Rather than take it for granted, the link between an image and an affective state (of desire, fear, exultation, or contempt) taking hold of people in the theater of politics seems to me in need of interpretation. For, after all, the power of metaphors does not reside in the images themselves but, as Fernandez has noted, in their connection to our experience

---

2. There are a number of important studies that have complicated the mapping of the nation, on the topography of family, either by politicizing the family or complicating the nation through a topography of loss. See, for example, Borneman (1992), Satner (1990), Ivy (1995).

3. There are of course important exceptions. Three wonderful examples are Ivy (1997), Berlant (1997) and Siegel (1998).

through rich and equivocal condensation. It is this equivocal nature of metaphor, its play of presences and absences, of the absent present, that interests me here. What I propose is to explore such equivocality through a reading of Fernandez's work sensitive to psychoanalysis.

There is much affinity with psychoanalysis in Fernandez's theory of tropes, even though such an affinity remains inchoate in Fernandez' work, searching for expression in rich metaphors such as "the dark at the bottom of the stairs." The major achievement of psychoanalysis was the discovery of the unconscious. For Freud, the royal road to the unconscious was the interpretation of dreams. Condensation and displacement are the major operations by which meaning is generated in dreams,[4] and it is through these operations that the discourse of the unconscious is produced. For Lacan, condensation is "the structure of the superimposition that metaphor takes as its field" (1977: 160), while displacement is "that veering off of signification that we see in metonymy, and which from its first appearance in Freud is represented as the most appropriate means used by the unconscious to foil censorship" (1977: 160). Lacan argues that the function of condensation and displacement in the dream-work is the same as that of metaphor and metonymy in discourse; and, we could add, following Fernandez, in culture.[5] Fernandez's theory of culture reminds me of Freud's theory of dreams. For Freud, the dream is a rebus. And is not the "argument of images" (that for Fernandez defines culture) also a rebus—a puzzle deriving its meaning from a particular semantic field, or "qualitative space"? The interpretation of metaphoric images leads Fernandez to a topographic model of culture, just like the interpretation of dreams led Freud to a topographic model of the psyche. "I am inordinately attracted to it," Fernandez says before he describes it in this way: "Culture is a quality space of dimensions of continua, and society is a movement about the pronouns [we could say subjects] within this space" (1986: 12).[6] The privileged force moving "pronouns" (subjects) is, for Fernandez, metaphor. Metaphors not only provide identity, they *do* things; most notoriously, they "accomplish affective movement" (1986: 38), and in so doing, "facilitate [or inhibit, as the case may be] performance" (1986: 7). In this article, I am particularly interested in this capacity of metaphor to "do" things, this force not only to move people but to change scenarios. And I am particularly intrigued by the question of how this operation is performed in the space of political culture.

---

4. Victor Turner took also condensation and displacement as the basic operations through which symbolic meaning is generated in culture.

5. See for example Fernandez's seminal article "The Mission of Metaphor in Expressive Culture" (1974) reproduced in Fernandez (1986).

6. I am using subject in brackets to clarify the meaning of pronoun for those readers who might not be very familiar with Fernandez's work. In at least one instance, Fernandez uses the term subject as a synonym for pronoun: "A metaphor is a predication upon a subject of an object of a domain to which the subject belongs only by a stretch of the imagination." "The Mission of Metaphor in Expressive Culture" (1986: 37). The inchoate pronoun seems to me to be close to post-structuralist theories of the subject, where the subject is not constituted by an originary essence (consciousness, the soul...) but is constituted through the predicaments of culture and social institutions.

"Metaphors," Fernandez says, "arise in fantasy" and are then put into action (1986: 21). But how does fantasy relate to the work of metaphor? What are the states and fantasies that make metaphors not just significant, but forceful? Much of Fernandez's work concentrates on the semantic and affective effects of metaphoric predication, but what is happening in the space between the metaphoric signifier and the signified? In other words, between the pronoun (subject) and the metaphor? For Lacan, "the creative spark of the metaphor does not spring from the presentation of two images, that is, of two signifiers equally actualized. It flashes between two signifiers, one of which has taken the place of the other in the signifying chain; the occulted signifier remains present through its (metonymic) connection with the rest of the chain" (1977: 157). In other words, metaphors are signifying condensations which, by virtue of metonymic displacements, organize and disguise signification, and in the affective domain, organize and disguise (unconscious) terror, desires and fantasies. If the argument of images in culture closely resembles that of the dream, then, like the dream, it may function through disguise as much as through predication. And if disguise is what makes metaphoric predication both possible and powerful, then attention to metonymic circumventions appears crucial to understand the performative effects of metaphor. In an article devoted to metonymy, Durham and Fernandez (1991) discuss the ethnographic importance of metonymic association. Yet the question of affect, so important to most of Fernandez's work on metaphor, is oddly absent in the article on metonymy. In this article, I try to recapture the affective moves linked to metonymic association as they play in the arena of nationalist politics. I am interested in the imaginary space opened up by metaphoric predication and disguise, in the ways this imaginary space enables performances, and in what those performances may or may not do.

Of Hens and Ducks: Struggling for Figuration

Let me turn first to Northern Ireland, where a scene takes place in the streets of Belfast during the terrifying and turbulent time of the early 1970s:

The British army had swiftly transformed from a peacekeeping force to a force of occupation. Their focus had shifted from an initial mission of protecting Catholic neighborhoods from the attacks by Protestant mobs, to that of neutralizing the emerging yet rapidly-growing Irish Republican Army (IRA). The IRA had been part of Irish political culture for a long time. It fought the war of independence against Britain and played a part in the civil war that ensued after the signing of the agreement to partition the island in 1922. In Northern Ireland, however, it had been become nothing more than a nominal force and by the early 1960s, it had practically disappeared. However, the repression of the civil rights movement in the late 1960s, and the accompanying intimidation of Catholics, led to a resurgence of the IRA. Its initial purpose was to defend Catholic neighborhoods against mobs of police and Protestant loyalists, before the British army was sent in to keep the peace. The reborn IRA was composed mainly of ordinary young people drawn to it by the political situation of widespread intimidation. In an attempt to curtail its development, the government introduced a policy of internment without trial. Internment led to the arrest of hundreds of young people in the poor Catholic districts of Belfast with catastrophic political consequences. Not only did it fail to dismantle the IRA, but it antagonized the whole Catholic minority who felt victimized again.

The British army raided houses at night when they could catch people by surprise. It was then that Irish women decided to take action and organize themselves to alert neighbors of the presence of the British army in the vicinity, protest against the raids, and, if possible, prevent the arrests of relatives and neighbors. Groups of working-class women began to leave their houses at night to patrol the streets in an attempt to defend their neighborhoods against the surprise of the British Army. My neighbor Claire laughed as she narrated the story one evening in her living room:

> We got together a group of women in the neighborhood. Men and boys were being arrested all the time and the situation got so bad that we decided we had to do something. So we went out at night armed with whistles and garbage bin lids, and as soon as we saw a military patrol we started to bang the lids against the pavement and blow the whistles. Now, the military were called duck patrols so we called ourselves the hen patrols for a laugh and our mission was to follow the soldiers everywhere they went and make noise. We made a lot of noise, and noise can be frightening. I remember a soldier saying that he could handle the men but not the women. We really made them nervous; they really didn't know how to react. One time there was a fellow being arrested in a house and we were outside [on the street] making a lot of noise, and when the soldiers came out [of the house] we suddenly disappeared. You could hear a pin dropping, you know, the silence was very intense after the noise. The soldiers who had all their rifles and had been kicking us in the demonstrations were shaking, panicking, while we were in my house giggling away behind the curtains. They were terrified! We waited five minutes and went back to the street and started all over again. There was this woman in my house whose son had been interned, and she said, "My god, Claire, I never saw a color like that in their face." They were yellow, terrified! All was over when the fellow was finally taken away. Generally there was nothing you could do but bang the bin lids but that time we went home and left them in the street wondering what was going to happen to them, if somebody was going to shoot them. We had some laughs but it was very frightening.

In telling her story Claire still relished the power of women's performance to reverse a situation of disempowerment, if only temporarily. If metaphors can create a scenario, then certain performances demand appropriate metaphors. Women's resistance to a threatening army might become more effective if it is placed in the plane of parodic subversion through which a group of disempowered women can transpose political action to an imaginative scenario, where both parties are still different "species" (ducks and hens), but more comparable in power. At the level of public culture, the metaphor is operative, however, through its associative metonymic links that remain implicit in the metaphoric performance. Hens are domestic animals while ducks are not. This domesticity establishes a link of continuity between hens and women both associated with the area of the domesticity in the culture of Northern Ireland. At the same time, the attacks on Catholic areas and the introduction of internment had endowed the public space (streets) of these areas with the kind of intimacy, complicity and inner knowledge characteristic of the familial, domestic domain associated with women. Claire's narrative is a good example of that intimate complicity. Family and community constituted a semantic continuum rather than separate fields. While the whole Catholic areas became domestic, the British Army became occupying and violent foreigners and Protestant loyalists threatening outsiders. Since these areas are Irish Nationalist, and the soldiers were British, community became associated with the Irish nation, again under colonial assault. Thus, in many ways what makes this metaphoric predication of the hen patrols powerful is the opposition between intimate domesticity and violent outsiders, in which the position of power is reversed by suggesting an image of the domestic (hens-women-community-nation) sending the invading outsiders (ducks-men-state) flying away. This is also a reversal of the colonial structure played out in the Catholic working-class communities of Northern Ireland. These are some of the metonymic links, traces of the history and social culture that, being implicit and probably unconscious to the performance of the metaphor, make such performance socially and personally forceful. These associations may also explain the joyous feeling of humor and laughter that the evocation of the hen patrols unfailingly triggered in women and often in men, too. For the metaphor also embodies an image of gender reversal that empowers women and which is at the core of the pleasure that women feel in recalling the experience. But the laughter that Claire could still summon years after the event, speaks also of terror. For the humor of the parody of hens chasing ducks, of women frightening fully-armed soldiers with garbage bin lids and whistles, disguises the fear of military violence, the terror of a situation that becomes manageable by virtue of metaphoric predication and humorous reversal; a tragicomedy where political actors can also be performers.

If this story of metaphoric subversion speaks of the power of metaphor to shift feelings and shift social scenarios, opening thus novel forms of agency, it also speaks of the indeterminate character of the metaphoric operation, its signifying instability subject to multiple associations and the forces triggered by performance. The metaphoric play that permits political subversion can just as easily be canceled out by literalization aimed at separating ruthlessly blurred domains of experience.

The hen patrols, in their audacious and raucous defiance, became an image of community and indeed nationalist resistance. The containment of such resistance was then predicated on metaphoric destruction, a re-instauration of a scene of disempowerment where women could be deprived of empowering associations and thus put "in their place." The military began to shoot women who were part of the hen patrols—an unthinkable act at the time. In so doing, the military was not just killing women but also community resistance. Yet by doing so, the army also created a new scenario, one in which the bodies of women rather that their agency became a metaphor of the nation. Metaphors thus not only move people in an affective space, sometimes they move them independently of their will by moving political scenarios. The metonymic associations that make possible the performative effects (and affects) of metaphor, can also move social forces in unpredictable ways. This play of forces is, of course, a play of power that has some implications for how we think of the inchoate as it plays in political affairs.

What Metaphor Denies, or the Travails of Identity

Although metonymy has not received much attention by scholars, including himself, Fernandez nevertheless remains us that, as Levi-Strauss noted, the transformation of metaphor is achieved in metonymy (Fernandez 1986: 45; Durham and Fernandez 1991: 193). How is such a transformation accomplished in social reality? Metonymy, Lacan tells us, is "the most appropriate means by which the unconscious foils censorship" (1977: 160). In this sense, metonymic associations are like a series of clues about what is denied or obscured in the social workings of metaphor. These clues do not follow a straight path but a meandering and elusive one that requires for its interpretation a knowledge "dependent upon an immersion in culture" (Durham and Fernandez 1991: 196). The next example comes from my own land—the Basque Country—whose political culture has been part of my life and is my object of research. My goal here is to follow the metonymic clues of a powerful political metaphor—*cipayo*—which has proved to be quite pernicious in contemporary Basque political culture. I intend to provide a context of associations that might provide an understanding of what this metaphor *cipayo* does, and what it disguises by virtue of its predication. I am interested in the affects and ideas that give rise to the metaphor, and in those that the metaphor triggers. I want to know how those affects and ideas are linked to performative scenarios. I will begin by recounting a recurrent political performance, the scene of a riot.

The Riots of Betrayal

In 1997, I accompanied my mother in a demonstration in support of a negotiated peace process in the Basque Country that for more than thirty years had been the motivator of much political violence, emanating as much from the radical group ETA as from the security forces of the state. The demonstration aimed to pressure the Spanish government to negotiate a cease-fire with ETA. It took place in my home town, San Sebastián, and attracted many people of all ages who walked peacefully through the main streets of the city. The demonstration finished in the historic center of the city with a series of speeches by well-known personalities of the cultural and political world. This old part (*parte vieja*) of the city is a residential and commercial area of narrow cobbled streets and old buildings colored by the presence of political banners, posters, and graffiti. It has become a major space of entertainment, bustling with the activity of its endless bars and restaurants. With the political speeches now over, my mother and I ventured into the old streets of the *parte vieja* to enjoy an evening stroll and a sampling of the excellent *tapas* for which San Sebastián is famous. The area was now filled with people leisurely moving through the streets, in and out of bars. Soon after we began our stroll, I saw a group of about forty teenagers with their faces covered with kerchiefs and hoods advancing through a side street with Molotov cocktails (homemade petrol bombs) in their hands. People walking in that street headed for the closest intersection to get out of the way, and stood there watching the action, just as we did. The youths walked toward the boulevard that separates the *parte vieja* from the modern part of the city, where a van of the *Ertzaintza* (Basque police) is usually stationed. When they came within throwing distance, they launched their Molotov cocktails at the *Ertzaintza*, while at the same time calling them *cipayos asesinos* (assassin *sipais*). Within a few minutes, several more *Ertzaintza* vehicles arrived on the scene. Policemen jumped out and barricaded themselves at one end of the street from where the youths had thrown the petrol bombs. They were in full riot gear, their faces hidden under black balaclavas, riot-control arms and shields in their hands. By now, the youths had taken cover behind the corner of a street intersection and were shouting insults, calling the police *cipayos* and assassins. The *ertzainas* (Basque policemen and policewomen) started shooting rubber bullets and occasional tear gas cans. The youths threw firecrackers and stones at them. The *ertzainas* retaliated with more rubber bullets. Then the youths played a diversionary tactic and began the same routine in other streets, forcing the engagement of more *ertzainas*. A battle between masked police and masked youth had developed under the eyes of bystanders, who interrupted their stroll from bar to bar to watch the spectacle from the safety of the side streets. Most of us spectators were unmolested while the battle between *cipayos* and the hooded transgressors evolved into a series of sophisticated skirmishes, until the youths at last disappeared as swiftly as they had appeared in the scene. The *Ertzaintza* finally took control of the area, just as the sun was setting and the street lights were being turned on for the night. The whole episode had lasted about two hours.

Riot scenes like the one just described between Basque police and Basque radical nationalists became ritualized political performances during the second part of the 1990s. In their routinization, these performances have come to constitute a public spectacle that dramatizes the dilemmas and tensions of defining Basque identity in the contemporary Basque Country. The trope *cipayo* is key to understanding what these performances are about as well as the underlying tensions they both signal and negate. Rioting has been a recurrent part of the political culture in the Basque Country since the late 1960s, the last years of the Franco regime. It continued through the democratic transition that began after Franco's death in 1975, and persists up to the present time. Yet the form of rioting emerging during the 1990s was quite distinctive. During the 1970s and 1980s, rioting would typically break out after the Spanish police had actively charged against a demonstration. The use of guns and wooden batons by the police forced people to run for cover, and led the more courageous (and often younger) demonstrators to respond with stones, rubber bullets, tear gas, and sometimes live ammunition. These were dangerous moments when one could be injured, killed, or arrested. Because these riots were carried out against the Spanish police—a security force associated with decades of authoritarianism—and because riots were usually linked with demands for Basque autonomy, they often became a dramatization of Basque resistance against Spanish oppression. By the late 1980s, however, Spain was reorganized into a democratic state of autonomous regions. The Basque Country now had an autonomous government, a parliament, and their own emerging police force. These governing institutions resembled those of a state, even if they were sub-ordinated to the general dictates of the Spanish constitution and the central (Spanish) government. In Basque political culture, no other institution represents the state more clearly than the police.

The *Ertzaintza*, or Basque police, is a young force. It did not make its debut as enforcers of the law until the very end of the 1980s. The Basque police was intended to be the trusted civil police that the Basque Country never had except for a brief period during the civil war. Unlike the Spanish police forces, whose officers were born and raised in other parts of Spain and were in the Basque Country only for a transitory service period, the Basque police was formed by local men and women. Unlike the Spanish police forces who often lived in separate compounds on the outskirts of the community, *ertzainas* lived among the local population, had families and friends within the Basque geography, and thought of themselves as part of the community. The image of the *Ertzaintza* was a metonymy of the imagined Basque nation-state. Yet as a police force, the *Ertzaintza* had to assume the task of enforcing the law, which was still Spanish law. The ambiguity of Basque police enforcing the (Spanish) law created distrust not only from radical nationalists but from the Spanish government as well.

During the 1990s, the *Ertzaintza* proved itself as a police force that could violently repress demonstrations, gather intelligence, and conduct anti-terrorist operations. In other words, it proved itself capable of conducting the same functions as the Spanish police. This meant that the *Ertzaintza*, this metonymy of a desired Basque state, was using violence against other Basques, and more specifically against radical nationalists, the very people who most intensely desired an independent Basque state. In acting as metonymy of the state, the *Ertzaintza* introduced a threatening shift in the culture of Basque nationalism which, as with other nationalisms, rests on the fraternal unity of the imagined Basque nation (Anderson 1983). The rhetoric of a unitary national subject—Basque people—against the oppressive Spanish state was seriously threatened by the existence of a national police force acting against nationalists.

At the beginning of the 1990s, the special anti-terrorist unit of the *Ertzaintza* killed a member of ETA while attempting an arrest. The killing presented a shock for Basque radicals, for it meant that the political conflict in the Basque Country could not be articulated as one existing between a national self and a dominating Other, but rather as one existing *within* the national self. In performing as state (the Basque state), the *Ertzaintza* had introduced an unbearable ambiguity at the core of the nation. The ambiguity was compounded by the fact that this (Basque) "state" was enforcing Spanish law and thus could be seen as Spanish as well as Basque. It was at this point that the metaphor *cipayo* appeared on the scene. As I will try to demonstrate, this metaphor had the mission of covering up the ambiguity, best articulated as the problematic character of national identity riddled as it is with unrecognized difference. It did so by redrawing the boundaries of identity in a rigid manner so that difference was strictly positioned outside the boundaries of national identity and not within it.

Cipayo: The Intolerable Ambiguity of Being

I first encountered the term *cipayo* in 1993 when I was spending part of the summer in the Basque Country. It was part of some graffiti painted on the wall of a public building that read "*cipayos asesinos*." I remember my puzzlement, for the graffiti pointed at something that seemed important to Basque political culture and about which I knew nothing in spite of my intimate knowledge of that culture. I asked the friend accompanying me who these mysterious *cipayos* were. I learned from her that *cipayos* was the name given to the *Ertzaintza* by radical nationalists. *Cipayos*, she said, was the name for the soldiers of Indian origin serving in the British colonial army. The graffiti began to make sense. Radical nationalists were accusing the *Ertzaintza* of violent betrayal. I was still unaware of the motivations triggering such metaphoric predication, much less the train of its complex associations. But after I saw its accusatory presence for the first time, it was suddenly everywhere. I realized that radical nationalists habitually referred to the *Ertzaintza* as *cipayos* in their everyday speech. This, I thought, was more than a passing accusation. The transmutation of identity operated by metaphoric predication appeared to be taking root in the everyday political culture of radical nationalists. Then I saw them. It was in Rentería, an industrial town near San Sebastián, where I had gone to have dinner with a group of women at one of the many local *sociedades*, a mixture of bar/restaurant and social club organized as a cooperative of members. Not far from the *sociedad*, I saw a gathering of policemen in what appeared to be Spiderman outfits. Their uniforms were different from those of the familiar Spanish police. They were dressed in full riot gear: red and black uniforms, boots, helmets, bullet proof vests, faces covered with black balaclavas, and carrying riot arms. They were the *cipayos*, I was told, and the reason they were there was because there was a demonstration by radical nationalists scheduled to take place that evening. My only image of the *Ertzaintza* until that moment was that of harmless men and women dressed in rather folkloric fashion with white shirts and Basque berets, bereft of arms and standing in front of local government buildings. I had obviously missed some important developments during my stay out of the country. Equally interesting was the talk following my inquiries about the *Ertzaintza*. My friends were preoccupied with what they saw as a growing animosity between radical nationalists supporting the violence of ETA and other nationalists who supported the established autonomous institutions. The fabric of social life so closely woven in the Basque country was dangerously rupturing and my friends feared what they called a Balkanization of the Basque Country. The term *cipayo* was now associated with another metaphor: Balkanization.

In the political culture of the Basque Country, the metaphor *cipayo* appears as both a manifestation of anxiety about the rupturing of identity, and an attempt to repair that rupture. In this sense, a metaphor can also be a form of concealment. In this case, what the term *cipayo* conceals are different thoughts and feelings people have about what it means to be Basque. This alterity at the core of ethnic identity translates into divergent political projects. The metaphor of *cipayo* negates that alterity and symptomatizes a profound social anxiety about it. By predicating the identity of traitor onto the Basque police, radical nationalists are suggesting that the Basque police are not truly Basque. By extension, neither are those who support them, including the Basque Government, which is directly responsible for the actions of the *Ertzaintza*. What is being affirmed is a unitary dogmatic vision of Basque identity that denies contradictions or practices of power. But in so emphatically denying difference, radical nationalists actually reproduced it by making it a constant presence.

Nationalist Ambivalence: The Colony We Never Were

There are two dimensions to the image of *cipayo* that require further exploration if we want to understand what this metaphor *does* in the field of Basque political culture. One is the image itself; the other is the predication of betrayal. Here I present what Jane Gallop has called "a metonymic reading": "Whereas a metaphoric interpretation consists in supplying another signifier which the signifier in the text stands for [for example, *cipayo* representing *Ertzaintza*] a metonymic interpretation supplies a whole context of associations" (1985: 129). Let us look more carefully into this context. Radical nationalists could, of course, call the Basque police simply "traitors" or "assassins," as they called the Spanish police in response to outrageous acts of violence. Or they could predicate on them the metaphor of *txakurra* (dog), long used to debase the police to the category of the subhuman, thus legitimating the use of violence against them.[7] Instead of direct accusations or familiar metaphors that could have equally legitimized violence against the *Ertzaintza*, they chose the new, rather obscure image of *cipayo*.

What the image of *cipayo* does that the other images do not, is to frame the political conflict in the Basque Country in colonial terms. By predicating on the *Ertzaintza* the identity of *cipayos*, radical nationalists are not only casting on them the identity of betrayers, they are also positing a relation of analogy between the Basque Country and colonial India. In so doing, they are stating that the Basque Country is a part of the Spanish state by virtue of a colonial relation. By virtue of its inherent domination, this colonial relation is one of polarized opposition between colonizers and colonized that admits no middle ground. In the argument constructed by these images, the Basque Country remains colonized as long as it remains part of the Spanish state, regardless of how independent its autonomous institutions might be. Within this logic, the Basque Government and Basque parliament are not truly Basque as long as they remain part of Spain. The *Ertzaintza* are betrayers because they act in the interest of a colonizer state when they suppress the resistance of radical nationalists. The *cipayo* metaphor points to a colonial scenario by establishing a metonymic link between the Basque Country and Spain. Within this fantasy scenario, national identity is delineated along a polarized line—Basque/Spanish—that does not admit mediation. In this situation, violence is legitimized by the identification of Basque with the colonized, who in turn must use any means to get rid of the colonizer. In this polarized scenario, the predication of betrayal legitimizes violence against the Basque

---

7. See in this respect Zulaika (1988).

police, who by virtue of their subordination to the Spanish state are not Basque anymore. And yet the predication of betrayal reasserts the Basqueness of the *Ertzaintza*, for one cannot betray those with whom there is no intimate connection.

The associative chain described above has led to a political and social situation of increasing polarization, hostility, and violence within the Basque Country from the 1990s to the present. In some ways, this revival of colonial logic is a regression to the political logic predominant in the radical nationalism of the late 1960s and early 1970s, when Spain was still under a dictatorship and the Basque Country was the site of brutal cultural and political repression. It is ironic that this logic would surface at a moment when the Basque Country enjoys a great deal of freedom in organizing its cultural, social, and political affairs. But this is also a moment when the meaning of Basqueness is not taken for granted, but rather, subject to debate and contestation; a moment of rearticulation of what it means to be Basque in an increasingly globalized world. What the metaphor of *cipayo* conceals is the anxiety and uncertainty that this rearticulation produces, the fear that in developing a flexible and multiple identity, the line between self and other might be blurred and one's identity might disappear altogether.

For radical nationalists, the existence of autonomous institutions such as the Basque Government, parliament, and police within the boundaries of the Spanish nation-state poses a threat because while these elements are a metonymy of the Basque state that radical nationalists are fighting to achieve, they are also part of the Spanish state, indeed a salient trait of Spanish contemporary identity. The ambiguity of institutions that represent at once the imagined Basque nation and the law of the Spanish state is very threatening for radical nationalists. It is this ambiguity that radical nationalists have tried desperately to erase through the colonial scenario arising out of the metaphor of *cipayo*. But it could also be that what is really feared and resisted is the dissolution of a fantasmatic unity of identity bound to occur with the disappearance of an outside enemy.

The colonial scenario evoked by the metaphor *cipayo* is also linked by metonymic contiguity to the scenario of the independent nation. This is a scenario where the unity of the anti-colonial struggle gives rise to internal division, struggles of power, and violence. Indeed, India is a good example of this, and it is telling that the chosen image to accuse the *Ertzaintza* would be taken from that context. One could argue that the actual political reality of the Basque Country with its autonomous institutions, political parties and police force, constitutes a preview of the independent nation. The violent resistance of radical nationalists to this scenario of nationhood by predicating a colonial situation would suggest that a resistance to achieving an independent nation coexists with a desire to form it. Thus, if *cipayo* attempts to dispel political ambiguity, it also manifests profound ambivalence towards the national object. This would explain why the growing indiscriminate violence of radical nationalists threatens to destroy the very nation it purports to construct. Over the years, this violence has not only damaged the fabric of social relations considerably, it has also played in favor of anti-nationalist parties who have notably risen in recent elections.[8] Let me explore the play of ambiguity and ambivalence a bit further by returning to the treacherous identity that *cipayo* predicates.

National Intimacy

I have said that *cipayo* attempts to dispel the ambiguity of a Basque "state" that is simultaneously Spanish. It does so by effecting a move that divests the *Ertzaintza* (metonymy of the Basque state) of Basque identity by accusing it of betrayal and placing it firmly on the Spanish side of the Basque/Spanish boundary. Once this is done, the *Ertzaintza* becomes a legitimate target of nationalist violence and the boundaries of national identity are clearly reestablished. During the last several years the *Ertzaintza* has indeed become a ritualized target of radical nationalists' harassment and violence. And yet, as I said before, the notion of betrayal that *cipayo* conveys suggests a bond, a (national) intimacy that cannot quite be shaken out. Unlike the invader, or the stranger, the traitor retains a trace of us. He was one of us and his/her betrayal has separated us. But this separation is not complete, for if it were, there would be no betrayal. The betrayal itself ties us together, it makes the betrayer part of me, a wounded part to be sure, but still a part that cannot be extricated until the betrayal itself has disappeared, forgotten. The image of the *cipayo* contains the traumatic residue of an imaginary unity that has not been given up, while it signals the fact that it no longer exists. It is thus an ambivalent object, a threat and an object of identification. This ambivalence complicates the relationship between radical nationalists and the Basque police with an excess of affect that is absent in the relationship with the Spanish police. This excess manifests itself in practices of disclosure, such as openly revealing the identity of individual *ertzainas* in towns and villages, lead to their public humiliation and punishment, and ritualized attacks and riots. Such practices are, de facto, policing practices aimed at enforcing the boundaries of ethnic identity by punishing those who are considered to threaten them. They suggest a movement where the trauma of difference is repeatedly played out without resolution. The *cipayo* is thus a threat and a necessity, the despised object that challenges their fantasized ethnic community and the one which by virtue of evoking the Basque state is an object of desire; the despised object that stands in the way of unity and the one which by suggesting a colonial setting legitimizes nationalist violence.[9]

This ambiguity and ambivalence of an image that, at the same time, represents national betrayal and nationalist identification, can be tracked in the metonymic traces

---

8. A well-known politician and former mayor of Barcelona explicitly affirmed that (Basque) terrorism had benefited the right wing Partido Popular (PP, currently in government), helping them achieve an absolute majority in the last parliamentary elections. The PP government is virulently anti-nationalist and has systematically refused to negotiate a cease fire with ETA. It would seem that radical nationalists are doing everything possible not to achieve their goals.

9. There are many examples of the ambiguity associated with the Basque police. The latest appeared in the form of a communiqué published by all the major newspapers on May 24, 2000. In the communiqué, radical nationalist youth accused the *Ertzaintza* of being *cipayos* for arresting a group of youths charged with arsonist activities. The communiqué accuses the *Ertzaintza* of acting against the Basque people and being a servant of Spanish parties, and ends by threatening the *Ertzaintza* if they stand in the way of national sovereignty (*El País*, May 24, 2000, and *Gara*, May 24, 2000).

contained in the signifier *cipayo*, as it shifts etymologically from a representation of the colonial British army in India—*sipahi*—to a representation of anti-colonial force emerging with the mutiny of *sipahies* against the British in 1857, then to a representation of the police—*sipai*—in the postcolonial nation.[10] This etymological history points to the ambiguity of the *sipai* as a threat not only to national liberation but to colonial rule as well. This ambiguity is disguised, yet present, in the trope of the Basque *cipayo*, which acts simultaneously as a metonymy of the Basque nation and a metonymy of the hegemony of the Spanish state. Such ambiguity and its concomitant ambivalence manifests itself in the distrust periodically expressed by the Spanish government in relation to the *Ertzaintza*, and the suspicion voiced by radical nationalists that the *Ertzaintza* is infiltrated by the secret services of Spain.[11]

Conclusion

I have argued, in a rather tortuous way, that the play of tropes can productively direct us beyond predication to the dark spaces of fantasmatic identifications, where metaphoric predication and metonymic sliding weave arguments of images that shape performative scenarios through operations of concealment and disclosure. I have tried to show the inherent instability of metaphoric predication by exploring the context of metonymic associations that make them possible. These metonymic associations have led me to troublesome ideas and affects that are condensed in metaphor yet obscured or denied by the image they predicate. I have argued that the performative scenarios that metaphor facilitates can have a life of their own, leading to the creation of new metaphors or to the rigid, crippling enforcement of an authoritarian metaphor. I have done so by concentrating less on the metaphoric predicate than in the slippery space between signifiers, "the dark at the bottom of the stairs." For it seems to me that it is in this space between that we can find the complicated logic of our social arguments, the logic hidden from discourse that articulates an archeology of wounds, desires, and identifications that ultimately constitute our often violent social intimacy. The exercise might be worth it, for if we are not willing to look at "the dark at the bottom of the stairs," our impulse to return to the whole might become a wounded repetition of an ever-widening social chasm, threatening to engulf us in a terrifying feeling of disconnection.

---

10. See Lewis (1997), Metcalf (1964) and Mukherjee (1984) for more extensive etymology of the word *sipahi*, and for a history of the rebellion of 1857 in India.

11. See, for example, articles in the newspapers *El Mundo*, January 15, 1997, and *Egin*, January 15, 1998, April 22, 1997, and April 20, 1997.

CHAPTER 11

Playing Terrorist: Ghastly Plots and the Ghostly State[1]

At the end of December 1994 the public confession of two policemen triggered a major political crisis in Spain by implicating the democratic state in the use of paramilitary terror. Not since the attempted coup d'état of 1981, which brought the phantom of military rule to the surface of Spain's new democracy, had a national scandal so deeply shaken the core of Spanish democratic identity. It was as if the shock of a ghastly "real" had erupted through the cracks of democratic discourse, disturbing it with a growing anxiety about the (bad) nature of the state.[2] What was this state that was concurrently a state of law and an "outlaw"? And what was this democracy that rested on violent secret operations all too reminiscent of a former authoritarian regime? It is the "nature" or "being" of the state and its operations that concerns me in this article.

The nature of the state has perplexed social scientists and cultural critics alike. The difficulty in studying the state, as sociologist Phillip Abrams noted in a seminal paper (1988), resides in the fact that the state—as unified political subject or structure—does not

1. Originally published in the *Journal of Spanish Cultural Studies* 1.1 (2000): 43–58. A previous version was published as "A Fictional Reality: Paramilitary Death Squads and the Construction of State Terror in Spain," in *Death Squad: The Anthropology of State Terror*, edited by Jeffrey A. Sluka (Philadelphia: University of Pennsylvania Press, 2000), 47–69. Earlier versions of this article were presented at the MIT seminar series on *Peoples and States*, and at the Departments of Anthropology at Columbia University, University of Texas-Austin, Rice University, and Princeton University. I have benefited from the comments and suggestions made by faculty and students at these venues. I am especially grateful to Josetxo Beriain, Hildred Geertz, Michael Hanchard, Michael Herzfeld, Jean Jackson, Yael Navaro-Yashin, Mary Steedly, Katie Stewart, Stanley Tambiah, Michael Taussig, Julie Taylor, Jacqueline Urla, Kay Warren, Kamala Visweswaran and Joseba Zulaika. Research was made possible by grants from the Wenner-Gren Foundation for Anthropological Research, the American Council for Learned Societies, and the George Lurcy Charitable and Educational Trust.

2. This sense of unease about democracy was reflected in all the major newspapers that, after December 1994, printed daily reports on allegations of state terrorism and on the subsequent judicial inquiry into government and military officials. In the next two months, the secretary of state security was jailed along with other officials, and the former head of the Civil Guard left the country while under order of arrest. During the months that followed, the daily reports in all Spain's major newspapers on the various demands for political accountability, and the mutual accusations by political leaders of different parties, reflected a mixture of political opportunism and democratic anxiety. See, for example, *El Mundo* and *El País* during the first three months of 1995. See also the manifesto written by prominent Spanish intellectuals demanding democratic accountability in *El Mundo*, January 14, 1995, 12. For an explicit connection between the GAL and Francoism, see the historian Gabriel Jackson's "Urge una reforma," published in *El País Internacional*, July 22, 1996, 8.

exist; it is a collective illusion, the reification of an idea that masks "real" power relations under the guise of public interest.[3] For Abrams (1988: 58),

> The state comes into being as a structuration within political practice: it starts its life as an implicit construct; it is then reified—as the res publica . . . —and acquires an overt symbolic identity progressively divorced from practice as an illusory account of practice. The ideological function is extended to a point where conservatives and radicals alike believe that their practice is not directed at each other but at the state; the world of illusion prevails.

This illusion is sustained in no small measure by the shroud of secrecy surrounding the "being" of the state, which as Michael Taussig (1992) has noted, following Durkheim, invests it with the fabulous power of the sacred.[4] For Abrams, as for other scholars, the state is the effect of disparate power relations, a contradictory and dislocated set of discourses and apparatuses.[5] Thus for him, as for other scholars, the state should lose its mystifying power when it is unmasked as being an effect of power rather than the unified agent it appears to be.[6] Yet this is not the case. The gaze into the labyrinthine "interiority" of the state being does not necessarily dispel its "magical" power. On the contrary, it seems to augment it by triggering an endless proliferation of discourses about the state in the most diverse areas of social life. At least, this is what happened in the Basque Country with the unfolding of the convoluted story of state terrorism at the end of 1994. The presence of the state in a variety of social fields not only calls into question the separation between state and civil society, but makes the state in late modernity more and more an all-pervasive ghostly presence, a threatening force shaped by the collective experience of being overshadowed by an unfathomable power which can shape social life as a dangerous universe of surfaces and disguises.[7]

Nobody has shown better than Kafka that the illusion of a state-subject is no less real or any less socially powerful for being an illusion. The question is not the reality or unreality of the state-subject but, as Taussig has put it, "the reality of [its] powerful insubstantiality" (1992: 113). In this article I take the reality of this insubstantial state-being seriously and ask how it is imagined by the people who experience it, what its particular manifestations and forms of operation are, and what kind of subjectivity it comes to embody. The confession of Amedo and Dominguez is a particularly interesting text for, through it, the state-being is constructed not as subject of the law, nor as rational subject, but as subject of mimetic desire. It is this *jouissance* of the state, linked in Amedo's and Dominguez's narrative to practices of terror, that had the effect of a shock on the national body, as the public gaze was given a view of the forbidden and secret nature of the

---

3. For a development of Abrams's argument, see also Mitchell (1991).

4. See also Taussig (1992).

5. See also Brown (1995), especially chapter 7.

6. See Abrams (1988: 82), also Mitchell (1991).

7. There is a growing body of literature that challenges the separation between state and civil society. See, for example, Mitchell (1991), Gupta (1995), Navaro-Yashin (1998), Herzfeld (1992), Warren (1998).

state. This secret nature is what Walter Benjamin (1978) identified as the terrible ambiguity resulting from the blurring of law and violence at the heart of a state of Law, an
ambiguity springing according to him from the fact that, while the law is intended to
defend the public interest, it is also by definition an exercise of traumatic force legitimized
solely by its own existence.[8] For Benjamin (1978), the autonomous violence of the law creates the state as a spectral space, a no-man's-land where disavowed social violence flourishes. I will examine this spectral presence of the state in my last section, as the other side
of the violent *jouissance* of the state. For, among radical nationalists in the Basque Country at least, the dirty-war scandal gave rise to an experience of the state as a formidable
and elusive ghostly power. In my first section, I examine the "being" of the state by looking at the narrative of those who embody it most clearly: the two policemen arrested for
organizing political terror.

The State as Terrorist

In 1983, one year after the socialist electoral victory symbolically completed the transition
from dictatorship to parliamentary democracy, a new series of assassinations of Basque
radical activists began under the acronym of a new paramilitary organization that called
itself the GAL (Grupos Antiterroristas de Liberación, Antiterrorist Liberation Groups).
From 1983–87, this new paramilitary squad claimed responsibility for the assassination
of twenty-six Basques.[9] Some victims were members of the radical nationalist armed
group, ETA (Euskadi Ta Askatasuna, Basque Land and Freedom), living as refugees in
the French Basque Country.[10] Some were members or supporters of the legal political
movement for Basque independence, Herri Batasuna.[11]

There is a history of right-wing paramilitary groups in the Basque Country. There
had been a succession of them during the turbulent years that followed the death of General Franco. There were, for example, the Guerrilleros de Cristo Rey (Warriors of
Christ the King), the Batallón Vasco Español (Spanish Basque Battalion), the Acción
Apostólica Antiterrorista (AAA, Antiterrorist Apostolic Action), and a host of ubiquitous,
unnamed *incontrolados* (literally "uncontrolled," ultra right-wing elements, some in the secu-

---

8. For a commentary on Benjamin's obscure essay on violence (1978: 277–301), see Derrida (1991).

9. For assassinations attributed to the GAL, see Miralles and Arques (1989) and Rubio and Cerdán (1997). See also
the dossier on the GAL published by the newspaper *Egin* in its annual report for 1995 (*Egin* 1996: 257–302).

10. The French Basque Country was a sanctuary for political refugees during the Franco dictatorship. Basque activists
persecuted by the Spanish police took refuge there, forming a community of refugees that, until the mid-1980s, was relatively undisturbed by the French Government. The ETA leadership and its known activists have historically operated from
this "safe haven" outside Spain. The killings carried out by the GAL made a tremendous impact, creating a climate of insecurity and fear among Basque refugees.

11. Herri Batasuna was created in 1978 as a coalition of four political parties and a number of independent individuals. From the start, it was conceived and functioned as the core of a political movement acting as an umbrella for a variety of social organizations: youth, feminists, ecologists, trade unions, civic associations. HB now functions as a political
party but is still the center of a movement that extends beyond its members. For an excellent sociological study of HB, see
Arriaga Landeta (1997).

rity forces, who carried out terrorist acts in autonomous fashion, without the sanction of a host group). In the Basque Country, it was *vox populi* that these groups were linked to the security forces and in particular to the Civil Guard, a much-hated branch of the army empowered with policing functions.[12] Thus, when in December 1983 the GAL made their debut with radio communiqués and menacing graffiti, there was a ready popular frame within which to place them. Yet the old habits of the dictatorship were utterly incongruent with a socialist administration that represented a clear break with the past, a new state. What was this democratic state that was new yet linked to old practices of violence, an emblem of the new order of law and yet at the same time an outlaw?[13]

In 1987, José Amedo and Michel Dominguez, two police inspectors working for the intelligence department of the Spanish police, were charged and convicted of organizing the GAL. Along with Amedo and Dominguez, a number of mercenaries were arrested in connection with the assassination of Basque activists. The policemen assumed full responsibility for the creation of the GAL and, after their convictions, the judicial case was closed. Seven years later, in December 1994, the two policemen decided to reveal their (state) secrets. This revelation was made in a long, exclusive interview published in one of Spain's major newspapers, *El Mundo*. It appeared in four parts over the course of four days, like a serialized novel.[14] The story had a tremendous impact, triggering huge controversy in the political culture of Spain already disenchanted by economic and political corruption. In the Basque Country, the story came to confirm the worst fears and anxieties about the haunting power of the State.[15] The story was gripping. A cross between the confessional and the thriller genres, it had the addictive quality of a soap opera, with its extravagant scenarios, secret conspiracies, spy networks and hired assassins, briefcases stuffed with public money, stolen intelligence documents charting the dirty war, and cryptic handwritten communiqués. At the story's center were top-ranking officials in the government, public administration and security forces.[16] *El Mundo* sold out on the first

---

12. The connections between right-wing paramilitary groups and the state security forces have recently been demonstrated by a number of journalists: for example, Miralles and Arques (1989), Rubio and Cerdán (1997), and Rey (1996). But they became a matter of public controversy with the indictment of General Rodríguez Galindo and other Civil Guards for their participation in the assassinations carried out by the GAL. During the late 1970s, popular demonstrations against "*la Guerra sucia*" ("dirty war") denounced the connections between the state and right-wing paramilitary organizations. Reports and photographs of these demonstrations can be found in Basque newspapers of the time. There is also an extensive archive of ephemera, magazines, and political documents related to this issue in the Benedictine Monastery of Lazkano in the province of Gipuzkoa.

13. See Taylor (1993) for a comparative discussion of the military in Argentina as the embodiment of an outlaw state.

14. See *El Mundo*, December 27–30, 1994.

15. This was particularly the case after the discovery of the remains of José Antonio Lasa and José Ignacio Zabala, who disappeared in 1983. The inquiry into their disappearance implicated the Civil Guard General, Rodríguez Galindo, as well as other civil and military officials. The judge in charge of the inquiry was Javier Gómez de Liaño. See *El País*, March 22, 1995, as well as *El Mundo*, *El Diario Vasco* and other major newspapers on the same and following days. In the Basque Country, the discovery of Lasa's and Zabala's remains triggered riots by radical nationalists and increased political tension. See, for example, *El País*, March 26, 1995, 19; *El Diario Vasco*, March 22, 1995, 2, 8; *El Diario Vasco*, March 23, 1995, 6; and *El Diario Vasco*, March 25, 1995, 6.

16. See *El Mundo*, December 27–30, 1994.

day. On the second day, there were no newspapers left in my area of San Sebastián by 10 a.m.

The Story of the GAL as Narrated by Its Authors

After Amedo's and Dominguez's confessions, the judicial inquiry into the GAL reopened and the case became a regular feature in the press, avidly perused like the local news or sports page. The daily installments made a crime story the frame within which the state was publicly envisioned and materialized. It became a fictional reality which held everyone captive, within whose logic events made sense regardless of the supporting evidence.[17]

What follows is a story about state officials who become terrorists for the purpose of eliminating Basque terrorism, and to that end invent a terrorist organization called the GAL. It is a tale about the phantasmatic universe in which terror and desire are mutually constituted in acts of violence. Although there were a small number of acts of violence connected to the GAL's formation (notably, the disappearance of two young men in 1983),[18] the first action officially claimed by the GAL—the first action that gave it birth as a political subject—was the kidnap of a French citizen, Segundo Marey. It is this kidnap that occupies the major narrative space in the confession of Amedo and Dominguez, the two convicted policemen, who are both narrators and protagonists of the story that follows. In their narrative, this kidnap has the status of a tale of origins that constructs the state as an excitable body, a loosely connected ensemble of characters and bureaucracies held together by a phantasmatic identification with terrorism—a tale that narrates state terror as a Kafkaesque comedy of errors[19]—for the GAL's foundational act was a mistake. Here is my rendition of their story:[20]

The events go back to December 4, 1983. José Amedo waited at the frontier separating the towns of Irún in Spain and Hendaye in France. He had cleared, with the mili-

---

17. In saying that the stories were shot through with rumor and speculation, I do not mean that they were untrue or that the whole affair of the dirty war was an invention. The protagonists of the story told here have since been convicted and sentenced by the Spanish Supreme Court (*El País Digital*, July 27, 1998). I mean that, at the time, Amedo's and Dominguez's confessions were little more than oral narratives, yet in the Basque Country, at least, they seemed perfectly plausible and compelling. By "fictional reality," I mean the configuration of a "real"; that is, structured like fantasy, and a fantasy, a plot, a scene that configures reality by articulating forms of knowledge and social practices. For discussion of the notion of fantasy and its political impact see Žižek (1989, 1997).

18. The discovery of Lasa's and Zabala's remains just three months after the revelations of Amedo and Dominguez added a macabre edge to the GAL affair. The editorial of *El País* on March 22, 1995 was titled "*Nuevos espantos nacionales*" ("New National Horrors") and asked: "After yesterday's revelations, what new horrors await us in relation to the dirty war deployed by the state against ETA?" (p.1). The editorial connected the dirty war with authoritarian practices inherited from the former regime. The inquiry into Lasa's and Zabala's disappearance led to the conviction of General Rodríguez Galindo and those Civil Guards involved in the GAL's terrorist operations. See, for example, *El Diario Vasco*, May 24, 1996, 31, *El Mundo*, May 24, 1996, 18–19, and *El Mundo*, June 9, 1997, 20. For a new generation of young Basque activists, this event was the cognitive and emotional turning point that delegitimized Spain's democracy and constructed it as the authoritarian rule of a foreign power.

19. For Kafka, the comic dimension is inextricably linked to the horror of modern institutions. It accentuates the horror by separating it from the grandeur of the tragic. See Kundera (1987).

20. Taken from *El Mundo*, December 17, 1994.

tary police controlling the frontier, the transit of a car expected to arrive at 7 p.m. Evening turned to night and the expected car did not appear. Amedo got a phone call from the Bilbao chief of police. The latter told him to go immediately to an obscure frontier post in the Pyrenees, where he was to pick up someone who would be waiting for him. When he got there, a policeman guarding the frontier told Amedo that there was, indeed, a man waiting for him and that the Civil Governor had given instructions for him to accompany him. The man told Amedo, "Let's go." It was a dark, cold night. They went up a twisting mountain road. Amedo: "When we reached the top, I got out of the car and saw a big fat man in a T-shirt and beside him an old man wearing striped pajamas, shivering with cold." The man accompanying him and the fat man were mercenaries, both later arrested in 1987. Amedo continued: "I saw the three of them and remembered that Sancristóbal, Alvarez and Planchuelo [the Civil Governor, Chief of Police, and Head of Intelligence respectively] had told me they were going to kidnap a prominent member of ETA. And then, looking at the old man, I asked 'Who is that?' and Talbi [one of the mercenaries] replied, 'Segundo Marey.'" "Chapter II follows tomorrow," concluded the newspaper, blurring the boundaries between fiction and reality.

Chapter II began with the telephone conversation in the small Pyrenean police post between Alvarez (the Chief of Police) and Amedo over the fate of Segundo Marey: "[His detention] is a mistake, should we let him go?" Amedo asked. The police chief consulted with the Civil Governor and the Head of Intelligence at the other end of the line. They decided to continue with the kidnapping "to exploit it politically."[21] There followed a car journey from the Pyrenees to Bilbao, with the kidnapped man, from one car to another in various tunnels, until finally he was taken to an abandoned house on another mountaintop. Segundo Marey was kept for ten days in the kitchen of the derelict house with no electricity, water or heat, blindfolded in his pajamas, guarded by two mercenaries and two police officers.[22] I am struck by the proliferation of people who have become embroiled with the kidnap in the course of this narrative. Michel Dominguez described the house the day before Segundo Marey was liberated with horror and disgust:

> When I saw the situation I was taken aback. The house was an old stone building, completely derelict, everything was filthy. The ceilings had half collapsed, there was no furniture. Marey was on the floor, in the kitchen, blindfolded. He was wearing the same pajamas as on the day of his detention. He had no coat or anything, just a blanket, an army blanket. The officers guarding him were fed up.[23]

In Dominguez's story, the mimesis of terrorist transgression turns into the ambivalence of unheroic abjection for those who represent the state at the bottom, or perhaps one should say the "state's bottom:" that is, those who are in touch with the dirt of its

---

21. *El Mundo*, December 28, 1994, 8–9.
22. *El Mundo*, December 29, 1994, 10.
23. Ibid.

"sewers"—a recurrent metaphor for the dubious operations of the state.[24] No such ambivalence is imputed to those scheming in the offices of state buildings. On the contrary, the state officials playing terrorist in the Governor's office got carried away by the excitement of transgression and the sensation of omnipotence it brings.[25] They put aside their war against Basque terrorists to play a war against another state. Marey, the kidnap victim, would be used to blackmail the French state into collaborating with the antiterrorist plans of the Spanish government.

The first communiqué signed by the GAL was hand written by the Governor himself, translated into French and sent to the radio. In that first communiqué, the GAL demanded from France the release of Spanish policemen arrested for attempted kidnap, in exchange for Segundo Marey, who was accused of collaborating with Basque terrorism. Shortly after, there followed a second communiqué, issuing an ultimatum to the French authorities: either they release the Spanish policemen detained in France or the French citizen Segundo Marey would be killed.[26]

After the second communiqué, according to Amedo, the Governor (promoted to head of state security a year later) and a prominent leader of the PSOE (the governing Spanish socialist party), Ricardo García Damborenea, suggested that Segundo Marey be killed to avoid complications. "They were very euphoric, very full of themselves," Amedo insisted.[27] The socialist leader, García Damborenea, seems to have been obsessed with terrorism. In 1987, the year when the GAL ceased to operate after the detentions of Amedo and Dominguez, he published a short book titled *Manual del buen terrorista* ("A Manual of the Good Terrorist"), a sarcastic indictment of Basque terrorism that can barely disguise his fascination with it.[28] This fascination with terrorism was also manifest in the efforts of state officials to replicate the sign-things that make terrorism not just an action but a material entity, a subject. Sign-things such as an acronym, a seal, and communiqués endow Basque terrorism with the materiality of a political subject by providing a permanence and continuity that the act of violence alone cannot provide. So the state officials, in turn, produced not only an acronym for their terrorist actions but, according to the investigations of the well-known journalists Antonio Rubio and Manuel Cerdán, a seal as well. As described by them, the GAL seal was an inverted replica of the seal of ETA which

---

24. See Stallybrass and White (1986: 125–48) for a discussion of the trope of the sewer in the bourgeois imagination. In relation to the ambivalence of abjection see Kristeva (1982). See also Mary Douglas's seminal work (1966) which highlights pollution ("matter out of place") and abjection as symbols of social transgression and category confusion.

25. *El Mundo*, December 28, 1994, 10.

26. *El Mundo*, December 29, 1994, 10. The communiqué has the iconic function of conferring materiality and truth on Amedo's and Dominguez's narratives. They insist on these pieces of paper, of which they kept secret copies, reproducing the record-keeping function of the state that they embodied as agents of the law and as de facto terrorists. In this story of state terrorism, the communiqués also acquire a fetishistic character, at once the icon of a surreal, fantastic reality (the secret production of terrorism in the banal setting of government offices) and the empirical matter that embodies such reality by linking a person to the letters handwritten on tangible, reproducible paper.

27. *El Mundo*, December 28, 1994, 10.

28. See García Damborenea (1987). Basque bishops warned the Prime Minister (Felipe González) about García Damborenea's "excesses." See *El País*, June 9, 1997, 17.

represents a snake wound around an ax. The GAL seal represented an ax severing the head of the snake representing ETA. Like the acronym and the communiqués, the seal had the character of a fetish and pointed to a mimetic identification with the phantasm of Basque terrorism. This phantasmatic character of state terrorism, and of terrorism in general, extended to the details, taken from the nebulous world of conspiracy, of the seal's production. According to Rubio and Cerdán, it was ordered by General Andrés Cassinello, the Civil Guard chief of staff, who had served in the Basque Country and was believed by radical nationalists to be obsessed with eliminating Basque separatists (1997: 74–75).[29] Rubio and Cerdán claim that it was made at the headquarters of the army intelligence unit, where the course of the GAL was charted in a top-secret document made public only last year after much wrangling.[30]

Luckily for Marey, France released the detained Spanish policemen, and the Spanish state representatives decided to free Marey, although not without previously implicating the Spanish minister of the interior as the person responsible for authorizing the kidnap victim's release. Marey was freed, in France, on December 14, 1983. Dominguez later admitted that he himself sent the communiqué, written for the occasion, to the radio from a public telephone:

> Given the increasing number of assassinations, kidnappings and extortions perpetrated by the terrorist organization ETA on Spanish soil, planned and orchestrated from French territory, we have decided to put a stop to such things. The Antiterrorist Liberation Groups (GAL), founded to that effect, communicate the following: 1) every assassination perpetrated by the terrorists will elicit an appropriate response; 2) we affirm our intention to attack French interests in Europe because the French government is responsible for permitting terrorists to operate from its territory with impunity. As a sign of goodwill and convinced by the French government's gesture, we release Segundo Marey, arrested by our organization for collaborating with ETA terrorists. You will be hearing from the GAL again in the future.[31]

According to the two policemen's narrative, the positive "political" outcome of Segundo Marey's kidnap left its artificers even more euphoric than the actual operation. They got carried away. Like the terrorists of ETA, they, too, decided to organize an extortion system or "revolutionary tax," in this case levied on French industrialists, so as to intimi-

---

29. General Andrés Cassinello was indicted by Judge Baltasar Garzón for the assassination of four refugees claimed by the GAL (Egin, May 11, 1996, 11). During my research in the Basque Country in 1997, I found that radical nationalists had little doubt that Cassinello was obsessed with Basque separatism and involved in the GAL affair. Journalist Pepe Rey attributes to Cassinello a document entitled "*Hablemos de terrorismo*" ("Let's Talk About Terrorism") in which the perception of a war against terrorism is elaborated at length; see Rey (1996: 275–77).

30. The secret document of the CSID (military intelligence service) which charted the dirty war was known as its "Acta Fundacional" ("Foundational Act") and was published after much controversy by all major newspapers on March 23, 1997, when the Spanish Supreme Court lifted the government ban on its disclosure. See also Rubio and Cerdán (1997: 74–75), who publish the "Acta Fundacional" as an appendix.

31. *El Mundo*, December 29, 1994, 9. Several experts confirmed that Julián Sancristóbal, head of state security at the time, also wrote various communiqués signed by the GAL. See *El Mundo*, December 31, 1994, 10.

date the French authorities into collaborating in the war against ETA.[32] The Governor told Amedo to "bring a list of French industrialists, you can take it from the phone directory or whatever, because we are going to levy a revolutionary tax on the French," and they compiled a list of potential targets, but the project did not get off the ground. Instead, the GAL was funded by Spain's public treasury through the so-called "state reserved funds," the secret nature of which is an object of continued speculation. A long list of assassinations of Basque activists followed until 1987, when Amedo and Dominguez were arrested along with several hired assassins employed by them.

For four years, the dirty war was the object of huge political controversy. The judicial cases that followed one another during these years triggering constant debate, as well as conflicts within different branches of the judiciary, and between the judiciary and the government. Crucial pieces of evidence contained in papers of the military intelligence service, CSID, remained undisclosed until 1997.[33] And indeed, the top-ranking officials that figured prominently in the story of Segundo Marey's kidnapping and the subsequent assassinations have only recently been charged for their crimes.

Disorganized Mimesis, or the State as Terrorist Desire

There is a crucial dimension of state violence emerging from the story about the GAL by Amedo and Dominguez, conforming to what Theodor Adorno and Max Horkheimer have called "organized mimesis"; that is, an organized mimesis of terrorism as the constituting force of the state as subject. Yet what is salient in the Amedo's and Dominguez's confessions is the disorganized character of this "organized mimesis"; in other words, its amateurism, which led Francisco Alvarez Cascos (vice president of the Partido Popular (PP) government that succeeded the PSOE in 1996) to label it "bar terrorism," as if it were something out of Joseph Conrad's *The Secret Agent*.[34] There is an excess in the story that reveals the state more as parody than as mimicking agent. Indeed, the kidnap of Segundo Marey reads less like a copy of Basque terrorism than a parody of stock representations of Basque terrorists. It imitates the landscape and actions associated with ETA in cinema, fiction, and the media: the obscure frontier passes in the Pyrenees, the hide-out in the mountains (a terrain familiar to ETA experts), the secret contacts and meetings, the hidden documents charting events, even the seal and acronym.[35] All of this belongs to the genre of Basque terrorism and in varying degrees to the genre of terrorism in general, forming part

---

32. *El Mundo*, December 30, 1994, 9. The "revolutionary tax" levied against Basque industrialists is a key feature of ETA, and continues to be its main source of funding. It is a major headache for both Spanish and Basque governments, which have unsuccessfully tried to break it.

33. Prominent among these papers was a document titled "Acciones en el sur de Francia" ("Actions in the South of France") and known to the public as "Acta fundacional de los GAL" ("Foundational Act of the GAL"). This document outlined the plot of the dirty war. The government refused to disclose the secret papers to members of the judiciary investigating the GAL, triggering huge controversy over democratic practice. See for example *El País*, August 5, 1995, 10.

34. *El País International*, October 7, 1996.

35. This mimetic fascination with terrorism was publicly perceived by many people. See, for example, Xabier Arzallus, president of the Partido Nacionalista Vasco (PNV, Basque Nationalist Party), who, on March 25, 1995, declared to the press that the GAL was a mirror image of ETA. Reported in *Egin*'s Annual report for 1995 (1996: 44).

of what literary critic Joseba Gabilondo (1997) has called "the national production of terrorism" through cinema, fiction, film, and the media.[36] In this story, what is copied is not terrorism but a fantasy of terrorism, for the terrorist—like the savage—can exist only in fantasized form, as "the other" of an imaginary relation.[37] What is produced in this mimetic engagement of the state with the representation of terrorism is, precisely, terror: a traumatic real of dead bodies and intense affects—exhilaration, anger, and fear. And not only terror, but the state itself as subject, is produced in the act of producing terror—a restless state subject characterized by uncontrolled excitement.

The state "crafted" through Amedo's and Dominguez's confessional narrative departs from the image of bureaucratic routines and regulatory practices described by Foucault, veering off into a comic Kafkaesque nightmare of institutional surrealism. There is little rational about this state. It is suffused with affect: it gets excited, exhilarated at trespassing on the fantastic space of terrorism, carried away in its own fantasy of the terrorist's omnipotence, uncontained by the rule of law, unrestrained by the symbolic rules defining the "civilized" reality of parliamentary democracy.

The state as body politic is an ensemble of disorganized organs that wants to kill Marey and plots to copy the terrorists' extortion system. In its desire to overcome the terrorist's power, the state becomes the imagined terrorist. It is not the rational goal that matters, it does not matter that the kidnap victim is the wrong man; what matters is the power emanating from mimetic action, the enactment of the desire to be a terrorist. It is the act of kidnapping, killing, extorting that makes terrorism—like the state—real and effective, by binding its actors to and in an imaginary relation that constitutes an alternative reality. On the stage of the state being, fantasy cannot be separated from the calculated objectives that originally triggered the actions of terror. Indeed, it is through the enactment of fantasy in mimetic performance that terror becomes real and the state powerful. From the lustful fantasies of terrorist appropriation that constitute the state as subject, I turn now to the stories of terror—or "horror stories"—which constitute the political real for radical Basque nationalists in the Basque Country and which construct the state as a powerful ghostly presence.

Tales of Terror: The Ghostly State

Soon after I arrived back in the Basque Country at the beginning of 1997, I went to a local university to hear a talk about the Basque youth movement.[38] As I entered the

---

36. For a discussion of how the discourse of terrorism is structured around fictional tropes and genres, see Zulaika and Douglass (1996).

37. For the time-honored figure of the savage as the Other of Western civilization, see White (1978: 150–83). Zulaika and Douglass (1996) have argued that the figure of the terrorist is the contemporary embodiment of the former image of the savage.

38. The Basque youth movement comprises a number of different political organizations and cultural associations involved in a diverse array of activities. Much of the information for this section comes from personal interviews with activists involved in anti-militarist struggles, *gaztetxes* (unofficial youth centers), musical groups, free radios and political organization. For discussion of the youth movement, see Ramírez Goicoechea (1991), Lahusen (1993) and Urla (1995). See also the study commissioned by the Department of Culture of the Basque Government (Various Authors 1994).

Department of Fine Arts where the talk was taking place, I saw a slogan scrawled on the door in black ink, denouncing the state as an enemy: "Death to the damned state." A huge banner hanging in the hall of the building explained why: the state was, it seems, a kid napper. The banner demanded the freedom of an arrested student: "Freedom for Alatz, kidnapped by the Spanish state."

After the talk, my friend Antonio, who had been a radical activist in his youth, explained to me that Alatz had been arrested for carrying out arson attacks against the state.[39] He introduced me to some young activists for the book I was writing about youth politics. They appeared less interested in talking about their politics than in talking about what the state embodied for them in the person of the police, particularly the newly-formed Basque police. As we walked through the labyrinthine, narrow streets and squares of Bilbao's old quarters looking for somewhere to have lunch, one of these young activists, Jesús, began to talk about the *Ertzaintza* (Basque police) as if prompted by memories springing from the urban landscape: "The Ertzaintza are crazy," he said.

> They'll put down by force anything that evades their control. The other day, for example, the *parados* (unemployed) were holding a meeting in this square, as they do each week, and all of a sudden the police turned up with their vans and sirens, dressed up in riot gear, and told them to disperse in two minutes flat. For no reason whatsoever! They'd always met there. The *Ertzaintza* have got more and more belligerent and aggressive.

I would hear many stories about the "craziness" of the Basque police in the months to follow. "The way the *Ertzaintza* are acting is excessive," said Jesús, "I think they are conducting experiments on some towns, Hernani and Rentería, for example."[40]

Jesús and the rest of us have entered one of the many bars dotting the city's old quarters and we are sitting at a table eating lunch. It is late for lunch and there are very few people in the bar and indeed out in the streets, but Jesús is whispering and looking down at the ground and around him, as if to check no one is listening. "They broke my arm after a demonstration. There wasn't even a riot or anything, and suddenly this *ertzaina* throws me to the ground shouting "*puto vasco de mierda*" (shitty little Basque) and starts beating me with his wooden baton. And they're Basques, too! I haven't gone to a demonstration since then. I'm too scared." "He's been followed by the Civil Guard, too" said my friend Antonio. "For three months," says Jesús. "You'd get into the car and there'd be three other cars behind. You could go through a road block with no problem, they'd see the police cars behind you and let you through. There were several plain-clothes policemen behind me all the time, wherever I went. It makes you panic and feel paranoid," he said. "It's very scary and it's hard to stay calm. Some people react violently and get themselves a gun" (he means that they join the armed organization ETA). "People don't know it's happening," says Jesús, "because you don't see it, it's never reported, the media distort

---

39. To protect the identity of my informants, I have replaced their real names with invented ones.
40. The towns of Hernani and Rentería have a reputation for being strongholds of radical nationalism.

reality. They're manipulating the facts. What happened to that guy for example—what was his name? Anuk—was terrible." "What happened?" I asked.

> He was kidnapped by the Basque police and they did all sort of things to him, trying out drugs and psychological techniques on him. Then they let him go, but they kept following him all the time. He managed to send a letter to the ETA leadership—he was an activist, you see—telling them what was happening. A few days after kidnap, he was standing with a toy gun in his hand in front of an old garage; almost immediately the Basque police and the Spanish police appeared on the scene and fought among themselves to arrest him. It was clear they were waiting for him, that it was a set-up job. And then the national police took him to their headquarters and he obviously couldn't take it anymore and threw himself out the window.

Anuk's death was reported in the national press. In the Basque Country, it rekindled an ongoing debate about police treatment of detainees. His letter to the ETA leadership was published by the radical newspaper *Egin* shortly after his death, as an indictment of the police.

Anuk's letter was billed as an account of the *Ertzaintza*'s secret practices. It is a delirious narrative featuring all the anxieties about the state that populate the political imaginary of Basque radicalism: video surveillance, information chips, and the use of drugs. The narrative begins on the newspaper's front page under a headline across the whole page: "The *cipayos* detained and drugged me."[41] The letter constructs a universe dominated by the shadow play of a ghostly state in the guise of the Basque police, not unlike the universe of *The X-Files*. Here are some excerpts:

> I'm convinced they detected me from the beginning [of his militancy in ETA], they let me move around freely, keeping my movements under strict control. They wove a spider's web around me. The guy at the *Herri Hurrats* [a popular celebration in the French Basque Country, in favor of Basque-language education] who video-taped me was a *cipayo* disguised as a *picolo* [Civil Guard)]. You think that's absurd? The *cipayos* did that to confuse me, and after all, the *cipayos* and *picolos* have worked together. Anyway, the *cipayos* detained me, drugged me, hypnotized me, brainwashed me, and then let me go. They've used me and they still are. I feel like an instrument of the enemy.[42]

From this point on, the narrative becomes totally delirious: Anuk leaves his house at night, feels he is being followed by the police, goes to various places, and panics, feeling persecuted all the time. Reality becomes de-realized. Everything is appearance, shadow. Everywhere he sees police in disguise. He goes for a walk in the woods:

---

41. The use of *cipayo* as a derogatory term for the Basque police is recent (dating back less than ten years). It derives from the name given to soldiers of Indian origin serving in the British colonial army. The connotations of betrayal and collaboration with an occupying force are obvious. The term is commonly used by Basque radical nationalists of all ages, but especially among young people who never use the name *Ertzaintza* to refer to the Basque police.

42. *Egin*, September 28, 1993, 3.

As I came down the mountainside, they ambushed me. They were all over the place. What nobody knows is that they have a hidden camp (*"una base escondida"*) there. From the outside it looks like a farm house (*"caserío"*) but it's all very well organized. They were doing training or something like that. They all had yellow windbreakers on. There were people of all ages there but lots of very young people. And lots of guards with long weapons, at observation posts. I started walking through some bushes and had the impression they were playing with me. I thought I saw two guys with video cameras in a tree. I couldn't quite believe it, then I stumbled on the cable. Every now and then they'd turn on a light. It was probably for the filming, we'll see what kind of *mise-en-scène* they come up with this time . . . I was totally surrounded by *cipayos*, and in the foreground there was something that looked like a space ship. There were five or six people inside, observing my every reaction. I felt helpless. Nobody spoke, they kept on with their game. They showed me a video with images of a dead body, drugs and other things. I'm sure they interrogated me but I can't remember. At some point they brought me a cup of coffee; I drank it, and soon I felt a lump and pain in my stomach. Later, they told me a guy called Damián was waiting for me in a van. They pointed to a path. It was raining. The path was full of brambles. At the end of it were more vans, obviously *cipayos* in disguise.[43]

The delirious character of the letter does not escape the attention of radical nationalists but does not de-authorize it either. On the contrary, it proves the power of the police—which is to say the state—to drive you mad. For radical nationalists, this surreal narrative is not an indication of the mental heath of a particular individual, but proof that the *Ertzaintza* were using drugs on people. It is read as a revelation of hidden facts, of things that happen in the shadows. The point is not the narrative's rational coherence or lack of it, but that it constitutes an epistemological entry into a plausible "real" whose fullness of being cannot be grasped. For radical nationalists, everything is possible, or at least plausible, with the police. For, after all, we now know that the CSID was experimenting with drugs to be used against ETA militants, and we know this is true because the director resigned in a hurry when the scandal hit the public.[44] There is nothing so unreal in Anuk's surreal, delirious narrative, which is why Javi, who gave it to me, read it as a statement of hidden truth and wrote "mescaline" in the margin of his copy of the published letter, at the point where Anuk wondered what kind of drug the police might have given him. In a political universe where the surreal seems factual, and the rational and reasonable order of things mere appearance, the question is not whether or not Anuk was crazy, but the fact that his delirium articulates an experience, a sense of the real that is, for radical nationalists, masked. It is, for them, the "really real" in spectral form: a specter that has recurrently erupted into Basque political life, becoming its center, its most important referent. In the street narratives of police terror that circulate freely in the dense public sphere of the Basque Country, the state figures as a "ghostly" reality, a universe of surfaces, held

43. Ibid., 4–5.
44. See Rubio and Cerdán (1997: 277–82).

together by fear, apprehension and anger, by kinds of excitement that make the bodies of young radical nationalists, like the body of the state, nervous bodies.[45]

Subjectivity, Truth, and the "Real" of the State

One could object that I have left out the crucial question of the truth-value of these stories of violence, and thus the issue of how real this violence is. I have deliberately left out the issue of truth, not because I do not think it is important, but because, in its conflictive claims, it tends to obscure what I think is really crucial: that is, the "truth effects" of the stories which themselves constitute an immediate, affective, charged political reality. To conclude, I should like to retrace the connections between truth and subjectivity that constitute the political real of the state in the case discussed. Let me first go back to Amedo's and Dominguez's narrative. The fact that this narrative of state terror is a confession as well as an indictment of top-ranking officials has important implications for its social effects. One effect is the truth effect attached to the act of confession by virtue of its performative force; as Foucault notes: "by its own mechanics, the verbal act of confession . . . is the proof, the manifestation of truth" (1997: 223). Since this truth effect stems from the revelation of a hidden interiority, confession has, since early Christianity, been a privileged vehicle for the construction of subjectivity. The two policemen's confession becomes a narrative through which a particular subjectivity is crafted. As the narrative unfolds, one realizes that it is not so much the subjectivity of the policemen that is shaped through its confession as the subjectivity of a state-being to which the two policemen belong. For what is revealed is a particular "interiority," not of the policemen themselves, but of the state.

The state-subject which emerges in this confessional story is at odds with the common Weberian definition of the state as a bureaucratized rationality. Rather, the state emerges as a disjointed subject of feeling, driven by desire as much as, if not more than, by (state) reason. This feeling body of the state becomes real, not so much through the confluence of reason and violence that is the hallmark of the modern state, as through the performance of mimetic violence against a fantasized terrorist enemy. However, what is striking about this narrative is not so much the "events" of state terror it recounts, as the narrative excess discernible in the surreal vicissitudes of the plot which—like the manifest content of a dream—appear to point to a "repressed" side to the account of events.[46] What I hope to have shown is not just that the state is constituted through the narrative proliferation of excess, but that it is constituted as nothing but excess. The spectral form of this excess makes its appearance in the stories about police violence which I encountered among radical nationalists in the Basque Country during 1997. The political reality of these activists appears as an effect of their imaginary relation to an all-powerful phan-

---

45. I am alluding here to Taussig's idea (1992) that the state should be regarded as an enervated body.

46. I am drawing here on Žižek's discussion of narrative excess as indicative of a story's repressed content (1997: 41n13).

tom state. By "imaginary" I do not mean "illusory" or "not real"; rather, in a variant version of Lacan's theory of the mirror phase, I mean a reality in which the subject is constituted through the misrecognition of itself in the mirrored image of an "other." Nationalist activists are constituted as political subjects in an imaginary relation to the state, just as the state is constituted as subject in an imaginary relation to the phantom Basque terrorist. However, neither the state nor radical nationalists constitute a homogeneous or coherent subject. Both are loosely connected and contradictory ensembles of institutional bodies, apparatuses, fantasies, political groups.

In the stories told in this article, both nationalist violence and state violence are produced, not arbitrarily, but within what Derrida (1994: 97) has called a "phantomatic mode of production": a structure and modus operandi which produce both the state and terrorism as fetishes of each other, constructing reality as an endless play of mirror images. This play of terrorism is what makes the State (with a capital *S*) and Terrorism (with a capital *T*) so real, organizing political life as a phantasmatic universe where the "really real" is always somewhere else, always eluding us.

CHAPTER 12

A Hall of Mirrors: On the Spectral Character of Basque Violence[1]

> What matters when one tries to elaborate upon some experience,
> isn't so much what one understands, as what one doesn't understand.
>
> Lacan, *The Seminar of Jacques Lacan, Book 1.*

I begin with a story that most people in the Basque Country probably know. It is about things that happen somewhere midway between dream and reality, in the space some would regard as the unreal materialized, or that others might consider to be inapprehensible reality, the domain of trauma and fantasy. On December 10, 1995, Mikel Otegi, 23 years old, took the shotgun hanging on the wall of his farmhouse, went outdoors, and killed two *ertzainas* (Basque policemen) who had come to inquire about his fast driving. He then called the authorities to report the crime and surrendered. In his deposition, Otegi testified that he could not remember what had happened, and only remembered that he "lost it" ("*se salió de sus casillas*"). He said that he saw the two policemen by the side of the road while driving. When he arrived home, he went to bed. Then he heard the dogs barking, came out to see what was happening, and saw the two policemen, one of them near his car. He testified that he told them to go away, but the *ertzainas* ignored him. He then "lost it," went inside the house, and could not remember what happened next. Otegi also stated that the Basque police had harassed him over the previous two years; that he was beaten by them once, and that, since then, he had been feeling constantly accosted (Forest 1997: 247–48).

1. Originally published in *Basque Politics and Nationalism on the Eve of the Millennium.* Basque Studies Program Occasional Papers Series, No. 6, edited by William A. Douglass et al. (Reno: Basque Studies Program, University of Nevada, Reno, 1999), 115–26. Based on a paper presented at the conference, *Basques in the Contemporary World: Migration, Identity, and Globalziation,* Reno, Nevada, July 5–10, 1998. The research for this article was funded by grants from the American Council for Learned Societies (ACLS), Wenner-Gren Foundation for Anthropological Research, and the George Lurcy Educational and Charitable Trust. A version of this piece has been published as "Lo 'real'. Violencia política como realidad virtual," in *La Cuestión Vasca. Claves de un conflicto cultural y político,* edited by Josetxo Beriain and Roger Fernandez (Barcelona: Proyecto A Ediciones, 1999), 106–17. The names of people used in this article are pseudonyms.

This episode touched a deep nerve within an already nervous political world of the Basque Country. It became a symptomatic event, one triggering heightened emotions and deeply contested interpretations. I begin with this episode to talk about the violent exchange between radical Basque nationalist youths and the young *ertzainas* that has dominated the political climate during the late 1990s until ETA's recent cease-fire [1998–99]. During the last decade, the *Ertzaintza* (Basque police force) has progressively assumed the police functions accorded previously to the Spanish national police, including riot control and conducting the anti-terrorist campaign. One consequence has been that young activists coming of age during this decade frequently encountered the power of the state in the guise of the *Ertzaintza*, and therefore made it a target of the violence within an escalating strategy of rioting and sabotage against the state. Because the violence occurring between Basque police and radical nationalist activists falls within the "imagined community" of the Basque nation (in contrast to a former symbolic structure in which the "Basque people" was opposed to the "Spanish state"), such violence has evoked, for many Basques, the specter of fratricide and a corresponding deep anxiety over national (Basque) identity. After Otegi's killings, for example, the phantom of fratricide haunted the reports, editorials, and articles published by the *El Diario Vasco* newspaper.[2] The brother of one of the policemen killed voiced it by saying that "we are killing ourselves,"[3] meaning the Basques. Professional experts reinforced this specter of civil confrontation.[4] Whether created or reinforced, the anxiety of fratricide has been actively fed by the mass media in its ongoing reports referring to monstrous ethnic violence and active metaphorical comparison of the Basque Country with the Balkans.

While anxieties over violence occur across the nationalist political spectrum, moderate and radical nationalists blamed each other for generating it and jeopardizing the nation-building project. This opposition between nationalists has changed with ETA's cease-fire, a development that has given rise to a regrouping of all nationalist forces in the struggle for self-determination, and that has reestablished the older opposition between Basque nationalists and the Spanish state. Yet, despite this shift, young activists have continued to deploy the kind of urban violence called *kale borroka*, which has been infused more than before with the aura of fratricidal spectrality. The street violence is a threat to the recent nationalist alliance (and the current structure of political opposition between Basque nationalists and Spanish state) because it underscores an inherent tension within nationalism. Inasmuch as the Basque institutions assume state powers in the development of government and its security apparatuses, opposition to the state by radical activists continues to fall within the mission of their version of Basque nationalism,

---

2. An editorial in *El Diario Vasco*, December 11, 1995, 3, explicitly invoked the phantom of fratricide: "The demonstrations in support of the aggressor accompanied [by] threats to the *Ertzaintza* bring to the surface how the cancer of fanaticism is weaving a fratricide strategy with very perverse effects on the future."

3. *El Diario Vasco*, December 13, 1995, 1.

4. Javier Elzo, in *El Diario Vasco*, December 12, 1995.

or at least within the contested space of "Basqueness," thereby framing national identi-ty as split and shifting construction. I would suggest that the realization of a divided and conflicted national identity has a traumatic impact, one that gives political violence its spectral form.

In this article, I am interested in tracking the ghostly character of this violence between Basque police and young radical nationalists, its structure and manifestations for those who engage in it and whose everyday lives are marked by its presence. I will argue that for those agents and sufferers of the violence whom I interviewed—*ertzainas* and young activists alike—violence is engendered, materialized, and reproduced as, and within a realm of, violence and terror woven by the rumors of abuse and death circulating within the Basque Country's dense public sphere; that is, in bars and streets, in posters and news-papers, as well as through the ritualized interactions and performances of young *enca-puchados* (hooded activists) and masked police. In this sense, I suggest that violence in the Basque Country is better understood as a fantastic reality than as an ideological prod-uct. To speak of violence as a fantastic reality is not to say, however, that it is illusory, or the product of some kind of social pathology; rather, it means that in the Basque Coun-try the experience of violence corresponds to a *different* mode of reality, one whose visibil-ity is that of the invisible, a spectral mode not unlike that of witchcraft. I use fantasy here in a psychoanalytic sense; that is, neither as a deformation of an original event nor as a purely illusory construction, but as a form of reality in its own right, one that structures the lives of subjects and that might become, in fact, the only truly *Real*.[5] Otegi's feelings of persecution by the police might or might not correlate with actual police harassment, but the violence of being accosted was for him—as it is for many other youths—real, and it produced its own reality effects and its own corresponding violence. The same, I will argue, can be said about the *Ertzaintza*, whose feelings of harassment by young *encapucha-dos* were/are as real, and are equally capable of triggering their own forms of institution-alized (albeit illegal) violence.

This spectral space of trauma and fantasy constitutes what Benjamin saw as a kind of no-man's-land of the modern state, where the police cease to maintain the law but instead take it into their own hands.[6] Yet the ghostly violence of the police is underscored by a profound ambivalence toward the law, which is simultaneously maintained, trans-gressed, and experienced as a punitive agency. The Basque police share with their radical youth counterfoils the experience of Law as oppressive agency. In articulating collective anxieties about Basque national identity, the mimetic exchanges between these opposing forces engender violence as another reality, a presence that erupts into the order of nor-mality, disrupting it and giving it a sense of surreality.

---

5. See Laplanche and Pontalis (1989).
6. See Walter Benjamin's essay, "Critique of Violence" ([1921] 1978: 277–300).

The Space of Trauma

The Specter of the State

I first heard about Otegi in the course of a whispered conversation held as we walked through the bars and streets of Bilbao, invested with the political intimacy of secret knowledge that can become dangerous in the possession of the wrong person. My friend Antonio had introduced me to two other young men, and told them that I was interested in writing about "street fights." He was careful not to use the term "street violence," as young activists attribute that expression to the attempts of the mass media and the state to discredit them. As we walked through the labyrinthine streets and plazas of the old part of the city, Jesús suddenly began to talk about the *Ertzaintza*, as if prompted by memories sprouting up out of the urban landscape:

> The *Ertzaintza* are crazy," said Jesús, "they are ready to repress anything that goes out of their control. The other day, for example, the *parados* (the unemployed) were in this plaza having a meeting like they do every week and the police appeared all of a sudden with their vans and their sirens, dressed in riot gear, and gave them two minutes to disperse. For no reason! They had always met there. They are increasingly belligerent and aggressive.

I heard many stories about the "craziness" of the Basque police during those first months of 1997. "The way the Basque police are acting is excessive," said Jesús. "I think they are experimenting with some towns, like Hernani and Rentería." Itziar, a girl from Hernani, told me on another occasion that they used to laugh at the Basque police, but "now we don't laugh anymore. We are frightened. With the national police or the civil guard you always knew what they were up to, they either beat you or they didn't, but with the Basque police you never know... you can be doing nothing and they come and beat the hell out of you—they're crazy."

We entered a bar. There were very few people within or, indeed, out in the streets, but Jesús was whispering and looking over his shoulder from time to time as if to make sure that nobody was listening. "They broke my arm after a demonstration," he said. "There was not even a riot or anything, and suddenly this *ertzaina* throws me to the ground, *puto vasco de mierda*, and started beating me with his wooden baton. And they are Basque! I haven't gone to a demonstration since then. I'm too scared." His friend said that he had also been followed by the police. "For three months," said Jesús. "You got into the car and it was you and three other cars behind. You could go through a road block with no problem, they will see the police cars behind you and let you pass. There were constantly several plain clothes policemen behind me all the time, no matter where I went. It creates a lot of panic and paranoia," he said. "It's very frightening and it is difficult to remain calm. Some people react violently and just go and get a gun." This is when I heard about Otegi for the first time, in the company of Anuk, a young member of ETA who claimed to have been abducted by the *Ertzaintza*. Jesús continued, "This poor guy, Otegi, who shot two *ertzainas* . . . it could have happened to anybody . . . it is terrible that there are two persons dead, but it's not strange. The presence of the *Ertzaintza* is very suffocating."

As he spoke, I remembered the conversation the night before in one of the radical bars in the old part of Bilbao. Somebody had told a story about the *Ertzaintza* waiting for some high school students in front of their houses, intimidating them with threats of violence if they continued with their radical activities. The story provoked the outrage of all those present and prompted a string of similar tales. "That is what they are doing now," said Marga, "and they have taken to strip-searching women detainees, that is how they terrorize the girls." "People don't know about this" stated Jesús, "because you don't see it, it is never reported; the mass media is distorting reality. They are manipulating what is happening. What happened to this guy, Anuk, was terrible." "What happened?" I asked.

> He was kidnapped by the Basque police and they did all sorts of things to him, experimented with him by giving him drugs, and using psychological techniques. They let him go, but they were following him all the time. He managed to send a letter to the leadership of ETA—you see he was a militant—in which he told what was happening. He appeared a few days after they had taken him with a toy gun in his hand in front of an old garage and almost immediately the *Ertzaintza* and the Spanish police appeared on the scene and fought among themselves [for the right] to arrest him. It was clear that they were waiting for him, that this was something prepared. And then the national police took him to their station and, obviously, he couldn't take it anymore, so he threw himself out of the window."

"Have there been more cases like this one?" I asked. Javi produced a cynical smile and said, "Well, now they hang themselves with a rope," alluding to a Basque political prisoner (Jose Mari Aranzamendi) who had been found hanging dead in his cell, his feet and hands tied, his eyes covered with a kerchief. The next day the town was plastered with posters denouncing the death as political assassination by the state. Prison authorities said he had committed suicide.

Antonio had his theory of suicide as a new form of dirty war after the GAL scandal,[7] which implicated Spanish state officials in paramilitary assassinations of Basque radicals, had made overt killing difficult. "Nobody believes the suicide! They [the state authorities] are trying to create terror, send a message to Basque radicals that says "this is what awaits you." In the discourse of the everyday speech of radical nationalism, the state is a phantom, an authoritarian and violent agency that is everywhere yet nowhere in particular; a ghostly presence that haunts the political imaginary of Basque radicalism and organizes it around stories of violence and death.

---

7. From 1983 to 1987, a new right-wing paramilitary organization called GAL (Grupos Antiterroristas de Liberación, Antiterrorist Liberation Groups) claimed the assassinations of more than thirty Basque activists. In 1994, two policemen revealed the implication of the Spanish government and the military in organizing the GAL.

For the young *encapuchados* involved in defacing the state with Molotov cocktails, the *Ertzaintza* has become, alongside the Spanish police or the Civil Guard, the embodiment of the state. For the radicals, the state's ghostly power permeates the actions of the *Ertzaintza*, cloaked in the black masks that they call *verdugillo*. For Tasio, an *ertzaina*, the mask is self-defeating because it betrays fear and manifests, all too iconically, the blurred line between terrorism and policing, between the terror of Law and the law of Terror. "When you see the images of the police with masks and the arrested leaders of Herri Batasuna without them, you realize that the police has failed as such," says Tasio. For him, the masked police emblematize the state as outlaw and signify its mimetic performance of terrorism.

The power of the state circulates in the form of rumors and stories about the sudden appearances of the police, their abuse and their unfathomable motives. Ekaitz, an old radical, thinks that the Basque police is totally infiltrated by the CSID (the Spanish Secret Service) and that nothing Basque or autonomous remains in it. Like Ekaitz, young radicals also think that the body of the *Ertzaintza* that once represented the image of an imagined Basque state, has been possessed by the Spanish state. Therefore, for them, the Basque police force is simply not Basque anymore, it is another state's body. And like the body of the possessed, the *Ertzaintza* speaks and acts as someone else (De Certeau 1988: 246). Consequently, for radical nationalists it becomes doubly alien, an object of fear and resentment, a powerful shadow that is and isn't, a familiar figure turned stranger, a betrayer that has to be uncovered by unmasking its duplicitous identity with the derogatory designation: *cipayo*. The term *cipayo* refers to the soldiers of Indian origin serving in the British colonial army, and therefore carries the implicit meaning of betrayal.

These rumorous stories of unpredictable police violence and dirty wars circulate freely in the dense public sphere of Basque politics: in the bars, on the streets, and in informal conversations. My friend Maria assures me, as we walk along the ocean in San Sebastián, that a couple of young guys disappeared in the area of Mondragón, reappearing hours later without knowing where they had been. She has no doubt that this was the work of the Basque police, even though she cannot answer any of my concrete queries about when, how, and who.

In this maze of rumors it is not truth that counts, for it cannot be extracted from the narratives. What matters are the stories themselves, delineating as they do a traumatic space where the uncanny sense of the real erupts in the form of spectral exchange. Like the police, whom they violently engage, these young activists have a ghostly reality as well. Appearing and disappearing with their faces covered, they suddenly strike against a building or a police van, like an eruption of another *reality* upon the mundane surface of politics, their masks mirroring those of the police in a hide-and-seek game, a repetitive *fort-da*, that iconizes the power of concealment.

A Hall of Mirrors

The *encapuchados* are the agents of a new form of political violence focused on the defacement of the state and performed by radical youngsters ranging from fourteen to twenty-two years of age. In the years before the ceasefire, it became an increasingly quotidian occurrence for a pack of these youngsters to invade the central streets and plazas, their faces covered with hoods and kerchiefs and their hands bearing the Molotov cocktails that were destined to burn public buses, police vehicles, telephone booths, ATM machines, the headquarters of conservative political parties, court houses, and other public buildings, only to disappear as swiftly as they had appeared. For the *encapuchados,* this was sabotage of the state. During 1995 and 1996, according to the counts by Gipuzkoan authorities,[8] there were 408 and 440 such acts in the province respectively, and they increased by a further 25 percent during 1997. More so than the violence of ETA, the presence of the *encapuchados* has struck a deep nerve in Basque society.

Like the police, the *encapuchados* trigger all sorts of rumors about their identity. Jayone, who is a patrolling *ertzaina,* thinks that the *encapuchados* are manipulated by older radical nationalists. "Some of those people are dogmatic, they are like a sect and you cannot talk to them because they do not listen or think by themselves." She thinks that some might be idealists, but others are simply hired to create trouble. "A fellow officer told me," she said, "that his sister was caught in a riot and took refuge in the entry hall of an apartment building, along with a group of young guys; and then an older man entered the building, took his wallet out of his pocket and gave 5,000 pesetas [approximately $40] to each person. The officer's sister took the money and left, afraid to say anything." Jayone is convinced that at least some *encapuchados* are paid and she said that most *ertzainas* think so too.

As she talked, I remembered the story told by my neighbor, a woman in her fifties who, like many of her generation, does not approve of the sabotage and arbitrary rioting, even though she sympathizes with radical nationalists. She, too, wonders about the identity of the *encapuchados* and thinks some of them might be paid by the "state" to create bad press for radical nationalists. "They are not our people," she says. And her story followed the same plot as that of Jayone, even though they occupied opposed positions within the political spectrum. My neighbor assured me that she personally once saw how, after a riot in the old city, an old man gave 5,000 pesetas to a young fellow. She said she told them they were shameless and they both lowered their heads. This was how she knew that it was payment for stirring up trouble.

Those studying political violence know that the story of "agents" being paid for organizing riots is a common one in many places (Tambiah 1997). Juan, a savvy cultural activist, laughs at the story when I ask him what he thinks about the rumors of paid *encapuchados.* "Oh sure, I have also heard them, all the stories have the same plot," he says as he repeats it right down to the 5,000 pesetas. "So you, too, have heard them?" I ask. "Of course, it's part of the political folklore." To me it seems like an attempt to seize the

---

8. For more information, see the annual reports of the Fiscalía de la Audiencia Provincial de San Sebastián, during the years 1995 and 1996.

ghostly reality of violence. For the *Ertzaintza*, such spectral violence has crystallized into what has been called *grupos Y*.

These spectral *grupos Y* project the experience of being a Basque police-person as one dominated by fear.

> The central experience as patrolling *ertzainas* is fear. The *encapuchados* are a source of fear. With the *encapuchados* you have a sense of helplessness, a sense that you can be attacked at any moment and you cannot do anything, because they are the ones who throw stones or explosives or Molotov cocktails at you. And you are in there trapped in the small space of a van or a car and are just an easy target. And if you hit somebody you can be punished. You feel very impotent and vulnerable, particularly with the judicial system because they are anxious to find a culprit and the penalties are then higher than the ones they give to these youths.

Jayone tells how the *Ertzaintza* was called one night to a small town, "because somebody had set ablaze a trash container." A police van responded and it turned out to be an ambush. More than a hundred *encapuchados* emerged, suddenly throwing stones. The *Ertzaintza* started firing rubber bullets and somebody hit one of the *encapuchados* in the eye. There was a thorough investigation that supposedly discovered which officer had caused the injury, which is something very difficult to know because "there are several people shooting at once and all of them are wearing masks." Jayone tells the story of the ambush as an illustration of the *Ertzaintza's* vulnerability in the face of both social transgression and the Law which she herself embodies. Thus, in her story, the Basque police force appears as a particularly alienated body: at once the agent of the Law and the subject who fears it, a split subject, who is at once the Law and the outlaw.

Jayone's story mirrors, remarkably, the rumors of young radicals. Like the latter, the *Ertzaintza* experiences the *encapuchados* as spectral subjects of violence, a reality governing their lives yet inapprehensible. As in the case of the *encapuchados,* such spectral violence can erupt unexpectedly at any moment and works through the production of fear, which then circulates within a strange cultural economy spawning a universe of mimetic practices between the young radical *encapuchados* and the police (the other *encapuchados*), a ritualized *fort-da* play that futilely attempts to master the absent presence of the other. An example is when Tasio says that there is an urgency among *ertzainas* to "do something" about the *encapuchados*.

> And what do you do? You go and try to unmask them, even though you might know who they are, because that unmasking gives you the feeling of doing something, of having some control, some power. Even though you haven't done anything, it gives you the sense that "at least now we know who they are." But you see in most towns you know already who they are before the unmasking. However, you get sucked into that game.

So the *ertzainas* also resent and distrust the Law which, in the form of judicial restraints, can turn against them. As with the young radicals, for the police the production of, and need for, a culprit is an arbitrary process that renders them vulnerable. There is a measure of arbitrariness in the detention and charging of radical youngsters, since the activists are hooded and generally have their faces uncovered only upon being arrested. So there is little chance of determining who was doing what. Jayone's description of the production of a culprit after the shooting of a young man with a rubber bullet echoes, ironically, the same predicament.

The sense of defenselessness that the police feel in the face of the Law reached the level of paroxysm upon the outcome of Mikel Otegi's trial. In a shocking verdict, the jury found Otegi not guilty, heeding the defense's argument that his killings were the consequence of a heightened feeling of persecution that translated into a moment of mad rage. Otegi was set free. "That was *very, very* hard," said Jayone,

> it hurt very deeply because you felt totally vulnerable and impotent, totally at their mercy; it is like *they* [the Law] had given *them* [radical nationalists] impunity to do anything. There are two persons dead and he is *free*!! He is not in a psychiatric hospital or anything like that, he is free. And next day you are on the street on duty and see a demonstration of young radicals shouting "*Mikel Askatua*" ("Mikel Free") and applauding, and you have to be there listening to it, and you cannot do anything because they are not doing anything illegal, they are just shouting! I saw my fellow officers cry out of anger.

Anger and fear organize the structure of feelings of the Basque police and young radicals alike. They constitute the experience of violence as a mimetic relation that makes the sense of what is *real* for the Basque police and for the *encapuchados* mirrors of one another. This *reality* of violence is not ordinary reality, but rather what seeps through the order of reality and ultimately shapes it as a space of trauma and terror. This *reality* of violence makes reality a play of surfaces and what some call political madness a reality.

CHAPTER 13

Out of Their Minds?: On Political Madness in the Basque Country[1]

On March 9, 2001, the Basque separatist group ETA (Euskadi Ta Askatasuna—Basque Land and Freedom) killed Iñaki Totorika, a patrol officer in the Basque police force, with a bomb planted under his patrol car. It was the first time that this organization targeted a regular officer of the *Ertzaintza* (or Basque police), and the news caused another convulsion in the long list of events that had shaken the Basque Country since ETA broke a fourteen-month ceasefire in December 1999. A well-known political journalist characterized this killing as "a qualitative change in terrorism" in an article entitled "*Terror a la Deriva*" ("Terror at a Loss"), a title suggesting a violent intervention that had lost direction, a terror out of control and making no sense. The killing of Totorika, said Alberto Surio, the journalist, extended this criminal phenomenon to the social body of the *Ertzaintza* and their families and friends. It seems, he said, that analysts in the Basque police had thought about the possibility "of a major bloody action, an indiscriminate massacre [that] performed a kind of kamikaze craziness extending the panic everywhere."[2] The expression came, he wrote, from a high-ranking nationalist in the Basque government. The protagonist of this horror scene, imagined, anticipated, and feared by the high-ranking nationalist, was none other than "a mad ETA ready to burn all bridges, needing to show an image of invincibility." The background to this scenario, wrote Surio, was "a political context marked by a confrontation between institutional and radical nationalism." With this background, the scenario created with the death of the police officer points, he continued, to the Basque Nationalist Party (Partido Nacionalista Vasco, PNV) that is dominant in the Basque government, as a target of ETA. This last scene is the epitome of nationalist dystopia—a horror story that ends in self-destruction of the national self. But Iñaki Totorika, the Basque policeman, was not only important because he symbolized the violent opposition between nationalist projects, and signaled a profound rupture within Basque

---

1. Originally published in *Empire & Terror: Nationalism/Postnationalism in the New Millennium*, edited by Begoña Aretxaga, Dennis Dworkin, Joseba Gabilondo, and Joseba Zulaika, Conference Papers Series No.1 (Reno: Center for Basque Studies, University of Nevada, Reno, 2004), 163–75. Based on a paper presented at the conference, *Nationalism, Globalization, and Terror: A Debate on Stateless Nations, Particularism/Universalism, and Radical Democracy*, Center for Basque Studies, University of Nevada, Reno, April 7–9, 2002.

2. Alberto Surio, "Terror a la Deriva," *El Diario Vasco*, October 3, 2001.

nationalism as a whole, but because his affiliations signaled also the complexities of Basque identity in the Basque Country today. For while Inaki Totorika was a member of the PNV—that is, a nationalist himself—he was also a member of a Spanish socialist labor union, Unión General de Trabajadores (UGT, General Workers' Union). It is precisely this kind of ambiguity, in which Basqueness is not defined in a relation of exclusion to Spanishness, that ETA has tried to eliminate since the end of the ceasefire. I will come back to this ambiguity later, but first let me return to the theme of madness in the article I referred to above.

During the second half of the 1990s, madness became a prominent trope in the discourse on Basque politics, signaling a fear of unpredictable nationalist or state violence. Here I will restrict my discussion to the figure of madness in relation to nationalist violence. Madness has become the domain of anguished paroxysm after the separatist group ETA called off its ceasefire in December 1999, and initiated an all-out campaign for national sovereignty (called "Now"), which has reached a toll of about thirty assassinations so far [2000–2001], as well as a high number of arson attacks and widespread intimidation performed by radical nationalist youth. Since the break of the ceasefire, the violence of both ETA members and young radicals has targeted members of non-nationalist parties such as the PSOE (Spanish socialist party) and the right-wing Partido Popular (PP), the party of the Spanish government, as well as journalists, intellectuals, and artists, who have voiced their disagreement with nationalist violence; it has also intimidated members of the moderate nationalist PNV (dominant in the Basque government). A nationalist town councilor described the situation in this way: "There is a kind of madness now in which everybody could be a victim." From the perspective of the ideological history of ETA, which has been leftist in character, the new campaign of violence does not make sense. Some of those killed had leftist histories and had served prison terms for their activities against Francoism. Others were representatives in small town councils or figures known for favoring a politics of dialogue with ETA, rather than military confrontation. This was the case with Ernest Lluch, a professor and former health minister in the socialist government, who had strongly advocated negotiating with ETA as a solution to the ongoing nationalist violence. Negotiation has been a long-lasting demand on the part of radical nationalists, although one strongly resisted by the Spanish government. In killing Lluch, ETA appeared to be eliminating a space of mediation necessary for a potential political negotiation. The killing didn't seem to make any sense. The communiqué signed by all political forces condemned "*la sinrazón de ETA*" (the unreason of ETA).[3]

The violence unleashed by ETA after the ceasefire is increasingly foreclosing the space of the political as the space of the nation. Furthermore, it has had the seemingly paradoxical effect of reinforcing the anti-nationalist Spanish right-wing in the Basque Country, as well as debilitating the social fabric that constitutes Basque nationalism at the local level. In other words, rather than *strengthening*, the violence of ETA and of the young

---

3. "Todas las Fuerzas Políticas Condenan la Sinrazón de ETA," *El País*, November 22, 2000.

activists has the effect of *weakening* nationalist aspirations and the possible political avenues to achieve them. The harder the radical nationalists try to will into being an independent Basque nation (which they portray as imminent) through discourse and violent action, the lower is the desire for national existence among the Basque population. So bewildering is the new strategy of Basque radicalism, and so much in the profit of the right-wing party in the Spanish government, that it would seem that ETA had been cleverly infiltrated by the Spanish state to provoke the destruction of Basque nationalism once and for all. But this, of course, is nonsensical conspiracy theory. For Juan Jose Ibarretxe, the president of the Basque government and a member of the PNV, "ETA is out of reality."[4] At a loss for other explanations, the most common reaction of commentators is that radical nationalists have gone totally out of their minds. But what exactly is insane about it?

In this paper, I would like to reflect on this figure of madness as the categorization of a violent politics that destabilizes epistemological and political certainties. What does it signify? What does it do? And ultimately what *does it say?* In asking this last question, I want to suggest a connection between a form of political intervention that is deemed deranged and a kind of knowledge that the political subject of radical nationalism might not want to know. I follow here the lead of a large body of scholarship that, from Freud to Lacan, and Nietzsche to Foucault and Derrida, has posed madness as a problem of knowledge: "Madness fascinates," says Foucault, "because it is knowledge . . . intimate knowledge, which is offered and at the same time evaded" (1988: 21–22). Recently, Johannes Fabian (2000) has made a related argument; namely, that the knowledge produced in the colonial encounter was not the product of rational epistemologies, but the outcome of various states of insanity. My goal here is not to discuss the conditions of knowledge production, but rather, to ponder what kind of intimate knowledge a putative political madness might point to, and to wonder what "the strange paths" of this knowledge (Foucault 1988: 25) might say about the complicated (dis)articulation of the nation-state form more generally. Let me first discuss, albeit briefly, the political background of this discourse on political madness in the Basque Country.

Background

The trope of madness became prominent during the 1990s at a moment when a Basque police force entered the scene of Basque politics and a moment when a new youth movement emerged as an aggressive nationalist subject. Let me backtrack a little: ETA was born in 1959 as a response to the military regime of Francisco Franco. ETA's ultimate goal was the unification of the French and Spanish Basque provinces into an independent nation-state. Until the death of General Franco in 1975, however, its actions had an essentially anti-fascist character. Most of ETA's targets during that period were members of the Francoist security forces. After Franco died, Spain undertook a period of democratic

---

4. "Comunicado del Presidente del Gobierno Vasco," *El País*, November 28, 1999.

reform, called (not very originally) "*La Reforma*" (the Reform). The Constitution of the current democratic regime was a cornerstone of the *Reforma* and was endorsed by the Spanish people in a referendum held in 1977, but not approved in the Basque Country, where there was a 70 percent combination of abstention and negative votes for not including "the right to self-determination" for the *nacionalidades,* or ethnic regions within the Spanish state—that is Catalunya, the Basque Country, Galiza. What the Constitution envisioned, instead, was a process of increasing regional autonomy, and so during the following ten years—from 1975 to 1985—the Basque Country developed an array of state-like institutions: a government and parliament, judicial and educational apparatus, its own police force, and even its own revenue system—a unique structure in the whole of Spain. Although this set of administrative and political institutions is subordinated to the Spanish Constitution and legislation, they enjoy a considerable degree of autonomy that, for all practical purposes, produces state effects in the everyday lives of individuals living in what is officially called "the Autonomous Community of the Basque Country."

In this scenario, where the goal of an independent Basque Country could be pursued through the conventions of democratic politics—say, by growing popular demand—ETA's armed strategy was expected to stop. But it did not. Its rationale was that the regime had not really changed, and that, despite the appearance of democracy, there was still a dictatorial state. This rationale was aided by a succession of emergency legislative measures in the Basque Country, which permitted the infringement of civil and human rights of those accused of having some relationship with Basque terrorism. In spite of the blows suffered by radical nationalists during the democratic transition, ETA survived and even attracted the sympathy of a vibrant youth movement, making its appearance during the mid 1980s. By the mid 1990s, a time when ETA was extremely weak after its leadership had been arrested in toto, a new brand of radical nationalist youth became the stars of the Basque political theater.

This new breed of nationalist youths became the subject of a new kind of urban insurgency, characterized by arson attacks on public buildings and services, as well as police vehicles and rioting; a violence that for the first time systematically transgressed the moral boundaries of local communities, by intimidating and attacking both neighbors and peers who opposed their politics, including other nationalists. This new form of violence was largely incomprehensible to the majority of the population, triggering a heightened anxiety about civil confrontation (and more importantly about the radicalization and widening spectrum of nationalist violence). Jabi, one of the leaders of this youth movement who has now disappeared, most likely into the ranks of ETA, explained its logic, which he called "*la lógica del tensionamiento*" (the logic of tensing):

> After 1992, with the leadership of ETA in prison, the enemy says that's it, we have finished with them, and then the enemy springs a trap in the form of a debate about whether the armed struggle is good or bad for the political process, if we should take part in the institutional dynamic . . . and radical nationalists fell into this trap and it is then that Jarrai [a radical youth organization] and ETA itself says *that's it,* this is a false debate that only leads us to kill ourselves. And from then on, the question for us is that if we are going to have

an adequate peace at the end of the war, then what we have to do is to make sure that there is war and not to deactivate it. So we redirect that false debate about violence and we begin to put things in their place. This is when we enter into the strategy of *tensionamiento* [tensing], which means that in order for it to be distension [untensing] there needs first to be tension. That is to say we are not going to sign a peace at which we arrive as defeated, so if they want peace what we have to do is to tense the political climate so that then both parts can talk about distensing. The enemy itself takes you to that path.

But who is the enemy? Jabi: "During the years of pseudo-democracy, certain judicial people, certain journalists, politicians, etc. have positioned themselves in defense of the current political system, in defense of the state, and have shown total disrespect for Basque national aspirations; those people can only be catalogued as enemies."

In September 1998, after, indeed, a very tense few years, ETA called a ceasefire as part of a new political agreement with moderate nationalists (PNV and EA, Eusko Alkartasuna (Basque Solidarity), a social democratic nationalist party). The support for radical nationalist politics, which had been steadily diminishing in the last years, changed overnight with the end to violence and higher vote counts in the following elections, with the result that the radical nationalists became the second largest nationalist force, the third largest force after the socialist party in the Basque Country. Their support made possible a nationalist government in the Basque Country that could govern without the support of non-nationalist parties, the PSOE (or its Basque variant, PSE-EE) and conservative PP. This was the first time that such a configuration was actualized in the Basque Government. Overnight, radical nationalism had passed from a socially marginalized force to a center-stage political player, showing that there was substantial support for their leftist political program, although conditioned on ending violence. Political possibility was in the air, and the ceasefire triggered, within the political culture of the Basque Country, a new sense of excitement and a general demand for political negotiations with ETA that would make its break in fighting permanent. The Spanish PP government stalled on the negotiations for a definite peace, using as an excuse that youth violence and intimidation (now labeled "low-intensity terrorism") had not disappeared. Frustrating popular expectations in the Basque Country, the Spanish government seemed to be doing everything possible to indeed deter the peace process.

On December 3, 1999, after more than a year of lack of progress on a possible negotiation between ETA and the Spanish government, ETA called off the ceasefire. A good number of political organizations and analysts blamed the Spanish government for the break of the ceasefire. But shortly thereafter, ETA published a communiqué in which it explained that the ceasefire never had as a goal the attainment of peace, but rather wanted the building of a sovereign Basque State. ETA said that that was an opportunity to "change the old juridical-political framework that unfolded from the reform of the dictatorship in favor of a new juridical-political framework based on democracy for the Basque People." ETA contended that it halted the ceasefire because *el proceso* ("the Process") had been stalled by the PNV, their nationalist allies, who had "attempted to modify the very nature of the peace initiative, which was a process of national construction ['*construcción del*

Pueblo [*Vasco*]'] and which they tried to make into a mere process of peace ['*un proceso de paz sin contenido*'].[5] The time, ETA said, was ripe for the Basque people to act as a de facto sovereign nation by creating a Constituting Sovereign National Assembly, elected by all Basque citizens in the provinces divided now between the French and Spanish states. This proposal seemed so far from the current horizon of the politically possible that an elected representative from within the radical nationalist coalition was prompted to say that "ETA was confusing desire with reality."[6]

If ETA confused desire with reality, it was determined to make the logic of desire prevail.

After the ceasefire, ETA emerged radicalized in its actions that targeted local politicians, journalists who wrote against ETA, former state officials, university professors, and, finally, in March 2000, also the *Ertzaintza,* the Basque police who had become an official legitimate target because, as "a repressive body subject to Spain," it was incessantly repressing Basque society.[7] The common denominator connecting the victims was their association with what ETA called "the Spanish project" ("*el projecto de España*"). The logic of "tensing," which was associated with youth street violence during the late 1990s, had now come to find its full dramatic expression in the killings of ETA.

More so than before, ETA's violence was restructuring the semantics of social space around the mutually exclusive categories of Basque and Spanish. What seemed crazy was the ease with which one could be violently expelled from the field of Basqueness into the dangerous field of Spanishness, such that the sphere of Basqueness, strictly identified as a national space—the idealized Basque People, or Euskal Herria (a term encompassing the totality of Basque provinces in the Spanish and French states)—was increasingly being reduced to a hard core of radical nationalists. It was thus the disjunction between a discourse of citizenship, national sovereignty, and institutional building, and the violent reduction of those who were supposed to constitute the national community; the disjunction, that is, between a discourse of democracy and a ruthless authoritarian policing of identity; in sum, the disjunction between an idealized national object and the disappearance of national or even nationalist community. These were the disjunctions that precipitated the worried conclusion that there was no rational explanation, not just in the rhetoric of the mass media but in the concerned commentary of friends and acquaintances. Radical nationalists, in short, were out of their minds.

The Local Semantics of Madness

Let me now come back to my initial question. What defines this state of insanity? At the local level, what is signaled by the figure of madness is a state of incomprehensibility, an

---

5. Declaración de Euskadi Ta Askatasuna (ETA) en la que anuncia el final de la tregua (ETA declaration in which it announced the end of the ceasefire), November 1999. At http://www.filosofia.org/his/h1999eta.htm.

6. Milagros Rubio, *El Diario Vasco,* December 2, 1999.

7. *El País,* March 31, 2001.

impossibility of making sense; a state, in fact, of epistemological arrest: ETA's actions are undermining the very goal of national sovereignty it is pursuing. Madness is also associated with a breach in the moral order that bounds local (and political) community, a breach that constitutes a traumatic excess, a violent eruption within the familiar order, of that, which—in its inability to be apprehended—defamiliarizes it. The gasoline bombing of a bookstore that is a symbol of leftist resistance to Francoism, because its owner is a member of the socialist party; the intimidation of an elderly and well-known artist, Agustin Ibarrola, because he expresses his opinion against nationalist violence; the harassment of neighbors who openly disagree with radical nationalists—all of these are examples of this traumatic breach of the moral community that is felt as a state of madness. More than anything, madness figures a fracture in reality, articulated not just in action but also in a discourse that takes the form of a delirium in which radical nationalists figure as the people-nation occupied by foreign enemies. In the communiqué issued after breaking the ceasefire, for example, ETA asserted its "commitment to defend Euskal Herria—the Basque people-nation—from the oppression, occupation, and attacks by Spain and France."[8]

I would argue that to pose the question of violence in the Basque Country as a question of madness vis-à-vis democratic (shall we say State) reason is already to perform a particular kind of operation by which this violence is severed from the realm of the political. To oppose violence to the reason of a state of law is to entrench nationalist violence in the space of unreason, as well as to open a space of pure confrontation where the possibility of dialogue between these positions is eliminated. Patxo, a high-ranking journalist for the newspaper *El País* who has written widely against nationalist violence and who is now under police protection because of death threats (like some 700 other people) issued by ETA, put it to me very clearly: "To kill a man is to kill a man," he said. "You cannot talk with ETA because they don't listen to reason. The only thing to do is to apply the law!" This is, of course, the position of the Spanish government, which counteracts violence with growing repressive legislation. Yet in the Basque Country, the law has an ambiguous character, inscribed as it has been in a long history of police abuse. A politics of violent confrontation feeds into the logic of occupation of radical nationalism, reproducing a spiral of endless violence.

Yet if this critique of the figure of madness as sustaining the violence of state reason allows us to see a configuration of the political as an increasingly polarized and foreclosed space, it does not bring us any closer to the reality animating the seemingly incomprehensible and traumatic violence of ETA and radical youth: the paradox that this form of *willing* the nation into being appears to be destroying it.

---

8. ETA and radical youth have indeed taken the position of sovereignty, as defined by Giorgio Agamben (2000b), that is a position of absolute force, of the law as absolute force from which only they are excluded. In two recently issued communiqués, one in January, the other in March of this year, ETA announced that anybody in the Basque police, from officer to those in command, are now targets of its violence as well as political forces that position themselves against nationalist violence.

Madness as Secret Knowledge

I want to take seriously this figure of madness, not as a figure organizing a discourse of political exclusion, but instead as a domain of knowledge, one characterized in the words of Lacan by "a fault, a point of rupture in the structure of the external world that finds itself patched over by fantasy" (1993: 45). Part of the knowledge of this political madness signal refers to the violence of the Spanish Civil War (1936–39) and the thirty-six years of dictatorship (1939–75), buried but not dead, after the death of Franco and over which silence the birth of the democratic regime was pacted. Mario Onaindia, a member of ETA in the early 1970s and condemned to life in prison by the Francoist regime, thinks of ETA as the only "leftover of Francoism,"[9] while Felipe González, former socialist president of the Spanish government, wrote of ETA in one article as a "phantom of the former regime that we have not overcome."[10] If the silence of the civil war and the dictatorship organized the reality of the democracy as a fissureless state of law, what organizes the reality of the current nationalist violence as a madness? By *reality* I do not mean an external reality, but rather what Freud called "psychic reality" and what French psychoanalysts Nicolas Abraham and Maria Torok ([1959] 1994) have defined as "what is rejected, masked, denied precisely as *reality;* it is that which *is* all the more so since it must not be known; in short Reality is defined as a secret." What I intend to do in the rest of the paper is to discuss the Reality, thus understood, that organizes the dynamic of radical nationalist violence. To do so, I will focus on what Abraham and Torok would call a phantomatic word; a word that is strange to the vocabulary of the subject, yet one that organizes a stage within which the Reality of the subject is revealed as it is simultaneously disguised. Lacan puts it in similar fashion: "Beginning with an utterance, a game is instituted" (1993: 51). In Basque nationalist madness, the word, the utterance that institutes the game and organizes the scenario of madness, is the term *cipayo,* which is used by radical nationalists to address the *Ertzaintza,* or Basque police.

Let me briefly say that during the 1990s the *Ertzaintza* proved itself as a police force that could violently repress demonstrations, gather intelligence, and conduct anti-terrorist operations. In acting against radical nationalists, the *Ertzaintza* challenged the latter's ideology that nationalist violence was the result of a conflict between Spain and the Basque Nation, situating that violence squarely within a Basque field. In performing as state (the Basque state), the *Ertzaintza* had introduced an unbearable ambiguity at the core of the nation imagined by radical nationalists. Moreover, this ambiguity was compounded by the fact that this (Basque) "state" was enforcing Spanish law, and could, thus, be seen as Spanish as well as Basque. It was at this point that the word *cipayo* appeared on the scene. As a metaphor, *cipayo* had the mission, to echo James Fernandez (1986), of covering up this ambiguity, best articulated as the problematic character of Basque identity (riddled as

---

9. Emilio Alfaro, "Doblemente Condenados," *El País*, February 4, 2001.
10. See Felipe González, "Chile, Argentina y las Comisiones de la Verdad," *El País*, April 22, 2001.

it is with unrecognized difference). It was to do so by rigidly redrawing the boundaries of ethnic identity, so that difference was strictly positioned outside the boundaries of national identity and not within it.

Cipayo: The Intolerable Ambiguity of National Being

I first encountered the term *cipayo* in 1993 as part of some graffiti that read "*cipayos asesinos.*" I remember my puzzlement at this word, about which I had no previous knowledge. A friend explained that *cipayos* was the term used by radical nationalists to insult the *Ertzaintza*. *Cipayos,* she said, was the name used some hundred and fifty years ago for the soldiers of Indian origin serving in the British colonial army. The graffiti then began to make sense to me. Radical nationalists in Basque Country were accusing the *Ertzaintza* of betrayal of their own people and culture. I was still unaware of the motivations triggering the election of such an obscure word, much less of the train of its complex associations. But after I saw its accusatory presence for the first time, it was suddenly all around me. I realized that radical nationalists habitually referred to the *Ertzaintza* as *cipayos* in their everyday speech. Equally interesting was the talk that followed my inquiries about the *Ertzaintza*. Friends and acquaintances from different sides of the political spectrum were preoccupied with what they thought to be a growing animosity between radical nationalists supporting the violence of ETA and people supporting the established autonomous institutions. The fabric of social life having been so tightened in the Basque Country now appeared to them to be rupturing, and my interlocutors feared what they called a Balkanization of the Basque Country.

The metaphor/insult *cipayo* appears both as a manifestation of an anxiety about the rupturing of identity and as an attempt to repair it. By attributing a treacherous identity to the Basque police, radical nationalists suggest that the Basque police are not truly Basque. By extension, neither are those who support the police truly Basque, particularly those in the Basque Government, which is directly responsible for the actions of the *Ertzaintza*. What *cipayo* conceals, though, is the existence of different forms of being Basque that do not coincide with a nationalist project—an alterity of being that lies at the core of Basque identity and that translates into divergent political projects. The term *cipayo* negates that alterity and symptomatizes a profound anxiety about it. What *cipayo* asserts by exclusion, then, is a unity of identity projected into a utopian national community.

Nationalist Ambivalence: The Colony We Never Were

There are two dimensions to the metaphor *cipayo* that I would like to explore further. One is the image associated with the signifier *cipayo*, and the other is its predication of betrayal. Here I move to what Jane Gallop has called "a metonymic reading": "whereas a metaphoric interpretation consists in supplying another signifier which the signifier in the text stands for [for example, *cipayo* represents *ertzaintza*, in our case] a metonymic interpretation supplies a whole context of associations" (1985: 129). Let's then look more carefully into this context. Radical nationalists could, of course, call the Basque police simply traitors, assassins, or *txakurras* (dogs), terms with a long history of use in debasing the Spanish police, for example.[11] Instead of direct accusations or readily available insults that could have equally legitimized violence against the *Ertzaintza,* radical nationalists chose, however, the new and obscure term *cipayo.*

What the metaphor *cipayo* does that the other words do not is frame the political conflict in the Basque Country in colonial terms. By associating the *Ertzaintza* with the figure of *cipayo,* radical nationalists are not only calling them betrayers, they are also positing a relation of analogy between the Basque Country and a colonial context. In so doing, they are stating that the relation between the Basque Country and Spain is a colonial one. By virtue of its inherent domination, this colonial relation can only be one of polarized opposition between colonizers and colonized that admits no middle ground. Indeed, it is as if radical nationalists had reinvented the Battle of Algiers. In the discourse constructed by these associations, the Basque Country remains colonized as long as it stays part of the Spanish state, regardless of how autonomous its "autonomous" institutions might be. Within this logic, the Basque government and Basque Parliament are not truly Basque as long as they remain part of Spain, nor as long as they do not encompass *all* the Basque provinces in France and Spain. It is precisely to reinforce this scenario that a new significant word, *partition,* made its debut in radical nationalist political discourse. ETA issued a communiqué in February 2000 to affirm that, "The institutions of the *partition* not only are useless [*muertas,* literally "dead"] but they have become a total obstacle to overcome the conflict [between Euskal Herria and Spain] and as a consequence they constitute the conflict itself."[12] The *Ertzaintza* are *cipayos* and not merely betrayers, because they act in the interest of a colonizer state and a state of partition, when they suppress the resistance of radical nationalists now figuring as the homogeneous totality of Basque citizens. In this fantasy scenario of a colonial context, violence is legitimized by the identification of "Basque" with "the colonized," who must use any means to get rid of the colonizer, thus legitimizing violence against the Basque police, who, by virtue of their subordination to the Spanish state, are not Basque anymore.

The associative chain described above has led to a political and social situation of increasing polarization, hostility, and violence within the Basque Country from the late 1990s to the present day, when those who disagree with the colonial scenario staged by the metaphor *cipayo* are being violently excluded from the sphere of Basque identity. Txema Montero, a former representative in the European Parliament for Herri Batasuna (the radical nationalist party) in 1988, and now outside this organization as a result of his disagreement with the violent politics of ETA, expressed it this way in an interview, when he said that, "ETA seeks an ideological war between two communities, something that did not exist except in the war of 1936." This colonial scenario emerges at a moment

---

11. See in this respect Zulaika (1988).
12. *El País,* May 11, 2000. The communiqué was issued by ETA at the end of February.

when the meaning of Basqueness is not taken for granted, but instead is subject to debate and contestation, a moment of rearticulation of what it means to be Basque in an increasingly globalized world. What the metaphor of *cipayo* conceals is the anxiety and uncertainty that such rearticulation produces. But it could be also that what is really feared and resisted is the dissolution of a fantasmatic unity of national identity that was bound to occur with the disappearance of an outside enemy. Let me elaborate.

The colonial scenario evoked by the metaphor *cipayo* is also linked by metonymic contiguity to the scenario of an independent nation. This is a scenario where the imaginary unity produced in the anti-colonial struggle might give rise to internal division, as well as struggles of power and violence—it is telling, for example, that the image chosen to accuse the *Ertzaintza* was taken from the British/Indian context. One could argue that the actual political reality of the Basque Country, with its autonomous institutions, political parties, and power relations, constitutes a preview of an independent nation. Radical nationalists' violent resistance to this scenario of nationhood, by predicating a colonial situation, would suggest that a resistance to achieving an independent nation coexists with a desire to form it. Thus, if *cipayo* attempts to dispel political ambiguity, it also manifests profound ambivalence toward the national-state form. This would explain why the growing indiscriminate violence of radical nationalists threatens to destroy the very nation it purports to construct. During the last few years, this violence has not only considerably damaged the fabric of social relations, it has also played in favor of anti-nationalist parties that have notably risen in recent elections.[13] Let me explore the play of ambiguity and ambivalence a bit further by returning to the treacherous identity that *cipayo* predicates.

National Intimacy

I have said that *cipayo* attempts to dispel the ambiguity of a Basque "state" of being that is simultaneously Spanish. It does so by effecting a move that divests the *Ertzaintza* of Basque identity through the accusation of betrayal, and placing this police body and those who support it firmly on the Spanish side of the Basque/Spanish boundary. Once this is done, the *Ertzaintza* becomes a legitimate target of nationalist violence and the boundaries of national identity are clearly reestablished. And yet, the notion of betrayal that *cipayo* conveys suggest a bond, a (national) intimacy that cannot quite be shaken off. Unlike the invader, or the stranger, the traitor retains a trace of self. The betrayal itself ties betrayer and betrayed together. It makes the betrayer part of the betrayed—a wounded part, to be sure, but still a part that cannot be extricated until the betrayal itself has disappeared or been forgotten. The *cipayo* contains the traumatic residue of an imaginary unity that has not been given up, while it signals the fact that it no longer exists. It is thus an

---

13. A well-known politician and former mayor of Barcelona explicitly affirmed that (Basque) terrorism had benefited the right-wing Partido Popular (PP) currently running the government, helping it achieve an absolute majority in the last parliamentary elections. The PP government is virulently anti-nationalist and has systematically refused to negotiate a ceasefire with ETA. It would seem that radical nationalists are doing everything possible *not* to achieve their goals.

ambivalent object, a threat, and an object of identification. This ambivalence complicates the relation between radical nationalists and the Basque police with an excess of affect that is absent in the relation with the Spanish police. This excess manifests itself in practices of disclosure, such as the public uncovering of individual *ertzainas* in towns and villages, their public humiliation and punishment, ritualized attacks, and now assassinations. Such practices of ritualized attacks are, de facto, policing practices aimed at enforcing the boundaries of ethnic identity by punishing those who are thought to threaten them. In recent years, these policing practices have extended to other Basques who openly condemn nationalist violence. These practices suggest a movement in which the trauma of difference within national identity is repeatedly played out without resolution. For radical nationalists, the *cipayo* becomes, then, both a threat and a necessity, a despised object that challenges the fantasized unity of the national community and one that by virtue of evoking the Basque state is an object of desire; a despised object that stands in their way of unity and the one that by suggesting a colonial scenario legitimizes nationalist violence.[14]

This ambiguity and ambivalence of a figure that represents, at once, national betrayal and nationalist identification, can be tracked in the metonymic traces contained in the signifier *cipayo,* as it shifts etymologically from a representation of the colonial British army in India *(sipahi),* to a representation of anti-colonial forces emerging with the mutiny of *sipahies* against the British in 1857, to a representation of the police *(sipai)* in the postcolonial nation.[15] This etymological history points to the ambiguity of the *sipai* as a threat, not only to national liberation, but to colonial rule as well. This ambiguity is concealed, yet present, in the use of the Basque *cipayo,* which acts simultaneously as a metonymy of the Basque nation and a metonymy of the hegemony of the Spanish state. Such ambiguity and its concomitant ambivalence manifests itself both in the distrust periodically expressed by the Spanish government in relation to the *Ertzaintza,* and in the suspicion voiced by radical nationalists that the *Ertzaintza* is infiltrated by the secret services of Spain.[16]

To recapitulate, then, a kind of madness can be seen in the violence of Basque radical nationalists. But this madness is not defined by their belief that they embody the nation-people, or that the moment is ripe to achieve national independence now. That is the fantasy that hides a reality unspeakable and rather shameful, organized around the knowledge that an actual nation-state would necessarily entail the loss of an idealized unified nation as a utopian object of desire. The possibility of such loss engenders a deep

14. Many examples can be found of the ambiguity associated with the Basque police. The latest appeared in the form of a communiqué published by all major newspapers on May 24, 2000. In the communiqué, radical nationalist youth accuse the *Ertzaintza* of being *cipayos* for arresting a group of youths charged with arsonist activities. The communiqué accuses the *Ertzaintza* of acting against the Basque people and being "a servant of Spanish parties," ending by threatening the *Ertzaintza* if they stand in the way of national sovereignty (*El País,* May 24, 2000; *Gara,* May 24, 2000).

15. See Metcalf (1964) and Mukherjee (1984) for more extensive etymology of the word *sipahi,* and for a history of the rebellion of 1857 in India.

16. See, for example, *El Mundo,* Jan. 15, 1997; and *Egin,* January 15, 1998, April 20, 1997, and April 22, 1997.

ambivalence toward the actual possibility of a nation-state. In fact, never was the Basque Country more on a fast track to national sovereignty than during the ceasefire, when a coalition of nationalist forces began to orchestrate institutional forms for self-government, with wide popular support. Calling off the ceasefire and the radicalization of ETA's violence has destroyed those initiatives for self-government and triggered a great deal of hostility and distrust toward a project of national sovereignty. Thus, while radical nationalists strive madly indeed to obtain their object of desire—a Basque nation-state—they do everything possible to ensure that it will not happen.

Yet I would like to suggest that this political madness unfolding in the Basque Country might be an expression of something intrinsically mad, or maddening, in the nation-state form itself. I would argue that something is profoundly at odds in this hegemonic form of the modern polity that engenders a constant tension between the logic of nationhood as a utopian, fraternal community sustained by imaginary acts of identification, and the practice of statehood as a force of law sustained by multiple relations of power. For radical nationalists throughout the Basque Country, the state effects produced by a variety of institutions and political processes are reified into a subject that is still experienced as a forceful enemy, yet one that also constitutes an object of identification. This identification is best manifested in the sanctioning form of ETA's violence that acts as a sovereign power. And thus we have this ongoing state of paralysis characterized by increasing violence on the part of ETA, young radicals, and the different manifestations of Statehood, which seems geared to perpetuate itself ad infinitum. Why? Because while the nation is an object of desire, radical nationalists can maintain a unified sense of national self as colonized people and can continue to figure as main characters in a story that in Samuel Weber's view, is split into a present that is never complete and a future that never fully arrives. It is precisely this state of expectation that the electoral poster produced by radical nationalists for the oncoming elections to the Basque government illustrates.

The nation is represented here not as a political community, but, literally, as a body of imaginary identification, a body that in the form of the fetus is anticipated but not quite born yet. Notice that the state/father is absent from this picture—a patent force nowhere to be seen.

CHAPTER 14

Maddening States[1]

Introduction

During the past decade, the field of knowledge that we call the state has become the object of renewed academic reflection by anthropologists and scholars in other fields. During the 1980s and mid 1990s, studies of globalization seemed to point to the radical weakening and transformation, if not disappearance, of the modern state (Appadurai 1993, 1996; Hannerz 1996; Michael Kearney 1995; Ong 1999; Tsing 2000). States' borders and economies were being challenged, if not erased, by neoliberal transnational corporations, by higher order political processes of unification such as the formation of the European Union, or by those set in motion by the fall of the Berlin Wall and the transitions from authoritarian regimes to democratic ones. War and war economies in Africa, Latin America, and Asia made a joke of the monopoly of state violence by showing the crucial role of other actors (warlords, guerrillas, drug traffickers) in inflicting violence, displacing populations, and organizing economic and political networks (Steinmetz 1999). Refugees and migrants were crossing state borders and challenging both territorial sovereignty and homogeneous definitions of the nation-state. Diasporic forms of identification coexisted (if not competed) with nationalist identities. So, too, the traditional functions of the state as regulator of diverse areas of social life such as law, education, health, crime, national security—what Althusser (1971) called the "state apparatus"—were being substituted by private companies and institutions. To give just one example, the penal system, which was once the paradigm of the modern, panoptic disciplinary sovereignty accompanying the emergence of the modern state, has become in the United States a large, private, profitable business that has abandoned any pretension to reform and has embraced a racialized logic of pure containment and abandon, where the simultaneous enticement to, and suppression of, violence seem to be the only rule (Hallinan 2001). So, too, have nongovernmental organizations (NGOs), aid organizations, and transnational entities like the World Bank, rather than local communities or state officials, determined development and political projects (Ferguson 1990; Gupta 1998; Hale 2002; Trouillot 2001).

---

1. Originally published in the *Annual Review of Anthropology* 32 (2003): 393–410.

And yet, in spite of this inexorable logic of neoliberal capitalist globalization, or as Comaroff and Comaroff call it, "millennial capitalism" (2000a), which has eroded those functions of the Weberian state that were once its defining feature, the state form can hardly be said to have withered away (Comaroff and Comaroff 2000a; Trouillot 2001). Since 1945, the number of states has more than quadrupled. From 1989, when the Berlin Wall fell, to 1994 there were twenty-two new states created (Nagengast 1994), and the number has increased since then. The desire for statehood continues to be intense in many parts of the world, in spite, or perhaps because of, the hollowed-out character of the state. Struggles for statehood help to sustain ethnic conflicts, processes of insurgency and counterinsurgency, war economies, international interventions, refugee camps, and torn societies. The commanding power of the state form can partly be understood because the state holds a sort of meta-capital (Bourdieu 1999), its hallowed form commanding an imagery of power and a screen for political desire as well as fear. There is also real capital circulating through the elusive body of the state in the form of international aid, development projects, and capitalist ventures of various kinds. This aura of capital associated with the state is often transformed into a discourse of corruption when people encounter the doubtful practices of local bureaucrats (Gupta 1995). The corrupt state also acquires visibility through highly publicized events highlighted by the mass media (Navaro-Yashin 2002). In marginal locales the images of corruption mix with those of consumption giving rise to discourses and sentiments of abandonment by the state (Berdahl 1999). Globalization is not only compatible with statehood; it has actually fueled the desire for it, whether to have access to resources and powers experienced, imagined, or glimpsed, or to defend an ethnic group against the violence of another state, one of the arguments forwarded by Basque insurgents in the Basque Country.

Foucault's analysis of power as a field of multiple forces challenged the notion of the state as a unitary center of power, and more specifically it challenged the notion that the state was necessarily the most important target of political struggles (Foucault 1978, 1979, 1991). His inquiries into governmentality and bio-power inspired a whole field of research of power that were outside the field of state studies. The notions of governmentality as well as bio-power have returned, however, to rethink the notion of the state in a new light as a contradictory ensemble of practices and processes (Brown 1995; Mitchell 1991; Trouillot 2001) and as new managements of life and death (Agamben 1998). Repositioning the question of the state in relation to the meaning of sovereignty also seems to me particularly crucial, especially after September 11, 2001.

The question of desire, as well as fear, becomes most crucial in rethinking the kind of reality the state might be acquiring at this moment of globalization, not only of capital, services, and culture, but also of security operations and states of emergency. The question of subjectivity emerges as critical in a variety of ways. On the one hand, there are the subjective dynamics that link people to states, something that Weber already pointed out; and on the other there is what one could call the subjectivity of the state being (Taussig 1992: 111–40, 1997). How does it become a social subject in everyday life? This is to ask about bodily excitations and sensualities, powerful identifications, and uncon-scious desires of state officials (Aretxaga 2000a, 2002); about performances and public representations of statehood; and about discourses, narratives, and fantasies generated around the idea of the state. The state cannot exist without this subjective component, which links its form to the dynamics of people and movements. A major part of this essay is therefore devoted to this problem.

There are other dimensions of statehood I have left out for reasons of space and preference, not for reasons of importance. These are questions relative to state formation and postcolonial state practices. I use state form to emphasize the notion of a powerful state devoid of content, which then serves as a screen for a variety of identifications and as a performative mask (Abrams 1988) for a variety of power discourses and practices. In using the notion of state form, I echo Balibar's notion of national form as a reposito-ry of ideas, images, and ideologies, which are not predetermined (Balibar and Wallerstein 1991; Žižek 1993). In this way I attempt to leave the state as both an open notion and an entity, the presence and content of which is not taken for granted but is the very object of inquiry. By thinking about the state in this way, I want to emphasize the power it still conveys; its social and political presence can hardly be ignored.

The Untenable Hyphen

It has been difficult to think of the state outside the hyphenated dyad "nation-state." States have appeared as actively promoting national cultures (Handler 1988), creating national narratives (Borneman 1993, 1998) that could organize and give shape to collective sub-jectivities. They have actively engaged in the production of national fantasies of commu-nitas (Berlant 1993; Grant 2001) in a variety of ways, from monumentalization of hero-ism aimed at creating collective memory and myth, to monumentalization of fable and folktale projecting the erasure of memory and the infantilization of the nation. In studies of nationalism, states often figure as being actively involved in creating "imagined [nation-al] communities" (Anderson 1991 [1983]), cultural intimacies through narrative, media, ritual, pageantry, and public works that link the public sphere to the domestic and local scenes (Borneman 1998; Herzfeld 1997). Nationalist movements have also aspired and fought for states of their own, linking the desire for statehood to nationalist proclama-tions and often to opposition to another state (perhaps seen as oppressor or colonizer).

Yet if the nation and state are joined in ambiguous ways (Trouillot 1990), the notion of the nation-state has also obscured the instability and deeply problematic nature of such a seemingly self-evident link. On the one hand, the fantasy of a unified, imagined nation-alist community clashes with internal differences and power struggles. Differences in class, gender, ethnicity, and status create de facto differences in citizenship. The impact of state power is felt differently at various levels of the national community. At the margins of the polity and at the local level, encounters with the state are often experienced in an intimate way where power is experienced close to the skin, embodied in well-known local officials, through practices of everyday life (Das and Poole 2004). This encounter with the state at the local level often takes the form of a discourse of corruption (Gupta 1995), but it can also take the form of profound ambivalence and a discourse of abandonment, as in the remote areas of Colombia where who acts as the state is disputed among a number of actors: the military, the guerrilla, the drug lords (Ramírez 2001). Local officials are caught in a situation divided by impotence and responsibility to their communities, always uncertain about the impact of state power in its different incarnations. The imagined national state, which is supposed to provide for its citizens, seems remote and careless, not fulfilling its obligations and generating a discourse of state deficit, an insufficient state which has abandoned its citizens. In fact, there is not a deficit of state but an excess of statehood practices: too many actors competing to perform as state. Longings for a good paternalistic state coexist with a nationalist discourse of citizenship. At the margins of polities and global economies, the desire for a good state can take the form of struggles for full citizenship (Aretxaga 1997; Hardt and Negri 2000; Ramírez 2001; Warren 1993). The nationalist discourse of citizenship remains attached in the social imaginary to the state but clashes with the actual experience of marginalization, disempowerment, and violence.

The experience of disjunction in the status of citizenship is sometimes covered up by what Girard (1979) called the "scapegoat," an outsider, or an outsider-insider, a ritual repository of the jarring violence inhabiting the national community. Riots against ethnic others can be an example of such attempts to rid the imagined national space of its inherent violence (Tambiah 1997). While it is certainly the case that all sorts of manipulations and political interests are part of what triggers ethnic violence (Brass 1997; Das 1990; Warren 1993), we should also direct close attention to a recurrent dynamic that exceeds strategic manipulation in which violence within the national community is displaced to an insider-outsider, a familiar stranger forcefully cast out of the polity.

In the centers of global power such displacements have also become the norm. In Europe, immigrants often become targets of practices of violence by state institutions, right-wing organizations, and disaffected citizens (Balibar and Wallerstein 1991; Žižek 1997). Processes of unification, such as those of eastern and western Germany, have created their own targeted lesser citizens too (Berdahl 1999). In societies where old regimes have given rise to new ones there are often deep fissures between state and government, a corollary of a situation in which the bureaucracy and the administration are left in place while the government changes. In places like Russia, organized crime can function as a veritable para-state (Comaroff and Comaroff 2000a).

Discourses of patriotism and practices of war against a magnified enemy such as terrorism disguise differences in power and the internal violence of the nation around a national unity to combat a common enemy (Aretxaga 2002; Zulaika and Douglass 1996). Yet the violence of security apparatuses can also turn into the homeland policing of the state's own citizens in a paranoiac gaze that curtails civil rights and extends terror through the social field. It is in the studies of violence that the state—what we imagine as the state, what we call the state, that ensemble of discourses and practices of power, that elusive subject that can so much affect the life of citizens—appears most clearly as working against the nation (Trouillot 1990). The very concept at the heart of the nation, "the people," becomes an object of fear and violence by a state that wants to have absolute control of a nation it is at once dividing and destroying. "The people" is invoked and torn apart through the creation of ever-present enemies: criminals, communists, subversives, guerrillas, terrorists (Daniel 1996; Denich 1994; Nelson 1999; Ramírez 2001; Siegel 1998; Taylor 1997).

There is also a gender dimension to the instability of the nation-state link. In societies torn by the terror of the violence of military rule, such as Argentina and Guatemala, the state is represented and enacted through military performances of masculinity while the nation is feminized into idealized, desexualized maternity. Actual women, who remain outside this imaginary of idealized motherhood, are a reminder of what cannot be fully controlled in the nation—the object of sexual-political violence in endless performances of violent control of the body of the nation by the state body (Nelson 1999; Taylor 1997). So, too, in societies torn by ethnic violence or war, women have become the embodiment of a threatening nation or a threatening ethnic other; their bodies become the field through which violent statehood not only enacts but draws its power (Aretxaga 2000a; Das 1996b). This is the case not only in Bosnia but also in Algeria, India, Rwanda, and South Africa. The imaginary of the nation-state is organized in a variety of ways: as romance or idealized domestic space and inhabited by an ongoing nightmare of sexualized and racialized violence in which the masculinity of statehood becomes a constant threat rather than a benevolent agent. This is a situation in which a repetition-compulsion of violence might be coupled with a compulsion of desire for a harmonic but illusory nation-state. The state should then be thought of in ways that are not necessarily totally dislodged from the nation but neither attached to it. Rather one should consider a variety of relations that are ambivalent, ambiguous, hostile, violent, and porous—in which the nature of the hyphen is more a cipher than a self-evident reality.

The Government of Bodies

The violence and terror spread by totalitarian regimes or/and military bodies has often been considered an attack of the state on civil society; yet this sharp distinction between state and civil society has been questioned in recent scholarship on the state (Alonso 1994; Aretxaga 2000b; Borneman 1998; Brown 1995; Gupta 1995; Mitchell 1991; Navaro-Yashin 2002; Trouillot 2001). The separation between civil society and the state does not exist in reality. Rather, the state as phenomenological reality is produced through discourses and practices of power, produced in local encounters at the everyday level, and produced through the discourses of public culture, rituals of mourning and celebration, and encounters with bureaucracies, monuments, organization of space, and so on. The state has to be considered as the effect of a new kind of governmentality (Mitchell 1991); it appears as an open field with multiple boundaries and no institutional or geographical fixity (Trouillot 2001). It is recognizable through its multiple effects. The state has lost many of the ordering functions that produced the effect of a unitary force such as the organization of health care, education, economic production, imprisonment, and military and policing interventions, which are, in many cases, contracted to private companies; on the other hand, aid organizations, NGOs, private entrepreneurs, security companies, and warlords are acting as state and producing the same powerful effects.

> The paradox of what we call the state is at once an incoherent, multifaceted ensemble of power relations and a vehicle of massive domination—despite the almost unavoidable tendency to speak of the state as an "it" the domain we call the state is not a thing, system or subject, but a significantly unbounded terrain of powers and techniques, an ensemble of discourses, rules and practices cohabiting in limiting, tension ridden, often contradictory relation to each other (Wendy Brown 1995: 174).

One strategy for studying the state will be to "focus on the multiple sites in which state processes and practices are recognized through their effects" (Trouillot 2001: 126), looking for encounters that are not immediately transparent. The sites of everyday life become "a central domain for the production and reproduction of the state" (Navaro-Yashin 2002: 135).

Critiques of the state as a unitary center of power have drawn on Foucault's critique of state as the structure (Poulantzas 1978) or apparatus (Althusser 1971) that defines the locus of power. Foucault's studies of governmentality suggested the rise of a new kind of sovereign power from the eighteenth century, one in which the power of the absolute sovereign was replaced by an array of practices and discourses aimed at the ordering and control of bodies and populations. The emergence of statistics, new notions about health and contagion, madness and sanity, sexuality and reproduction, techniques of surveying and mapping and census, new institutions such as the clinic and the prison, and the discourses of the social sciences were aimed at rendering populations and bodies legible, disciplined, and controlled. State officials deployed this legibility to create their own fictions of reality. These fictions of the state then turn into nightmares animated by utopian visions of efficiency and technological and bureaucratic control:

> The economic plan, survey map, record of ownership, forest management plan, classification of ethnicity, passbook, arrest record and map of political boundaries acquire their force from the fact that these synoptic data are the points of departure from reality as state officials apprehend and shape it. In dictatorial settings where there is no effective way to assert another reality, fictitious facts-on-paper can often be made eventually to prevail on the ground, because it is on behalf of such pieces of paper that police and army are deployed —the categories used by state agents are not merely means to make their environment legible, they are an authoritative tune to which most of the population must dance (James C. Scott 1998: 83).

In the era of globalization, practices of legibility and control are carried by a variety of organizations and take a variety of forms that nevertheless produce state-like effects so that the state continues to be a powerful object of encounter even when it cannot be located. In the margins and borders of global spaces and polities, but perhaps also in the marginal spaces of western cities (Aretxaga 1997; Balibar and Wallerstein 1991), the will to legibility present in the violence of the checkpoint or the police questioning of immigrants turns into a repetition of illegibility and uncertainty about the outcome of the encounter; de facto, an arrest of temporality (Das and Poole 2004), an intimate secrecy in which the fictions of the state about the people it fears, gets locked in with the fictions people at the margins have about the state (Taussig 1997). What is interesting here is that it is not only the people who imagine the state, but also the state itself in its multiple incarnations that has, and enacts, its own fantasies (Siegel 1998). This mirroring dynamic, between the imaginary relation of those embodying the state and those who encounter their effects in everyday life, emerges indirectly from studies of the state (Taussig 1993, 1997). This idea suggests a subjective dynamic that produces and reproduces the state as objects of fear and attachment, of identification or disavowal, as subjects of power, elusive, unlocatable, ever present, immensely powerful, or impotent. It alerts us to what Judith Butler has called "the psychic life of power" (1997).

The Power of a Fiction

The subjective dynamic that sustains the state as a powerful, inescapable social reality has been noted by anthropologists and other social theorists. Weber, who defined the state as "a compulsory association which organizes domination" through the means of physical force (Gerth and Mills 1946), also understood that "in reality, obedience [to the legality of the state] is determined by highly robust motives of fear and hope—fear of the vengeance of magical powers within the power-holder, hope for reward in this world or in the beyond—and besides all this, by interests of the most varied sorts" (Gerth and Mills 1946). So, too, does George Simmel call attention to this subjective dynamic that makes the state a powerful reality (1955). Early political anthropology also wrestled with the notion of the state. In his introduction to the classic *African Political Systems*, Alfred R. Radcliffe-Brown makes explicit that the state as a unitary entity is a fiction:

> In writing on political institutions there is a good deal of discussion about the nature and origin of the State, which is usually represented as being an entity over and above the human individuals that make up a society, having as one of its attributes something called "sovereignty," and sometimes spoken of as having a will (law being often defined as the will of the State) or as issuing commands. The State in this sense does not exist in the phenomenal world; it is a fiction of the philosophers (Fortes and Evans-Pritchard 1940: xxiii; Taussig 1992: 111–40; Trouillot 2001).

In a seminal paper, Phillip Abrams also calls attention to the fictional character of the State (Abrams 1988), strongly questioning (like Radcliffe-Brown) the materiality of this "fictional reality" (Aretxaga 2000a). The difficulty in studying the state resides in the fact that the state—as unified political subject or structure—does not exist; it is a collective illusion, the reification of an idea that masks real power relations under the guise of public interest:

> [T]he state is not the reality which stands behind the mask of political practice. It is itself the mask which prevents our seeing political practice as it is ... It starts its life as an implicit construct; it is then reified—as the *res publica* ... and acquires an overt symbolic identity progressively divorced from practice as an illusory account of practice. The ideological function is extended to a point where conservative and radicals alike believe that their practice is not directed at each other but at the state. The world of illusion prevails (Abrams 1988: 58).

The illusion of the state as the subject of domination hiding behind political practice is sustained in no small measure by a shroud of secrecy surrounding the being of the state (Taussig 1992: 111–40, 1997). The secrecy and the anxiety that accompany this ungraspable character of power are elaborated in public culture in a variety of ways, including news reporting (Navaro-Yashin 2002) and television series like the American-produced *X-Files*, generating a derealization of reality, or a sense of the state as virtual reality (Aretxaga 1999a), like the powerful Wizard of Oz determining people's lives. In locations where the state is felt as arbitrary violence, the force of the state is experienced as a traumatic emergence of the Real that breaks the parameters and assumptions of ordinary reality—as, for example, with the discovery of the extent of information about people accumulated by the Stasi secret police in East Germany or the discovery that close relatives had acted as spies (Lukens and Rosenberg 1993). This sense of an invisible, all-powerful subject has been elaborated beautifully in creative literature as well. One only has to think of Milan Kundera's *The Book of Laughter and Forgetting* (1981), in which the Soviet state appears as the invisible hand that alters history by erasing public figures from official photographs. This is the kind of traumatic power over life and death held by the fictional reality of the state elaborated by Kafka in *The Trial* (1964) and other stories. In places like Argentina, with its spectacular disappearances, Guatemala, Colombia, Sri Lanka, the former Yugoslavia, and a great part of Africa, violence enacted by different armies, not just by the state but by those aspiring to statehood, has created un-nameable "spaces of death" (Taussig 1986) without borders; nightmarish realities in which the habitual references that organize reality have been systematically broken, giving rise to powerful phantasmatic states or state-like organizations (Comaroff and Comaroff 2000b; Daniel 1996; Malkki 1995; Nelson 1999; Suarez-Orozco 1992; Tambiah 1996; Taylor 1999; Warren 1993).

For Abrams, as for other scholars, the mystifying illusion of a center of power called the state must be unmasked for the reality of disparate relations of power to emerge. Yet to gaze into the labyrinthine interiority of state being (as in truth commissions or when the archives of the Stasi were opened) does not necessarily dispel its mystifying, magical power. On the contrary, such mystifying power often seems to be augmented by such unveiling of the state's scandalous life, triggering an endless proliferation of discourses about the state at all levels of social life. But to talk of the state as a fiction does not necessarily mean falsity but rather, as Clifford Geertz (1973) said long ago, a certain genre of representation, a particularly powerful one. If the fictional reality of the state is socially powerful, then scholars must focus not only on those discourses and practices that produce this state form as real but also on the actual social and subjective life of this formation we call the state. If the state appears and acts as having a life of its own, then we are in the presence of a fetish and must ask for the powerful ways in which this fetish works (Nelson 1999; Taussig 1993, 1997). To look for state effects is also to follow the ways in which those identified as the state enact their fantasy vis-à-vis those others it considers its enemies (Taussig 1997; Zulaika and Douglass 1996).

Fantasy, Fetish, Sensuality

One of the areas where fantasy has entered state discourse and practice has been the expanding field of terrorism. On the one hand, official documents reproduce plots and narrative forms from novels or films about terrorism. On the other hand, journalists covering terrorist subjects often turn to fiction writing about terrorism (Zulaika and Douglass 1996). In much of the literature about terrorism, "the brandishing of stark facts goes hand in hand with great leaps into discursive fantasy" (Zulaika and Douglass 1996: 4; Aretxaga 2002). The boundaries between fiction and reality become indistinguishable, endowing encounters between the state and terrorism with a phantom quality (Zulaika and Douglass 1996: 14; Aretxaga 2002). Such indistinguishability creates not only forceful interventions within particular political fields (military interventions, unjustified arrests, torture) but also political cultures "of uncertainty and fear [that] mark the bodies of its subjects to the point of haunting them" (Navaro-Yashin 2002: 181). Such haunting by the persecutory power of the state does not face in only one direction. Those identified as state—government officials, politicians, military personal, policemen, judges, prosecutors etc.—are also haunted by the perceived power of terrorists, subversives, guerrillas, or criminals (Aretxaga 2000a; Siegel 1998; Taussig 1986). This mirroring paranoid dynamic often takes the form of powerful identifications and obsessive fascination, as when the state engages in terrorist or criminal practices in order to appropriate the power it attributes to its enemies, criminals, subversives, or terrorists (Taylor 1997). These are not just moments of repression against enemies that are already there; they are fields in which the state and its enemies are created and recreated as powerful fictional realities (Siegel 1998) through what Derrida has called "a phantomatic mode of production" (1994: 97), a structure and *modus operandi* that produces both the state and its threatening Other as fetishes of each other, constructing reality as an endless play of mirror images. It is in the act of killing, kidnapping, disappearances, and imprisonment that the state materializes as a powerful spectral reality, which marks the bodies and souls of those subjected to its practice. In some parts of the world, the increase in criminal "phantom states" has been associated with the development of an increasingly spectral neoliberal economy, the violence of which has called into being old specters such as witches, zombies, and ghosts (Comaroff and Comaroff 1999, 2000a).

Criminal states alert us to the fact that the power of the state is harnessed not so much from the rationality of ordering practices, as from the passions of transgression, in which the line between the legal and the illegal is constantly blurred. One has to recall Bataille and Foucault and think of what this particular blurred border may mean for the exercise of state power. To go back to fantasy, a good deal of the literature on the state and violence shows the state not as the product of rational technologies of control but as the subject of excess that bypasses any rational functionality. What articulates this excess is fantasy (the fantasy of statehood, the fantasy of total control, the fantasy of appropriation of the other, the fantasy of heterosexual domesticity, and so on), which appears as a major component of political life and a key factor structuring power relations. Fantasy here is not meant as a purely illusory construction, but as a form of reality in its own right, a scene whose structure traverses the boundary between the conscious and the unconscious (Laplanche and Pontalis 1989). Fantasy in this sense belongs to the "objectively subjective" (Žižek 1997). It is not opposed to social reality but constitutes its "psychic glue." The state can be considered then as "a privileged setting for the staging of political fantasy in the modern world" (Rose 1996: 4; Agamben 1998).

This is not to say that rational technologies of control are unimportant to the materialization of state power; it is to say that they are animated by a substrate of fantasy scenes that betray complicated kinds of intimacy, sensualities, and bodily operations. If the state is constituted as an effect of discourses and practices, this is an embodied and sensual effect. It depends on the continuous recreation of the body of national heroes (Navaro-Yashin 2002; Weiss 2002), on corpses and funerals as acts of possession and rebirth. The corpse mediates between the state and the people (Siegel 1998; Taussig 1997) in a process that seems intrinsic to the materialization of the state. In Indonesia, the emergence of a notion of criminality coincides with the suppression of the people under Suharto's New Order. The obsession with the criminal springs from the fact that the criminal mediates a realm of death "leading towards a force the state felt it lacked and which in mastering the criminal [massacring them], it hopes to have for itself" (Siegel 1998: 6). Is this process not also undergirding the obsession with guerrillas, ethnic rebels, and terrorists? There is an uncanny quality to the production of the state through the production of an enemy because often the criminal or terrorist or threatening Other is a familiar face, familiar but strange, strange in its familiarity, such as neighbors. Nothing distinguishes them from the rest except the fact of their death, kidnapping, disappearance, or arrest (Balibar and Wallerstein 1991; Siegel 1998; Taussig 1997; Warren 1993).

It is impossible, with all this, to ignore the discourses and practices of sexuality involved in the production and reproduction of the state. The systematic rapes of women and men that often accompany state formation, and that reached the proportions of genocide in the case of Bosnian Muslims and in Rwanda, have been linked by some scholars to the institutions of territorial sovereignty and heterosexuality. This collective sexual-

political violence "is not the cause of anything but the effect of sexual political categories—of the interimplication of heterosexuality and territorial sovereignty" (Borneman
1998: 284). The embodied being of what counts as the state is not a neutral body, but is
instead a thoroughly sexualized one, whose sexual operations are invested with political
power (Aretxaga 2001b; Das 1996b; Taylor 1997). There is a strange intimacy between
the state and the people. The state excises from the polis those subjects and practices that
question or threaten homogeneous models of territorial sovereignty and heterosexual
forms of political control, which are fundamental to national narratives of harmonious
domesticity. This intimacy that filters and subverts modern disciplinary practices and
rational technologies of control was already noticed by Foucault in his study of modern
forms of punishment:

> The training of behavior by a full time-table, the acquisition of habits, the constraints of the
> body, imply a very special relation between the individual who is punished and the individ-
> ual who punishes him . . . The agent of punishment must exercise total power which no
> third party can disturb; the individual to be corrected must be entirely enveloped in the
> power that is being exercised over him. Secrecy is imperative and so too is autonomy at
> least in relation to this technique of punishment. (Foucault 1979: 129)

The modern will to reform seems to have been abandoned to mere forms of confinement of those who are excluded from the social-political community. The camp as a
form of exclusion and total control seems to have replaced the Foucauldian prison as a
model of total control over life (Agamben 1998). Yet such total control over life and death
only makes more acute the presence of terrifying forms of intimacy. In some ways, "the
'estrarity' of the person held in the sovereign ban is more intimate and primary than the
extraneousness of the foreigner" (Agamben 1998: 110; Agamben 2000a; Berlant 1997;
Siegel 1998; Žižek 1993).

There is a relation of simultaneous attraction and repulsion that holds together this
sovereign power and those reduced to bare life, life that can be killed without accountability (Agamben 1998; Hardt and Negri 2000). There is a will to legibility here as a state
effect that is focused on bodies perceived as both familiar and opaque, an object of fascination and threat. The official gaze constantly scans these bodies for signs (of the criminal, the terrorist, the immigrant, the undocumented), in an attempt to render them transparent, to extricate the secret opacity of its uncanny familiarity. Practices of legibility are
not detached but invested with affect. Ideologies of difference take the form of bodily dia-
critics that fuel the obsession to render threatening bodies and people legible. Yet these
intense practices of legibility often produce more opacity, as subjects manipulate stereotypes, so that the state in its military, police, or legal embodiment may see everything and
yet see nothing, as in the case noticed by Fanon (1967) of women in the Algerian anti-
colonial war who don the veil in order to carry arms unnoticed, while the army focuses
on veiled women as the object of terrorist threat (Aretxaga 1997, 2000a; Bhabha 1990;
Das and Poole 2004; Fanon 1967). The terrifying force of the management of bodies and

people that characterizes the modern state, coupled with the intimacies that invest it, is not unrelated to the power of the law as it has come to represent the sovereign power of the state. The intense affect of this power, its "obscene enjoyment" (Žižek 1993), ingeniously portrayed by Kafka in his famous novel *The Trial*, has a hold not only on one's life but also on one's soul. It has the capacity to drive people mad, madness that comes from being "oversaturated with law" (Berlant 1991), with the force of law without signification (Aretxaga 2000a; Santner 1996).

The State of Exception

On the one hand, for some scholars it is precisely when we set aside the problem of sovereignty that the state comes into view as a complex problem of power, an ensemble of techniques and tactics of domination that Foucault defines as more crucial than the state for those interested in power (Foucault 1979, 1991). Yet for others, the continuous desire for political sovereignty in the form of statehood makes unavoidable the question of what sovereignty means in the age of Empire (Hardt and Negri 2000). On the other hand, sovereignty takes the form of homogeneous territorial sovereignty justifying all sorts of violence against those defined as outsiders (Borneman 1998). Yet the claim to sovereignty from states and those aspiring to statehood entails a larger problematic, of how power is articulated and imagined today in a global world where democracy has become the form and discourse of political legitimation. It entails also a reflection of the mystifying force of the law (Derrida 1991). What defines sovereignty for some scholars is the power to call a state of exception, a social-political space of force ruled by a law beyond the law, where the distinction between fact and law has become blurred (Agamben 1998; Hardt and Negri 2000; Schmitt [1922] 1985). The state of exception is not decided by a situation of conflict or chaos, although this is often its discourse of legitimation; rather it is decided to affirm a juridical order in which lawfulness, right, is suspended in the name of law.

In this particular order, lawfulness and unlawfulness, execution and transgression of the law become indistinguishable "such that what violates a rule and what conforms to it coincide" (Agamben 1998: 57). Sovereignty then presents itself as the law, which stands outside the law. In this sense, to claim state sovereignty is to embody a juridical order that cannot be held accountable. The state in this sense is and is not the law. The lack of distinction between transgression and execution of the law that characterizes the state of exception, within which anything can happen, leaves the law as a terrifying force devoid of meaning from which one cannot escape. There is no position of exteriority to the power of a law that shows itself as arbitrary, ruthless, and invested with excitement (Žižek 1997), as Kafka so masterfully illustrated. And "what after all is a state that survives history, a state sovereignty that maintains itself beyond the accomplishments of its telos, is it not a law that is in force without signifying?" (Agamben 1998: 60). The question is, "what is the place of this law that is beyond the law?" (Foucault [1975] 1982: 198).

In his "Theses on the Philosophy of History," Walter Benjamin noted that "the state of emergency in which we live is not the exception but the rule" (Benjamin 1968: 257). What the state of exception brings to the fore is the spectral domain of the law in the form of military and police violence, which takes, in the state of exception, an autonomy that was previously hidden. In this sense "the exception gives rise to a form of right which is really a right of the police" (Hardt and Negri 2000: 17). Yet the spectral domain of the law as the form of the state not only pertains to situations of military alert but also is the rule in the life of democratic states. Such spectrality comes from the violence of pure performativity in which the law simply affirms itself in a tautological form: "the law's interest in a monopoly of violence is not explained by the intention to preserve legal ends but, rather, by that of preserving the law itself; that violence when not in the hands of the law, threatens it not by the ends that it may pursue but by its mere existence outside the law" (Benjamin [1921] 1978: 281). More than in any other act, law (as the state) reaffirms itself in the exercise of power over life and death (Agamben 1998; Benjamin [1921] 1978; Hardt and Negri 2000; Siegel 1998; Taussig 1992: 111–40, 1997). This lack of ultimate legitimation of law reveals something disturbing: "[A]t its foundation the rule of law is sustained . . . by the force/violence of a tautological enunciation—'the law is the law'" (Santner 1996: 10). Emptied of content, the violence of law, as sovereign power, becomes ghostly and persecutory, giving rise to forms of paranoiac acting from the state as much as from the subjects who encounter it. The ghostly, persecutory power of law is incarnated in the police, a haunting figure invested with formless power (Benjamin [1921] 1978), whose effects are seen as disappearances, corpses, arrests, and internments but whose identity remains mysterious, as objects of constant speculation, rumor, and fear. "The police become hallucinatory and spectral because they haunt everything; they are everywhere, even there where they are not, in their *Fort Dasein* to which we can always appeal. Their presence is not present, but the presence of its spectral double knows no boundaries" (Derrida 1991: 1011). Like in the king's two bodies, Ernst Hartwig Kantorovitch's famous theory of sovereignty, the spectral double of the police acts like the permanent body of the state, a presence interiorized as the law, at once fearful and paternalistic, familiar and strange, uncanny, a presence that one cannot shake out of oneself. Is this not what is at stake in Althusser's famous example of interpellation, when a hail by the police, "Hey you," compels one to turn around even when one knows one has done nothing wrong (Althusser 1971)? It is not the particular policeman as much as the spectral double, the state's other body wrenched with sovereign power, which, as a haunting law, makes one turn around when being hailed by the police. For Althusser, this hailing is not about meaning or significance but about performative force. What transpires in this performance of the spectrality of the state is an imaginary and violent relation with the state but also a paternalistic one.

This confluence of annihilating violence and paternalistic intimacy present in the regulations of the law/state is precisely what produces an uncanny feeling in relation to the police (Wendy Brown 1995; Freud 1958, 1967; Gerth and Mills 1946). It is what can drive people mad, as it did German Judge Daniel Paul Schreber, Freud's famous case of paranoid schizophrenia (Santner 1996). It is not only the coupling of rationality and violence as Weber suggested (Gerth and Mills 1946; Taussig 1992: 111–40) that defines the state, for what is at stake in modern forms of sovereignty is not merely the management of bodies and populations, the power over life, but the intensification of bodies and intimacies that result from those technologies of management. What Schreber's diary of his illness illustrates is what happens "when law becomes entangled in the management of life," a state of affairs that for Foucault characterized modern forms of sovereignty: "a sustained traumatization induced by exposure to, as it were, fathers who knew too much about living human beings" (Santner 1996). Schreber's father was obsessed with disciplining the body through a variety of modern regimes and disciplines. But the question one can extract through his case is that one could easily replace *fathers who knew too much* with *states who knew too much* about the bodies and lives of people. The confluence of violence and paternalism, of force and intimacy, sustains the state as an object of ambivalence, an object of resentment for abandoning its subjects to their own fate and one desired as a subject that can provide for its citizens (Wendy Brown 1995; Ramírez 2001). The state is split into good and bad state, triggering an imaginary of the state in which desire and fear are entangled in a relation of misrecognition from which one cannot be extricated. Such inextricability from the state as law rests on an imaginary relationship with the state, which presupposes a passionate attachment to the law (Butler 1997). The hold of the law, the impossibility of extricating oneself from it, rests on the force of its performance which, lacking symbolic content, can create an obsessive attempt at interpretation, at translation of mere force into the language of reason. What is ultimately untranslatable about the performance of the law, the dimension of pure performativity that constitutes the law's authority, is the arbitrariness of its power to decide life and death.

The relationship to the law is one of being abandoned to the force of its own performance, of being transformed into bare life, at least for those who are excluded from its domain. This exclusion is always present as a potentiality, a sine qua non of the law and the state as an embodiment of its form. The state needs constant exclusions: Those who are excluded are included through their exclusion. These exclusions are always present as potentiality, a sine qua non of the law and the state as embodiments of its form, best seen in the camp as the emerging nomos of the political and as the space where the state of exception coincides with life, in which anything can happen (Agamben 1998).

CHAPTER 15

Terror as Thrill: First Thoughts on the "War on Terrorism"[1]

Los Desastres de la Guerra

A few days before September 11, I was in Madrid at an exhibition of Goya's series of drawings entitled "Los Desastres de la Guerra" (The Disasters of War). The drawings are impressive in their stark depiction of the brutality and ironies of a war that came to occupy an epic status within Spanish history: the 1808 war of independence against Napoleon's occupation, a war that some consider the first guerrilla war in history. Uncompromising in his vision, Goya masterfully and relentlessly depicts a devastating reality hidden behind the rhetoric of national freedom: the sacrifice of poor people to the coalescing interests of religious and sovereign power. The war of 1808 was a popular war in the sense of being triggered by popular revolt against a foreign power and fought by peasants and artisans. It was immortalized in folk memory as a battle between the people and a well endowed foreign army. Reality was more ironic and complicated. The guerrilla war succeeded in ousting French troops and with them the liberal reforms they had introduced in the country. In its place came the despotic administration of an absolutist king, Fernando VII, whose regime of paranoid terror was first directed against the liberals and then against the impoverished population that had, ironically, restored him to his throne in the first place.

I cannot help but think now about Afghanistan and about the way the new disasters of war taking place in that remote country are skillfully cut off from the thriller-like media images of the war against terrorism. Among Goya's *desastres*, there is one entitled *Murió la Verdad* (*Truth Died*). The drawing shows a young woman as allegory of truth lying down on the ground. A bishop stands over her body, officiating, surrounded by a crowd held at bay by priests, while on the side Justice cries desperately. The drawing conveys the perverse ideological function of organized religion in the production of a version of reality in

1. Originally published in *Anthropological Quarterly* 75.1 (2002): 139–50.

the service of sovereign power. Truth and Justice are sacrificed to the official reality of church and sovereign.

As in Goya's drawing, the truth of the "War against Terrorism" is also disappearing fast in the interest of national security and patriotic unity. In its place, fantasies organize reality as fear and thrill.

The Scene of the War

I watched the attack on the World Trade Center (WTC) with the same sense of unreality as everyone I know. In the Basque city of San Sebastián where I grew up and where I was visiting, it was 3:00 pm, prime time news. An annual international festival was about to begin and small snippets of film were repeatedly shown on television. For a moment, the attack on the WTC seemed like a film preview had crawled unannounced into the wrong place. The very familiarity of the scene, already seen in popular Hollywood disaster movies, made reality unreal and shocking. It was not that a terrorist attack on the United States was unimaginable, it had in fact been imagined to satiety in films like *Independence Day*. Not only had the imaginary of a disaster saturated public culture with apocalyptic anxieties during the last decade, but so too had filled the imagination of the United States Department of State. After the end of the Cold War, terrorism had become the object of obsessive publishing by the state department, replacing the old figure of communism as a spectral enemy.

The anxious scene of foreign terrorists attacking the United States was not new but was in fact in place and ready to be occupied. Fantasy constitutes a scenario within which real action can take place and be interpreted. What was unimaginable was then not the attack itself, but that the fantasy of the attack could materialize. If inside the United States there was trauma, outside the country what followed the stunned moment of seeing the impossible materialized was fear, not of terrorism, but of a military intervention by the United States and its consequences for the rest of the world. The fear was made stronger by the mix of religious trascendentalism and cowboy justice in which the response to the attack was initially cast. The President of the U.S., George W. Bush spoke about a monumental "crusade" of good against evil, while demanding Osama bin Laden's body "dead or alive." The attack was immediately framed as an attack on American values which, under attack, appeared all of a sudden obscurely pristine; then it was framed as an attack on Western values, then an attack on civilization. The "War against Terrorism" was presented as both inevitable and epic: "a war to save the world," as George Bush said just before starting the bombing in Afganistan, a "just war."

For me, the "War against Terrorism" resonated against the (badly called) Spanish Civil War (1936–39), the war triggered by the military uprising of General Francisco Franco against an elected republican government of socialist majority. Veiled, fragmented, mysterious, but persistent references to "the war" punctuated my childhood, organizing life around a dense absence that acquired cosmic proportions as the disaster that radically changed the lives of those around me, and even life itself. That war was also framed by Franco as a "crusade" to save the world, in his case, against the peril of communism. The national "crusade" of General Franco against communism redeemed Spain from the hopes of social justice and claimed the country for God and for Franco himself. The nearly forty years of Francoist dictatorship were characterized by a timeless time filled with the silence of massive violence, a silence that structured the terror of the regime as permanent absent presence. The silence of this violence also organized the transition to democracy that followed the death of Franco and is still screaming through the violence of a new generation of Basque radical nationalists.

The current "War against Terrorism" is unfolding too around a double temporal structure, as an arresting time in which historical time itself, as "the indeterminate, the unfolding, and the continual eruption of the new" (Grosz 1999: 28) is arrested. In contrast to historical time, the structure of this timeless war is characterized by the temporality of waiting, waiting for the next attack, waiting for the spread of a virus, waiting for the killing of terrorists, waiting . . . as a prolonged moment of suspension and anxiety, of terror transformed into spectacle, of terror that is also a thrill, of terror that focuses and binds into new sense of patriotic affect. For most people in the U.S., waiting characterizes the situation of being in war, a situation in which one gets to play a part by being vigilant, attentive, ready to discover un undefined suspicious movement that might betray a terrorist plot. Waiting is an atemporal temporality where fantasy flourishes.[2] Here, then, is the flourishing fantasy of Terrorism (with a capital *T*), a fantasy that, as in the film *Independence Day*, the war against this archenemy can ultimately restore order out of chaos and return us to a lost innocence.

The Specter of Terrorism

> Each figure seemed to be somehow, on the borderland of things, just as their theory was on the borderland of thought. He knew that each one of these men stood at the extreme end, so to speak, of some wild road of reasoning.
>
> G.K. Chesterton, *The Man Who Was Thursday.*

The war against terrorism has been represented by much of the media as inevitable, a war to save the world no less; this is a war, we are told, that will be long, undefined, unlocatable, unknowable, in a word timeless. This is represented as a war with great unknowns and simple verities of good and evil where, as U.S. Secretary of Defense Donald Rumsfeld said on the Cable News Network (CNN), "the important thing is that we know who the bad guys are" even if we don't know anything else. The space of the war against Terrorism is a space of fictional reality defined by a fantastic enemy where the real and the unreal are indistinguishable. War maneuvers have to be secret we are told,

---

2. Vincent Crapanzano (1986) has written about the existential situation of waiting.

the operations unaccountable. We are left with a security system that operates autonomously in a variety of secret ways. Secrecy is the key word of this war. And isn't that what terrorism is all about?

There is something incongruous and imbalanced in the assembling of a world war coalition against Terrorism; there is something jarring and surreal in the movement of troops and aircraft to Afghanistan—a poor and devastated country with a famine crisis and virtually nothing to bomb—to get an indeterminate number of suspected terrorists out of unreachable caves. The demonstration of imperial military might against a little-known Islamist organization incarnated in the figure of a mostly obscure man has conferred on bin Laden and al Qaeda the status of a powerful state force. Focusing on him has transformed a criminal act of unknown authorship into a global transcendental conflict, double-staged as a fight between western civilization against religious fundamentalism on the one hand, and dispossessed Islam and western imperialism on the other. Is this not the political dream of Osama bin Laden cum Taliban regime?

Although the United States has attempted to counteract the scenario of a U.S. military intervention against Islam by enlisting the support of as many Muslim countries as possible into its war, the fragility of such alliances was already evinced after the first day of bombing in Afghanistan. This is not surprising, since the alliance against terrorism is based on two crucial and volatile factors. First is the power of the U.S. to induce support from reluctant Muslim countries who, in acquiescing, risk fueling the alienation of their own populations at home. The second crucial factor in this alliance is the political profit that particular states are extracting from it in legitimating their own dubious, and often very brutal, policies towards their own minority populations. This is the case, for example, of India in relation to Kashmir, Turkey in relation to the Kurds, Russia in relation to Chechnya, Spain in relation to Basque separatists, and, of course, Israel, which hopes to eliminate the Palestinians through some sort of permanent erasure. These ambivalent alliances are not only unpredictable in the middle and long run, they are already contributing to the expansion of a radical Islamist movement, a movement capable of capitalizing on the discontent and dispossession of large masses of people throughout the Muslim world. This would seem to be a primary goal of Osama bin Laden, transformed by the U.S. into prophet and martyr of an Islamist crusade. Thus the U.S. cum NATO, for all its military force, seems to be out of control, playing bin Laden's game and thereby becoming an instrument for bin Laden's larger objective of an imagined Muslim polity.

For much of the Muslim world, the United States is perceived as the terrorist while Osama bin Laden is the unjustly persecuted saint. To elaborate, bin Laden has emerged as a master of effects. Appearing against the background of a rock the same day George Bush announced the beginning of air strikes in Afghanistan, relaxed, enveloped in the imagery of the desert and speaking softly about justice and the end of Muslim humiliation, Osama bin Laden is—as he warns the U.S.—the mirror image of George Bush at the very moment he launches the U.S. attack on Afghanistan. The mighty military power of a world alliance bombing a devastated Muslim country contrasts with the single, outdated rifle leaning against the rock wall next to Osama bin Laden; the image of a single anachoret facing an empire, the word "terrorism" binding them in a circular accusation of phantom terror. We are in what Derrida (1994) has called "a phantomatic mode of production," caught in the production and actualization of mirroring phantoms: Islamist and Western terrorisms.

Making Terrorism

> To break up the superstition and breaking of legality should be our aim. Nothing would please me more than to see Inspector Heat and his likes take to shooting us down in broad daylight with the approval of the public. Half our battle will be won then; the disintegration of the old morality would have set in its very temple. That is what you ought to aim at.
>
> Joseph Conrad, *The Secret Agent.*

For all its proclaimed novelty, the layout of the war has been quite conventional and follows a well-known routine of American military intervention: display of military might, surgical airstrikes and covert operations. On the part of the Taliban cum bin Laden network the war takes the form of guerrilla warfare against Western imperialism and particularly the United States. This war takes place in the invisible space of the terror imaginary of the U.S. (attacks on buildings and government, germ infection, etc.) and in the visibly impoverished landscape of Afghanistan. If bin Laden's objective is to galvanize support for a radical Islamist movement, the medium is the spectacle created by the imbalance of the struggle, and imbalance that evokes Western imperialism, historical humiliation and arbitrary violence. On the one hand, the war triggers outrage and sympathy among the discontented population of the Middle East, on the other hand, it justifies (and even demands) the suicide attacks on the American population. These two moments are bound together through the psychic mechanism of identification, already signaled by Freud as the primary glue of social groups. First there is identification with the carefully built figure of martyrs in the face of unjust and overpowering violence; then identification with the paladins of justice wielding the sword of God. Of course, this process is mirrored in the U.S.: identification with the victims gives way to identification with the warring government through the binding affective force of patriotism.

At the level of public representation, the double figure of martyr and state-like force, these two poles of identification were incarnated in the figures of Osama bin Laden and his aide Sleiman Abou-Gheith. While the first spoke of injustice and peace for Palestinians, the second, in a more stately appearance, threatened a continuing "storm of airplanes."[3] The extreme craftiness at using modern technology to tap and recreate anew an old cluster of religious images, contradicts the opinion that assigns to Islamic radicalism an entrenchment in past tradition. The Taliban, like Osama bin Laden's brand of radi-

---

3. John F. Burns, "More Strikes Against US Threatened," *New York Times*, October 10, 2001, B8.

calism, does not represent the force of timeless tradition, but a contemporary creation of tradition, a concomitant effect of modernity well known to students of nationalism. If the "invention of tradition" (Hobsbwam and Ranger 1983) is not new to students of political movements, neither are the tactics that bin Laden is using. The use of an outrageous attack as a provocation for massive use of force, preferably employed indiscriminately, is typical of anti-colonial guerrilla warfare. A brutally illustrative example of this tactic is Gillo Pontecorvo's now classic film, *The Battle of Algiers*. State force with its accompanying dirty wars, secret operations and special commandoes or death squads—that is, the use of terror to combat "terrorism"—reproduce the very terrorist practices they want to eliminate, creating a closed dynamic of mimetic violence that can reproduce organized terror ad infinitum, narrowing if not closing the space for political engagements of other kinds.

At the level of the political imaginary, we are assisting the discursive and military construction of Terrorism with capital *T*, a political figure that was in the making for some time, but which has finally made its world debut after September 11, as an absolutized enemy of a phantasmic character, rapidly becoming, in the midst of the anthrax scare, mystery and thrill, something like the figure of the Joker in the film *Batman*. Secretive by their very nature, terrorist organizations acquire reality as a political and social force not only through the effects of their violence but also through the production of material culture: anagrams, seals, communiqués, uniforms, videos, and so on. But what counts as a terrorist organization for government institutions responds not to a single reality, but to a variety of very different historical and socio-political realities. Terrorism with capital *T*, however, is a fictional reality, the object of a particular genre of popular novels and film thrillers. Thus, for example, what was initially a faceless attack, and then an organization, has become a vast network of unknown proportions constituting what, according to the *New York Times*, an intelligence officer called "a global state"[4] (a characterization that incidentally appeared three days after the initial bombing and justifies what has been called "America's New War"). Similarly, we have been seeing the emergence of some of the staple ingredients of the thriller genre of terrorism: enigmatic documents, chilly manuals, horripilating bloody videos. The document encountered in the luggage of Mohamed Atta, now believed to be the mastermind of the attacks, might be a preparation guide for suicide operations. Yet its language sounds stereotypical; it resonates all too much with the popular fiction of terrorism not to appear virtual, and perhaps because of that has the capacity to evoke a chilling terror.[5] Similarly, a manual for terror is also discovered, suggesting the brainwashed character of fanatic terrorists. It is entitled "Military Studies of the Jihad against Tyrants." The first mission stated in the manual is "to end the godless regimes and substitute Islamic states for them."[6] And in Spain, the detention of an Islamic commando uncovers thirty-two videotapes depicting bomb attacks, the slashing of

---

4. Raymond Bonner, "Experts Doubt Iraq Role in Latest Terror Attacks," *New York Times*, October 11, 2001, B7.

5. Neil A. Lewis and David Johnston, "Document That May Have Been Used to Prepare the Attacks is Reported Found," *New York Times* Electronic Edition. September 2, 2001.

6. "El Manual del Terrorista. 'Asesinar soldados y turistas'," *El País*, October 4, 2001.

throats, and training camps. For all we know, the videos might be genuine training material, but they don't seem very different from the staple thrillers found at the average video-store. The headline of the news report ("The Bloody Videos of the Sleepy Cell") signals the horror of a reality which is located midway between fairy tale and thriller movie. It is the little details, such as the date on the videos ("September 1, 1999") or the Arabic language of the documents, that endows this fictional reality with the stamp of truth. On October 6, the *New York Times* published an article in its op-ed section that drew a parallel between the war on terrorism and the Cold War against communism. The article was type-set around a large image of a book with the title, "The Terrorist Manifesto by Osama bin Laden," thus invoking old phantoms in a new light. In the middle of the image there is the trademark of terrorism, a ski mask—even though Islamist radicals don't use ski masks.

This "material culture"—these "things"—has, like the fetish, the power to incarnate the absent presence of terrorism. Their power resides in the capacity to evoke a threatening presence about which we have little knowledge, a presence whose reality is deeply entangled in ideological and popular fantasy.[7] What we are witnessing now, I want to suggest, is the materialization of this fictional reality of Terrorism, as an actual enemy of war: the displacement of this fictional reality from the screens of the movie theaters onto the screens of the television newscasts. What we are assisting now, and experiencing, is the entrapment of political life into virtual reality, at least at a new scale; or as the *New York Times* put it: the line between government and show business is being blurred.[8] An indication of how deeply the reality of terrorism is embedded into the scenarios of fantasy is the recruitment of Hollywood by the U.S. military "to brain storm about possible terrorist targets and schemes in America and to offer solutions to those threats."[9] The virtual reality of Terrorism has the potential to become an actual reality. If Terrorism remains the overarching enemy without organizational, cultural or historical distinctions, and which becomes the pretext for all kinds of policing and military practices, then we might very well find ourselves with a phenomenon of violence characterized by close links between different organizations that might not have collaborated before. So, too, may the scenarios of spectacular violence provide the amplifying voice and claim to fame of otherwise obscure and marginal organizations. What I am suggesting is that the war on Terrorism might indeed create the very enemy it is seeking to eradicate; it might create Terrorism in a new way, setting the stage of war not as state of exception, but rather as a permanent state of affairs in which the state of exception has become the juridical norm and the legitimating right of police and military intervention.[10] This permanent state of

---

7. See in this respect Zulaika and Douglass (1996).

8. See, for example, the report on George Bush enlisting the aid of Hollywood and of the popular show *America's Most Wanted* for the hunt of terrorists. Alessandra Stanley, "President is Using TV Show and the Public in Combination to Combat Terrorism," *New York Times*, October 11, 2001, B2.

9. Dailynews.Yahoo.com/htx/nm/20011008/en/people-terrorists.

10. See in this respect Hardt and Negri (2000), where the authors argue that the state of exception will articulate a new form of "right" in the new global order.

exception does not eliminate practices of terror; rather it instrumentalizes terrorism for a new kind of social, political and economic production.

War on Terrorism: America Resolved

From September 11 to the beginning of the bombing in Afghanistan, the newspaper *The Austin American Statesman* reported the war news daily under the same first page headline: "War on Terrorism: America Resolved." While the paper alluded to the determination of the country in its war against terrorism, the headline revealed the fact that the war could be a form of resolution for the major ailments of the country and the current administration. For a start, the war has produced a passionate nationalist unity and intense feeling of patriotism focused on the charged figure of the American citizen. While the meaning of this patriotic fervor is not yet clear and its direction is still volatile, there is little question that for the moment it has erased from view the scabrous issue of ongoing class and racial violence. It has obscured from view the social abandonment and police containment of poor communities, and managed to blame terrorism not only for the downturn of the economy but for the layoffs of workers as well. This is, of course, not new. Wars often serve the purpose of diverting social tension. Not only are deeply entrenched inequalities within the U.S. obscured by patriotism, but the surge of nationalist passion has elevated the popularity of an administration whose legitimacy before September 11 was doubtful. Social policies and progressive agendas are falling fast from sight, giving space to a new set of discourses and practices about national security that police dissent and censor information. For the time being, the war is productive for conservative agendas and the security and military industries. The link between patriotic discourses and the machinery of the security is best exemplified by the battery of counter-terrorist measures for which U.S. Attorney General John Ashcroft, summoned the most awkward descriptive title ever given to a counter-terrorist package: "Provide Appropriate Tools Required to Intercept and Obstruct Terrorism Act 2001," a title which only makes sense when translated into its acronym form: PATRIOT Act 2001. Patriotism and national betrayal are emerging as the organizing terms of political discourse. The bill—scaled down from its initial draft, which called for the indefinite detention of immigrant terrorist suspects—still gives wide authority to the police and secret services to arrest suspects, wiretap conversations and monitor e-mail communications.[11] Other measures proposed by the administration include increased militarization of borders, tightening immigration procedures, and expanding the power of intelligence agencies. What all these antiterrorist measures amount to is the suspension of civil liberties characteristic of a state of exception; one that will, no doubt, target some populations more than others. The state of exception, of course, is not new either, how else can we conceptualize the politics of containment,

---

11. Neil A. Lewis and Robert Pear, "Negotiators Back Scaled-down Bill to Battle Terror," *New York Times*, October 2, 2001.

intensive surveillance and industrial imprisonment of poor inner city communities legitimized by the war on crime and the war on drugs?

The question is whether this new state of exception redefines the juridical dimension of the new world order. And if so, what form will this redefinition take? What implications will it have? Some scholars, such as Giorgio Agamben, have already warned about the increasing redefinition of the law by an ongoing state of exception in late modernity. One of the consequences of this new state of law is, to quote Agamben, "that in the state of exception, it is impossible to distinguish transgression of the law from execution of the law, such that what violates a rule and what conforms to it coincide without any reminder" (1998: 57). This indistinguishability between execution and transgression of the law, is also what characterizes the kind of guerrilla warfare that is often grouped under the rubric of terrorism. A war against Terrorism, then, mirrors the state of exception characteristic of insurgent violence and in so doing it reproduces it ad infinitum. The question remains: What politics might be involved in this state of alert as normal state? Would this possible scenario of competing (and mutually constituting) terror signify the end of politics as we know it? Will it mean the subordination of the political to a state of right defined by security demands and military operations, as Hardt and Negri (2000) have suggested? And what would constitute the passions that would sustain such an ongoing confrontation? In the poor regions and neighborhoods of the Muslim world, where Islamist radicalism has found resonance, passions might be fueled by a vision of a society in which one is redeemed from suffering, marginality and alienation. But in the U.S., what would feed the passions necessary to endure the suffering and support the violence of an unpredictable war? Would this be the thrill of terror provided by the spectacle of violence itself, as it becomes routinized into timeless temporality? If the fundamental question of widening inequalities and growing injustice that this neoliberal globalization is creating is not addressed, and if U.S. foreign and domestic policies are not seriously reconsidered to stop the massive loss of human life that goes on unspectacularly behind the scenes, then there is little hope of ending terrorist forms of violence, including those practiced by state or state-like organizations. If a military strategy against a fictionalized and absolutized enemy predominates as a convenient and productive scapegoat against untenable everyday violence, then we might find ourselves in a social space characterized by the timeless time of unending war, the fictional realities of a permanent state of exception and the spectacle of violence; this is a scene that is already in place in many areas of the world.

EPILOGUE

The Intimacy of Violence and a Politics of Friendship[1]

JOSEBA ZULAIKA

I had the good fortune that Begoña Aretxaga wrote an epilogue to one of my books.[2] This book's title was taken from an adage by Nietzsche, "Enemies, there is no enemy!" (Zulaika 1999). In the work, I advocated the need for a new "politics of friendship" to resolve the endemic Basque/Spanish conflict, and Begoña's essay was entitled "The Intimacy of Violence" (see chapter 8 of this volume). I was flattered by her willingness to engage with my work, but also challenged since she was critical of some of my positions. I take this opportunity to further that conversation, fully aware that the fact she will not reply this time does not imply she would agree with some of my positions, but also aware that there is nothing she would want more from me than to continue this debate. Furthermore, the war in Iraq adds relevance to issues she raised in that essay.

On the basis of ethnographies such as Jeanne Favret Saada's *Witchcraft in the Bocage*, Philippe Bourgois' *In Search of Respect* and my own on *Basque Violence*, Aretxaga confronts the "moral dilemmas" posed by the "situation of being simultaneously victim and victimizer," to then ask herself: "From which vantage point that isn't already, in one way or another, that of accomplice, can one judge this violence? None," she replies. "For there is no external position—now that God and Reason have been replaced as guides of universal values—that functions as a moral guarantee and redeems us from the personal burden of moral responsibility." For her, such complicity with the informants is tied to anthropology's professional ethics, which require researchers not to harm the lives of their informants, and which, while similar to professional situations in other fields such as journalism or psychology that rely on inter-subjective relationships, in no way imply a moral

1. Paper presented at the American Anthropological Association Symposium in honor of Begoña Aretxaga, Chicago, November 2003.
2. See Chapter 8 of this volume, "The Intimacy of Violence."

relativism or indifference. Aretxaga concludes that, "Ultimately, the ethical and moral dilemmas confronted by the anthropologist are no different in nature to those confronted by our informants." Her position regarding nationalism and violence is that, "there is no position that remains 'uncontaminated'"; that is, "that does not take part, consciously or unconsciously, in the power games that the discourse of terrorism itself has demarcated beforehand."

The issue of the intimacy of violence cannot be avoided in situations such as the Basque case, argues Aretxaga, or in the case of Iraq, when the "terrorists," far from being social outcasts or psychopaths, are frequently your neighbors, friends, and even family members. To render those "terrorists" into the embodiment of an evil which must be tabooed and extirpated, is to deny that they are an integral part of the ordinary reality of those societies. Such denials become counterproductive and in the end, result in further violence.

The daily reality in a city such as San Sebastián, Aretxaga's hometown, is that the media's impersonal "terrorist" is "a next-door neighbor, your high-school friend's brother, an acquaintance with whom you've had a drink on several occasions, or that guy from your college class." If, following Michael Herzfeld's notion of "cultural intimacy," social groups are stereotyped according to their lifestyles by power positions outside the group, we can imagine the degree to which members and sympathizers of a pro-ETA political party such as Batasuna, bonded by repression and self-victimization, become a community of intense intimacy against a world that accuses them of complicity with terror. The media routinely report ETA's more than eight hundred murders during its bloody history, to which the other side adds the less-known fact that some 40 per cent of Batasuna sympathizers, who had regularly made up 15 percent of Basque voters, have had problems with the police and fear torture. This tortured body of the nation becomes a community of loss, fear, and mourning. Anderson's "imagined community," argues Aretxaga, is also a community that one cannot imagine outside of the affective domain based on spaces of intimacy. Beyond historical circumstances or beyond the recent invention of the concept of "nation," only a community of sentiment can explain the intense emotional attachment to national realities.

Yet the one thing this community of mourning cannot do is to stop the excesses of violence. Suddenly one neighbor kills another of your neighbors alleging political treason, or you see an old friend that you once visited in prison, now drinking champagne to celebrate the killing of your own brother, and the question that resists any easy and self-serving political answer emerges at the heart of that cultural intimacy: "But how can that be?" It is the presence of the Lacanian Real, "the trauma of a violence among close friends in which the completely incomprehensible and the incredibly mundane come together." This is also the birth of morality, the beginning of law and culture at the very moment in which the Freudian sons kill their father. The response, "But how can that be?" refers to the moral limits of a community in which such violence among intimates is possible, and ultimately questions the value of a community based on the violent exclusion of some of its members.

A crucial aspect of this logic of violence requires understanding the production of the figure of the enemy. This is where the mutual dynamics between the State and ETA, in a war mentality in which both feed on each other, take center stage. Such a vicious circle has clear benefits for each side: the State can blame all its mistakes and deficiencies on terrorism, while ETA can find justification for its own perpetuation by pointing to the State's violence. Beyond merely instrumental interests, Aretxaga sees in this relationship "an imaginary intimacy, a mutual obsession and fascination that dominates and defines the joint identity of these two politico-mythological actors." She illustrates this mimetic appropriation of terrorism by the State by way of the infamous Spanish case of the "dirty war" known as GAL, in which the socialist government replicated the very methods of the terrorists, and which betrayed "an imaginary identification with the figure of the terrorist, whose power resides not in the law, but in its transgression."

There could not be a more starkly opposed position to President Bush's mantra that we are in a war between good and evil than Aretxaga's careful analysis, based on her Irish and Basque ethnographic experience, which stresses that: "'the state' and 'terrorism' form part of the same political imaginary and their actors make up a phantasmic relationship that links them intimately, with each one depending on the other for its own definition and legitimacy." When ETA maintained a ceasefire for over a year in 1998–99, the Spanish Government's reaction was not one of jubilation; in the Basque Country, it was widely perceived as one of obstructionism to a possible solution. Similarly, ETA's followers never truly agreed to the idea of a political settlement without further violent struggle. The implication of this insight, crucial for the Basque case, but also for other cases such as the Israeli/Palestinian one, and in the end for the entire "war on terror," is that there cannot be a true peace process without revisiting this relationship between the State and Terrorism and that, in Aretxaga's words, "the success of any peace process will depend on the capacity to confront, face-to-face, our political phantoms."

If we look through the lens of the ongoing political discourse we hear every day, this anthropological perspective may appear as hopelessly naive. But, emphatically, it is not. Everything we have learned in anthropology says that the priest and the murderer are the same person, and that it is by the logic of tabooing people that today's intimate friends become tomorrow's arch-enemies. Bin Laden and Saddam Hussein, Manuel Noriega or the blind Sheik Omar Abdul Rahman, were in the past human enough to be our closest allies. This is "the intimacy of violence" Aretxaga is concerned about. Is the solution to the present violence to now turn that past collaboration into a religiously sanctioned "war on terror," a "crusade" with no middle ground but mutual destruction between "them" and "us"? Should we believe that the current policies on terrorism provide a better perspective than the one put forward by Aretxaga and other anthropologists, which urges us to look at the imaginative and ritualistic basis of the entire terrorism discourse and practice? The argument that the premises of the discourse itself may contribute crucially to furthering the violence (whether it is McVeigh, Sheik Rahman, or bin Laden) is one that we will not hear in the media, but one that we anthropologists are well equipped to make.

Edmund Leach spelled out best the dangers of a terrorism discourse which assumes such a complete lack of shared moral values with the terrorist "other" that, "every form of terroristic atrocity is not only attributed to the other side but becomes permissible for oneself. Indeed, counter-terrorism becomes, in a bizarre sense, a religiously sanctioned moral duty" (1977: 36). Should we be surprised by what has happened in Guantánamo or Abu Ghraib? Not after we take into account the discourse of terrorism.

How can we overcome these Manichean politics in which each position becomes an inverted reflection of the irreducible opposite? This is where I proposed, for the Spanish/Basque situation, and on the basis of the new European and global supra-state institutions, a politics based on the model of friendship that would overcome the centuries-long enmity between the two communities. Aretxaga liked my substituting a multiplicity of democratic alternatives for the bipolar world of the unending struggle dominated by the archetypal figure of "the enemy." But she felt uncomfortable with my postulating "friendship as a metaphor for this new political subjectivity" and what she understood as its "utopian" dimension. Friendship, which is born of mutual trust and affection, cannot be forced on anyone, she argued; whereas in politics pragmatic considerations lead us to recognize the position of the other side without having to feel sympathy for it. Friendship can be affected by politics, but politics, as the domain of power differences, cannot exhaust the field of friendship. Aretxaga illustrates the ideal quality of a politics of friendship by invoking Levinas' ethical imperative, an author to whom various anthropologists have lately granted special attention; his radical care and responsibility for the Other includes the political dimension as well. This would certainly be a radical departure from politics as we know it, but Aretxaga wonders whether in the end that position would erase the political dimension altogether. In a situation of historical violence, for example, can you suddenly erase it in order to propose a new politics of friendship? Can you become friends with the one who tortured your daughter or the one who killed your brother? Aware that a friendship demanded by politics would cease to be true friendship, Aretxaga concludes that "It is precisely the awareness of belonging to the same community and feeling free to not be 'friends' with someone that, in my view, makes genuine dialogue about political differences possible."

I agree with Aretxaga that friends are chosen, not imposed, whereas as citizens we cannot avoid the impositions of politics. Friendship, if it is to be sustaining, may even require a certain separateness and valuing of differences. And any readiness to model political relationships on the principles of friendship requires an awareness that there can be no good friendship when a fluid negotiation of the power differentials in the relationship is lacking. The danger is to disguise such differentials with the rhetoric of friendship while imposing acts of demeaning charity.

But there is a sense in which Aretxaga's own acceptance of the Levinasian obligation to care for the Other is close to an obligation for the asymmetrical and gift-like qualities of friendship relationships. It is true, as Aretxaga observed, that Levinas' distinction between the political and the ethical undermines any attempt at subsuming politics under the rubric of ethics or, by extension, friendship. Still, whereas the ethical remains in the realm of individual moral duty, friendship is ultimately a "second person" relationship and therefore it can be made to belong as much to the realm of politics as of ethics, as Aristotle showed.

Following Hannah Arendt, there is also a sense in which the Kantian categorical imperative, of having to act on the maxim that what you want for yourself should become a universal law, may be translated as an imperative for friendship. In Arendt's thinking, it is better to suffer wrong than to do wrong, because you can remain the friend of a sufferer, but who would want to be the friend of a murderer. In other words, it is better not to murder, the quintessential duty of the military and the cornerstone of the politics of enmity, because it makes friendship, which is the greatest good, impossible. A politics that makes half the world friends and the other half enemies fails this categorical imperative by its unwillingness to universalize what we want for ourselves. In this regard, friendship is prior to justice, for, in Aristotle's words, "when men are friends they have no need of justice, while when they are just they need friendship as well" (1941: 1155a26–27).

What this debate points to are the difficulties in conceptualizing new political subjectivities beyond the friend/enemy dichotomy. Are you with us or against us? This is also the alternative we hear from our politicians after they have taken us to war once again. The attackers of the Twin Towers on 9/11 surely were our enemies. Or were they? It is well documented that the perpetrators of the first attack on the Twin Towers had been our friends during years of fighting side by side against Reagan's "Empire of Evil" in Afghanistan. Their spiritual leader, Sheik Omar Abdul Rahman, had repeatedly come to this country with visas provided by the CIA to indoctrinate the future anti-communist crusaders. Sheik Omar was confined to a New York prison on conspiracy charges which, according to an editorial in the *New York Times* (no friend of terrorists), "only required [the Government] to prove *the intention* to wage a terror campaign" and despite "only the sketchiest connections [being] established between Sheik Abdel Rahman and the alleged mastermind of that crime, Ramzi Ahmed Yousef." This was done on the basis of the testimony of one Mr. Salem, who had been paid a million and a half dollars by the government, and which sounded to the *New York Times* "like sheer fantasy." There was, of course, someone who had paid Sheik Omar's expenses while he was in the U.S. and who was keeping score. He was Osama bin Laden, another former CIA protégé who had been our warrior friend but now became our arch-enemy. So the larger question becomes, not just who are our friends and who our enemies, but what type of politics creates such "friendships" and "enmities," and what logic pushes "friends" into becoming our future "enemies."

It is here that Aristotle's definition of friendship as a political relationship becomes most relevant. And it is here that Nietzsche's call to the enemy—"Enemies, there is no enemy!"—becomes a radical departure from politics-as-usual. It has certainly been the case throughout history, in Carl Schmitt's classical argument that the figure of the enemy was central to the very notion of politics, to the point that if you lose the enemy you lose politics. The dissolution of the figure of the enemy implies a revolution by introducing the aporia of friendship as a relationship that goes beyond the logic of reciprocity (Derrida 1997). This is also the logic of Blake's imperative: "Do be my enemy for the sake of friendship." Such a call to the enemy converts the enemy ipso facto into a friend, while the friend is asked to become an enemy as well. This is no longer "love your enemy" in a Christian sense. It is simply love before being loved or the disproportionate, excessive logic of the gift; it is the Nietzschean transposition of values or the Levinasian/Derridean responsibility for the Other before the Other.

Aretxaga's question remains, however: when defined as friendship, does politics disappear? In other terms, what would happen to the real structure of the political without the friend/enemy opposition? But this was precisely Nietzsche's crime, his overturning of values, the perverse necessity to make opposites turn into each other. In Derrida's commentary, losing the enemy is a crime on the order of the political or against the political itself. From the axiom that the very opposition between friend and enemy constitutes politics, Schmitt derived that ignoring the enemy would even be an essential risk for humanity. He further established a crucial distinction between enmity and hostility; the political antithesis of friendship is not enmity but hostility, he argued. The enemy is something "public" and opposition to the enemy has nothing to do with private sentiments of hatred. This is a lesson soldiers must learn at the outset and which is intrinsic to the military's hierarchical culture; the decisions never belong to the individual, who is even forbidden to use the first-person pronoun, "I." The soldier must simply destroy the enemy target; harboring hostile or friendly feelings towards the enemy is simply irrelevant. In fact, the first inversion implied by the *amicus/hostis* opposition is that even the friend can be an enemy. Far from a rarity, this is rather the norm in a civil war. In the Christian tradition, the maxim "love your enemy" didn't mean love your political enemy; that is, be tolerant of, say, the Muslims during the crusades. Europeans had to fight Islam to the end in the name of universal Christianity while loving the Muslims as neighbors. This is also the predicament in which Bush's war on terror puts us all. We are told that this is not a war against Muslims but against terror. The catch is that of the hundreds of terrorist suspects, in Guantánamo or in the anonymity of the U.S. prison system, they are all, almost without exception, Muslims.

These are not inconsequential semantic games. The distinction between enmity and hostility was a product of a Christian Europe which could thus fulfill the Christian duty of loving the neighbors while murdering them for being Muslims. As Derrida comments, this was not just any war, but combat with the political at stake, a struggle for politics. Similarly, in the ongoing war on terror, the inaugural semantic act which defines the terrorist enemy and creates its own genre of politics, a politics that is quite novel rhetorically but whose direct inspiration we could find in the European crusades against Islam, is the crucial operation that legitimizes and frames such politics. Terrorism provides for us what the crusades provided for Christian Europe: the excuse for the creation of a political enemy so barbaric that its elimination requires going to war. The war on terror confronts us with vast redefinitions of the very nature of warfare and law —regarding premises such as preemption, for example, to say nothing of the impact on basic laws and civil liberties that affect the entire political domain; this too is a moment for the "struggle for politics." And nothing is more subversive to Bush's politics than Nietzsche's adage, "Enemies, there is no enemy!"

Regarding the war on terror, the challenge for Aretxaga was to show how both sides are not really opposed but reinforce each other. This is similar to Slavoj Žižek's argument of "the temptation of a double blackmail," namely, either the unconditional condemnation of Third World Evil that appears to endorse the ideological position of American innocence, or drawing attention to the deeper socio-political causes of Arab extremism which ends up blaming the victims of 9/11. Each of the two positions are one-sided and false. Pointing to the limits of moral reasoning, Žižek resorts to the dialectical category of totality to argue that: "From the moral standpoint, the victims are innocent, the act was an abominable crime; however, this very innocence is not innocent—to adopt such an 'innocent' position in today's global capitalist universe is in itself a false abstraction." This does not entail a compromised notion of shared guilt by terrorists and victims; "the point is, rather, that the two sides are not really opposed, that they belong to the same field. In short, the position to adopt is to accept the necessity of the fight against terrorism, BUT to redefine and expand its terms so that it will include also (some) American and other Western powers' acts" (2001: 46–47).

Which is why, in this struggle for the true meaning of politics, it might be helpful to recall the canonical texts on "friendship" by writers such as Aristotle, Montaigne, Nietzsche or Derrida, and invoke a "politics of friendship"; that is, take certain features of friendship and expand them to construct a model of a political community. Friendship is not here a mere "metaphor," but an epistemic model which introduces the promise of a radically different logic in politics. An interesting example of how to provide paradigmatic status to friendship can be found in Lorraine Code's search for a feminist epistemology which, beyond the traditional Cartesian subject/object interaction, will create richer subjectivities. Even recognizing that friendly relations are never pure or unmediated, still friendship recognizes, beyond the impartiality and neutrality of individualistic "I" thinking, that people are essentially "you," second persons. Friendships can accommodate growth and are able to confront ambivalences and ambiguities. The virtues of friendship were first described by Aristotle, who devoted two entire books of his Nichomachean Ethics to the topic. His view that man is essentially a political creature is connected to the view that friendship is the best form of living with others. For Aristotle, friendship is as much epistemological as affective, as we need, beyond trust, the cognitive capacity to know the character of a good friend. Besides benevolence and commitment, friendship recognizes the self-sufficient other's separateness and independence. It requires a common moral and legal status, which is why in his times true friendship was not possible between master and slaves, nor among men and women considered inferior. Because of its basis in the knowledge of a friend's character, well-chosen friends enrich our lives, unwisely chosen friends damage us.

The Aristotelian closeness between politics and friendship derives from his under-standing of politics as an activity that is primary to all other activities, whether public, as in government, or private, as in family and personal practices. Thus, friendship as a par-adigm "can point the way to a relational analysis of subjectivity that is at once morally accountable, politically engaged, and located in 'second person' dialogues" (Code 1991: 101). It is the epistemic potential of friendship, as a place for knowing other people, as well as its political potential, as a locus for positive allegiances, that my initial treatment of the topic left undeveloped, therefore making Aretxaga feel uncomfortable with it. She thought I was using friendship as a "metaphor" for politics, when my argument wanted to echo the Aristotelian closeness between friendship and politics while arguing that, in the terrorism-prone world of nuclear military technology in which we live, the creative poten-tial of friendship can best substitute the Schmittean paradigm of politics as constituted by the figure of the enemy.

In its final consequence, the logic of friendship implies the radical dissymmetry, even the excess, of the logic of the gift which goes beyond the demands of reciprocity. Politi-cally, this points to a democracy to come that goes beyond numerical proportionality. Such logic of disproportion is confronted with the problematic of trust, the paradox that subjectivity is unstable yet friendship and political allegiance require reliable trust.

Arendt aligned thinking with friendship. She claimed, following the Greek philosophi-cal tradition, that "the dialogue of thought can be carried out only among friends" (1971: 189). Begoña Aretxaga was a singular practitioner of such an alliance between thinking and friendship. She had to think and write because so many of her friends in Ireland and the Basque Country, her colleagues and students, needed her work. The goal of her ethno-graphic and theoretical sophistication was to reveal the subjective core of the people she had come to know and be intellectually responsible for. She wrote as if intellectual failure was also a failure in friendship, and as if lost friends, which she did have, were somehow the result of intellectual errors that could be avoided. Like many of you, for years I enjoyed the gift of her thinking as inseparable from the gift of her friendship. As if it need-ed any further proof, her illness provided the final occasion to reveal the extraordinary fortitude and lucidity of her mind, the witty and selfless generosity of her spirit. She had to make the effort to write as passionately and as brilliantly as she did because, in these times of danger, she deeply cared for us, her friends.

Bibliography

Abraham, Nicolas, and Maria Torok. *The Shell and the Kernel.* 1959. Edited, translated, and with an introduction by Nicholas T. Rand. Chicago: The University of Chicago Press, 1994.

Abrams, Phillip. "Notes on the Difficulty of Studying the State." *Journal of Historical Sociology* 1.1 (1988): 58–89.

Abu-Lughod, Lila. *Veiled Sentiments: Honor and Poetry in a Bedouin Society.* Berkeley: University of California Press, 1986.

Agamben, Giorgio. *Homo Sacer: Sovereignty and Bare Life.* Translated by Daniel Heller-Roazen. Stanford: Stanford University Press, 1998.

———. *Remnants of Auschwitz: The Witness and the Archive.* Translated by Daniel Heller-Roazen. New York: Zone Books, 2000a.

———. *Means Without End: Notes on Politics.* Translated by Vincenzo Binetti and Cesare Casarino. Minneapolis, MN: University of Minnesota Press, 2000b.

Alonso, Ana Maria. "The Politics of Space, Time and Substance: State Formation, Nationalism and Ethnicity. *Annual Review of Anthropology* 23 (1994): 379–405.

Althusser, Louis. "Ideology and Ideological State Apparatuses: Notes Towards an Investigation." *Lenin and Philosophy and Other Essays.* Translated by Ben Brewster. New York: Monthly Review Press, 1971. 127–86.

Amnesty International. *Report of an Amnesty International Mission to Northern Ireland.* June, 1977.

Anderson, Benedict. *Imagined Communities: Reflections on the Origin and Spread of Nationalism.* London: Verso, 1983. Revised edition, 1991.

Anghiera, Peter Martyr. *De Orbe Novo (The Decades of the Newe Worlde or West India).* 1555. Translated by Richard Eden. Ann Arbor: University Microfilms, 1966.

Appadurai, Arjun. "Patriotism and Its Futures." *Public Culture* 5 (1993): 411–29.

———. *Modernity at Large: Cultural Dimensions of Globalization.* Minneapolis: University of Minnesota Press, 1996.

———. "Dead Certainty: Ethnic Violence in the Era of Globalization." *Public Culture* 10.2 (1998): 225–47. Reprinted in *Development and Change* 29 (1998): 905–925.

Ardener, Shirley. "Sexual Insult and Female Militancy." In *Perceiving Women.* Ed. Shirley Ardener. London: Dent and Sons, 1975. 29–53.

Arendt, Hannah. *The Life of the Mind*. Vol. 1. *Thinking*. New York: Harcourt, Brace, Jovanovich, 1971.

Aretxaga, Begoña. *Los funerales en el nacionalismo radical. Ensayo antropológico*. San Sebastián: Baroja, 1987.

——. "Striking With Hunger: Cultural Meanings of Political Violence in Northern Ireland." *The Violence Within: Cultural and Political Opposition in Divided Nations*. Ed. Kay B. Warren. Boulder, CO: Westview Press, 1993. 219–56.

——. "Dirty Protest: Symbolic Overdetermination and Gender in Northern Ireland Ethnic Violence." *Ethos* 23.2 (1995): 123–48.

——. *Shattering Silence: Women, Nationalism and Political Subjectivity in Northern Ireland*. Princeton: Princeton University Press, 1997.

——. "What the Border Hides: Partition and the Gender Politics of Irish Nationalism." *Social Analysis* 42.1 (1998): 16–32.

——. "Lo 'real'. Violencia como realidad virtual." *La Cuestión Vasca. Claves de un conflicto cultural y político*. Ed. Josetxo Beriain and Roger Fernandez. Barcelona: Proyecto A Ediciones, 1999a. 106–17.

——. "La intimidad de la violencia." Epilogue. *Enemigos, no hay enemigo*. By Joseba Zulaika. Donostia: Erein, 1999b. 233–253.

——. "A Fictional Reality: Paramilitary Death Squads and the Construction of State Terror in Spain." *Death Squad: The Anthropology of State Terror*. Ed. Jeffrey A. Sluka. Philadelphia: University of Pennsylvania Press, 2000a. 47–69.

——. "Playing Terrorist: Ghastly Plots and the Ghostly State." *Journal of Spanish Cultural Studies* 1.1 (2000b): 43–58.

——. "Engendering Violence: Strip Searches of Women in Northern Ireland." *History in Person: Enduring Struggles and Practices of Identity*. Ed. Dorothy Holland and Jean Lave, Santa Fe, NM: School of American Research Press, 2001a. 37–61.

——. "The Sexual Games of the Body Politic: Fantasy and State Violence in Northern Ireland." *Culture, Medicine and Psychiatry* 25 (2001b): 1–27.

——. "Terror as Thrill: First Thoughts on the 'War on Terrorism.'" *Anthropological Quarterly* 75.1 (2002): 139–50.

Aristotle. *Nichomachean Ethics*. Translated by W.D. Ross. *The Basic Works of Aristotle*. Ed. Richard McKeon. New York: Random House, 1941.

Arriaga Landeta, Mikel. *Y nosotros que éramos de HB. Sociología de una heterodoxia abertzale*. San Sebastián: Aramburu, 1997.

Asad, Talal. "Notes on Body Pain and Truth in Medieval Christian Ritual." *Economy and Society* 12.1 (1983): 287–327.

Balibar, Etienne, and Immanuel M. Wallerstein. *Race, Nation, Class: Ambiguous Identities.* Translation of Etienne Balibar by Chris Turner. London and New York: Verso, 1991.

Baudrillard, Jean. "La conjuration des imbeciles." *Libération*, May 7, 1997. An English version, "A Conjuration of Imbeciles," translated by Francois Debrix, is available at http://www.uta.edu/english/apt/collab/texts/conjuration.html.

Bauman, Zygmunt. *Intimations of Postmodernity.* London: Routledge, 1992.

Bell, J. Bowyer. *The Secret Army: The IRA 1916–1979.* Cambridge, MA: MIT Press, 1980.

Benjamin, Walter. "Theses on the Philosophy of History." In *Illuminations: Essays and Reflections.* Translated by Harry Zohn. Ed. Hannah Arendt. New York: Schocken Books, 1968. 253–64.

———. *Reflections: Essays, Aphorisms, Autobiographical Writings.* 1921. Translated by Edmund Jephcott. New York: Harcourt Brace Jovanovich, 1978.

Berdahl, Daphne. *Where the World Ended: Re-Unification and Identity in the German Borderland.* Berkeley: University of California Press, 1999.

Beresford, David. *Ten Men Dead: The Story of the 1981 Irish Hunger Strike.* London: Grafton Books, 1987.

Beriain, Josetxo, and Roger Fernandez, eds. *La Cuestión Vasca. Claves de un conflicto cultural y político.* Barcelona: Proyecto A. Ediciones, 1999.

Berlant, Lauren. *The Anatomy of National Fantasy.* Chicago: University of Chicago Press, 1991.

———. "The Theory of Infantile Citizenship." *Public Culture* 5 (1993): 395–410.

———. *The Queen of America Goes to Washington City: Essays on Sex and Citizenship.* Durham: Duke University Press, 1997.

———., ed. *Intimacy.* Special issue of *Critical Inquiry* 24.2 (1998).

Bhabha, Homi. "Of Mimicry and Man: The Ambivalence of Colonial Discourse." *October* 28 (1984): 123–33.

———., ed. *Nation and Narration.* London and New York: Routledge, 1990.

Bilbao, Jon. *Eusko-Bibliographia.* 9 vols. San Sebastián: Auñamendi, 1970–1976.

Boland, Eavan. *A Kind of Scar: The Woman Poet in a National Tradition.* LIP Pamphlets. Dublin: Attic Press, 1989.

Borneman, John. *Belonging in the Two Berlins: Kin, State, Nation.* Cambridge: Cambridge University Press, 1992.

———. "Uniting the German Nation: Law, Narrative and Historicity." *American Ethnologist* 20.2 (1993): 288–311.

———. *Subversions of International Order: Studies in the Political Anthropology of Culture.* Albany: State University of New York Press, 1998.

Bourdieu, Pierre. "Rethinking the State: Genesis and Structure of the Bureaucratic Field." *State/Culture: State Formation after the Cultural Turn.* Ed. George Steinmetz. Ithaca: Cornell University Press, 1999. 53–72.

Bourgois, Philippe. *In Search of Respect: Selling Crack in El Barrio.* Cambridge and New York: Cambridge University Press, 1995.

Brass, Paul R. *Theft of an Idol: Text and Context in the Representation of Collective Violence.* Princeton: Princeton University Press, 1997.

Brown, Norman O. *Life against Death: The Psychoanalytical Meaning of History.* Middletown, CO: Wesleyan University Press, 1959.

Brown, Terence. *Ireland: A Social and Cultural History, 1922 to the Present.* Ithaca: Cornell University Press, 1985.

Brown, Wendy. *States of Injury: Power and Freedom in Late Modernity.* Princeton: Princeton University Press, 1995.

Bruner, Edward M. "Ethnography as Narrative." *The Anthropology of Experience.* Ed. Victor W. Turner and Edward M Bruner. Urbana: University of Illinois Press, 1986. 139–55.

Burton, Frank. *The Politics of Legitimacy: Struggles in a Belfast Community.* London: Routledge and Kegan Paul, 1978.

Butler, Judith. *Gender Trouble: Feminism and the Subversion of Identity.* New York: Routledge, 1990.

———. *Bodies That Matter: On the Discursive Limits of "Sex."* New York: Routledge, 1993.

———. *The Psychic Life of Power.* Stanford: Stanford University Press, 1997.

Butler, Judith, and Joan Scott, eds. *Feminists Theorize the Political.* New York: Routledge, 1992.

Cairns, David, and Sean Richards. *Writing Ireland: Colonialism, Nationalism and Culture.* Manchester: Manchester University Press, 1988.

Cameron Report, The. *Disturbances in Northern Ireland: Report of the Cameron Commission.* London: Her Majesty's Stationery Office, Command 532, 1969.

Canetti, Elias. *The Human Province: Notes 1942–1972.* New York: Seabury Press, 1978.

Canny, Nicholas P. "The Ideology of English Colonization: From Ireland to America." *William and Mary Quarterly* 30 (1973): 575–98.

———. *From Reformation to Restoration: Ireland 1534–1660.* Dublin: Helicon, 1987.

Cardinal, Marie. *The Words to Say It: An Autobiographical Novel.* Cambridge, MA: Van Vactor & Goodheart, 1983.

Castoriadis, Cornelius. *The Imaginary Institution of Society.* Cambridge: Polity Press, 1997.

Chatterjee, Partha. "Colonialism, Nationalism and Colonized Women: The Contest in India." *American Ethnologist* 16.4 (1989): 622–33.

———. *The Nation and Its Fragments: Colonial and Postcolonial Histories*. Princeton: Princeton University Press, 1993.

Clark, Robert P. *The Basque Insurgents: ETA, 1952–1980*. Madison: University of Wisconsin Press, 1984.

Code, Lorraine. *What Can She Know? Feminist Theory and the Construction of Knowledge*. Ithaca and London: Cornell University Press, 1991.

Collins, Tom. *The Centre Cannot Hold*. Dublin: Bookworks, 1984.

Comaroff, Jean, and John Comaroff. *Of Revelation and Revolution: Christianity, Colonialism and Consciousness in South Africa*. Chicago: University of Chicago Press, 1991.

———. "Alien-nation: Zombies, Immigrants, and Millennial Capitalism." *South Atlantic Quarterly* 4 (1999): 779–806.

———. "Millennium Capitalism: First Thoughts on a Second Coming." *Millennial Capitalism and the Culture of Neoliberalism*. Special Issue of *Public Culture* 12.2 (2000a): 291–343.

———. "Naturing the Nation: Allies, Apocalypse, and the Postcolonial State." *Hagar: International Social Science Review* 1.1 (2000b): 7–40.

Community for Justice. *Strip Searching – A Moral Issue*. Published by the Community for Justice, 1987.

Coogan, Tim Pat. *The IRA*. London: Fontana Books, 1980a

———. *On the Blanket: The H-Block Story*. Dublin: Ward River Press, 1980b.

Copjec, Joan, ed. *Radical Evil*. New York: Verso, 1996.

Corcuera Atienza, Javier. *Orígenes, ideología y organización del nacionalismo vasco (1876–1904)*. Madrid: Siglo XXI, 1979.

Cornell, Drucilla. *Beyond Accommodation: Ethical Feminism, Deconstruction and the Law*. New York: Routledge, 1991.

———. *Transformations: Recollective Imagination and Sexual Difference*. New York: Routledge, 1993.

———. "Rethinking the Beyond of the Real." *Levinas and Lacan: The Missed Encounter*. Ed. Sarah Harasym. New York: State University of New York Press, 1998. 139–81.

Coronil, Fernando. *The Magical State: Nature, Money and Modernity in Venezuela*. Chicago: The University of Chicago Press, 1997.

Corrigan, Phillip, and Derek Sayer. *The Great Arch: English State Formation as Cultural Revolution*. New York: Basil Blackwell, 1985.

Coulter, Carol. *Ireland: Between the First and the Third World*. LIP Pamphlets. Dublin: Attic Press, 1990.

———. *The Hidden Tradition: Feminism, Women and Nationalism in Ireland*. Cork: Cork University Press, 1993.

Crapanzano, Vincent. *Waiting: The Whites of South Africa*. New York: Vintage Books, 1986.

Curtis, Lewis Perry. *Anglo-Saxons and Celts: A Study of Anti-Irish Prejudice in Victorian England.* New York: University Press, 1968.

———. *Apes and Angels: The Irishman in Victorian Caricature.* Washington, DC.: Smithsonian Institution Press, 1971.

Curtis, Liz. *Ireland: The Propaganda War: The British Media and the "Battle for Hearts and Minds."* London: Pluto Press, 1984.

Daniel, Valentine E. *Charred Lullabies: Chapters in an Anthropography of Violence.* Princeton, NJ: Princeton University Press, 1996.

Darby, John, ed. *Northern Ireland: The Background to the Conflict.* Belfast: Appletree Press, 1983a.

———. *Dressed To Kill: Cartoonists and the Northern Ireland Conflict.* Belfast: Appletree Press, 1983b.

Das, Veena. *Mirrors of Violence: Communities, Riots, and Survivors in South Asia.* Delhi and New York: Oxford University Press, 1990.

———. *Critical Events: An Anthropological Perspective on Contemporary India.* Delhi and New York: Oxford University Press, 1995.

———. "Language and Body: Transactions in the Construction of Pain." *Social Suffering.* Special issue of *Daedalus* 125.1 (1996a): 67–93.

———. "Sexual Violence: Discursive Formations and the State." *Economic and Political Weekly* 31 (1996b): 2411–25.

Das, Veena, and Ashis Nandy. "Violence, Victimhood and the Language of Silence." *Contributions to Indian Sociology* 19.1 (1985): 177–95.

Das, Veena, and Deborah Poole, eds. *Anthropology in the Margins of the State.* Santa Fe, NM: School of American Research Press; Oxford: James Currey, 2004.

Deane, Seamus. *Civilians and Barbarians.* Field Day Pamphlet, No. 3. Derry: Field Day Theatre Company, 1983.

———. *Heroic Styles: The Tradition of an Idea.* Field Day Pamphlet, No. 4. Derry: Field Day Theatre Company, 1984.

———., ed. *Field Day Anthology of Irish Writing.* Vol. 3. Derry: Field Day Publications, 1991.

De Certeau, Michel. *The Practice of Everyday Life.* Translated by Steven Randall. Berkeley: University of California Press, 1984.

———. *The Writing of History.* Translated by Tom Conley. New York: Columbia University Press, 1988.

Denich, Bette. "Dismembering Yugoslavia: Nationalist Ideologies and the Symbolic Revival of Genocide." *American Ethnologist* 21 (1994): 367–90.

Derrida, Jacques. "Force of Law: The Mystical Foundations of Authority." *Cardozo Law Review* 11 (1991): 920–1045.

———. *Specters of Marx: The State of the Debt, the Work of Mourning and the New International.* Translated by Peggy Kamuf. New York: Routledge, 1994.

———. *Politics of Friendship.* Translated by George Collins. London: Verso, 1997.

Dorfman, Ariel. *Death and the Maiden.* 1991. New York: Penguin, 1994.

Douglas, Mary. *Purity and Danger: An Analysis of the Concepts of Pollution and Taboo.* London: Routledge and Kegan Paul, 1966.

Draculic, Slavenka. "Women Hide Behind a Wall of Silence." *Why Bosnia? Writings on the Balkan War.* Ed. Rabia Ali and Lawrence Lifschultz. Stony Creek, CT: The Pamphleteer's Press, 1993. 116–21.

Durham, Deborah, and James Fernandez. "Tropical Dominions: The Figurative Struggle over Domains of Belonging and Apartness in Africa." *Beyond Metaphor: The Theory of Tropes in Anthropology.* Ed. James W. Fernandez. Stanford: Stanford University Press, 1991. 191–210.

Edwards, Ruth Dudley. *Patrick Pearse: The Triumph of Failure.* London: Gollancz, 1977.

Egin. "La Guerra sucia 1975–1995." *Euskadi 1995.* Hernani: Orain, 1996. 257–302.

Elshtain, Jean Bethke. *Women and War.* New York: Basic Books, 1987.

Elzo, Javier, ed. *Planteamientos para unas actuaciones sobre la subcultura de la violencia y sus repercusiones en la juventud vasca.* Deusto: Gobierno Vasco, 1995.

European Law Centre. *European Human Rights Reports.* Part 10. London: European Law Centre, 1981.

Evason, Eileen. *Against the Grain: The Contemporary Women's Movement in Northern Ireland.* Dublin: Attic Press, 1991.

Fabian, Johannes. *Out of Our Minds: Reason and Madness in the Exploration of Central Africa.* Berkeley: University of California Press, 2000.

Fairweather, Eileen, Roisin McDonough, and Melanie McFadyean. *Only the Rivers Run Free: Northern Ireland: The Women's War.* London: Pluto Press, 1984.

Fallon, Charlotte. "Civil War Hungerstrikes: Women and Men." *Éire-Ireland* 22 (1987): 75–91.

Fanon, Frantz. *A Dying Colonialism.* Translated by Haakon Chevalier. New York: Grove Press, 1967.

Farrell, Michael. *Northern Ireland: The Orange State.* London: Pluto Press, 1976.

Favret-Saada, Jeanne. *Deadly Words: Witchcraft in the Bocage.* Translated by Catherine Cullen. New York: Cambridge University Press, 1980.

Feldman, Allen. *Formations of Violence: The Narrative of the Body and Political Terror in Northern Ireland.* Chicago: University of Chicago Press, 1991.

———. "Violence and Vision: The Prosthetics and Aesthetics of Terror." *Violence and Subjectivity.* Ed. Veena Das, Arthur Kleinman, Mamphela Ramphele, and Pamela Reynolds. Berkeley: University of California Press, 2000. 46–78.

Ferguson, James. *The Anti-Politics Machine: "Development," Depoliticization, and Bureaucratic Power in Lesotho*. Cambridge and New York: Cambridge University Press, 1990.

Fernandez, James W. "Persuasions and Performances: Of the Beast of Everybody and the Metaphors of Everyman." *Daedalus* 101.1 (1972): 39–60.

———. *Persuasions and Performances: The Play of Tropes in Culture*. Bloomington: Indiana University Press, 1986.

Flackes, W.D., and Sidney Elliott. *Northern Ireland: A Political Directory, 1968–1988*. Dublin: Gill and Macmillan, 1989.

Forest, Eva. *¿Proceso al jurado? Conversaciones con Miguel Castells*. Hondarribia: Hiru Argitaletxe, 1997.

Fortes, Meyer, and E.E. Evans-Pritchard, eds. *African Political Systems*. London: International Institute of African Languages and Cultures; Oxford University Press, 1940.

Foster, R.F. *Modern Ireland 1600–1972*. London: Penguin, 1988.

———. *Paddy and Mr. Punch: Connections in Irish and English History*. London: A. Lane, 1993.

Foucault, Michel, ed. *I, Pierre Rivière, Having Slaughtered My Mother, My Sister, and My Brother . . . A Case of Parricide in the 19th Century*. Translated by Frank Jellinek. Lincoln and London: University of Nebraska Press, 1975. Reprint, 1982.

———. *The History of Sexuality*. Vol 1. *An Introduction*. Translated by Robert Hurley. New York: Vintage Books, 1978, 1980; Pantheon Books, 1979.

———. *Discipline and Punish: The Birth of the Prison*. Translated by Alan Sheridan. New York: Vintage Books, 1979, 1980.

———. *Madness and Civilization: A History of Insanity in the Age of Reason*. Translated by Richard Howard. New York: Random House, 1988.

———. "Governmentality." *The Foucault Effect: Studies in Governmentality*. Ed. Graham Burchill, Colin Gordon, and Peter Miller. Chicago: Chicago University Press, 1991. 87–104.

———. *The Politics of Truth*. New York: Semiotext(e), 1997.

Freud, Sigmund. "The Uncanny." 1925. *The Standard Edition of the Complete Psychological Works of Sigmund Freud*. Ed. by James Strachey et al. Vol. XVII. London: Hogarth Press and the Institute of Psychoanalysis, 1955. 217–56. Reprint, *On Creativity and the Unconscious*. Ed. Benjamin Nelson. New York: Harper Torchbooks, 1958. 122–61.

———. "Moses and Monotheism." 1939. *The Standard Edition of the Complete Psychological Works of Sigmund Freud*. Ed. James Strachey et al. Vol. XXIII. London: The Hogarth Press and the Institute of Psychoanalysis, 1964. 3–137. Reprint, translated by Katherine Jones. New York: Vintage Books, 1967.

———. *The Interpretation of Dreams*. 1899. Cutchogue, NY: Buccaneer Books, 1985.

———. *Civilization and Its Discontents*. 1930. Translated and edited by James Strachey. New York: W.W. Norton, 1989.

Gabilondo, Joseba. "Masculinity's Counted Days: Spanish Postnationalism, Masochist Desire, and the Refashioning of Misogyny." *Anuario de Cine y Literatura en Español* 3 (1997): 53–72.

Gallop, Jane. *Reading Lacan.* Ithaca: Cornell University Press, 1985.

García Damborenea, Ricardo. *Manual del buen terrorista.* Madrid: Cambio 16, 1987.

Garland, David. *Punishment and Modern Society: A Study in Social Theory.* Chicago: University of Chicago Press, 1990.

Garmendia, Jose Mari. *Historia de ETA.* San Sebastián: Haramburu, 1979.

Garmendia Lasa, Elixabete, et al. *Yoyes. Desde su ventana.* Iruña: Garrasi, 1987.

Geertz, Clifford. *The Interpretation of Cultures.* New York: Basic Books, 1973.

Gerth, Hans Heinrich, and C. Wright Mills, eds. *From Max Weber: Essays in Sociology.* New York: Oxford University Press, 1946.

Girard, René. *Violence and the Sacred.* Translated by Patrick Gregory. Baltimore: Johns Hopkins University Press, 1979.

Goffman, Irvin. *Asylums: Essays on the Social Situation of Mental Patients and Other Inmates.* New York: Anchor Books, 1959.

Gordon, Avery. *Ghostly Matters: Haunting and the Sociological Imagination.* Minneapolis: University of Minnesota Press, 1997.

Grant, Bruce. "New Moscow Monuments, or, States of Innocence." *American Ethnologist* 28.2 (2001): 332–62.

Grattan, Henry. "Speech in the Irish Parliament, April 16, 1782." *The Field Day Anthology of Irish Writing.* Vol. I. Ed. Seamus Deane. Derry: Field Day Publications, 1991. 918–21.

Graziano, Frank. *Divine Violence: Spectacle, Psychosexuality and Radical Christianity in the Argentine Dirty War.* Boulder, CO: Westview Press, 1992.

Grosz, Elizabeth. *Volatile Bodies: Towards a Corporeal Feminism.* Bloomington: Indiana University Press, 1994.

———. *Becomings: Explorations in Time, Memory and Futures.* Ithaca: Cornell University Press, 1999.

Gupta, Akhil. "Blurred Boundaries: the Discourse of Corruption, the Culture of Politics, and the Imagined State." *American Ethnologist* 22.2 (1995): 375–402.

———. *Postcolonial Developments: Agriculture in the Making of Modern India.* Durham, NC: Duke University Press, 1998.

Hackett, Claire. "Self-Determination: The Republican Feminist Agenda." *Feminist Review* 50 (1995): 111–16.

Hale, Charles R. "Does Multiculturalism Menace? Governance, Cultural Rights and the Politics of Identity in Guatemala." *Journal of Latin American Studies* 34 (2002): 485–524.

Hallinan, Joseph T. *Going Up the River: Travels in a Prison Nation.* New York: Random House, 2001.

Hammoudi, Abdella. *Master and Disciple: The Cultural Foundations of Moroccan Authoritarianism.* Chicago: Chicago University Press, 1997.

Handler, Richard. *Nationalism and the Politics of Culture in Quebec.* Madison: University of Wisconsin Press, 1988.

Hannerz, Ulf. *Transnational Connections: Culture, People, Places.* New York: Routledge, 1996.

Hardt, Michael, and Antonio Negri. *Empire.* Cambridge, MA and London: Harvard University Press, 2000.

Harlow, Barbara. *Barred: Women, Writing and Political Detention.* Middletown, CT: Wesleyan University Press; Hanover, NH: University Press of New England, 1992.

Hayden, Robert M. "Imagined Communities and Real Victims: Self-Determination and Ethnic Cleansing in Yugoslavia." *American Ethnologist* 23.4 (1996): 783–801.

Heaney, Seamus. "Act of Union." *Selected Poems 1965–1975.* London: Faber and Faber, 1980.

———. *An Open Letter.* Field Day Pamphlet, No. 2. Derry: Field Day Theatre Pamphlets, 1983.

Herr, Cheryl. "The Erotics of Irishness." *Critical Inquiry* 17.1 (1990): 1–34.

Herzfeld, Michael. *Anthropology Through the Looking Glass: Critical Ethnography in the Margins of Europe.* Cambridge: Cambridge University Press, 1987.

———. *The Social Production of Indifference: Exploring the Symbolic Roots of Western Bureaucracy.* Chicago: University of Chicago Press, 1992.

———. *Cultural Intimacy: Social Poetics in the Nation-State.* New York: Routledge, 1997.

Hillyard, Paddy. "Law and Order." *Northern Ireland: The Background to the Conflict.* Ed. John Darby. Belfast: Appletree Press, 1983. 32–61.

Hobsbawm, Eric, and Terence Ranger, eds. *The Invention of Tradition.* Cambridge and New York: Cambridge University Press, 1983.

Hodgen, Margaret T. *Early Anthropology in the Sixteenth and Seventeenth Centuries.* Philadelphia: University of Pennsylvania Press, 1964.

Ifeka-Moller, Caroline. "Female Militancy and Colonial Revolt: The Women's War of 1929, Eastern Nigeria." *Perceiving Women.* Ed. Shirley Ardener. London: Dent and Sons, 1975. 127–59.

Irigaray, Luce. *This Sex Which Is Not One.* Translated by Catherine Porter. Ithaca: Cornell University Press, 1991.

Ivy, Marilyn. *Discourses of the Vanishing: Modernity, Phantasm, Japan.* Chicago: University of Chicago Press, 1997.

Jáuregui Bereciartu, Gurutz. *Ideología y estrategia política de ETA. Análisis de su evolución entre 1959 y 1968.* Madrid: Siglo XXI, 1981.

Jones, Ann Rosalind, and Peter Stallybrass. "Dismantling Irena: The Sexualisation of Ireland in Early Modern England." *Nationalisms and Sexualities*. Ed. Andrew Parker et al. New York: Routledge, 1992. 157–71.

Juaristi, Jon. *El bucle melancólico. Historias de nacionalistas vascos*. Madrid: Espasa, 1997.

Kafka, Franz. *The Trial*. Translated by Willa and Edwin Muir. New York: Modern Library, 1964.

Kearney, Michael. "The Local and the Global: The Anthropology of Globalization and Transnationalism." *Annual Review of Anthropology* 24 (1995): 547–65.

Kearney, Richard. *Transitions: Narratives in Modern Irish Culture*. Manchester: Manchester University Press, 1988.

Kelly, Fergus. *A Guide to Early Irish Law*. Dublin: Dublin Institute for Advanced Studies, 1988.

Kelly, John. *A Politics of Virtue: Hinduism, Sexuality and Countercolonial Discourse in Fiji*. Chicago: University of Chicago Press, 1991.

Kiberd, Declan. *Inventing Ireland: The Literature of the Modern Nation*. Cambridge, MA: Harvard University Press, 1995.

Kilfeather, Siobhan. "Strangers at Home: Political Fictions by Women in Eighteenth Century Ireland." Ph.D. Diss. Princeton University, 1989.

Kristeva, Julia. *Powers of Horror: An Essay on Abjection*. Translated by Leon S. Roudiez. New York: Columbia University Press, 1982.

———. "Strangers to Ourselves: The Hope of the Singular." *Visions of Europe*. Ed. Richard Kearney. Dublin: Wolfhound, 1992. 99–107.

Kundera, Milan. *The Book of Laughter and Forgetting*. Translated by Michael Heim. New York: Alfred A. Knopf, 1980. Reprint, New York: Penguin, 1981.

———. *El arte de la novela*. Barcelona: Tusquets Editores, 1987.

Lacan, Jaques. *Ecrits: A Selection*. Translated by Alan Sheridan. New York: Norton, 1977. Reprint, 1982.

———. *The Four Fundamental Concepts of Psychoanalysis*. Translated by Alan Sheridan. New York: Norton, 1981.

———. *The Psychoses*. Book III. *The Seminar of Jacques Lacan 1955–1956*. Translated by Russell Grigg. New York: W.W. Norton and Co., 1993.

Laclau, Ernesto, and Lillian Zac. "Minding the Gap: The Subject of Politics." *The Making of Political Identities*. Ed. Ernesto Laclau. London: Verso, 1994. 11–39.

Lahusen, Christian. "The Aesthetic of Radicalism: The Relationship between Punk and the Patriotic Nationalist Movement of the Basque Country." *Popular Music* 12.3 (1993): 263–80.

Laplanche, Jean. *New Foundations for Psychoanalysis*. Translated by David Macey. Oxford and New York: Basil Blackwell, 1989.

————. *Essays on Otherness*. Ed. John Fletcher. London and New York: Routledge, 1999.

Laplanche, Jean, and Jean-Bertrand Pontalis. "Fantasy and the Origins of Sexuality." *Formations of Fantasy*. Ed. Victor Burgin, James Donald and Cora Kaplan. New York: Routledge, 1989. 5–34.

Larrañaga, Vicente. *La ideología Carlista (1868–1976)*. San Sebastián: Diputación Foral de Guipúzcoa, 1984.

Leach, Edmund. *Custom, Law, and Terrorist Violence*. Edinburgh: Edinburgh University Press, 1977.

Lewis, Ivor. *Sahibs, Nabobs and Boxwallahs: A Dictionary of the Words of Anglo-India*. Delhi: Oxford University Press, 1997.

Lloyd, David. "The Conflict of the Border." Unpublished manuscript. N.d.

Loughran, Christine. "Armagh and Feminist Strategy." *Feminist Review* 23 (1986): 59–79.

Lukens, Nancy, and Dorothy Rosenberg, eds. *Daughters of Eve: Women's Writing from the German Democratic Republic*. Lincoln: University of Nebraska Press, 1993.

Lyons, F.S.L. *Culture and Anarchy in Ireland 1890–1939*. Oxford and New York: Oxford University Press, 1979.

MacBride, Seán. Introduction. *One Day in My Life*. By Bobby Sands. London: Pluto Press, 1983.

MacDonagh, Oliver. *States of Mind: A Study of Anglo-Irish Conflict 1780–1980*. London: Allen and Unwin, 1983.

Malkki, Liisa. *Purity and Exile: Violence, Memory and National Cosmology Among Hutu Refugees in Tanzania*. Chicago: University of Chicago Press, 1995.

Mani, Lata. "Contentious Traditions: The Debate on *Sati* in Colonial India." *Recasting Women: Essays in Indian Colonial History*. Ed. Kumkum Sangari and Sudesh Vaid. New Brunswick, NJ: Rutgers University Press, 1990. 88–125.

Marron, Oonagh. "The Cost of Silencing Voices Like Mine." *Unfinished Revolution: Essays on the Irish Women's Movement*. Ed. Frances Devaney et al. Belfast: Meadbh Publications, 1989.

McCafferty, Nell. *Armagh Women*. Dublin: Co-Op Books, 1981.

McCann, Eamonn. *War and an Irish Town*. London: Pluto Press, 1980.

McCann, Mary. "The Past in the Present: A Study of Some Aspects of the Politics of Music in Belfast." Ph.D. Diss. Queen's University, Belfast, 1985.

McVeigh, Robbie. *It's Part of Life Here . . . the Security Forces and Harassment in Northern Ireland*. Belfast: Committee on the Administration of Justice, 1994.

Meaney, Gerardine. *Sex and Nation: Women in Irish Culture and Politics*. LIP Pamphlets. Dublin: Attic Press, 1991.

Medbh, Maighread. "Easter 1991." *Feminist Review* 44 (1993): 58–60.

Memmi, Albert. *The Colonizer and the Colonized*. Boston: Beacon Press, 1965.

Metcalf, Thomas R. *Aftermath of Revolt: India, 1857–1870.* Princeton. Princeton University Press, 1964.

Miralles, Melchor, and Ricardo Arques. *Amedo. El estado contra ETA.* Madrid: Plaza & Janes/Cambio 16, 1989.

Mitchell, Timothy. "The Limits of the State: Beyond Statist Approaches and Their Criticism." *American Political Science Review* 85.1 (1991): 77–96.

Mohanty, Chandra Talpade, Ann Russo, and Lourdes Torres, eds. *Third World Women and the Politics of Feminism.* Bloomington: Indiana University Press, 1991.

Morris, James. *Farewell the Trumpets: An Imperial Retreat.* New York: Harvest/HBJ, 1978.

Morrison, Toni. *Beloved: A Novel.* New York: Alfred A. Knopf, 1987.

Mosse, George L. *Nationalism and Sexuality: Middle-Class Morality and Sexual Norms in Modern Europe.* Madison: University of Wisconsin Press, 1985.

Muenster, Sebastian. *Cosmographiae Universalis.* Basilea: Henrichum Petri, 1554.

Mukherjee, Rudrangshu. *Awadh in Revolt, 1857–1858: A Study of Popular Resistance.* Delhi: Oxford University Press, 1984.

Murphy, Brenda. "A Curse." *Territories of the Voice. Contemporary Stories by Irish Women Writers.* Ed. Louise DeSalvo, Kathleen Walsh D'Arcy, and Katherine Hogan. Boston: Beacon Press, 1989. 226–27.

Nagengast, Carole. "Violence, Terror, and the Crisis of the State." *Annual Review of Anthropology* 23 (1994): 109–36.

Nairn, Tom. *The Break Up of Britain: Crisis and Neo-nationalism.* London: NLB, 1977.

Nandy, Ashis. *The Intimate Enemy: Loss and Recovery of Self under Colonialism.* Delhi: Oxford University Press, 1983.

Nash, Catherine. "Remapping and Renaming: New Cartographies of Identity, Gender and Landscape." *Feminist Review* 44 (1993): 39–57.

National Council for Civil Liberties (NCCL). *Strip Searching: An Inquiry into the Strip Searching of Women Prisoners at Armagh Prison Between 1982 and 1985.* London: National Council for Civil Liberties, 1986.

Navaro-Yashin, Yael. "Travesty and Truth: Politics of Culture and Fantasies of the State in Turkey." Ph.D. Diss. Princeton University, 1997.

———. "Uses and Abuses of 'State and Civil Society' in Contemporary Turkey." *New Perspectives on Turkey* 18 (1998): 1–22.

———. *Faces of the State: Secularism and Public Life in Turkey.* Princeton, NJ: Princeton University Press, 2002.

Nelson, Diane M. *A Finger in the Wound: Body Politics in Quincentennial Guatemala.* Berkeley: University of California Press, 1999.

Nietzsche, Friedrich. *The Genealogy of Morals.* Translated by Francis Golffing. New York: Anchor Books, 1956.

Nordstrom, Carolyn. "Rape: Politics and Theory in War and Peace." *Australian Feminist Studies* 11.23 (1996): 149–62.

Nordstrom, Carolyn, and JoAnn Martin, eds. *The Paths to Domination, Resistance and Terror.* Berkeley: University of California Press, 1992.

Norval, Aletta J. "Thinking Identities: Against a Theory of Ethnicity." *The Politics of Difference: Ethnic Premises in a World of Power.* Ed. Edwin N. Wilmsen and Patrick McAllister. Chicago: University of Chicago Press, 1996. 59–70.

Obeyesekere, Gananath. *Medusa's Hair: An Essay on Personal Symbols and Religious Experience.* Chicago: University of Chicago Press, 1981.

———. *The Work of Culture: Symbolic Transformation in Psychoanalysis and Anthropology.* Chicago: University of Chicago Press, 1990.

———. *The Apotheosis of Captain Cook: European Myth Making in the Pacific.* Princeton: Princeton University Press, 1992.

O'Dowd, Liam. "Church, State and Women: The Aftermath of Partition." *Gender in Irish Society.* Ed. Chris Curtin, Pauline Jackson, and Barbara O'Connor. Galway: Galway University Press, 1987. 3–33.

O'Dowd, Liam, Bill Rolston, and Mike Tomlinson. *Northern Ireland: Between Civil Rights and Civil War.* London: CSE Books, 1980.

Óh Ógáin, Dáithí. *The Hero in Irish Folk History.* Dublin: Gill and Macmillan, 1985.

Olujic, Maria B. "The Croatian War Experience." *Fieldwork Under Fire: Contemporary Studies of Violence and Survival.* Ed. Carolyn Nordstrom and Antonius C.G.M. Robben. Berkeley: University of California Press, 1995. 186–204.

O'Malley, Padraig. *Biting at the Grave: The Irish Hunger Strikes and the Politics of Despair.* Boston: Beacon Press, 1990.

Ong, Aihwa. *Flexible Citizenship: The Cultural Logics of Transnationality.* Durham, NC: Duke University Press, 1999.

Ortelius, Abraham. *Theatrum Orbis Terrarum.* Antuerdiae: A.R. Sandensen, 1570.

Owens, Rosemary Cullen. *Smashing Times: A History of the Irish Women's Suffrage Movement 1889–1922.* Dublin: Attic Press, 1984.

Parker, Andrew et al. *Nationalisms and Sexualities.* New York: Routledge, 1992.

Pearse, Patrick. "The Murder Machine." 1916. *Field Day Anthology of Irish Writing.* Vol. II. Ed. Seamus Deane. Derry: Field Day Publications, 1992. 288–93.

Pérez-Agote, Alfonso. *La reproducción del nacionalismo. El caso vasco.* Madrid: CIS; Siglo XXI, 1984.

———. *El Nacionalismo vasco a la salida del Franquismo.* Madrid: Siglo XXI; CIS, 1987.

———. "Self-Fulfilling Prophecy or Unresolved Mourning: Basque Political Violence in the Twenty-First Century." *Empire & Terror: Nationalism/Postnationalism in the New Millennium.*

Conference Papers Series, No.1. Reno: Center for Basque Studies, University of Nevada, Reno, 2004. 177–98.

Peteet, Julie. "Male Gender and Rituals of Resistance in the Palestinian Intifada: A Cultural Politics of Violence." *American Ethnologist* 21.1 (1994): 31–49.

Plunkett, Joseph. *The Poems of Joseph Mary Plunkett.* Dublin: Talbot, 1916.

Poulantzas, Nicos. *State, Power, Socialism.* Translated by Patrick Camiller. London: New Left Books, 1978.

Ramírez, María Clemencia. *Entre el Estado y la Guerrilla. Identidad y Ciudadanía en el Movimiento de los Campesinos Cocaleros del Putamayo.* Bogotá: Instituto Colombiano de Antropología e Historia, 2001.

Ramírez Goicoechea, Eugenia. *De jóvenes y sus identidades. Socio-antropología de la etnicidad en Euskadi.* Madrid: CIS, 1991.

Ramos, Agustín. "Crítica de los procesos de legitimación del Estado en Euskalherria." Undergraduate thesis, Universidad del País Vasco, San Sebastián, 1985.

Renan, Ernest. "What is a Nation?" 1882. *Nation and Narration.* Ed. Homi K. Bhabha. New York: Routledge, 1990. 8–22.

———. *The Poetry of the Celtic Races and Other Studies.* 1896. Translated, with an introduction and notes, by William G. Hutchinson. Port Washington, NY: Kennikat Press, 1970.

Rey, Pepe. *Intxaurrondo. La trama verde.* Tafalla: Txalaparta, 1996.

Riches, David, ed. *The Anthropology of Violence.* Oxford: Basil Blackwell, 1986.

Rolston, Bill. "Politics, Painting and Popular Culture: The Political Wall Murals of Northern Ireland." *Media, Culture and Society* 9 (1987): 5–28.

———. "Mothers, Whores and Villains: Images of Women in Novels of the Northern Ireland Conflict." *Race and Class* 31.1 (1989): 41–58.

Rosaldo, Renato. *Culture and Truth: The Remaking of Social Analysis.* Boston: Beacon Press, 1989.

Rose, Jacqueline. *States of Fantasy.* Oxford: Clarendon Press, 1996.

Rowthorn, Bob, and Naomi Wayne. *Northern Ireland: The Political Economy of the Conflict.* Cambridge: Polity Press, 1988.

Rubio, Antonio, and Manuel Cerdán. *El origen del GAL. "Guerra Sucia" y crimen de estado.* Madrid: Temas de Hoy, 1997.

Rulfo, Juan. "Pedro Paramo." *Obras.* Mexico: Fondo de Cultura Economica, 1987. 147–254.

Sahlins, Marshall. *Historical Metaphors and Mythical Realities: Structure in the Early History of the Sandwich Islands Kingdom.* Ann Arbor: University of Michigan Press, 1981.

———. *Islands of History.* Chicago: University of Chicago Press, 1985.

Said, Edward. *Orientalism.* New York: Pantheon Books, 1978.

Sands, Bobby. *Skylark Sing Your Lonely Song: An Anthology of the Writings of Bobby Sands*. Cork and Dublin: Mercier Press, 1982.

———. *One Day in My Life*. London: Pluto Press, 1983.

Sangari, Kumkum, and Sudesh Vaid. *Recasting Women: Essays in Indian Colonial History*. New Brunswick: Rutgers University Press, 1990.

Santner, Eric L. *Stranded Objects: Mourning, Memory and Film in Postwar Germany*. Ithaca: Cornell University Press, 1990.

———. *My Own Private Germany: Daniel Paul Schreber's History of Modernity*. Princeton, NJ: Princeton University Press, 1996.

———. *On the Psychopathology of Everyday Life: Reflections on Freud and Rosenzweig*. Chicago: University of Chicago Press, 2001.

Scarry, Elaine. *The Body in Pain: The Making and Unmaking of the World*. New York: Oxford University Press, 1985.

Schmitt, Carl. *Political Theology: Four Chapters on the Concept of Sovereignty*. 1922. Translated by George Schwab. Cambridge, MA: MIT Press, 1985.

Scott, James C. *Seeing Like a State: How Certain Schemes to Improve the Human Condition Have Failed*. New Haven, CT: Yale University Press, 1998.

Scott, Joan. "The Evidence of Experience." *Critical Inquiry* 17 (1991): 773–97.

Siegel, James T. *A New Criminal Type in Jakarta: Counter-Revolution Today*. Durham, NC: Duke University Press, 1998.

Simmel, Georg[e]. *Conflict*. Translated by Kurt H. Wolff. Glencoe, IL: Free Press, 1955.

Sluka, Jeffrey A. *Hearts and Minds, Water and Fish: Support for the IRA and INLA in a Northern Ireland Ghetto*. Greenwich, CT.: JAI Press, 1989.

Sommer, Doris. "Irresistible Romance: The Foundational Fictions of Latin America." *Nation and Narration*. Ed. Homi K. Bhabha. London and New York: Routledge, 1990. 71–98.

Sontag, Susan. *Against Interpretation and Other Essays*. New York: Octagon Books, 1978.

Spencer, Jonathan. "On Not Becoming a 'Terrorist': Problems of Memory, Agency and Community in the Sri Lankan Conflict." *Violence and Subjectivity*. Ed. Veena Das, Arthur Kleinman, Mamphela Ramphele, and Pamela Reynolds. Berkeley: University of California Press, 2000. 120–40.

Spenser, Edmund. *A View of the Present State of Ireland*. 1st ed. Dublin: Sir James Ware, 1633. Oxford: Clarendon Press, 1970.

Spivak, Gayatri. "Can the Subaltern Speak?" *Marxism and the Interpretation of Cultures*. Ed. Cary Nelson and Lawrence Grossberg. Urbana: University of Illinois Press, 1988a. 271–316.

———. "Forward to 'Draupadi' by Mahasweta Devi." *In Other Worlds: Essays in Cultural Politics*. New York: Routledge, 1988b. 179–87.

———. "Women in Difference: Mahasweta Devi's 'Douloti The Bountiful." *Nationalisms and Sexualities*. Ed. Andrew Parker et al. New York: Routledge, 1992. 96–120.

Stallybrass, Peter, and Allon White. *The Politics and Poetics of Transgression*. Ithaca, NY: Cornell University Press, 1986.

Steinmetz, George, ed. *State/Culture: State Formation after the Cultural Turn*. Ithaca, NY: Cornell University Press, 1999.

Stewart, A.T.Q. *The Narrow Ground: Patterns of Ulster History*. Belfast: Pretani Press, 1986.

Stewart, Pamela J., and Andrew Strathern. *Violence: Theory and Ethnography*. London: Continuum, 2002.

Stoler, Ann L. "Carnal Knowledge and Imperial Power: Gender, Race and Morality in Colonial Asia." *Gender at the Crossroads of Knowledge: Feminist Anthropology in the Postmodern Era*. Ed. Micaela di Leonardo. Berkeley: University of California Press, 1991. 51–101.

Stryker, Rachel. "Wee Girls or International Women: Strip Search and the Politics of Political Prisoners." Paper presented at the *American Anthropological Association Meetings*. Washington, DC, 1988.

Suarez-Orozco, Marcelo. "A Grammar of Terror: Psychocultural Responses to State Terrorism in Dirty War and Post Dirty War in Argentina." *The Paths to Domination, Resistance and Terror*. Ed. Carolyn Nordstrom and JoAnn A. Martin. Berkeley: University of California Press, 1992. 219–60.

Suleri, Sara. *The Rhetoric of English India*. Chicago: Chicago University Press, 1992.

Swift, Jonathan. *Gulliver's Travels*. 1726. London: Penguin, 1967.

———. "The Story of an Injured Lady (Written by Herself): Being a True Picture of Scotch Perfidy, Irish Poverty, and English Partiality." 1746. *The Prose Works of Jonathan Swift*. Vol. 7. Ed. Temple Scott. London: Bell and Sons, 1905.

Tambiah, Stanley J. "The Nation State in Crisis and the Rise of Ethno-Nationalism." *The Politics of Difference: Ethnic Premises in a World Order*. Ed. Edwin N. Wilmsen and Patrick McAllister. Chicago: The University of Chicago Press, 1996. 124–43.

———. *Leveling Crowds: Ethno-Nationalist Conflicts and Collective Violence in South Asia*. Berkeley: University of California Press, 1997.

———. "Obliterating the 'Other' in Former Yugoslavia." *Paideuma* 44 (1998): 77–95.

Taussig, Michael. "History as Sorcery." *Representations* 7 (1984): 87–109.

———. *Shamanism, Colonialism, and the Wild Man: A Study in Terror and Healing*. Chicago: University of Chicago Press, 1986, 1987.

———. *The Nervous System*. New York: Routledge, 1992.

———. *Mimesis and Alterity: A Particular History of the Senses*. New York: Routledge, 1993.

———. *The Magic of the State*. New York: Routledge, 1997.

Taylor, Diana. *Disappearing Acts: Spectacles of Gender and Nationalism in Argentina's "Dirty War."* Durham: Duke University Press, 1997.

Taylor, Julie. "The Outlaw State and the Lone Rangers." *Perilous States: Conversations on Culture, Politics and Nation.* Ed. George Marcus. Chicago: Chicago University Press, 1993. 283–305.

———. *Agency, Trauma, and Representation in the Face of State Violence: Argentina.* Brasilia: Departamento de Antropologia, Universidade de Brasilia, 1999.

Thompson, E.P. *The Making of the English Working Class.* London: Penguin, 1963.

Thompson, William Irwin. *The Imagination of an Insurrection, Dublin, Easter 1916: A Study of an Ideological Movement.* West Stockbridge, MA: Lindisfarne Press, 1982.

Timerman, Jacobo. *Prisoner Without a Name, Cell Without a Number.* Translated by Toby Talbot. New York: Alfred A. Knopf, 1981.

Toibin, Colm. *Martyrs and Metaphors.* Letters from the New Island Series. Dublin: Raven Art Press, 1987.

Trouillot, Michel-Rolph. *Haiti, State Against Nation: The Origins and Legacy of Duvalierism.* New York: Monthly Review Press, 1990.

———. "The Anthropology of the State in the Age of Globalization: Close Encounters of the Deceptive Kind." *Current Anthropology* 42.1 (2001): 125–38.

Tsing, Anna. "The Global Situation." *Cultural Anthropology* 15.3 (2000): 327–60.

Turner, Victor. *The Forest of Symbols: Aspects of Ndembu Ritual.* Ithaca, NY: Cornell University Press, 1967.

Urla, Jacqueline. "Outlaw Language: Creating Alternative Public Spheres in Basque Free Radio." *Pragmatics* 5.2 (1995): 245–61.

Various Authors. *El proceso de socialización en los/las jóvenes de Euskadi.* Vitoria-Gasteiz: Departamento de Cultura, Gobierno Vasco, 1994.

Ward, Margaret. *Unmanageable Revolutionaries: Women and Irish Nationalism.* London: Pluto Press, 1983.

———. *A Difficult, Dangerous Honesty: Ten Years of Feminism in Northern Ireland, A Discussion.* Belfast: Women's Book Collective, 1987.

———. "The Women's Movement in the North of Ireland: Twenty Years On." *Ireland's Histories: Aspects of State, Society and Ideology.* Ed. Seán Hutton and Paul Steward. London: Routledge, 1991. 149–63.

Warner, Marina. *Alone of All Her Sex: The Myth and the Cult of the Virgin Mary.* New York: Vintage, 1983.

Warren, Kay B. *The Symbolism of Subordination: Indian Identity in a Guatemalan Town.* 2nd ed. Austin: University of Texas Press, 1989.

———. "Interpreting *La Violencia* in Guatemala: Shapes of Mayan Silence & Resistance." *The Violence Within: Cultural and Political Opposition in Divided Nations*. Ed. Kay B. Warren. Boulder, CO: Westview Press, 1993. 25–56.

———. *Indigenous Movements and Their Critics*. Princeton: Princeton University Press, 1998.

———. "Epilogue: Toward an Anthropology of Fragments, Instabilities, and Incomplete Transitions." *Ethnography in Unstable Places: Everyday Life in Contexts of Dramatic Political Change*. Ed. Carol Greenhouse, Beth Mertz, and Kay B. Warren. Durham: Duke University Press, 2002. 379–392.

Weiss, Meira. *The Chosen Body: The Politics of the Body in Israeli Society*. Stanford, CA: Stanford University Press, 2002.

White, Hayden. *Tropics of Discourse*. Baltimore: John Hopkins University Press, 1978.

Whitehead, Neil, ed. *Violence*. Santa Fe, NM: School of American Research, 2004.

Whitney, Craig. "Belfast Amid the Strife: Wrenched but Not Ruined." *New York Times*, Sunday, October 30, 1988.

Whyte, John. *Interpreting Northern Ireland*. Oxford: Clarendon Press, 1990.

Williams, Raymond. *Keywords: A Vocabulary of Culture and Society*. London: Fontana Paperbacks, 1976.

Winkler, Cathy, and Penelope J. Hanke. "Ethnography of the Ethnographer." *Fieldwork Under Fire: Contemporary Studies of Violence and Survival*. Ed. Carolyn Nordstrom and Antonius C.G.M. Robben. Berkeley: University of California Press, 1995. 155–84.

Women Against Imperialism. *Women Protest for Political Status in Armagh Gaol*. Women Against Imperialism, April 9, 1980.

Woodworth, Paddy. *Dirty War, Clean Hands: ETA, the GAL and Spanish Democracy*. Cork: Cork University Press, 2001.

Yeats, W.B. *The King's Threshold*. 1st ed. London: A.H. Bullen, 1904. London: Macmillan, 1937.

Žižek, Slavoj. *The Sublime Object of Ideology*. New York: Verso, 1989.

———. "Enjoy Your Nation as Yourself." *Tarrying with the Negative: Kant, Hegel and the Critique of Ideology*. Durham: Duke University Press, 1993. 200–37.

———. *The Plague of Fantasies*. London: Verso, 1997.

———. *Welcome to the Desert of the Real*. New York: The Wooster Press, 2001.

Zulaika, Joseba. "Itziar: The Cultural Context of Basque Political Violence." Ph.D. Diss. Princeton University, 1982.

———. "The Tragedy of Carlos." *Basque Politics: A Case Study in Ethnic Nationalism*. Ed. William A. Douglass. Reno: Associated Faculty Press and Basque Studies Program, 1985. 309–331.

———. *Basque Violence: Metaphor and Sacrament*. Reno and Las Vegas: University of Nevada Press, 1988.

——. "Terror, Totem, and Taboo: Reporting on a Report." *Terrorism and Political Violence* 3.1 (1991): 34–49.

——. "The Anthropologist as Terrorist." *Fieldwork Under Fire: Contemporary Studies of Violence and Survival.* Ed. Carolyn Nordstrom and Antonius C. G. M. Robben. Berkeley: University of California Press, 1995. 205–22.

——. *Enemigos, no hay enemigo (Polémicas, imposturas, confesiones post-ETA).* Donostia: Erein, 1999.

Zulaika, Joseba, William A. Douglass. *Terror and Taboo: The Follies, Fables, and Faces of Terrorism.* New York and London: Routledge, 1996.

Credits

Editor's note: Most of the articles included in this compilation have been previously published, as noted below. Articles are reprinted as published except for minor editing for consistency of spelling and terminology throughout, correction of typographical errors, and minor style and formatting changes. In a few instances where we have noted incorrect information (dates, etc.), it has been corrected.

"Striking with Hunger: Cultural Meanings of Political Violence in Northern Ireland," was originally published in *The Violence Within: Cultural and Political Opposition in Divided Nations*, edited by Kay B. Warren (Boulder, CO: Westview Press, 1993), 219–56. Reprinted by permission of Westview Press, a member of Perseus Books, L.L.C.

"Dirty Protest: Symbolic Overdetermination and Gender in Northern Ireland Ethnic Violence," was originally published in *Ethos*, 23.2 (1995): 123–148 (American Anthropological Association/University of California Press). Reprinted with permission of the University of California Press.

"What the Border Hides: Partition and the Gender Politics of Irish Nationalism," was originally published in *Social Analysis* 42.1 (March 1988): 16–32. Copyright of Berghahn Books. Reprinted with their kind permission.

"Does the Nation Have a Sex? Gender and Nation in the Political Rhetoric of Ireland," was originally published as "¿Tiene sexo la nación? Nación y género en la rétorica política sobre Irlanda," *Arenal* (julio–diciembre 1996), pp.199–216. English translation by Cameron J. Watson.

"The Sexual Games of the Body Politic: Fantasy and State Violence in Northern Ireland," was previously published in *Culture, Medicine and Psychiatry* 25 (2001): 1–27 (Kluwer Academic Publishers). Published with kind permission of Springer Science and Business Media. Another version of this article was published as "Engendering Violence: Strip-Searching of Women in Northern Ireland," in *History in Person: Enduring Struggles, Contentious Practices, Intimate Identities*, edited by Dorothy Holland and Jean Lave (Santa Fe: School of American Research Press, 2001), 37–61.

"The Death of Yoyes: Cultural Discourses of Gender and Politics in the Basque Country," was originally published in *Critical Matrix* 4.1 (March 31, 1988): 83–113 (Program in the Study of Women and Gender, Princeton University). Reprinted with kind permission of the author's estate.

"Intimacy of Violence," was originally published as "La intimidad de la violencia," Epilogue, in Joseba Zulaika, *Enemigos, no hay enemigo (Polémicas, imposturas, confesiones post-ETA)*. (Donostia: Erein, 1999), 231–53. Published with permission of Erein. English translation by Cameron J. Watson.

"Before the Law: The Narrative of the Unconscious in Basque Political Violence," was previously unpublished. Published here with permission of the author's estate.

"Of Hens, Hoods, and Other Political Beasts: What Metaphoric Performances Hide," was previously unpublished. Published here with permission of the author's estate.

"Playing Terrorist: Ghastly Plots and the Ghostly State," was previously published in the *Journal of Spanish Cultural Studies* 1.1 (2000): 43–58. URL: http://www.tandf.co.uk. Published with their kind permission. Another version was also published as "A Fictional Reality: Paramilitary Death Squads and the Construction of State Terror in Spain," in *Death Squad: The Anthropology of State Terror*, edited by Jeffrey A. Sluka (Philadelphia: University of Pennsylvania Press, 2000), 46–69.

"A Hall of Mirrors: On the Spectral Character of Basque Violence." Paper presented at the conference Basques in the Contemporary World, Reno, Nevada, July 5–10, 1998, and published in *Basque Politics and Nationalism on the Eve of the Millennium*, edited by William A. Douglass, Carmelo Urza, Linda White, and Joseba Zulaika (Reno: Basque Studies Program, University of Nevada, Reno: 1999), 115–26.

"Out of Their Minds? On Political Madness in the Basque Country," was first published in *Empire and Terror: Nationalism/Postnationalism in the New Millennium*, edited by Begoña Aretxaga, Dennis Dworkin, Joseba Gabilondo, and Joseba Zulaika (Reno: Center for Basque Studies, University of Nevada, 2004), 163–75.

"Maddening States" is reprinted from the *Annual Review of Anthropology* 32 (2003): 393–410. Permission kindly granted by Annual Reviews, www.annualreviews.org.

"Terror as Thrill: First Thoughts on the 'War on Terrorism'" reprinted, with permission, from the *Anthropological Quarterly Journal* 75.1 (Winter 2001): 139–50, by the Institute for Ethnographic Research, The George Washington University.

Index

AA (Acción Apostólica), 217
Abou-Gheith, Sleiman, 273
Abraham, Nicolas, 248
Abrams, Phillip, 261–62
Abu-Lughod, Lila, 54n39
Acción Apostólica (AA), 217
Adorno, Theodor, 223
Afghanistan, 269, 272–73, 283
Africa, 71n10, 90–91, 259, 262
Agamben, Giorgio, 131, 132, 139, 177, 247n8, 277
Ajuria Enea Pact, 168, 168n4
Al Qaeda, 272
Aldanondo, Fran, 136–37
Algeria, 91n8, 109, 259, 265
Althusser, Louis, 255, 267
Amedo, José, 216, 218–24, 221n26, 228
Amnesty International, 55, 62, 181n9
Anderson, Benedict: on affective attachment for the nation, 166, 169n7, 202; on imagined community, 12, 31n2, 78–79, 93, 136n8, 257, 280; on nation and nationalism, 78–79, 83, 93–94, 100, 202; on national borders, 78–79
Anglo-Irish Agreement (1985), 89–90
Anthropological Quarterly, 14
Appadurai, Arjun, 171n10
Aranzamendi, Jesus, 235
Ardener, Shirley, 71n10
Arendt, Hannah, 283, 286

Aretxaga, Begoña: academic career of, 9–10; border crossing by, in Ireland, 76–80; contributions of, 9–10; death of, 9; and displacement, 133–34; education of, 9, 20, 22; ethnographic narratives and representational strategies for Northern Ireland field research by, 19–30; illness and dying of, 14, 15, 286; overview of research by, in Basque Country, 11–14, 21–22, 133–34; overview of research by, in Northern Ireland, 10–11, 19–30; political activism during youth of, 12, 22, 80, 133, 201–2, 207–8; terror during childhood of, 127–32, 270–71; writings by, 9–12, 21, 22, 24, 134
Argala, 150
Argentina, 218n13, 259, 262
Argument of images, 157n14
Aristotle, 283, 285–86
Armagh prison, 24, 28, 67, 68–73, 103, 104, 109–10
Arnold, Matthew, 84, 97, 98
Arregi, Joseba, 156
Arzallus, Xabier, 223n35
Arzamendi, 137
Ashe, Thomas, 37, 55
Assassinations: in Basque Country, 136, 137, 143–45, 147–62, 177–80, 184–200, 235, 242, 246; of Basque policemen by Otegi, 13, 144, 177–80, 184–200, 231–32, 233, 235, 239; by

Made in the USA
Charleston, SC
02 October 2012